VOTE FOR THE REFORMER
I

Byeong-Soo Min

Index 2

Introduction 3

Book I

PART 1 7
A journey into history

PART 2 11
2.1. From 1.5 million to 10,000 years ago (Evolutionary progress)
2.2. From 10,000 years ago to 1000 BC (Society and culture)

PART 3 31
3.1. From 1000 BC to 600 AD (The Ancient World)
3.2. From 601 to 1500 (The Middle Ages)

Book II

PART 4 91
4.1. From 1501 to 1800 (The Great Transformation)
4.2. The 19th Century (Why the West Matters)
4.3. The revolutions that built the modernity

PART 5 135
5.1. 20th century before WW II (Hope and Horror)
5.2. 20th century in WW II (Climax of confrontations)
5.3. The 20th century in WW II (Beyond WW II)
5.4. 20th century (Korean Modern History and War)

Book III

PART 6 207
6.1. The 21st Century (Issues)
6.2. The 21st Century (Society)

PART 7 266
7.1. Four Cases and three shifts
7.2. Suggestions for reform
7.3. Conclusion

Introduction

1. The reasons that motivated me to write this book.

For 32 years, from January 1989 to December 2020, I served shipping companies in Korea. During that time, I worked in a variety of shipping-related fields, including corporate strategy, ship finance, and new construction, the sale and purchase of used ships, human resources management, corporate performance management, internal auditing, and local office sales and operations.

I have worked primarily in Seoul, Korea, but I have also spent eight years in the United States (Irvine, California) and the United Kingdom (London). In 2021–2023, I also took the opportunity to work for the Korea National Park Service for two years, providing customer service in parking lots and campgrounds and conducting African Swine Fever and wild hog searches inside the national park's boundaries.

I wrote this book with two purposes for young adults:

    (i) to provide historical insights (Part 1-6) like ballast water in the ship to keep stability on rough sea,

    (ii) to suggest a behavioral pattern (Part 7) with the "Case C" and the "Be Yourself and Do Yourself"

My terminology of "young adults" as readership refers to the people who are studying in high school in their high teens, those in universities or colleges who are preparing for their careers, and those who are beginning careers in private or public enterprises in their twenties.

In pursuit of these purposes, I have considered the fact that young adults will live in a much more diverse, interconnected, and conflicting society, especially the time of the next three decades (2025 2055) which shall be far different from the three decades (1989-2024) that I have undergone. The drastic differences require new sets of being and doing to respond.to them.

Firstly, I have gone through history from Part I to Part 6 to identify the points to suggest the young adults for their living in the next three decades.

I have experienced the economic growth of the 1980s and 1990s, along with a string of crises in 1998 (the IMF's bailout of the Korean national economy), 2008 (the global financial crisis), and 2020 (the global immobility locked in the COVID-19), I have seen numerous instances of corporations and individuals rising and falling during crises that had an impact on other companies and individuals including themselves. Although the causes of the fortune shifts varied, it was evident that every setback was agonizing, heartbreaking, and regretful which cast a long shadow to recover from them. I have also made many mistakes in my being and actions during that time and this book is my confession which shall be condensed in the book.

Based on these experiences, I have dived into history to consider some practical points, which could help young adults better understand the contemporary world. I suggest some points that young adults may execute in the next three decades (2025-2055), which will be critical to whether society is made sustainable or not.

I am not an academic practitioner of history, and I don't mean to study history with this book, either, but

I just dived into history to know how the socio-political-economic environment of the 20th century and the early 21st century has been made, and how the next three decades (2025-2055) from the practical perspective for the young adults who will be living the prime time in their lives.

In this context, I put forward my suggestions in the hope that the knowledge and insights from history would help young adults to succeed in their careers, prevent or lessen losses and damage, if any, and create a sustainable future.

Secondly, I have encouraged young adults to express themselves in all social interactions by creating their identity strenuously (Be Yourself) and executing their belief set confidently (Do Yourself) to make society sustainable in the new world fraught with challenges and opportunities. As the book title "Vote for the Reformer" indicates, the practices of performing reforms and supporting reformers would be the most practical and legitimate way to make society sustainable.

As a native Korean, I have worked with various foreign counterparts in cross-cultural interactions, I have felt compelled to learn more about their history and culture, particularly regarding the need to understand how they have dominated business value chains and reaped greater profits through maintaining patents, royalty, entry barriers, legacies, exclusive associations, and premium service.

Furthermore, I occasionally experienced a sense of discomfort and isolation during both formal and informal meetings or social gatherings. I found it difficult to understand the unseen emotions of the Westerners in situations of a heated argument, a flash of jollity, or delicate tension in disputes in the somewhat clandestine air of exclusivity among themselves. I don't mean to be a flawless Asian to share the Western culture in natural mateship and collegiality with the Westerners; rather, I mean to feel included and at home so that you may express your pointed logic and reason compatible with ambient air nimbly, even if it isn't enough to lead the mood in it adroitly.

A solid foundation of knowledge of their history and culture, in general, may help broaden understanding of specific issues, so I believe we should start by seeking insights from historical knowledge. A set of cultural jargon and past experiences in such situations may also help us understand the topics and the mood. Furthermore, if there is something you do not understand you should not be afraid to ask them to clarify the points again.

I encourage young adults to be straight and convincing in expressing themselves and to never flinch from challenges or constraints. When they face any cases of unfair social convention, I urge them to defy them by speaking up about what they feel and demand, and never flinch from them nor pretend that they accept malpractice or unfair treatment.

The next three decades will be a divisive world where people are easy to conflict and hard to resolve it. This requires young adults to have a good understanding of the characteristics of morality such as moral reasoning, moral deviations, and moral choices to help themselves exercise the "Be Yourself" and "Do Yourself". Without a sound understanding of morality, they may get lost in a moral struggle or get stuck in an unbalanced moral bent which do no help them sustain the challenges in the next three decades.

During the process of working on this book, I have been thinking of the young people in business who will make their decisions in a condition that nothing is clear and firm, and there is no one-size-fits-all answer to most situations, but they will have to do it only with their knowledge and reasoning.

In my cases, I made many mistakes as well as some achievements in the decisions of works, petty or significant, in the areas of business development, investment or divestment, risk management, push and pull in negotiations, finding the right moment to speak and act, or being patient and scrutinizing, the balance between conflicting virtues like service quality for customers and business profit from customers, or hire and fire of staff.

I hope this book may help young adults with this book, especially the Part 7, when they are up to making their own decisions.

2. Structure of the book

The main purpose of going through history is to find the historical development of cases of "Be yourself and Do yourself" of the people who had undergone trials and tribulations at the time.

Book I is for the lead-in stage from the beginning of human history until it reached the turning point of history in the late 15th century.

It describes the process of hominization that developed a series of ancient civilizations on the spots of appropriate arable lands. Those developments resulted in the flowering of classical civilizations in Greco-Roman culture in the Mediterranean basin, the Indus Valley in India, and the unified China of the Chin and Han Dynastys.

The Middle Ages in the post-Roman period from 600 until the New World opened in 1500 had brought European feudalism and Christendom, Islam and its expansion, the invasions of the Vikings, Turks and Mongols together with the onslaught of the Black Death. The rise and fall of Chinese Empires, Sui, Tang, and Song. The fall of Constantinople marked the end of Roman footprints in the Mediterranean region.

Book II deals with the great transformation and new order that led to Western Supremacy with the discovery of the New World, the mind revolutions with the Reformation, the Renaissance, and the Enlightenment from the 16th to 18th centuries. The development of technology caused the Industrial Revolution to flourish in the form of mass production and employment. Combined with colonialism across the world, Europe as the frontrunner of industrialization wielded its imperialistic power with unrivaled Western supremacy and Eurocentrism.

The world was getting complex as well as getting prosperous. The hierarchy in the socio-political structure and the polarity among the layered people became entrenched which has brought diverse streams of thoughts such as liberalism, nationalism, socialism, imperialism, and communism. The world of industrialized countries was boiling with conflicts under monarchical suppression from which the French Revolution erupted. It had made transformative changes in all fields of European soil by dismantling the monarchical orders, freeing the people from restraints that administered coercive orders. Wars and revolutions occurred not only in Europe but in the New World.

Book III is the result of the historical developments in Book I and Book II on which I focus as a phase-in progress toward the 21st century of young adults. The historical significance of the Book III made its volume preponderant compared to the Book I and II. The late 19th century to early 20th century was the era of hope and horror. WW I was the war between the alliances in blocs which was, in nature, a global confrontation for imperialistic interests. The Soviet Revolution in late 1910s and the Great Recession in the late 1920s wreaked havoc on peace and prosperity during which extreme regimes such as communized Russia led under Marx-Leninism and Nazi under national socialism which laid the ground for wars around the globe.

The wars in Europe, WW II, especially the Nazi-Soviets War (1941-45), and in Asia, the Korean War (1950-53) were catalytic of establishing the modern world in the 1960s and onwards. The two wars were distinct from the heavy casualties of military and civilians, and the character of total wars that changed the strategy of wars in the following decades. These two wars deserve deeper thought to better understand the geo-political uncertainties in the contemporary world which is being fraught with wars between the Ukraine-Russia and Iran-Arabic countries, and growing tension between Taiwan and China.

As I am a Korean residing in Seoul, I have sourced examples and cases in the book from Korea, but I wish many of them would be universally compatible with the people outside the country.

Part 7 is the conclusion of the Book I, II, and III. It delineates the lessons, insights, and suggestions for young adults. Specifically, Case C in 7.1 is my conclusion that young adults need to move forward, and they are suggested to take actions to be themselves and to do themselves as delineated in 7.2.

Case C is the set of minds to be effective for dealing with problems in the 21st century. I suggested it as "alert and agile, innovative and resilient".

Specific actions that I suggest to the young adults are to be lean, agile, and principled, to be steady in alter ego, to be tough, humble, and resilient, to be watchful about motion in the motionless appearance, and to be positive when in uncertainty. When it motion, however, walk fast and run long. All these physical and mental activities will help move toward the Case C.

For the part of actions that I suggest to them is to exercise the three seconds-rule, to exercise the three one hundred-rule, to exercise the three years-rule, to defy it. Never take the status of underdogs for granted, and vote for the reformers.

The entire descriptions from Part 1 through Part 7 are epitomized in the last section of 7.2 as the conclusion of the suggestion to the young adults, that is, "Vote for the reformer" because reforms as the most effective and practical alternative to make their future sustainable in democratic world.

I acknowledge that any flaws and shortcomings in this book are entirely my own. I am profoundly grateful for my family(Jung Won, Lee, and Dong Kee, Hee Young and Dong Jin, Min)'s patience and support throughout this project. Additionally, I am deeply grateful for Sojin Lee, Soyeon Kim, and Nozomi Kusaba for generously sharing their ideas and offering comments and to my family for supporting me in the process of working on this book. Last but not least. My deep gratitude goes to Meehye Kim in the Applebook Co., Ltd. for editing and publishing this book.

Book I

PART 1

With Part 1, this book begins a journey into history until it reaches 2024 just before the start of the three decades (1925-1955) which is dealt with in Part 7 to help young adults build their future during the thirty-year time.

1. History in the past and for the future.

From a business perspective, history can be reduced to the following principle: an ambitious party succeeded in becoming ruling elites who established their supremacy and set up a kingdom, maintained equilibrium in thought, discipline in action, and ability to respond to emergencies, degraded to lose focus and diverted their attention to non-essentials or wastes; imploded when they were divisive, undisciplined or lethargic; or exploded as a result of external attacks; and finally, a challenger entered as replacement to carry on the story.

Every historical turning point has been at the juncture of success or failure. Along the process, there have been innovations in tradition and adaptations to changes. To put it short, I think, the gist of lessons from history is to make the organization sustainable by all means, and the most effective way for the organization is to reform itself proactively. Otherwise, it languishes and decays, the roots rot to death, a sizable force uproots the foundation, and finally it is reformed passively contrary to its intention.

The past has traveled the historical road in the linear form of facts to the present, but the present history stands at a point where a myriad of paths diverges into the future. Some of the paths look wider and flatter, which are likely to lead to success while some others are less encouraging. The perception of them, in its nature, is subjective, but an action following the perception will end up with an objective result of a certain success or failure.

When reading and thinking about history, remember that the people in the past stood at their points of divergence, too. When they made the decision either proactively or reactively, all of it led to the results that have accumulated to create the current situation. What is clear for now in history was far from predictable or secure at the time of the real decisions that were made by the people in the past only in confidence, desperation, or complacency.

History tells the story of what happened, but modern people may reconstruct the series of specific events, but they cannot clarify the causal connections of why and how it happened. Today, we make our own decisions based on a variety of causes that will result in a certain result. However, the people in the future may be also struggling to understand the causality even though the level of comprehension would be much higher than in the past times due to the help of data and algorithms.

So, it is crucial for us to be keenly aware of the causality in relation to each decision as much as we can, and as holistic as we can. Lessons from history should be ingrained in the mind, and a governing system has to be established to refine the process to reform proactively, sustain the adversities, and avoid collapse as much as it can.

History has tended to take unexpected turns and caused uncertainty and instability. However, these unexpected turns do not justify our negligence in detecting the changeover of the situation and devising plans to respond to them effectively. We must be alert to changes, agile in response, and proactive in reforms.

This book is not for historical knowledge but for clues or insights in understanding the issues in the contemporary world relevant to young adults. The historical topics and contents were chosen to serve the purpose of finding clues or insights for the young adults in their businesses and interpersonal relations, and for the old generations to reform now and here at the cost of themselves, not that of the young adults.

2. Historical developments

The rise of a nation or empire continues as long as the political entity maintains its leanness of mind and organization, discipline in individual or collective action, and resilience in the face of opposition and disruption.

On the contrary, it begins to degenerate into decline when it reaches a peak and begins to struggle against obsolescence, and the virtues of being lean, disciplined in action, and enduringly resilient are long gone. When the margin of vitality for survival is exhausted and the entity is full of internal divides and external threats, it cascades into decline and finally succumbs to the pressure of downfall.

History is in flux and mutation, and it is difficult to predict major turning points in history. Accidental occurrences often change the course of history. However, for example, if you look closely at the sudden appearance of a black swan, it is bound to show signs. People are shocked by the appearance of the black swan because they take no heed of the signs or ignore the omens.

Various factors influence human history, such as different geography, different climates, unique geopolitical situations, and different cultures. Despite these variables, one constant in history is people and humanity. In ever-changing circumstances, they determine their actions in the matrix of important or urgent (priority), internal or external (focus), short-term or long-term (perspective), and personal interest or common good (motivation).

As history unfolds according to the actions of the matrices, it is destined to get thrown off-balance which naturally triggers actions to redress the balance. Thus, the concern is how to deal with the unbalance in social issues, get the flow of history back on a virtuous track, and make history sustainable in the future. In the era of the Fourth Industrial Revolution that rapidly changes contemporary society, it becomes even more important to reform problems to make the future sustainable for future generations, especially the generation of young adults in 2024 who will be living in the first half of the century (2025-2055) in the third millennium AD.

Part 1 introduces a need to reform structured problems in societies that remain unresolved and pose the risk of perilous disasters. Without a timely reform, the next generation's sustainability is evidently at risk. Thus, this is not a matter of option, but of imperative. Specifically, the various structured problems in societies are getting worse: the pension crisis, climate change, demographic doom, government and household debt, social conflicts, the polarization of wealth and ideology, the threat of nuclear attack by North Korea, and the revolutionary changes brought about by the Fourth Industrial Revolution.

Mankind's history is littered with examples of reform failures to prevent catastrophes or to reverse downward trends that were not corrected in time. We find notable examples in the history

1) The late Roman Empire in the early fifth century didn't reform when barbarians started to humble the Pax-Romana by breaching the Roman territory beyond the Danube River.

2) The Byzantine Empire didn't reform when the Christian rescuing force of Hungarian crusaders was crushed at Necropolis in 1396 by the Turks before the Byzantium's collapse in 1453.

3) The Joseon Dynasty in Korea didn't reform when the king sneaked into the Russian embassy in Seoul for protection in 1896 with the royal stamp that approved official documents.

4) Nazi Germany didn't reform when the Allies pushed hard to Berlin from all directions on German homeland territory in January 1945.

5) Imperial Japan didn't reform when the United States Air Force was selecting the two cities from a list of Hiroshima, Kokura, Niigata, Nagasaki, and Kyoto to drop the atomic bombs on 6 August and 9 August 1945.

The geopolitical situation is combustible, and a new conflict can break out anytime if it is not properly controlled and mitigated. As of late October 2024, the Ukraine-Russian war gets complicated with the participation of North Korean troops in the war, and hostility between Israel and Arabic countries is expanding to armed conflicts between Israel and Iran.

Moreover, people are experiencing disorderly confusion and dynamic imbalance; social accountability is lacking irrationality overrides reason and common sense, empathy and social cohesion turn into hatred and indifference, people deliberately pull strings of opinion manipulation and conspiracy theories, and accumulating apathy or antipathy dispel a sense of volunteerism and solidarity.

Societies rot from ruling elites like dead fish rots from the head. When leaders descend into corruption, people become rebellious mutineers, dejected scapegoats, or dependent parasites. This economic and ideological middle class dwindles, and its function of rebalancing and moderating extremes by acting as a counterweight and social buffer in a polarized and polarizing society weakens.

For the sake of the next generation, leaders must strengthen the middle class, initiate reforms with determination, push them through the resistance of vested interests, and complete the reforms.

When problems abound in the frenzy of adversity, our experiences of the searing mood may become a source of counter energy to slow, contain, or reverse the adversarial trend. People have shown an unyielding virtue of adversity, turned the adverse trend around, and produced positive results in the end. The adversity that worked in concert with multiple negative elements has caused counteraction to breed inventiveness, like necessity, by forming an entrepreneurial culture.

The onslaught of irrationality and anti-intellectualism will reach a level of critical mass that will inspire a new round of modern versions of Renaissance, Reformation, and Enlightenment (collectively called "RR&E"). The new movement should be induced to rebuild reason and sensibility as the RR&E had done to illuminate the Dark Ages in the 16th century. When a new trend of the modern RR&E is placed and grows in the 21st century in conjunction with the Fourth Industrial Revolution, it will help avert many problems apparent in the turning era of history.

It is always important to strike a balance between short-term focus on immediate results and long-term focus on lasting effects. The leaders craft their visions and present them to the public. They invoke the unyielding virtue of adversity and condense the energy into reformative actions to finish the reforms. This is the imperative of the 21st century, namely a new Zeitgeist, to make a sustainable future for young adults.

The young adults also need to do their part by involving in reforms or expressing their demands through the media. There is no free lunch, and everything has its price that must be paid before it can be acquired. The most effective way is to "vote for the reformers" who strive to reform the structured problems relevant to the young generation.

PART 2.

2.1. From 1.5 million to 10,000 years ago (Evolutionary progress)

1) Primates to modern humans

This is a brief description of how human beings have evolved through a lengthy process of change. This shows how the modern human species came into being. Evolution will continue in the 21st century with the very different emergence of humanoids driven by AI (Artificial Intelligence) and the data revolution.

(1)   6 million years ago, the evolutionary lines of proto-human and proto-chimpanzee diverged from each other.

(2)   4 million years ago, Australopithecus roamed the globe; they were terrestrial, bipedal, ape-like primates that walked on two legs and had slightly larger brains than great apes.

(3)   1.5 million years ago, Homo erectus (upright human) and Homo sapiens (rational human) emerged with a more modern gait and body proportions. They crafted tools from stone, wood, and bone.

(4)   From 400,000 to 40,000 years ago, Neanderthals diverged from the Homo sapiens and inhabited Europe and the Middle East. They created fire, developed sophisticated stone tools, and built their own culture.

(5)   70,000 years ago, Homo sapiens emerged, the subspecies of the genus Homo to which modern humans belong. They developed more sophisticated cultures and cognitive abilities by using tools, living in small nomadic groups, and consuming a diet of meat and plants.

The modern humans slowly spread from Africa to the Middle East, from Australia to the islands of Southeast Asia, and also to Europe and the Americas.

From 12,000 to 11,000 years ago, the Holocene Epoch began as the Earth warmed, glaciers retreated, and tundra melted, leading to the extinction of large mammals like the mammoth and rhinoceros. At the same time, humans shifted to hunting smaller game and gathering plant materials to supplement their diet, in the process of forming civilizations and the Agricultural Revolution.

Cognitive capacity distinguishes humans from other animals, including primates. The process of hominization includes an increase in brain size and the development of bipedalism. In addition, learning and teaching played a crucial role in the transition from hominization to humanization.

(6)   Homo sapiens sapiens will be challenged for the apex of the evolutionary process because the future world will undergo a profound transformation with the AI-driven machine being in tandem with the continued existence of modern humans. We expect it to proceed through the convergence of humans and machines.

The transformation is developing at a rapid pace, as humans will soon begin to incorporate AI into their physical selves that will evolve into Homo Machina. The evolution of the machine being into intelligent hominids cannot be purely imaginary, nor a matter of the distant future, but a real existence in the near future.

2) Climate change

The last Ice Age, which occurred about 115,000 years ago, was divided into three phases: glacial advance, glacial maximum, and glacial retreat.

About 12,000 years ago, glaciers in North America and Eurasia melted and retreated as temperatures gradually warmed. This global sea-level rise caused significant erosion along the coastlines and resulted in the disappearance of the Bering Land Bridge.

10,000 years ago, the physical landscape of the world was similar to what it is today.

In the last 2,000 years, there have been four major climate changes: the Roman Warm Period (200 BC-150 AD), the Dark Ages Cold Period from the 2nd to the 9th century, the Medieval Warm Period from the 10th to the 13th century, and the Little Ice Age with some cold spells from the 4th to the mid-19th century.

One of the main factors that changed the climate was the eruptions. Among the numerous occasions of eruptions, three cases are noteworthy, which are the Minoan eruption in the Aegean island of Thera in c. 1600 BC, Mount Vesuvius, Italy in 79 AD, and Mount Etna in Sicily, Italy in 1669 AD. Nowadays, some people mention Mount Paiktu on the border of the Korean peninsula and China as one of the possible eruptions, but no one knows when or if it will happen.

The weather anomalies caused heat, drought, heavy rains, mold, floods, and storms, leading to famine, failed crops, and starvation. These events were often followed by plagues.

The issue of climate change has become more serious in modern times because of interaction between humans and nature and will be discussed in "6.1. Ten Critical Issues of the 21st Century" in Part 6.

The anthroposphere refers to such ecological human activities as all the human structures, human settlements, and modifications that impact the biosphere (the living organisms that inhabit the Earth), lithosphere (the rigid outer layer of the Earth), atmosphere (the layer of air or other gases around the Earth), and hydrosphere (the watery part of the Earth's surface).

Recently, carbon dioxide levels have passed the tipping point of 350 ppm (parts per million) and are now at 420 ppm, resulting in life-threatening levels of global warming.

If humans in the 21st century fail to reduce carbon dioxide levels below 350 ppm and prevent temperature increases from exceeding 1.5°C, humanity will face greater threats from extreme weather, water crises, biodiversity loss, and toxic pollution.

The population of the 21st century will either be the last generation to reverse climate change or the first to experience the effects of an unstable environment.

3) Human characters

Over six million years of evolution, the human species has revealed its characteristics.

(1) Larger brains enabled high intelligence and cerebral power for tool making, behavioral flexibility, social interaction, and problem solving. The human brain, which consumes twenty percent of the body's energy, required more food to meet its energy needs, but as brain use increased, muscle size and strength decreased.

(2) Bipedalism freed the arms for complex tasks, allowing the production and use of sophisticated tools and interaction with others. It also improved vision and mobility but led to back pain and stiff necks.

(3) Humans developed complex social skills and met social challenges. It fostered strong bonds for interaction, innovation, and cohesion. Moreover, it takes a tribe to raise a social human, since constant

support from family and neighbors is essential.

(4) Human language differs from all other forms of animal communication because of its compositional nature. Humans can create and share information, allowing them to express intangible concepts and imaginative ideas.

(5) Humans can adapt to changes in climate, food, security, and population density. They often work together to meet challenges.

(6) Humans cannot be free from randomness or, in other words, a providential mystery that determines the fate of individuals. For example, the birth of a person decides the underlying fate. For example, Koreans born under Japanese rule from 1910-1945 became the people of the colonized, while those born in North Korea (the DPRK) at present have to live in sub-human conditions.

Primitive hunter-gatherers formed egalitarian societies based on family ties in loosely knit communities where they practiced cooperative work and shared values by living in close proximity to one another. They valued order and harmony within their societies, and those who lacked commonality or refused to respect it were sidelined, ostracized, or even killed.

Tribalism took the form of primitive communism, in which people hunted for prey or gathered edible resources together. People shared the fruits of foraging or games of hunting based on individual needs, without authoritarian rule or hierarchy. Social stratification occurred when they settled in a place in a much larger group, creating private property and putting an end to egalitarian society.

Thomas Hobbes (1588-1679, English philosopher) and Jean-Jacques Rousseau (1712-1778, Swiss philosopher) conceptualized pre-societal human life in response to the question of human nature. While Rousseau idealized pre-societal human life, Hobbes believed that the natural state of humanity is harsh and hostile, and that only the civil state can prevent this.

Hobbes views human nature as driven by base and selfish desires that were evident in the state of nature. This uncivilized nature is subject to competition, oppression, hierarchy, greed, brutality, gross inequalities, barbaric practices, and terrible wars in a notion of "bellum omnium contra omnes" (war of all against all).

In contrast, Hobbes' negative view is balanced by Rousseau's positive perspective that human beings are inherently good in the state of nature. Rousseau believes that people become selfish and evil because of the evil influence of society. Human life was probably peaceful and compassionate before civilization corrupted it.

Hobbes believed that the natural state of humanity is harsh and hostile, and that only the civil state can prevent this. He viewed human nature as driven by base and selfish desires that were evident in the state of nature. This uncivilized nature is subject to competition, oppression, hier-archy, greed, brutality, gross inequalities, barbaric practices, and terrible wars in a notion of "bellum omnium contra omnes" (war of all against all) and social antagonism. By nature, hu-mans are selfish, aggressive, and quick to panic. suspicion, immorality, contempt and hostility. The veneer theory evolved from the notion that human beings revert to selfish beasts without the veneer of law, order, and authority.

In contrast, Hobbes' negative view is balanced by Rousseau's positive perspective that human beings are inherently good in the state of nature, and human life was probably peaceful and compassionate before civilization corrupted it. He idealized pre-societal human life that a primitive state preceding socialization is morally neutral in peaceful conditions. He also believed that people became selfish and evil because of the evil influence of society.

Since then, the concept of human nature has developed in a binary way.

On the one hand, there is an inherent goodness in humanity, where doing good is more natural than doing evil. The experience of egalitarian sharing reflects a strong sense of altruism, commitment to reciprocity, and community. By emphasizing cooperation, order, and harmony, people are encouraged to take greater responsibility and work together.

In another aspect, there is an unintellectual and irrational human nature. It holds a dim view of masses who are mostly cowardly and easily panicked, and lacking moral fiber that brings a breakdown of morale and mass hysteria in mental severity. Throughout history, humans have indulged in cardinal sins like greed and pride resulting in class warfare, horrific atrocities, wan-ton destruction, cruel exploitation, and inhumane slavery. This primitive mindset has led to gen-ocides in deadpan and callous manner such as the Holocaust and the Nanjing Massacre during World War II ("WW II").

4) Gender roles

Many societies have accumulated layers of differences between men and women. Those who dared to erase the boundaries were punished, but those who conformed were not rewarded. Both women and men can display similar levels of anathema, greed, and abuse, but men tend to express their aggression through raw physical violence due to their belligerent hormonal and masculine characteristics.

Gender roles have varied over time according to the mode of production.

In hunter-gatherer societies, the practice of gathering food led women to have only a few babies every two to three years, allowing them to breastfeed, and carry their infants while gathering food and moving for relocation. The maximum number of children was usually one or two when they moved around.

As agriculture developed, the division of labor increased the value of men in patriarchal societies where male machismo became prominent. Offspring became a source of labor; women focused more on childbearing and domestic chores than on participating in production alongside men. In this context, women were often subject to male influence. Male supremacy changed women's status from one of co-decision-makers with men to one of dependence and subordination. Patriarchy became universal and persisted through political upheavals, social revolutions, economic transformations, and cultural osmosis.

However, human history shows some cases of inverse relationships between physical prowess and social power. It is usually mental and social skills, rather than brute force, that determine the chain of power at the top of the social ladder. Ultimately, soft power has proven more effective in communication and leadership.

When it comes to matters of realpolitik in everyday life, an inclusive person is suited to placate, manipulate, and direct people by exercising the virtues of clemency, inclusion, and delegation. Throughout history, women have had such compatible leadership qualities, such as Cleopatra (r. 51-30 BC) of Egypt, Empress Wu Zeitan (624-705) of Tang China, and Elizabeth I of England (r. 1558-1603).

One of the epochal events in gender equality was feminism during the French Revolution of 1789. Some radical women revolutionaries demanded reforms to challenge male supremacy, but these efforts fell short of implementing changes that would ease the burdens of childbearing and motherhood and increase women's rights and benefits at the personal, civic, and national levels.

In today's sophisticated world, a new social trend is developing a new future. In addition to the inherent qualities of leadership, the trend of gender parity, debiasing in hiring practices and performance evaluation, and the growing need for caregiving responsibilities will require more women leaders.

Modern urban life made men the primary breadwinners, while women were often left as lonely homemakers and household managers or, for the working class, as overburdened outworkers, housekeepers, and parents. Not surprisingly, beyond the genteel parlors of enlightened society in the industrializing world, there existed a thriving underworld of prostitution, desperation, and early death for women.

In the era of gender equality in the modern world, women became co-decision-makers with men, as they had been in primitive hunter-gatherer societies, played significant roles as alpha females in the great empires, and contributed to the revolutionary zeal for gender equality. In addition, their use of soft power has proven more effective in leading people.

The traditional differences in gender expectations based on male supremacy are gradually fading, paving the way for gender equality in the 21st century. The gravitational pull of gender equality often shows signs of matriarchy or even female supremacy in some areas of society. Conversely, it can lead to gender conflict as men seek equal rights.

Every culture has its own beliefs, norms, and values, but these are in constant flux and upheaval. Gender is no exception. Gender culture, which includes gender roles, gender identity, and gender equality, can evolve during times of social change through various interactions among men, women, and gender minorities.

The process of gender evolution is, in some respects, full of confusion, disorder and contradiction, which will bring about a great wave of social transformation. People in the 21st century need to be aware of the impending transformation and should reshape their perspectives to effectively respond to specific gender issues in society. The revolutionary vision of feminist Olympe de Gouges (1748-93) in the French Revolution will finally be realized, or even more so, in the near future.

Harvey C. Mansfield delivers his thoughts on the roles of gender in gender-neutral society in his book, Manliness. He said our gender-neutral society is much stronger formally in public law than it is actually in private. A better education would make children and grown-ups more aware of themselves in franker and less manipulative than what we attempt now. A better public doctrine would give greater respect to the way to live as two genders in private.

The liberal state us based for the sake of impartiality between two genders on an abstraction; it is neither male nor female. But human beings cannot actually live that way, vigilantly stifling every thought or impulse due to one's gender. To protect women's career, we need a gender neutral state which assumes that the principle of our public lives must rule our private lives too. It makes women think that they are unfaithful to the cause of women if they do not behave like men.

Women should be free to enter on careers but not compelled, and men should be expected, not merely free, to be manly. A free society cannot survive if we are so free that nothing is expected of us.

2.2. From 10,000 years ago to 1000 BC (Society and culture)

Some readers may wonder what the ancient empires of thousands of years ago have to do with modern people in the 21st century. It is understandable for people living in a rapidly changing world to have such thoughts, given the vast gap in time, place, and culture between the ancient world and the modern world, and the strange names of the people and the exotic places.

However, from another perspective, the lessons and influences of the ancient people and their empires still resonate today. The rustic charms embedded in the relics and artifacts have remained virtually unchanged through the scores of centuries. Nothing is created in a vacuum. Their legacies in the ways of life have been mutated and passed down from generation to generation.

In addition to the historical connection between ancient empires and modernity, ancient people had their own belief systems. However, their way of thinking and acting to express their unique and specific minds was not so far from that of modern people. We can find connections between innate humanity and aesthetic values that ancient people got inspired and tried to express in the times of their cultures worldwide. See examples:

- The Altamira Bison, painted on the ceiling of the Altamira Cave, dates from around 15,000 BC. It brilliantly captures a realistic three-dimensional perspective with detailed depictions of the face, hair and hooves. It should not surprise us that it inspires contemporary artists and viewers if it were displayed as a modern work of art by an anonymous artist in a modern gallery.

- The hand stencils in the Cueva de las Manos (Cave of the Hands), dating from approximately 11,000-7,500 BC, demonstrate the artistic heritage of early Holocene hunter-gatherers in Argentina. The hand marks of left and right hands are grouped together but differ in size and direction. This means that there were many people with different characters. The seeming randomness of filling the space with their handprints is indistinguishable from that of modern humans.

- The Samara Plate, excavated near present-day Baghdad in Iraq and dating from around 5,000 BC, is on display at the Vorderasiatische Museum in Berlin. The pottery features swirling arrangements of fish and birds with abstract geometric patterns toward the rim. The bold outer ring reverses the direction of the swirl and contains a swastika at its center. In terms of design with its aesthetic implications, could we say that artistic design from seven thousand years ago is so archaic and irrelevant to modern art?

- The Thinker and the Sitting Woman of Cernavoda, dating from around 5000 BC and housed in the National Museum of Romanian History, are terracotta figures with exaggerated features such as large concave eyes and broad hips in a seated posture. When we appreciate the modern sculpture of "The Thinker" by Auguste Rodin (1840 -1917) at the Musée Rodin, it may not be easy to find a big gap in the feature of thoughtfulness between the two men spanning nearly 7,000 years.

1) Ancient empires and civilizations

Beginning around 10,000 BC, the Neolithic period saw the rise of civilizations in the Fertile Crescent along the Tigris and Euphrates rivers, northern China, Mesoamerica, and the Indus region of India.

These civilizations shared six key trends, with some variations:

(1) Diverse populations grew in size and density, leading to the development of cities.

(2) Subsistence farmers and artisans, armed with new tools and skills, produced more food and necessities.

(3) Politics with hierarchical layers of bureaucrats, standing armies, centralization, and social stratification were the price for the security provided by states.

(4) Economic activities became more specialized, resulting in structured inequality and injustice.

(5) New ideas emerged that shaped thought and action, promoting the common good, protesting rights abuses, and fostering a sense of fatalism while encouraging good karma for the next life.

(6) They all rose, peaked, declined, and collapsed in their own patterns.

Scientific knowledge, especially mathematics and astronomy, and ideological developments led to fundamental techniques and products: the growth of long-distance trade, the rise of merchants as a social class, the use of coins for trade, the adoption of phonetic alphabets (except in China), and the rise of religions centered on a dominant god, a guiding principle of life, or a code of conduct.

Empires have been a common and stable form of political organization for the past 5,000 years. They ruled over diverse cultures in vast territories. Great empires reduced human diversity and forged new and much larger groups by erasing the unique characteristics of many peoples.

History shows that wars have always played a role in the rise and maintenance of empires, occasionally interrupted by periods of peace. The peace during the intermittent period was obscured by dereliction of duties in complacency. As empires expanded, so did the frequency and scale of warfare.

Many empires arose through military conquest, but there are some exceptions where alliance, ethnic cohesion, or shared beliefs played a significant role. For example, the Athenian Empire was formed as a voluntary alliance of solidarity, the Holy Roman Empire relied on marriage alliances and feudalism, and the British Empire was built on a foundation of imperialism and democracy.

The existence of an empire usually involved slaughter and oppression during wars, enslavement, deportation, and genocide. In many cases, the fall of an empire hardly meant safety for the subjugated people, but a new empire crept into the power vacuum. The conquerors ravaged the land with pillage, slaughter, and robbery and called it peace.

Most conquered peoples were subjugated for hundreds of years or more, slowly absorbed by the conquerors until their distinct cultures were erased and forgotten. Empires have been overthrown by external invasions, internal divisions within the ruling elites, rebellions by the common people, or military coups.

Meanwhile, a significant portion of humanity's cultural achievements owe their existence to the exploitation of conquered populations during migrations and settlements for survival. For example, many remarkable advances in knowledge and insight were made by the Greeks, Romans, Islamic civilizations, Indians, and Chinese in the series of migrations and settlements.

The history of empires and civilizations from ancient empires to the Roman Empire

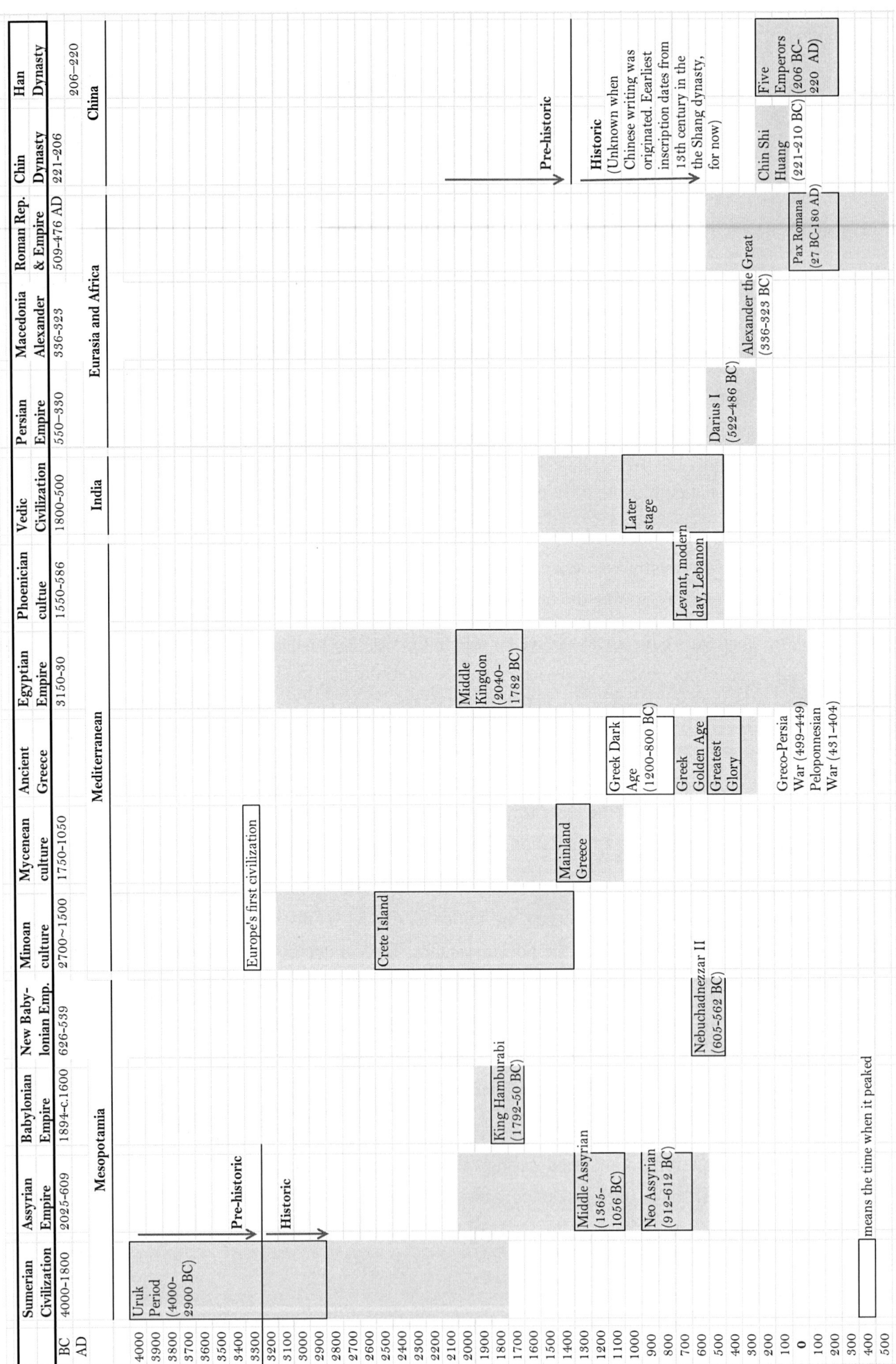

Sumerian Civilization (4000-1800 BC)

The first Mesopotamian civilization arose along the Fertile Crescent between the Tigris and Euphrates Rivers. The rivers overflowed in the spring, depositing fertile soil as the waters receded. The scarce rainfall prompted farmers to irrigate their fields with river water. This created a food surplus and encouraged population growth and community expansion.

The Sumerians invented wedge-shaped cuneiform writing around 3500 BC. It was the most important invention between the advent of agriculture in 7000 BC and the development of the steam engine in the 18th and 19th centuries during the Industrial Revolution. Sumerian writing was adopted by others for over 2000 years until the Phoenicians developed a simplified alphabet of only 22 letters in 1300 BC. We can see the ingenuity of human intelligence, but it made progress over time.

The story of the great flood was passed down through generations. Ut-napishtim, the king of Uruk, warned Gilgamesh of the impending disaster and told him to build a boat. The boat was a large cube, quite different from Noah's Ark (Genesis 6:14-16). After sealing this cube with bitumen, he loaded it with food, his family, personal belongings, animals, and skilled craftsmen.

The storm raged for seven days, leaving nothing but water. 12 days later, the cube came to rest on dry land. He sent out a raven, but it didn't return when the waters receded. As he left the cube, he made a sacrifice to the gods, who promised never to send another flood. In gratitude, they granted him and his wife immortality.

Astride the rivers, the people of Mesopotamia developed the refinements of civilization. Early Mesopotamian civilization established a government to govern society with clear distinctions of job descriptions, replacing the loosely organized communities of earlier agricultural societies (the verb "to govern" comes from the Latin gubernare, meaning "to steer").

This urbanization of cities was crucial in promoting trade and the exchange of ideas, which relied on food from neighboring regions and a government capable of running an administration and court system.

This civilization created a stratified social structure, with distinctions ranging from slaves treated as property to powerful kings and priests. It created gender inequality, valued aggressive behavior and warlike qualities, and prioritized the interests of leaders over the happiness of the common people. These characteristics have persisted in subsequent civilizations.

Akkadian Empire (2334-2154 BC)

It was the first ancient empire in Mesopotamia, ruling over both Akkadian and Sumerian speakers throughout the region, including the Levant (Syria and Lebanon). Around 2250 BC, Sargon the Great demonstrated a form of monarchy by forging the first empire that boasted over one million subjects and a standing army of more than five thousand soldiers.

The Akkadians developed the first postal system, using clay tablets to transmit messages. They were the first to use writing for more than commercial and temple records, producing several literary works. However, the Empire of Akkad only lasted 189 years until it collapsed in 2154 BC due to an invasion by the Guitams.

For the next 1,700 years, the kings of the Assyrians, Babylonians, and Hittites took their cues from Sargon the Great, claiming that they too had conquered the entire world. Around 2000 BC, various kingdoms began to emerge throughout the Middle East in an era of great upheaval.

Assyrian Empire (2025-609 BC)

Assyria was an ancient Mesopotamian civilization that existed as a city-state (21st-14th centuries BC), then as a territorial state, and finally as an empire (14th-7th centuries BC). During the Middle Assyrian period (1363-912 BC) and the Neo-Assyrian period (911-609 BC), Assyria was one of the two great Mesopotamian kingdoms, along with Babylonia to the south.

The Assyrians are known to have built roads in 2000 B.C., with paved strips 1.5 meters apart, on which their carts and chariots could run. The Neo-Assyrian state maintained a vital system of communication arteries for messengers and envoys traveling the roads on state business. This administrative innovation of roads and communication networks became a standard tool in the administration of empires.

King Shamshi-Adad V (r. 824-811 BC) married Sammu ramat (850-798 BC), the daughter of the Babylonian king Marduk-zakir-shumi. Shamshi-Adad V relied on his father-in-law's support to secure his kingship in the midst of a civil war against his brother, which resulted in a humiliating treaty.

After the death of his father-in-law and the accession of his brother-in-law, Shamshi-Adad V attacked Babylon (814 BC) and took him as a prisoner to Assyria. It is not known how the queen of Assyria, the sister of the captive, reacted to her brother's imprisonment.

At this point, Shamshi-Adad V declared himself king of Sumer and Akkad, disavowing Babylon and proclaiming Assyria as the true guardian of Babylonian culture and gods. However, he died young in 811 BC.

His son, Adad-nirari III (r. 811-783 BC), was still a child, so Shamshi-Adad's queen, Sammu ramat, took power. Since a woman on the Assyrian throne was unprecedented, she joined all previous Assyrian kings in calling herself "not only the queen of Shamshi-Adad V and the mother of Adad-nirari III, but also the daughter-in-law of Shalmaneser, King of the Four Regions".

Not sure if this is true, the old story says that Sammu-ramat seized power by asking her husband to give her the authority to rule the country for just 5 days. Once he agreed, she had him executed and took the crown for herself, becoming a significant figure in a male-dominated empire.

Assyria was at its strongest during the Neo-Assyrian period with the most powerful military in the world and ruled the largest empire in history, stretching from modern-day Iran in the east to Egypt and Cyprus in the west under the reign of Sargon II (722-705 BC) and his son Sennacherib (705-681 BC).

In 722 BC, the Assyrian army captured Samaria, the capital of the northern kingdom of Israel (2 Kings 17:6), and deported many Israelites. At that time, deporting the inhabitants of rebellious vassal states was a common strategy used by Mesopotamian empires to maintain control.

King Sennacherib conducted military campaigns in the Levant, most notably his invasion of the Kingdom of Judah and his destruction of Babylon in 689 BC after its repeated rebellions. He made Nineveh (modern Mosul in Iraq) his capital, built a new palace, and erected inner and outer city walls.

In 701 BC, the Assyrian king Sennacherib laid siege to Jerusalem, the capital of the southern kingdom of Judah. According to the Bible, 185,000 Assyrian soldiers died and Sennacherib withdrew (2 Kings 19:35-36).

On the contrary, the Assyrians told a different story. King Sennacherib's Clay Prism, unearthed at Khorsabad in northern Iraq in 1928, had six inscribed sides that recorded eight successful military campaigns against various peoples who refused to submit to Assyrian rule. As part of the third campaign in it, he besieged Jerusalem and imposed heavy tribute on Hezekiah, King of Judah.

History argues that the Hanging Gardens, one of the Seven Wonders of the Ancient World, were built either by the Assyrian King Sennacherib in Nineveh or by King Nebuchadnezzar II (605-562 BC) of the Neo-Babylonian Empire in Babylon for his homesick Median wife.

New Babylonia to the south was a constant preoccupation of the Assyrian kings. Despite many attempts to appease the New Babylonians, revolts were frequent. The revolt of 626 BC, combined with an invasion by the Medes under Cyaxares in 614 BC, led to the downfall of Assyria. Assur was sacked in 614 BC and Nineveh fell in 612 BC.

The last Assyrian ruler, Ashur-uballit II, gathered what remained of the Assyrian army at Harran, where he ruled for 3 years. The city was captured by Medo-Babylonian forces in 610 BC. His final attempt to retake the city in 609 BC failed, and he disappeared from history, marking the end of the ancient Assyrian kings and the great Assyrian Empire.

Babylonian Empire (1894-c.1600 BC)

Babylon was founded as a small city-state in central Mesopotamia in 1894 BC and lasted for a century until it was sacked by invaders in 1531 BC. However, everything changed during the reign of Hammurabi (1792-1750 BC). He was an effective ruler who established a centralized bureaucracy and introduced taxation. By 1776 BC, Babylon had become one of the largest cities in the world.

Hammurabi liberated Babylon from foreign rule. He then conquered all of southern Mesopotamia, bringing stability and renaming the region Babylonia. After Hammurabi's death, the Babylonian Empire quickly disintegrated into a small kingdom centered around the city of Babylon.

Hammurabi's Code, discovered on a stone tablet in Iran in 1901, was a collection of cases designed to establish general standards of justice. The code established a pecking order of superiors, commoners, and slaves that provides important insights into the social relations of the Babylonians:

"If a free person helps a slave to escape, the free person will be put to death,

If the robber is not caught, the man who has been robbed shall formally declare whatever he has lost before a god, and the city and the mayor in whose territory or district the robbery has been committed shall replace whatever he has lost for him

If a person owes money and Adad (the river god) has flooded the person's field, the person will not give any grain (tax) or pay any interest in that year

If a merchant increases interest beyond that set by the king and collects it, that merchant will lose what was lent

If a man has put out the eye of free man, they shall put out his eye

If a man strikes the cheek of a free man who is superior (in rank) to him, he shall be beaten with 60 stripes with a whip of ox-hide in the assembly

If a man strikes the cheek of a free man equal to him (in rank), he shall pay one Maneh of silver

If a man strikes the cheek of a villain, he shall pay ten shekels of silver

If the slave of a free man strikes the cheek of a free man, they shall cut off his ear" (The Code of Hammurabi).

Babylon asserted itself in the region with the Neo-Babylonian Empire (626-539 BC). Nebuchadnezzar II (r. 605-562 BC), known as Nebuchadnezzar the Great, was considered the greatest king of the empire. He is said to have built the Hanging Gardens of Babylon.

In 588 BC, the siege of Jerusalem began, and in the summer of 586 BC, Nebuchadnezzar II captured Jerusalem from the Kingdom of Judah. It ended with the sacking and destruction of the city. Jerusalem became a Babylonian province, marking the end of the Kingdom of Judah. It led to the Babylonian Captivity, as many Jews were captured and deported to Babylon.

The Babylonian Captivity is vividly depicted in Psalm 137 of the Bible, where the captive Israelites express their sadness by the rivers of Babylon, reflecting on the Jerusalem they left behind. The modern singers of Boney M. have sung this sentiment in a rhythmic tone with their song "By the Rivers of Babylon".

The Neo-Babylonian Empire was overthrown in 539 BC by the Persians, who ruled the region until Alexander the Great (356-323 BC) conquered it in 335 BC. Alexander conquered Babylon in 331 BC and held Babylon in high esteem until his death in Nebuchadnezzar II's palace in 323 BC.

Minoan and Mycenean cultures, and Ancient Greece

Their outdoor lives had been active due to the sunny weather. The terrain's islands and straits aided in the development of colonization, trade, and sailing abilities. They imported and developed their nearby older and more established civilizations. Their personalities were not all the same. The Greeks were portrayed as being virtuous, moderate, and serene, but they were also demeaning and superstitious, engaged in the unnatural vices of phallic pleasure and homosexuality, offered human sacrifices, and upheld slavery.

The twin peaks of Europe's first civilization were the Minoan culture (2700–1500 BC) in Crete and the Mycenean culture (1750–1050 BC) on mainland Greece. Both the mainland sites at Mycenae, Tiryns, and Pylos, as well as the palace sites on Crete at Cnossos, Phaestus, and Malia, have demonstrated complex social structures. The Minoan and Mycenean cultures shed light on prehistoric European history with the Trojans, who controlled the Straits of Dardanelles and Troy fell in 1184 BC.

Due to the veil effect of high-floating volcanic dust, the temperature in the northern hemisphere fell precipitously during the eruption in the Aegean island of Thera in 1628 BC. The first European civilization ended violently, as shown by prehistoric artifacts in the sites.

Since the Minoan culture was destroyed at Cnossos 3,500 years ago, Greece has achieved its heyday, Rome was constructed on Greek foundations, and Europe has subsisted on the artifacts of Rome. The cycle of active youth, confident maturity, and impotent decline was ingrained in the history of political and cultural communities.

The Athenian democracy emerged in the sixth century BC in the Greek city-state (called a polis) of Athens, and the first Olympiad in 776 BC marked the beginning of the golden age of Greek city-states (8th–4th century BC). During the interbellum period between the Greco-Persian War (499–449 B.C.) and the fratricidal Peloponnesian War (431–404 B.C.), Greek culture reached its pinnacle with the opening of the Pantheon at Athene in 438 BC. When Greece fell to the Macedonians in 338 BC, the core era of her greatest glory came to an end. The Macedonians and later Romans ruled over the Greek city-states.

People's perceptions were shaped by the Persian War, which made them believe that whereas the Eastern Persians were a place of slavery, cruelty, ignorance, and tyranny, Greece was a place of freedom and beauty. The foundation for the development of Western and European culture was created by this less than objective approach.

An individual from Macedonia named Alexander (r. 336-323 BC) was the first to see the entire world. The Hellenic Age began with Macedonian dominance and ended when Alexander's successors were overthrown by Rome's expanding might. Asking whether Prussia is German is equivalent to asking if Macedonia is Greek.

Greek historiography has left an indelible mark on history.

Herodotus (484-420 B.C.) was the father of history. He saw the past as a titanic contest between Europe and Asia, culminating in the Greco-Persian War (499-449 BC).

Thucydides (455-401 B.C.) was the most political autobiographer, and he was strictly impartial in recounting historical events with subjective opinions.

Greek civilization has been hailed as the "Mother of Europe" or the "Source of the West". Much of it was absorbed by the Romans, who passed it on to the Christian and Byzantine traditions, and it was rediscovered during and after the Renaissance.

2) Innovations

As the glaciers receded and Homo sapiens and sapiens developed, the innovations began. Sedentary communities replaced a nomadic lifestyle of hunting and gathering food. The emergence of farming and herding societies as a result of this shift caused a shift in diet from carnivorous to omnivorous. Human existence became healthier and safer as a result of these advancements.

History has been characterized by a constant struggle to harness ever-larger quantities of energy in ever more useful ways. From the earliest experiments with animal-drawn traction of plows helped humans advance agriculture, the march of material progress has been accompanied by increasingly sophisticated mastery of fuel and energy systems. It started from firewood to cook food, heat homes, brew barley into beer, and smelt metal ores into plowshare and spearheads.

Around 8000 BC, the Middle East saw the start of the Neolithic Revolution. The shift from hunting and gathering to an agrarian and settled way of life was crucial. It allowed for greater populations and established the groundwork for future empires by altering the sociopolitical systems compatible with empire-building.

The domestication of plants and animals was aided by advancements in stone technology, such as polishing, grinding, and boring. People started plow fields, weave cotton, make pottery, breed horses, farm livestock, and hybridize animals like mules. These developments assisted the mass urbanization and colonization of humans.

They created tools. Early urban building made use of copper and bronze, but these materials were costly to acquire and prone to blunting. Therefore, rather than being useful tools for work, they were primarily employed as ornaments or weapons for the minority.

Since iron ore was more plentiful than copper, methods for working with it were developed as a result of its discovery. Later, iron and carbon were combined to form steel. This invention made it possible to produce useful instruments that could endure temperature changes and wear, such as steel wheels, hoes, armor, cooking implements, plow points, nails, and needles. The hunt for the copper and tin, which were only found in isolated places, encouraged long-distance contacts.

The waves of migration, commercial trade, and invasions energized mobility and extent as the elements of invention. Conquerors, traders, and migrants came together in these movements, which led to a flurry of inventive ideas as well as difficulties embracing and adjusting to new customs. It is no less puzzling fact that the most comprehensive development of maritime transportation with investment in resources, time, and skill in the ancient world came from Egypt, a land associated more with sand than seafaring.

Many innovations in history were lost to history until the advent of printing. Archives and libraries were vulnerable, and conquerors and arsonists easily spotted and destroyed valuable knowledge.

The early origins of inventions were the result of serendipity as much as needs of the inventors, and they have been produced with little large-scale production management until the Industrial Revolution in the 19th century whose conditions were set with the wide-scale use of coal in England. A century later, oil and natural gas followed by a plethora of advanced technologies such as nuclear, solar, hydrogen fuel cells, wind farms, tidal and bio-fuel generation in modernity in the 21st century.

3) Agricultural revolution

Climate conditions in the Fertile Crescent became drier and cooler. People were exposed to sudden famines by natural events beyond their control, such as droughts, floods, tempests, frosts, blights, and hailstorms. Faced with the threat of starvation, they had two options since they could no longer maintain their previous way of life:

One was to move backward by returning to a nomadic lifestyle. This shift often led to a warlike organization aimed at raiding other tribes for food. Stone battle axes, flint daggers, and arrowheads became common tools of conflict as such warfare intensified.

Another was to develop agriculture. People gathered seeds from edible grasses and sowing them. They constructed ditches for farming, used animal dung to replenish the soil, drained marshlands, and dug wells. They also domesticated animals by enclosing them to induce artificial genetic selection and create new species. The process was often associated with divine power, a fertility goddess.

Agriculture, metallurgy, and livestock rearing were some of the advancements created by Homo sapiens sapiens that opened the door for many more technologies. Hunting was rendered obsolete by cattle rearing, metalworking gave people more control over the environment, and agriculture lessened the risk of food shortages.

The invention in metallurgy seemed to hammer the meteoric iron and native ores, to heat the metal to melting point, and then to temper it to make it harder. Other skills were to extract pure metals from ores by the process of burning or eliminating the impurities and to make copper-tin alloys in permanent stone or iron molds. In 4000 BC, people learned to melt and anneal it, and to extract and combine it with other metals.

Specifically, the Agricultural Revolution, also known as the Neolithic Revolution, marked a crucial transition in human history from small, nomadic bands of hunter-gatherers to larger settlements and early civilizations. The Agricultural Revolution started around 10,000 BC in the Fertile Crescent, a region in the Middle East where humans first embraced farming.

Shortly after agriculture was set in place in the Fertile Crescent, it spread in a wave of domestication of plants and animals. Farming techniques spread across the Middle East, China, and Central America. Civilizations and cities grew out of the Agricultural Revolution as the first industrial innovation. By the 1st century, most humans managed to feed themselves by agriculture unless natural calamities or man-made disasters disrupted agricultural activities.

We listen to the story of the Garden of Eden in the Bible, where Adam and Eve lived as foragers. The expulsion from Eden and the directive to toil envisage a feature of the Agricultural Revolution. Once humans stopped gathering food, they had to toil to cultivate the land filled with thorns and thistles and produce grain for their survival.

At the expulsion from Eden, an angry God condemns Adam *"Since you listened to your wife and ate from the tree whose fruit I commanded you not to eat, the ground is cursed because of you. All your life you will struggle to scratch a living from it. It will grow thorns and thistles for you, though you will eat its grains. By the sweat of your brow will you have food to eat until you return to the ground from which you were made. For you were made from dust, and to dust you will return"* (Genesis 3:17-19).

The countryside changed drastically due to slash-and-burn practices and repeated cultivation of the lands. Communities organized shelters to accommodate settlements and food storage, prioritizing efficiency in surveillance and protection, which evolved into modern town planning. Due to long-term cultivation, the soil has become weaker due to nitrogen exhaustion, which is also evident in the current practice of growing apples in orchards, salinization from improper soil management, and erosion from frequent flooding.

The agricultural revolution continues to evolve even in the 21st century. Over 70 percent of humanity will live in cities in the 2020s, and we need to produce 70 percent more food to feed nine billion people by 2050. Vertical farming allows food to be grown inside skyscrapers. Plants are monitored by sensors and their cultivation is optimized using big data and machine learning.

Compared to conventional farming, it uses a fraction of the water and yields more while operating in smaller areas. Additionally, it decreases the need for pesticides, decreases nutrition loss, and shortens the time it takes to get to customers. Techniques like hydroponics, which spray nutrients onto the roots of plants to enable them to thrive without soil, are gaining popularity.

This new farming approach hasn't solved all challenges in food production, but its growth potential is substantial. For example, cultured meat is cultivated meat grown in a lab from a few animal cells. It's real meat, but it doesn't require animals to be slaughtered the way traditional meat does. Although it doesn't require animals to be killed like regular meat does, it is still real meat. Faster production time, significantly lower labor and land requirements, and far higher cost-effectiveness characterize lab-grown meat. In the near future, humans might be the first creatures to obtain protein without depending on conventional cattle.

From a different perspective, there is an implication of the invention of agriculture. In addition to helping to grow population and feed and alleviate hunger, it also created the basis for all the problems of civilized society because the pre-agricultural people had less things to fight for. The civilized people had found more reasons to go to war than in a condition of absence of agriculture.

4) Pastoral nomads and barbarians

While agriculturalists settled on the most fertile land across the Eurasian continent, pastoral nomads made their living by following herds, hunting games, and gathering grains in the vast grassland known as the steppe, which stretch from east to west across the continent.

The nomads led a migratory lifestyle, moving their herds of horses, sheep, and cattle in search of green pastures. They traded salt, pots, textiles, and other manufactured goods for horses, meat, and honey. The relationship between settled civilizations and nomadic tribes was symbiotic based on mutual dependence.

However, when climate changes desiccated the grazing lands and depleted game populations, the nomads faced hunger and deprivation. With no help available, they migrated in search of more promising survival conditions. In their movements, they constituted fearsome fighting forces and exerted violence.

Pastoral nomads were seen as crude barbarians. They often raided the West and East, forcing those civilizations to fight back, pay tributes, or allow them to settle within their territories. Unfortunately, appeasement mostly turned out to be fatal as shown in the fall of the Roman Empire and Han Empire in between 300 and 600, and the losses from the Mongol invasions in the 13th century.

The experiences of Chinese dynasties illustrate vivid examples of strategies used to deal with nomadic threats: building defensive walls, bribing them for peace, forming marriage alliances, dispelling them out of territories, inciting internal conflicts within their ranks, or allowing them to fight amongst themselves.

At this point, we need to think about the efficacy of the wall, that is, the reasoning of the great wall builder who aimed to deter the mobile and sporadic nomads by the immovable and long-ranged wall for a long time. We also need to think about the efficiency of the wall, that is, the real cost, including opportunity cost, and human losses for building the wall and keeping it in line with its intended use for the long period.

Some opinions about the wall may include the following: a single penetration at a point of the wall by a powerful nomad could invalidate the entire ranges of defense, the deployment of a large number of defense forces along the long wall thinned out the defense itself, weakened its defense capacity to respond to the agile nomads in an agile manner, and costed a lot constantly that consumed the imperial treasury., and the last but not the least.

In my view, the wall-builders might have believed that they would be powerful enough for the long period to repel the attacks of nomads in the state of overcoming the problems of efficacy and efficiency relevant to the wall. Yet, the ideas went against the historical reality that all political entities that arose were destined to fall.

The builders of the Great Wall were great in their thoughts to fend off the barbarous nomads when they built the wall and maintained it for a certain period, but history didn't see it that way. In the short term. the Great Wall partly and temporarily succeeded in dispelling the nomads, but, in the long term, it contained themselves inside the wall and discouraged interaction and connection with those in the outside world who later overpowered the wall-builders and established their empires in China.

The notion of wall-builder and bridge-builder in the contemporary sense is dealt with in the Part 7.

5) Social interaction

Hunter-gatherers formed small-band societies that thrived in harsh environments. These societies were somewhat peaceful and egalitarian, characterized by low population densities spread across vast lands, with few possessions worth defending or acquiring. In contrast, sedentary agricultural societies were more populous, stratified, and had valuable properties and products that needed protection.

The necessity of carrying children during daily gatherings and periodic camp moves contributed to low birth rates. Women in the tribe could not afford to have more than one child at a time, leading to staggered births through practices such as sexual abstention, abortion, or infanticide.

The transition to agriculture resulted in a revolutionary transformation of these societies. This shift introduced elements of class division, established permanent state structures, created full-time bureaucracies, formed organized armed forces, and fostered an urban environment for protection and convenience. It also resulted in the subordination of women and the emergence of slavery as a societal norm.

In fixed agricultural villages, once children reached a few years old, they no longer needed to be carried. Larger families became more advantageous as a greater number of children meant more land could be cultivated in the future. As a result, it led to natural population growth.

As food production increased, no one was left to starve. However, they worked harder than foragers and often had a poorer diet due to the intensive labor involved and the unpredictability of harvests. When droughts, floods, or cold befell them, lots of grain producers starved to death.

War was far from being inevitable or predictably rational because it tended to be personal. It was the result of a series of bad judgments made by the powerful leaders involved. Even when men's conceptions were sound and reasonable to win discernment of actuality, they behaved in an unreasonable way that overturned the notion that reasons guided. In that sense, war was predictably irrational.

The ancient culture of war sometimes was to massacre everybody in the conquered cities, and to plunder animals and goods. It was not uncommon to practice ruthless devotion to their gods for grain or other beneficences by using the most innocent and vulnerable members of the community such as sacrifices of children and virgins

The agricultural surplus permitted people to be freed from subsistence activities to function as ministers of religion, concentrate on craft work, prepare for warfare, or exchange local products with others. The emergence of a significant division between agriculturalists who paid taxes and the ruling elites who collected them became the defining characteristic of civilization and cities.

The resolution to conflicts within hunter-gatherer bands involved either splitting up or individuals departing from the bands. On the other hand, agriculturalists did not have the same options once the land was cleared and planted. Instead, stored food became a target for both external raiders and internal conflicts, leading to violence over resources.

Worries about the future became a major focus for humanity. The agricultural economy faced challenges such as droughts, floods, and pestilence. Farmers had to produce more than they consumed to ensure a surplus for bad years ahead, and to pay taxes to ruling elites, often leaving them with only bare subsistence or even less.

Food shortages fueled politics, wars, art, and philosophy. Unlike hunter-gatherer societies, war became endemic in agricultural societies. This gave a further impetus for formal decision-making mechanisms to exercise social control. The loose band of tribalism gave ways to organize structures of administration and governance, accompanied by religious rituals and myths.

Civilizations engineered by the Agricultural Revolution and socio-political hierarchy built the great edifices, including the pyramids of Egypt, communal sites along the Yellow River Valley in China, the ziggurats of Iraq, the palace of Knossos in Crete, the fortresses at Mycenae in Greece, and the planned cities of Harappa and Mohenjo-Daro in the Indus Valley.

They gained the skills by osmosis to quarry, transport, erect, and carve massive blocks of stone for decoration with intricate artistic designs. In Eurasia and Africa, they also learned to obtain copper and tin from rock oxides, and eventually to fuse them into bronze for making ornaments and weapons.

The emergence of urban settlements was attributed to farming, livestock rearing, and trade that fueled the growth of cities and urbanism. This urban development has been closely linked with the formation of states, which required centralized authority, the emergence of hierarchies, gender disparities, and ultimately class divisions.

Grain storage symbolized the preservation of society because nothing was more important than to secure the grain in the era of frequent droughts, floods, famine, plagues, wars and heavy taxation. Those who supervised the granaries held power and they demanded the people's strict obedience. The biblical description hereinbelow illustrates how grain storage was critical during fluctuating harvests – seven years of bumper crops followed by seven years of famine. Unless the national risks are properly managed, the entire population can fall into a perilous state of mass extinction. The scarcity of stored food often drove desperate people to engage in warfare for control of these vital resources.

"Then Pharaoh gave Joseph a new Egyptian name, Zaphenath-paneah. He also gave him a wife, whose name was Asenath. She was the daughter of Potiphera, the priest of On. So, Joseph took charge of the entire land of Egypt. He was thirty years old when he began serving in the court of Pharaoh, the king of Egypt. And when Joseph left Pharaoh's presence, he inspected the entire land of Egypt. As predicted, for seven years the land produced bumper crops. During those years, Joseph gathered all the crops grown in Egypt and stored the grain from the surrounding fields in the cities. He piled up huge amounts of grain like sand on the seashore. Finally, he stopped keeping records because there was too much to measure.

During this time, before the first of the famine years, two sons were born to Joseph and his wife, Asenath, the daughter of Potiphera, the priest of On. Joseph named his older son Manasseh, for he said, "God has made me forget all my troubles and everyone in my father's family." Joseph named his second son Ephraim, for he said, "God has made me fruitful in this land of my grief." (Genesis 41:45-53).

At last, the seven years of bumper crops throughout the land of Egypt came to an end. Then the seven years of famine began, just as Joseph had predicted. The famine also struck all the surrounding countries, but throughout Egypt, there was plenty of food. Eventually, however, the famine spread throughout the land of Egypt as well.

And when the people cried out to Pharaoh for food, he told them, "Go to Joseph, and do whatever he tells you." So, with severe famine everywhere, Joseph opened up the storehouses and distributed grain to the Egyptians, for the famine was severe throughout the land of Egypt. And people from all around came to Egypt to buy grain from Joseph because the famine was severe throughout the world."

6) Social hierarchy

Ancient society viewed social distinctions based on birth – such as class, gender, race ethnicity, and locality – as natural, granted, and inevitable. For example, there were clear divides between freemen and slaves, men and women, and among ethnic groups. These distinctions resulted in the need for specific statuses and behaviors in the hierarchical structure.

The hierarchical system was run in a social structure in which the ruling elites such as kingship, aristocracy, priests, warlords, and nobles were usually appointed and succeeded in their exclusivity and heredity in social distinctions and division. Meanwhile, the ruled, such as freemen, commoners, and slaves were supposed to obey and follow the ruling elites. Each of them held a set of responsibilities and roles in the hierarchical system.

The vicious circle of hereditary hierarchy was translated into a rigid social system that had rotated in the dismal loop of fate: innate discrimination → lack of individual competence to break off → social prejudice and stigma → hopeless acceptance of one's fate → acquired discrimination. It was nearly impossible for those caught in the loop to escape.

A typical case is the closed social stratification of caste in India which began in 1500 BC. People are born into a specific category of four classes: the Brahmins, who are priests and scholars at the top, the Kshatriyas, who are political rulers and soldiers, the Vaishyas, who are merchants, and the Shudras, who are considered the lowest, often comprising laborers and servants.

The hierarchy, which was linked to Hinduism, served as the foundation for social ranking and unequal access to resources like as income, wealth, reputation, and power. The Brahmins adopted vegetarianism and banned the eating of beef as a sign of holiness, and they strengthened social distinctions by assigning occupational and tribal groups to their place of hierarchy.

The ruling elites used census data and tax records to maintain control over the populace, demanding agricultural goods as taxes and rents, and labor for the upkeep of their lands and properties. To ensure the obedience of the people, writing was indispensable in the system of religious rites and administrative governance.

The hierarchy enhanced production efficiency and offered security during the crisis, but it also charged taxes, drafted individuals for labor, and exploited the ruled in more negative ways. This hierarchical structure remained firmly established until the Industrial Revolution dismantled and replaced it with the industrial structure in the late 18th century.

Even in modern times, hereditary hierarchy endures in various forms, the rich get richer, the privileged dominate offices, the educated parents bring higher education to their kids, and the poor parents pass on their poverty to their children. For those who are trapped in structured discrimination, the sense of helplessness turns into hopelessness. The victims have a high likelihood of experiencing more victimization.

The hierarchy will remain in place as long as people live on, and it will take on different forms such as exploitation, abuse, or misappropriation. The privileged who hold the majority of positions in contemporary governmental structures, commercial systems, and cultural institutions claim to prioritize the welfare of the people, but the allegation often loses significance when the interests of the privileged are at risk.

The privileged seldom act in a way that benefits young people at the expense of their own interests. Young adults should, whenever possible, challenge some unfair treatment by the privileged by arming themselves with pertinent facts and arguments. When they seek equal opportunity and a fair process in their social interactions, they shouldn't feel defensive or guilty. They ought to knock till the door opens. One of the practical options is to vote for the reformers who strive to reform the structured problems for young adults.

PART 3

3.1. From 1000 BC to 600 AD (The Ancient World)

1) Civilizations in China: Chin and Han Dynasties

By 1750 BC, China began its recorded history with conquests and racial integration. As the Shang dynasty came to an end in 1125 BC, the Zhou(周) kingdom succeeded it and maintained order in a more relaxing manner. China went into confusion when the Huns came down and set up principalities, and local rulers became independent.

In Spring and Autumn and the Warring States (770-221 BC), philosophers such as Confucius (551–479 BC), Sun Tzu (544-496 BC), Mencius (371–289 BC), and Shang Yang (390–338 BC) flourished. The brutal Warring States period (403-222 BC) ultimately made the seven states: Chu(楚), Han(韓), Qin(秦), Wei(魏), Yan(燕), Qi(齊), and Zhao(趙).

At a time when Rome was uniting the Mediterranean basin, Chin Shi Huang (r. 221-210 BC) unified China, and became the first Emperor of China and the founder of the Chin Dynasty (r. 221-206 BC). Rather than holding the title of king, as previous rulers had, he assumed the newly invented title of emperor which would see continuous use for the next two millennia in China.

As emperor, he staged a series of reforms to establish a centralized administration for greater efficiency and control. He was a man of standardization. He standardized weights, measures, axle lengths of carts, language, and laws. A network of roads and canals was constructed, and the Great Wall was erected for defense against barbarian invasions from the north.

He went on inspection tours to ascertain his iron rule. Many dissident scholars were executed, and scholarly books were burned. He searched for the elixir of immortality in vain, but he left life-sized terra-coat soldiers and horse figures. His death led to the collapse of the Chin Dynasty when peasants revolted. The able leader was hardly able to be a humble and generous leader.

Gao Zu (r.202-195 BC) of the Han Dynasty (206 BC–220 AD) had been born a peasant. Weary of the backlash over the harshness of the Chin Dynasty and the cost of suppressing revolts, he ruled with a mix of heavy-handed force against dissenters and a promise of security for those who didn't oppose him.

Nomadic tribes to the north and west harassed China. In 202 BC, Emperor Gao Zu led an army to attack the Xiongnu but was captured instead; he managed to secure his release with a hefty ransom. Gao Zu adopted an appeasement strategy involving a gift-marriage alliance, but this proved unsustainable due to potential backtracking by either party, or it ultimately failed to defuse tension.

The policy changed to an offensive stance to remove the northern threat under Emperor Wu (r.141-87 BC). The Han-Xiongnu war (133 BC-89 AD) broke out, resulting in strategic successes against the Xiongnu. By 60 BC, China projected its influence deep into the Western Region (Xiyu 西域 or modern-day Xinjiang). To the West lay the Pamir mountains and, beyond them, a new world opened that led to a transcontinental network.

The Han Dynasty developed trade routes along the Silk Road, which traversed treacherous terrain. Its total length from China to Mediterranean ports was over 6,400 kilometers, with additional sea miles by shipping to final destinations in Europe. A round-trip journey along the Silk Road from China to

Rome in ancient times took two years along the traces of long-range traffic which are faint now but unmistakable. Rome's well-heeled citizens were by now able to indulge the most exotic and extravagant of tastes from China.

It was not only goods that flowed the silk Road that linked the Pacific, Central Asia, Indian, the Persian Gulf and the Mediterranean in antiquity; so did ideas. Intellectual and religious exchange made for a rich melting pot where ideas were borrowed, refined and repackaged. The religions of Christianity, Judaism, Zoroastrianism, and Buddhism spread across the Silk Road.

The Silk Road bridged the Han Empire in the east and Italy, the Byzantine Empire, the Middle East, and other states in Western Europe. The linkage brought huge benefits in knowledge and trade, but the same route was used by marauding nomads and infectious pathogens that devastated the European population for two millennia.

The Han dynasty (206 BC–220 AD) made developments in civil service and government structure; scientific advancements such as the invention of paper and compass, the use of water clocks and sundials for time measurement, the development of a seismograph, and the creation of stirrups that allowed the horsemen in heavy armor to ride without tumbling off.

The Han Dynasty faced the same threats that plagued all Chinese dynasties: decadent emperors, corrupt aristocrats, and ferocious court struggles in a blind obsession for power. They contended with raids of nomadic tribes, and tax revenue decreased due to social unrest and tax exemptions, revolts by peasants, and rebellions by nobles who were abused by emperors.

When history took a negative turn, it went from bad to worse in a series of adverse events. The same type of great pestilence that had shattered the Roman Empire under the reign (161-180 AD) of Marcus Aurelius, the last emperor of the Five Good Emperors, helped facilitate the fall of the Han dynasty in China in 220 AD.

The collapse of the Han Dynasty was a setback in Chinese history. The Han Empire was such a pivotal era that the majority ethnic group today still refers to themselves as the people of Han. Despite its power and technological innovations, the empire's collapse sent the country into disarray for four centuries until it was reunified during the Sui Dynasty (581–618 AD).

2) Civilizations in the Mediterranean: Persia and Greece

The Mediterranean is the inland sea and the geographical unit that connects the Middle East, North Africa, and Southern Europe. Europe is separated from Asia and Africa only by the narrow but navigable straits of the Bosporus and Gibraltar. Its sea lanes have provided a channel for cultural, economic, and political contacts which have been crucial since the Classical World.

The Minoan culture (2700-1500 BC) on Crete, and the Mycenaean culture (1750-1050 BC) in Greece were two pillars of Europe's first civilization in the Mediterranean. Under the reign of Caesars, it became a Roman lake as Roman territories surrounded the land and sea. Since the decline of Roman power, the sea powers have been subject to the land-based empires on its periphery.

Once Muslim states took root in the Levant (modern-day Israel, Jordan, Lebanon, Syria, southwest

Türkiye), Africa, and the Iberian Peninsula following the rise of Islam and the fall of Byzantium, the Mediterranean became an area of permanent division. The people inhabiting the northern shores had higher levels of civilization and dominated the southern neighbors.

In 550 BC, Cyrus the Great (r.550–530 BC) founded the Persian Empire (550–330 BC). Based in modern-day Iran, it became the largest empire in history, spanning from the Greek cities of Lydia in Asia Minor in the west, through West Asia as its base, to the majority of Central Asia in the northeast, and parts of South Asia (modern-day Pakistan in the Indus Valley) to the southeast.

He was a man of vision, strategy, and wisdom. He was the designer of the great Persian Empire, a strategist who involved the people in a shared vision, and a leader who exercised his power with discipline while sympathizing with the conquered. He set a perfect example of political leadership in human history.

In the process of empire building, his military campaigns were strategic, aimed at encouraging enemies to join the Persian Empire rather than forcing submission. When he fought in battles, he struck at the heart of opposing powers, opting for negotiation over brute force. After he conquered, he showed tolerance toward the people to retain their customs and beliefs.

Following the establishment of the empire, Cyrus the Great governed it with tact and dexterity, deference, and negotiation. He made everyone compatible with his vision of a new world, inspiring individuals from all walks of life to share it. He expressed his belief that only those who serve the people should be in positions of authority and framed his goals following how they would help the people.

The Babylonian Exile (or Babylonian Captivity) was the deportation and exile of the Jews of the ancient Israelite Kingdom of Judah to Babylon by Nebuchadnezzar II. The Babylonian exile is distinguished from the earlier exile of citizens of the northern Kingdom of Israel to Assyria around 722 BC. The exile in Babylon occurred in three waves from 597 to 581 BC as a result of Judean rebellions against Babylonian rule.

The Decree of the Cyrus the Great allowed the Jews to return to Jerusalem. Some Jews chose to remain in Babylonia and made themselves in the first Diaspora meaning Jewish people living outside Israel.

Historically, Jerusalem had been laid siege four times in 587-586 BC by the Babylonian king Nebuchadnezzar II (r.605-562 BC), in 70 AD by the Roman Empire under the Emperor Titus Caesar Vespasianus, in 1099 AD during the First Crusade of the European Christians, and in 1187 AD by Saladin of the Ayyubid dynasty of the Muslims.

The biblical expressions herein below illustrate the vivid scene of the joy of the Jews liberated from the Babylonian Captivity by the Decree of the Cyrus the Great in 538 BC

"Cyrus, the king of Persia, says, 'The Lord is the God of heaven. He has given me all the kingdoms on earth. He has appointed me to build a temple for him at Jerusalem in Judah. Any of his people among you may go up to Jerusalem and build the Lord's temple. He is the God of Israel. He is the God who is in Jerusalem. And may their God be with them. The people still left alive in every place must bring gifts to the people going. They must provide silver and gold to the people going up to Jerusalem. The people must bring goods and livestock. They should also bring any offerings they choose to. All those gifts will be for God's temple in Jerusalem" (Ezra 1:2-4)

Darius I (r.522-486 BC), aka Darius the Great, the third of the Persian rulers, made the Persian Empire to its peak. With massive resources and vast pools of manpower, the Persian Empire (c. 550-330 BC) under his rule became the world's first superpower. The Behistun Inscription, hewn into a cliff face at Behistun in Western Iran, tells the story how he put down revolts and uprisings, drove back invasions from abroad, wronged neither the poor nor the powerful, and tolerated the minorities. He completed the organization of the empire into Satrapies, a system initiated by Cyrus the Great, and fixed the annual tribute due from each province.

The Greeks developed their own distinct civilization. Greeks referred to strangers as barbarians because they thought their speech sounded odd, like *"bar bar bar"* noises. The seditious Greek city-states launched the Ionian Revolt (499–493 BC) in response to Darius I's subjugation of Thrace and Macedon on the European side of the Bosporus Strait, but it was ultimately put down.

The war between the Persians and the Greeks trailed on for a little more than twenty years.

The First Persian invasion of Greece (492-490 BC) was aimed at the Greek homeland. It was cut short when a storm blew up and wrecked the Persian navy on the rocks near Mount Athos. In the Battle of Marathon in 490 BC, the Greeks routed the Persian navy and the army on board and made a decisive victory that crushed the hope of the Persians to subdue the Greeks.

The historical accuracy of the runner is often questioned. The Greek historian Herodotus (484-425 BC) mentioned Pheidippides as the messenger who ran from Athens to Sparta asking for help and then ran back. He made no mention of the runner who ran from the Marathon to Athens where the people were agog with the result of the battle, and the runner burst into the assembly, exclaiming *"We have won!"* before collapsing and dying.

The story is said to first appear in "On the Glory of Athens" by Greek historian Plutarch (46-119 AD) in the 1st century AD, which quoted the lost work of Heraclides Ponticus (390-310 BC) and named the runner as either Thersipus of Erchius or Eucles.

Given that the Battle of Marathon took place in 490 BC, the first mention of the alleged runner was believed to have been done more than 100 years later, and the real scene happened about 500 years after the battle had occurred, making it unclear whether the story of the heroic runner was factual. An empirical observation nudges that something dramatic can be hardly true in full.

The Athenian victory has been regarded as a watershed in European history and the emergence of the rise of Classical Greece. The enslavement of Greece had been imminent until the Battle of Marathon by the subjugation to the Persians, but the Greeks withstood it thanks to intertribal cooperation.

Even the Spartans, to whom the war was a way of life, were impressed when they arrived a few days later and inspected the battlefield at Marathon. History recounts that more than 6,000 Persians lay dead, while the Greeks had lost less than 200 men.

Not surprisingly, Darius I did not want to leave the situation there. His conflicted emotions of pride and rage led him to launch an even more extensive war. Herodotus recounted his decision to launch a second, even more ambitious expedition against Greece, but his plans were derailed by an uprising in Egypt in 486 BC, and the expedition ultimately claimed the life of his son, Xerxes I, following the Persian defeat in the Second Persian invasion.

"When the report of the battle of Marathon reached Darius son of Hystaspes (i.e. 490 BC), who had already been thoroughly exasperated by the Athenians' attack on Sardis (namely, the Ionian Revolt in 499-493 BC), he now reacted with a much more intense fury and became even more determined to make war on Hellas (i.e. Greece) than he had been before. At once he began to issue commands and to send messengers throughout the cities of the empire with instructions to each of them to provide a great deal more than they had provided previously, including horses, food, warships, and transport boats. The announcement of these orders threw Asia" into commotion for three years as the best men were enlisted to serve in the army and to make preparations for war against Hellas. Then in the fourth year the Egyptians,' who had been enslaved by Cambyses, revolted from the Persians, which only increased Darius' desire to go to war, but now against both peoples." "The Landmark Herodotus" translated by Andrea L. Purvis, page 493).

The Second Persian Invasion (480-479 BC) was more impressive. Darius I and his successor, Xerxes I (r. 486-465 BC), prepared an army ten times larger than that of Darius. He crossed the Dardanelles in 480 BC.

At the narrow pass of Thermopylae located at the mouth of the Greek Peninsula, a force of combined Hellenic force of more than five thousand men from a dozen Hellenic cities camped at the pass and waited for the Persian army which was advancing south to enter the Greek mainland. Each contingent was led by the commanders assigned by their cities, but the most admired leader of the whole army was Leonidas.

Such a small number of the Greek forces formed ranks and repelled the attacks of the massive Persian army day after day, and King Xerxes was at a loss about how to deal with the impasse. It was, however, infiltrated through the path around the mountain under the guidance of a local traitor called Ephialtes.

At the sight of the sudden appearance of the Persian army, the Greek forces split up: those who lacked zeal to fight departed and scattered to their several cities, while the rest prepared to remain there Leonidas and the three hundred Spartans who thought that it would be ignoble to leave the pass for the glory and prosperity of Sparta. One of the Hellenic forces, the seven hundred Thespians led by commander Demophilos, was quite willing to stay with the Spartans and die with them.

The Greek forces fought with reckless desperation and no regard for their lives. By the time most of their spears had broken, they were slaying the Persian army with their swords in a violent struggle over the corpse. On the last spot of fighting, they defended themselves with daggers if they still had them, or if not, with their hands and teeth.

The Spartans and the Thespians alike proved themselves to be brave in the battle. They were buried where they had fallen. An inscription was erected there which said *"Three million foes were once fought right here, By four thousand men from the Peloponnes, Tell this, passerby, to the Lacedaemonians (another word for Spartans): It is here that we lie, their commands we obey"*

Xerxes I pushed on to Thebes and Athens. Thebes surrendered and the Athenians abandoned their city, and it was burnt. Greece seemed in the thrall to complete destruction, but again came victory against the odds. The large numbers of the Persian army and navy proved to be undoing in the narrow waters of the straits between the mainland and Salamis Island. The Greek fleet, though a third the size of the Persian, assailed it in the narrow straits and destroyed it.

Xerxes I found himself and his immense army cut off from supplies and his heart was broken when he retreated to Asia with one-half of his army, leaving the rest defeated at Platea (479 BC). The remnants of the Persian fleet were hunted down by the Greeks and destroyed at the Battle of Mycalae (479 BC) in Asia Minor. This would soon be the turn of the Greek civilization to overrun the Persian Empire.

Meanwhile, Greece had shown social leveling effects in the war mobilizations of the Athenian citizens bound by the culture of civil duties. This constrained the rise of inequality, and, consequently, the city-state civilization of ancient Greece enjoyed moderate levels of wealth and income inequality that helped sustain democracy.

Darius I made a blunder to invade Greece out of anger and pride, and his son, Xerxes I, made another blunder to do the same invasion.

Persian Empire declined as Darius I died in 486 BC and Xerxes I was assassinated in 465 BC. The heyday of the Empire that Cyrus the Great bequeathed in 530 BC lasted only for 60 years. It fell as the last emperor, the Darius III (r. 336–330 BC) was murdered in 330 BC by his kinsman when Alexander the Great pursued him after the Greek victory at the Battle of Gaugamela in 331 BC.

In the spring of 334 BC, Alexander crossed the Dardanelles (aka Hellespont) into Asia with at least 50,000 soldiers. He proceeded the Persian campaigns (334-327 BC), the Egyptian campaign (332 BC), and the Indian campaign (327-326 BC). At its peak, the Macedonian Empire of the Alexander the Great covered an area from the Balkan Peninsula, through Mesopotamia, to the Indian subcontinent.

In the ever-increasing expanse of the occupied lands, Alexander appeared to have become increasingly convinced that he was indeed all-powerful in the delusion that made his relations with his army sour. He pushed his army to the point of mutiny, and many thousands died on the journey home. Although the campaigns brought a Hellenizing influence to the growing empire, he made a blunder to push it beyond the operable limit.

It is contrasted with the border-restructuring of Emperor Hadrian (r.117-138) in the Roman Empire who paved the road to help make the Empire sustainable.

This refers to a case of the Alexander Great. A greater inducement to folly and danger is excess power because no one was able to resist the temptation of arbitrary power. In the first stage, mental confidence of Alexander succeeded in subduing territorial expansion across continents. In the second stage, when disagreements and disobedience happened, the initial principles of confidence of the great leader were changed to obsession and rigidity, and in the third stage, when the negative mood saturated, the failures enlarged the damages until Alexander died in 323 BC.

History witnessed that the imperial vision had passed from Cyrus of the Persian Empire to Alexander the Great, to Roman emperors, Muslim caliphs, Charlemagne in Europe, the Western politicians for imperial expansion in the 19th century, even Hitler in the Nazi and Stalin in the Soviet Union in the 20th century, and to American presidents in the Pax-Americana world.

3) The golden age of India

Between 1800 and 1500 BC, a watershed transformed life in India. The Indo-Aryan migrated from the central Asia Steppe into India which expanded into the Indus Valley and the Ganges Plain. This brought

Indo-European languages into India, like how the Steppe migrations into Europe around 3000 BC brought Indo-European languages to that region.

The Vedic Civilization (1800-500 BC) was centered in the northwestern parts of the Indian subcontinent and spread around 1200 BC to the Indo-Gangetic Plain, a flat and fertile land covering most of what is now northeastern India. It is named after the Rig Veda, the oldest scripture in Hinduism, composed during the early period of Vedic Civilization.

After the 12th century BC, Vedic society transitioned from semi-nomadic to settled agriculture. The development of iron axes and plows enabled the Indo-Aryans to settle the thick forests on the western Indo-Gangetic Plain. The agricultural expansion led to an increase in trade, competition for resources, and larger political units that coalesced many old tribes.

The Indus Valley region faced incessant threats from great powers in the West, such as the Persians' conquest that annexed the valley region by Cyrus the Great (r.550–530 BC) and Darius the Great (r.522-486 BC). It marked the beginning of outside influence in Vedic society and then Alexander the Great's campaign to India in 327-325 BC.

The Maurya Empire (320-185 BC) was the first pan-Indian empire, bordering the Greek Empire of Alexander the Great. At its zenith under King Ashoka (r.272-232 BC), it unified most of the Indian continent by crushing local revolts across India. It was just decades before Chin Shi Huang (r. 221-210 BC) unified China.

The Maurya monarchy established a highly centralized administrative system with a bureaucratic framework supported by a standing army and civil service, which helped operate the vast empire. It also flourished in economic activities, art, and architecture. Interestingly, Chin Shi Huang performed similar tasks to govern a unified China.

The religion of the Brahmans molded the mindset of craft and trade groups, leading to the establishment of a rigid social system with four castes: Kshatriyas (rulers and soldiers), Vaishyas (cultivators), and Sudras (toilers), the latter comprising conquered peoples. This system has persisted for millennia, even in the continued growth of trade and industry.

In contemporary India, some believe that market capitalism will ultimately erode the caste system, and the stratified society of India will be changing toward a free and open society. However, it looks sensible to assume for now that some people still face barriers to access to the markets and remain trapped in the vicious circle of debt and occupational inequality.

Some people in modern-day India think that market capitalism will eventually weaken the caste system and cause India's stratified society to shift toward freedom and openness. In some provincial states, many people adopted a single name to distance themselves from caste identity.

Despite the changes and reforms that have partially reduced caste inequality, caste identities remain strong, and last names often indicate a person's caste. The overall condition reveals that the caste system remains unscathed, especially in rural areas, where caste continues to be a significant force.

4) Roman Republic and Roman Empire

(1) Roman history

Rome conquered the people outside its territory. It began to mutate towards an empire as the people of power (the conquerors) controlled those of no power (the conquered). It was the same pattern as the precedent empires, for example, the Persians under Darius the Great (r.522-486 BC), and the Macedonians under Alexander the Great (r.336-323 BC) had done.

The Roman Republic (509-527 BC) was a city-state in 340 BC in Italy. It became the master of the peninsula by 264 BC, and it destroyed its archrival, Carthage, in the Punic Wars (264-146 BC). However, the Republic started to decline mainly due to internal conflicts, slave revolts, and the impoverishment of the peasantry. They showed a pattern mixed with subsistence and politics in violent protests. The mechanisms of practicing the Roman virtues such as a sense of responsibility and devotion to country, and the law did not function in good order.

Attempts at reform by the Gracchus brothers failed (133 BC, 122–121 BC) after both were murdered. Internal conflicts among Roman generals turned to civil wars, and the Senate was unable to effectively regulate the civil wars. Julius Caesar took power in 46 BC but was assassinated in 44 BC. A vicious circle of destruction was created between competition at home and aggressive warfare abroad.

The Roman Republic had tragically ended as Augustus became emperor in 27 BC.

The period of the Roman Empire (27 BC-476 AD) was marked by a series of incompetent and disoriented emperors, although it was interspersed with the rule of five capable and disciplined emperors for 84 years (96-180 AD): Nerva, Trajan, Hadrian, Antonius Pius, and Marcus Aurelius. The Roman Empire reached its zenith of power and territory expansion under Emperor Trajan (r.98-117 AD).

All empires inevitably experience a series of stages, beginning with their inception, followed by a period of dominance, maturation, and eventual decline, ultimately leading to their collapse. When indications of decline emerge, the political apparatus initially experiences a loss of coherence and subsequently undergoes a breakdown. The empire which was sustained by the exploitation of peasants and slaves dysfunctions.

The Roman Republic and the Roman Empire exerted a dominant influence on the global stage, utilizing the spoils of war to construct an extensive network of roads, aqueducts, basilicas, amphitheaters, monuments, baths, and bridges. Those of greater wealth grew, while citizen armies were deployed for longer periods and at greater distances from their homes.

A prevailing atmosphere of opulence and a sense of arrogance as their protective carapace emerged within the upper echelons of society, giving way to a reversal of the traditional virtues, which was now followed by a vicious decline. When the systems are no longer functional, the empire becomes susceptible to competition and challenges from external actors.

The decline of the Roman Empire commenced with the death of Marcus Aurelius, the last of the five good Emperors, in 180 AD. It persisted until the deposition of the last Emperor in the west, Romulus Augustus, in 476 AD. Emperor Constantine (r. 306-337 AD) legalized Christianity in 313 AD and officially dedicated Constantinople as the new capital of the Roman Empire in 329 AD. With the fall of the Western Roman Empire in 476 AD, the Dark Ages commenced and persisted until the 15th century in Western Europe.

The Roman period is divided into phases of political systems that existed in history from the founding of the Eternal City in 753 B.C. until the final destruction of the Eastern Roman Empire in 1453, which lasted 2,206 years. In the dimension of specific political and geographical entities, it can be detailed below:

- Roman Kingdom had existed for 244 years (753 BC-509 BC)

- Roman Republic for 482 years (509 BC-27 BC)

- Roman Empire which had been unified for 422 years (27 BC-395 AD)

- Western Roman Empire for 81 years (395-476 AD). When it is combined with the Roman Kingdom, Roman Republic, and unified Roman Empire, the total duration is 1,229 years (753 BC-476 AD)

- Easter Roman Empire for 1,058 years (395-1,453 AD). When it is combined with the Roman Kingdom, Roman Republic, and unified Roman Empire, the total duration is 2,206 years (753 BC-1,453 AD)

In summary, the greatness of the Roman world was caused by the various mechanisms of governance.

There was the physical bond of military garrisons and stone roads. The Roman roads facilitated travel between garrisons, all of which were connected to Rome itself, through which Roman laws and common standards of conduct were disseminated and applied, and the practices built the organizational bond. The Romans exercised psychological control by maintaining allegiance through a mixture of loyalty and fear, and those who did not pledge allegiance to Rome faced utter destruction and annihilation.

The greatness of Roman authority and its cohesiveness was impaired by the collapse of the Roman Republic caused by civil wars among generals and an incompetent political apparatus, and failures of the checks and balances in the Republicanism to serve its purpose and was inefficient in exercising its powers.

If we compare it to the Greek influence, the Greeks had grown from several scattered cities that spread by ships along the sea routes of the Mediterranean, while the Roman influence grew from a single organism. The Romans were land people, and they made territorial conquests with their legions marching along the Roman roads.

The Roman empirical system was not always active and principled in reforming itself and sometimes suffered from indiscipline, arbitrariness, and complacency in governing the vast empire with timely reforms. The decline began with the decadence and disintegration of Roman control in the 3rd century AD. It led to crumbling at the edges and demoralization at the center, as a succession of short-lived emperors signaled the empire's weakening.

The fish rots from the head. The great but underperforming and un-reforming Roman Empire followed the same pattern as the fish. All roads were connected to Rome, but the same roads led away from Rome as well.

(2) Roman mind

The Romans took their virtues as a code of conduct; 'gravistas' (a sense of seriousness and responsibility), 'pietas' (a sense of devotion to country and parents), and 'justia' (a sense of law, justice, and enforcement).

The Roman virtues were set by notable thinkers, including Marcus Tullius Cicero (106-43 BC), Lucretius (99-55 BC), Seneca (4 BC-65 AD), and Marcus Aurelius (r.161-180), who conveyed Greek philosophy to the Romans and developed the Latin terminology that formed the basis for the spreading of philosophy into the Middle Ages.

The Stoicism

One Greek school of thought, the Stoics, was founded by Zenon of Cyprus (335-263 BC) and took the name from the Athenian Stoa poikilê or 'the painted porch', where the group first gathered. They followed the conviction that human passions that cast calculation aside should be governed by reason and that the pursuit of virtue.

The vision of a universal fraternity, sense of duty, and disciplined training proved especially attractive to the Romans with their temperament. The Stoic creed of fortitude fleshed out its main postulate that the world was a theater for the display of human willpower and that the difficulties of human life were trials that appealed to Roman stubbornness and self-respect. However, its lack of natural sympathy for human suffering was not a shock to Roman pride.

The Stoics argued that the best, most virtuous, and most divine life was one lived according to reason, armed with calms and sensible mind of industry, discernment, and innovation, and levelheadedness, and unfettered exercise of the rational mind to sand humanity's rough edges, rather than the search for pleasure. This did not mean that humans had to shun pleasure; rather, it should be enjoyed in the right way. As human beings share reason and communal sense, humanity as a whole can be seen as a kind of community.

Stoics entered politics not for public approval, wealth, or power which were of no value to them, but they found meaning in improving the communities to which they belonged. Politics was painful as it would often prove for Cicero, but that was not so important because what mattered was the virtuous life loyal to the ideology.

Cicero was born in 106 BC into a wealthy Roman family from the town of Arpinum, southeast of Rome. His politics were much more traditional than blue-blooded radicals of noble births like Julius Caesar and the Gracchi brothers. His studies took him to Athens, where he was deeply influenced by the Hellenic philosophies of Plato and the Stoics, which shaped his thinking.

Cicero's generation did not create either Latin literature or the idea of a distinctive Roman educational canon, but they fixed both in their forms. Like most people of the ancient Mediterranean, Romans had lived for centuries in a world where culture meant Greek culture. No earlier than the 60s BC did the Romans create a complete and independent Latin literary culture.

In real life, Cicero was an orator, lawyer, politician, and philosopher. His powerful rhetoric not only swayed the Roman Senate but also profoundly shaped the art of speech in Western civilization. His life coincided with the decline and fall of the Roman Republic, and he was at the center of the turbulence of significant political events of his time.

Cicero subordinated philosophy to politics and he, therefore, tried to use philosophy to achieve his political goals. He hoped that the leaders of Rome would listen to his pleas to renew the Republic for which the Roman elites prioritized individual virtue and social stability over their desires for fame, wealth, and power.

Towards the end of the Roman Republic, internal political instability and power struggles for supremacy between high-ranking military leaders ultimately contributed to its collapse. Cicero was a staunch defender of the principles of the Republic, often in conflict with powerful figures promoting an autocratic agenda. Despite his best efforts, the Republic marked the end of the Roman Republic and the beginning of autocratic rule. Roman nobles maintained stoic restraint until the end of the Republic. However, once it came to an end, they were unable to continue their restraint.

He was murdered on 7 December 43 BC, but he was later revived by Tetrarch's discovery of Cicero's letters to his friend, Atticus, at Verona in 1345. It was regarded as a foundational moment of the Renaissance that brought to light the elements of Cicero's humanistic character. The view of him from the Renaissance was that he was a mortal, weak, timorous, and vacillating human, not superhuman.\

Seneca (4 BC-65 AD) was a major philosophical figure of the Roman Empire. As a Stoic, Seneca explored ethics and the importance of reason. He emphasized rationality and self-control to live in harmony with nature regardless of external circumstances. He also found himself in his role of checking and balancing on Emperor Nero as his minister and tutor until he retired.

Marcus Aurelius, the last one of five good emperors, was a man of the Stoicism who laid out the rules for virtue and happiness. Two other notable Stoic writers were Seneca and Epictetus. With the aid of Marcus Aurelius' powerful and moving writing in the "Meditations", Stoicism became a paragon of the virtue of Rome, although its actual practice depended on individuals.

"Meditations" were his private thoughts on how to make good on the responsibilities and obligations of his position. Trained in Stoic philosophy, he practiced a series of spiritual exercises almost every night —reminders to make him humble, patient, empathetic, generous, and strong in the face of whatever he was dealing with.

Here are a few selected phrases from Meditations that illustrate the main features Marcus Aurelius shared with himself:

"Finally, then, remember this retreat into your own little territory within yourself. Above all, no agonies, no tensions. Be your own master, and look at things as a man, as a human being, as a citizen, as a mortal creature. And here are two of the most immediately useful thoughts you will dip into. First, things cannot touch the mind: they are external and inert; anxieties can only come from your internal judgment. Second, all these things you see will change almost as you look at them, and then will be no more. Constantly bring to mind all that you yourself have already seen changed. The universe is transformation: life is opinion." (Meditations 4.3.4., Translated by Martin Hammond. Only for the underlined, meanwhile, it was translated by George Long).

Marcus Aurelius tried to achieve a man of composure who maintained a state of calmness and acceptance of one's fate (*amor fati*) by separating himself from the things that agonized him. He intended to keep the challenges from affecting his inner being because all of the things were in flux and upheaval, and the adversity might be turned into a different state when the time of change came.

"When you fret at any circumstance, you have forgotten a number of things. You have forgotten that all comes about in accordance with the nature of the Whole; that any wrong done lies with the other; further, that **everything which happens was always so in the past, will be the same again in the future, and is happening now across the world;** that a human being has close kinship with the whole human race — not a bond of blood or seed, but a community of mind. And you have forgotten this too, that every man's mind is good and has flowed from that source; that nothing is our own property, but even our child, our body, our very soul has come from that source; that all is as thinking makes it so; that each of us lives only the present moment, and the present moment is all we lose" (Meditations 12.26., Translated by Martin Hammond).

During his emperorship, Marcus Aurelius was confronted with a series of problems such as the German rebellions and the plague. Even in these daily burdens, he reminded himself of the things that he must remember that there is nothing new under the sun and everything that he owned was not his property. He just told himself. Live the day".

The Epicureanism

Epicureanism was named after Epicurus (342-270 BC) of Samos, Greece taught that people should devote themselves to the pursuit of happiness, fearing neither death nor the gods. They held that the road to happiness lay through self-control, calm, and self-denial.

The belief gained significant traction during the Roman era. It emphasized the pursuit of modest pleasure through achieving a state of ataraxia (a lucid state of tranquility or freedom from fear) and aponia (the absence of bodily or mental pain) through knowledge of the workings of the world and limiting desires. Correspondingly, they withdrew from politics because it could lead to frustrations and ambitions that would conflict with their pursuit of virtue and peace of mind.

Epicureanism was particularly influential in the late Roman Republic and early Roman Empire periods. It attracted followers like the poet Lucretius. Epicureanism is often misunderstood as a philosophy solely focused on seeking pleasure. Nonetheless, its fundamental principles placed a strong emphasis on avoiding pointless desires and anxieties in order to live a peaceful and pain-free existence.

Epicureanism and hedonism are both related to pleasure and happiness, but they have different approaches. Hedonism considers pleasure as the highest good and aim of human life. It strives to maximize net pleasure (pleasure minus pain) whereas Epicureanism advocates for modest pleasures, intellectual contemplation, and minimal pain as keys to happiness.

(3) Polarization

The structure of Roman society is commonly depicted as a social hierarchy, with emperors and senators at the top, taxed citizens in the middle who were taxed, and enlisted for military service, and enslaved individuals at the bottom.

The privileged few controlled interests in both peace and war – wealth generation, career opportunities, and booty of war. They acquired their wealth through heredity over generations or exclusive entitlements. The exploitative latifundia estate was illustrative of value extraction from the less privileged such as bonded labor and slavery.

Free men were the intermediate class between the privileged few and slaves. They were burdened to play the role of supporting the Pax Romana in its expansion and defense. They were technicians in social service and were subject to taxation. When they lost land or were heavily indebted, they had to do seasonal work or were reduced to enslavement.

Slaves were either born or made. Multiple reasons had them enslaved such as prisoners of war, captured and sold by pirates, kidnapped, abandoned, or defaulted on debt. They were considered the property of their owners, bought, sold, and mistreated at will. They had no personal rights to own property, enter into a contract, or marry legally while in servitude.

The seeds of destruction were planted as social polarization arose from the malfunction and imbalance in the stratified system. Society became polarized as the privileged few got wealthier, while free citizens became increasingly impoverished. The showy facade of great Roman pride and prowess was supported by flagrant polarization.

The pugnacious discrepancy bred a wave of civil conflicts that cracked the networked infrastructure, administration, and military power. It started with the Conflict of Orders (500-287 BC) between Plebeians and Patricians in the ancient Roman Republic for political equality and justice. The strife intensified over the following centuries.

History tells us that the problem bursts into an explosion if pressure is not defused in time. It is best to bridge the gap or reform the structured problem of polarity before reaching the boiling point of implosion. However, it is easier said than done because the relevant parties usually get stuck in perverse conviction, complacent hubris, unwillingness to change, or simply a sense of despair, and they cannot or will not reform themselves willingly. The great Romans were not exception.

(4) The Gracchus-brothers reforms

During its continuous expansion, the Roman Republic confiscated a lot of arable land from defeated enemies. The Romans converted it into public land that was either given to settlers or rented out. The portion of the latter came to benefit those who could only afford to cultivate in large tracts of land. It caused the public land to become concentrated in the hands of the wealthy.

The mass of free citizens and peasants who had fought and paid taxes for the Roman Republic got poorer. The backbone stratum was slowly perishing due to the influx of slaves and the concentration of land ownership. Their properties were at risk of forfeiture, and those who defaulted on debt fell into bonded labor or outright slavery.

Tiberius Gracchus (163-133 BC), from the oligarchic ruling class, won a tribuneship in 133 BC. The issue of land reform reached a critical point in 133 BC when he proposed a land redistribution program limiting land ownership to just over 300 acres of public land. He became a champion of the plebeians (from Latin plēbēius belonging to the people, from plēbs the common people of ancient Rome) who yearned for reform.

The plan required large landowners to redistribute the public land to poor citizens without proper compensation for prior investments. It further made the land inalienable to prevent the rich and powerful from buying out or displacing newly created smallholders, and it made efforts to enhance this program by providing settlers with startup funds.

On one hand, the land reform excited poorer peasants, leading them to flood into Rome to support his proposal, and ensure its passage through the Republic's assembly. On the other hand, it infuriated most of the rich senatorial class, who were horrified at the prospect of the amassing peasant mob.

The two forces proceeded in stages to the extent that the life of Tiberius Gracchus was endangered by enraged oligarchs. A body of senators pointing an accusatory finger at him for betraying the constitution clubbed him to death in 133 BC, while his followers were executed. Nevertheless, the repression did not deter the rising discontent among the impoverished peasantries.

Gaius Gracchus (154-121 BC), the brother of the murdered Tiberius Gracchus, was elected tribune in 123 BC. He was not in the mood of once bitten, twice shy when it came to reforming the Roman Republic. He attempted to make reforms. One of the reforms he supported was a bill promoting colonization programs for both Italians and foreigners, specifically in Carthage (an ancient city-state, on the North African coast near present-day Tunis. It was destroyed in the three-year siege by the Roman Republic during the Third Punic War in 146 BC. It was re-developed a century later as Roman Carthage) due to the lack of available land in Italy for resettlement.

The Senate didn't agree with it and appointed consul Lucius Opimius to attack Gaius Gracchus and his allies. Optimus and his supporters, along with mercenaries, murdered Gaius Gracchus and executed up to 3,000 of his supporters in 121 BC.

Tiberius and Gaius's land reform initiatives were intended to bolster the Roman Republic even if they sympathized with the plight of peasants. Should their reforms have been successful in redistributing the land and resettling the destitute, they could have addressed the social crisis of the plebians and helped transform the trajectory of Roman history.

The Roman Republic peaked in power around the first centuries of BC/AD, transforming the Mediterranean into a Roman lake for trade and tributes. It enriched the Romans beyond all recognition, but a great danger lurked in the shadow of the peak. Roman politics failed to defuse the tension from land conflicts, and it rendered one of the reasons that the Roman Republic started to degenerate.

It reveals the truth that reform is too important to be delayed or ignored when problems are evident from the lack of it. Many states' failures stem from no-reform or sluggish-reform by the reason of either the limited capacity (normally, they are a minority or ill-organized) of pro-reformers or the dragging heels of anti-reformers (normally, they are a majority or well-organized). Nothing is more important than timely reform. When the reform occurs too early, society may reject it; if too late, it may be too late for society to recuperate itself.

Standing in late 2024, President Yoon has taken steps to address a number of reform-issues in Korean society, such as the government, medical services, national pension, demographic shifts, household debt, student education, and the labor market. If these reforms are not addressed and completed in a timely manner, they could result in serious and immediate dangers. This has nothing to do with favoring or disfavoring a particular political figure; rather, it is about the vital interests of future generations in the 21st century, particularly the young people who will be directly impacted by the reform outcomes.

Everyone believes that reforms are necessary, but no one is willing to cover the associated costs, thus it is the leaders' art and science to move forward with the reforms. Restructuring current mechanisms to implement reform initiatives requires immediate attention. Although opposition to those reforms is not new, it must be overcome, accommodated, or disregarded in order to continue working toward the reforms and ultimately finish them.

They will undoubtedly burden or injure future generations if they are not appropriately reformed in a timely manner. Eventually, this will make society ineffective, which will lead to systemic failure, and collapse. Following the Gracchi brothers' unsuccessful reforms, the Roman Republic peaked a century later before gradually deteriorating until its fall in 476 AD.

By their very nature, the reform issues are likened to be time-bombs that will explode when the time comes. They will have an impact on those present at the detonation if the time bombs are not defused in a timely manner. Reform resisters are individuals who remain obdurate and casually pass the time bombs to those next to them without defusing them. They might be elephant-gazers in the room, recognizing the problems surrounding them but acting as though they don't exist. Such measures are all pointless and irresponsible, but only timely reforms are of importance and significance.

This refers to the "Vote for the reformers in the Part 7.

(5) Slave revolts

Slavery has existed in various places and times throughout human history, as have slave rebellions that emerged from the denial of human rights and property. It was the highest form of protest by those who were left with no option but to resist in the face of the most terrifying odds.

The entire Roman state and cultural apparatus was built on the exploitation of slaves to sustain itself. Regarded as no more than commodities, slaves were treated primarily to preserve their value as workers and assets for future sale. In the list of slave rebellions, three cases are chosen to illustrate the stark realities of servitude.

First, a revolt took place in Sicily from 135-132 BC, led by Eunus and aided by Cleon, both former slaves. Eunus revolted with 400 fellow slaves and took control of the island. Eunus proclaimed himself king, minted coins, secured supplies and formed a communal environment for ongoing protest. It ultimately involved tens of thousands of slaves, including herders and agricultural workers.

They received some support from local people who were delighted to see the rich were retaliated and killed. Indeed, while the slaves tried to maintain order and work the farms for themselves to sustain their protest, the free population engaged in looting the wealthy. The pattern of behavior was seen in other revolts as well.

The rebellion successfully repelled several Roman attempts to quell it for three years, aided by the treacherous Sicilian terrain. In 133 BC, consul Lucius Piso recaptured the city of Messana and put 8,000 prisoners to death. In 132 BC, consul Publius Rupulius marched on Enna, resulting in the death of Cleon, and around 20,000 prisoners were crucified in retribution.

A Second revolt erupted in the same island Sicily from 104-100 BC when a Senate decree called for the freeing of all freemen kidnapped and enslaved by pirates in the eastern Mediterranean. It meant that illegally enslaved freemen had the right to claim their freedom through manumission (literally meaning 'releasing from the hand').

Following the decree, the provincial governor, Publius Licinius Nerva, freed 800 slaves. This alienated the landed nobility who were concerned about losing their workforce, and they pressured the governor to hold it back. A rebellion broke out when the governor backtracked and ordered the enslaved back to servitude.

A slave by the name of Salvius amassed an army of more than twenty thousand slaves and organized them into infantry and cavalry units. Unlike the first rebellion, it lacked communal support, and a clear strategic objective was missing. It was massive in its size, but the revolt failed because of a lack of clear strategy and local support.

Third, a gladiatorial revolt broke out and threatened the very center of the Roman Republic in 73-71 BC. A band of more than 70 gladiators led by Spartacus broke off gladiatorial barracks in Capua and revolted demanding the abolition of slavery. His ranks were joined by runaways and herdsmen from the latifundia of southern Italy, swelling their ranks to about 70,000.

The rebellion remains the most successful slave resistance in the history of Rome. The slave army defeated hastily assembled Roman defenses while plundering the countryside. However, the very reasons for their initial success contributed to their eventual downfall. Their successes started to ruin them.

An opportunity existed for them to return to their native homelands beyond the Alps. Spartacus had no illusions of winning the slave war against the Roman army. He tried to convince the rebels to march through the Alps and scatter to their homelands in Gaul (modern-day, France and Germany) and Thrace (modern-day, south-eastern Bulgaria).

Filled with confidence and the allure of pillage and revenge, the rank and file did not heed his advice. While the rebels drifted through the countryside, Spartacus's army kept fighting, and they attempted to evade the Roman army by crossing the Straits of Messina to Sicily, where the first and second servile wars had been fought. They, however, made ill-timed and badly judged attacks on the Roman lines and were betrayed by pirates and finally rounded up in Apulia.

The revolting slave army eventually lost steam and ceased their movements. Spartacus died in a hard-fought battle at Senerchia, southwestern Italy. The six thousand captive slaves were crucified and showcased along the Appian Way (a Roman road connecting Rome to the southern Adriatic coast) over more than 100 miles.

The Spartacus rebellion marked the last of the major slave insurrections in ancient Roman history. It granted the sense and value of the slave laborers, and it induced the Roman landowners to treat their slaves more leniently and humanely. Emperor Honorius banned gladiatorial contests in about 404.

(6) Five good emperors and the others

"When the wicked rise to power, people go into hiding, but when the wicked perish, the righteous thrive" (Proverb 28:28). The Roman Empire (27 BC-476 AD) faced significant risks of succession, often plagued by morally decayed or self-indulgent emperors, except for an 84- year period (96-180) when five good emperors reigned, leaving the empire secure and stable.

Before and after the 84-year interlude, the Roman Empire was ruled by emperors of moral decay or self-indulgence. Some wicked emperors were the authors of ill and creators of misery, and cruel and sanguinary. It is said that beauty is defiled first from the core as dead fish rots from the head. The longlist of obnoxious emperors contained more than its share of degeneration. They are often cited as contributors to the decline of the Roman Empire due to their incompetent leadership and wicked behaviors.

This section examines the records of Caesar and the 23 Roman emperors from 59 BC to 193 AD to highlight issues of succession, leadership, and their effects. We can notice how succession succeeded or failed in achieving the common good for the Roman populace when we distinguish the periods before and after the five good emperors.

The records reveal that wayward emperors were rather common, while the series of five good emperors appeared unusual in the fragile succession system of the Roman Empire. This is just intended to know the issue of succession that significantly impacted the Roman Empires, including the training of successors or the presence of immature and eccentric leaders.

Everything has a cost, and nothing exists in a vacuum. In the course of emperorship, various causal elements determined whether an emperor was good or bad. As part of the succession plan, an heir apparent was chosen from the emperor's "household" and trained. The risk of succession would have been much reduced if the succession had been handled according to the principle of talent and personality for the imperial leadership rather than family inheritance.

Some readers may wonder why the descriptions of Roman Emperors below are lengthy. The answer is that, in terms of the Roman Empire's long-term sustainability, it is worthwhile to focus more on the shift from the Roman Republic to the Roman Empire, and the empirical leadership that had caused either positive or negative impacts. The accumulation of excesses and deficiencies made by numerous deviant emperors, along with the Senate's lack of checks and balances, led to the fall of the Roman Empire in 476 AD. A number of reforming emperors and leaders attempted to correct or lessen the excesses and deficiencies, but they were unable to stop the decline of the great Roman Empire until it reached the point of collapse.

The tangled successions of emperors before the Five Good Emperors

C. Iulius Caesar (r.59-44 BC, 15 years)

He was a celebrated Roman general and statesman, serving as the last Roman Republic consul, the conqueror of Gaul, present-day France, Belgium, Luxembourg, and parts of Switzerland, the Netherlands, Germany, and Northern Italy. (58–50 BC), victor in the civil war (49–45 BC), and dictator (46–44 BC). Caesar was launching a series of political and social reforms when he was assassinated by a group of nobles in the Senate House in 44 BC.

Endowed with a vitality that showed scarcely any sign of flagging and mastery in sword, pen, and tongue, he applied his talents with a swiftness of decision and a directness of aim that set him on a level with

Alexander the Great as a supreme man of action with a sovereign self-assurance that cast a spell on his friends and foes alike.

It was difficult to detect in him a vein of natural kindness. His subordinates gave him strict obedience but did not open their minds to him. Caesar's enemies were disgusted by his shameless bribing of the Roman populace, his manipulation of politicians, and the smash-and-grab policy of his military campaigns.

On 10 January 49 BC, Caesar shouted in a sort of passion "Alea iacta est!" which was the gambler's traditional cry: "Let the die be cast!" powered by political tensions and his desire for power. It was an act of defiance against the Roman Senate's ultimatum to disband his army and return to Rome. This decision opened the broad gates of civil war that ended the Roman Republic.

Caesar's capacity was most apparent in the administrative reforms: the land reform that distributed public land to the landless and limited the maximum amount of land an individual could own; the calendar reform that adopted a solar calendar; the expansion of citizenship that fostered a sense of belonging to the Roman Empire; and the Judicial reform to consolidate and codify Roman laws.

He was already becoming ambitious for power when he ruled Gaul. Some people thought that, from the time he started in politics, Caesar was aiming to become a king. But the facts show that he only decided to end the Republic later on. As he was further along in his plans to fix the main problems with the Roman system, he changed himself to be a dictatorial leader gradually.

His dictatorship with absolute power ended with his assassination by a group of republican conspirators headed by M. Brutus and C. Cassius Longinus. After Caesar's death, the leadership of the Caesarian party was assumed by his nephew, Octavian. The chaos that followed his death is no proof of failure in his statesmanship.

The responsibility for these falls on those who cut short their work of reform and reconstruction before it had been completed.

Although some of the trappings of people's representations remained and the personality of Caesar was contentious, the system of the Roman Empire from then on opened the door to the tyrannical rule of the Roman Emperors. The assassination of the benign dictator, Caesar, had set an example of pursuing personal privileges and influence by conspiracy, and it ended hopes of a return to the ideals of the Roman Republic. It was the blunder of the group of Roman senators who committed the assassination.

Augustus (r.31 BC-14 AD, 27 years)

The fortunate circumstances conspired to promote his political elevation: the adoption by Julius Caesar, the twelve-year triumvirate of Octavian, Mark Antony, and his ally Lepidus after Caesar's death, Mark Antony's bewitchment by Cleopatra, and his flattery and duplicity were the great instruments.

The naval battle of Actium on 02 September 31 BC was fought between Octavian's fleet and the combined fleets of both Mark Antony and Cleopatra VII of Egypt. The result, favorable to Octavian, ended the civil wars of the Octavian-Antony rivalry, finished off the Roman Republic, and gave Octavian the supreme title of Augustus, as the emperor of the Roman Empire.

With the fall of the Republic, the authority of the Roman Senate eroded under the monarchical system of government known as the Principate. It allowed for a dictatorial regime. Most Emperors upheld a facade of democracy, and in return, the Senate implicitly acknowledged the emperor's status as a monarch.

Augustus dramatically expanded the empire, including Egypt, Africa, Hispania, Britannia, Armenia, and Dacia, which took the form of the marvelous "Pax Romana", the 'Roman Peace.' This peace extended along the front lines from Hadrian's Wall to the Danube delta, whereby the provinces were firmly controlled, and wars were largely confined to the distant frontiers.

Under the stress of the civil wars and political convulsions, the population suffered heavy losses. With the restoration of political security during the reign of Augustus, the census returns of 28 BC and 13 AD registered an increase in the citizen-body by four to five million, which showed that the decrease during the preceding decades had been reversed.

Augustus's last duty to Rome was to provide it with a successor to his own position. In this tenet, he made it a rule that the imperial power should, if possible, remain in his household. But he persistently hesitated to make a final selection, and the eventual choice was made by a play of chance rather than by his own act after the tangle of succession was straightened out.

Whatever Augustus' shortcomings in his dynastic policy, he had been at pains to give each of his potential heirs through training in the art of government. In this respect, Tiberius was seen to be perfectly qualified to carry on Augustus' work, and the first and most important succession between emperors took place almost without a jolt.

The Julio-Claudian dynasty (Tiberius, Caligula, Claudius, and Nero).
Tiberius (r.14-37, 23 years)

He was chosen as the successor of Augustus only when he was the last man standing, as the young men Augustus had groomed for the throne – Gaius, Lucius, and Marcellus – died under mysterious circumstances. Some people suspected that Augustus' wife and Tiberius' mother, Livia, arranged their deaths.

Tiberius was a fearsome soldier, but he turned out to be a poor politician. He retreated from Rome to the island of Capri in the middle of his reign. Sejanus, the head of the Praetorian Guard, co-ruled as de facto ruler of the Roman Empire until he was accused of orchestrating a coup against Tiberius in 31 and was put to death.

Historian Tacitus (56-117) recorded him as a man of depravity: "He was atrocious in his brutality, but his lechery was kept hidden while he loved - or feared - Sejanus who was the head of the Praetorian Guard. In the end, he erupted into an orgy of crime and ignominy alike, when, with all shame and fear removed, he simply followed instincts with abandon".

He rarely trusted people. Not only did his morbid distrustfulness disrupt his family life, but it also weighed down his administration. His scandalous acts were characterized by stories of a perverted private life, such as painting the imperial palace with pornographic images, engaging in pedophilia with small children, raping sacrificial attendants, and throwing his opponents off island cliffs.

The rumors about his depraved life held true to some extent. In this, we also need a balanced thought of

Roman rumor mills that produced besmirching gossip deliberately. He left the Roman Empire, at least, secure in its expansion and defense, and financially solvent, which was important for the Roman people.

He nominated Caligula as his joint heir together with his grandson Tiberius Gemellus.

After he died 37, the Senate refused to vote Tiberius the divine honors that had been paid to Augustus. He set an example of unsuccessful successions in the Roman Empire, ignominious depravity and impertinent crimes of emperors who were impervious to the routine urgency and importance of imperial issues. They cracked the greatness of the Roman Empire to its collapse.

Caligula (r.37-41, 4 years)

At the support of praetorian prefect Macro, the senate accepted Caligula as a new emperor. He was at first welcomed as a relief from the depraved Tiberius. The young emperor, 25 years old, gave a promise of fulfilling the hopes of the people. Apart from having the young Tiberius Gemellus put to death, Caligula began his reign well, repealing some unpopular laws. He regaled the Romans with circus shows and beast-hunts, he displayed a shrewd judgment and wit in performing the imperial tasks.

But the honeymoon was to be short-lived. After a few months, he was taken ill, and when he returned to the public, he was a different person – self-important, megalomaniac, sadistic, irrational, deluded, and depraved. His reign betrayed his incapacity for the imperial roles. His lack of training led to reckless profusion of money and harsh over-taxation.

His temper and attitude were so overbearing that he conflicted with the Senate, and he exhibited autocracy by removing his rivals without the pretense of trial. He treated the Senate with utter disrespect, and he went so far as to imprison or slaughter individual senators he perceived as threats to his rule.

Although accounts of his behavior may have been exaggerated, there is little doubt that he indulged in the pleasures of the senses to an extreme degree hosting orgiastic parties with sexual perversions and enjoying killing for its own sake. Caligula spent money lavishly for public entertainment and construction projects as well as for buildings for his own glory.

By 40, Caligula seemed to have been fully convinced that he was a god, turning his palace into a temple, presenting himself dressed as various divinities, and demanding that he be treated as one.

The misdemeanor gave rise to disloyalty in the praetorian guard. In 41, a tribune in the guard murdered him in a corner of the palace. Caligula's wife and his daughter were also put to death. He was succeeded by his uncle Claudius. Caligula had the imperial treasury devastated and his tyranny led to the death of many innocent Romans.

When Emperor Tiberius chose Caligula as his successor, he had no reason to suspect that his heir would prove to be as mad as a box of frogs. He had made an inadvertent blunder. The story illustrated a need to build talents as heir-apparent in or outside the household with proper training before accession to the throne.

Claudius I (r.41-54, 13 years)

Tiberius Claudius Drusus, the uncle of the deceased emperor, was found crouching for concealment in the attic of the palace after the murder of Caligula. He was carried off by the praetorian guard and persuaded to accept imperial power. Claudius accepted it and promised a special bounty for the guard in return for their allegiance.

This transaction heralded a new pattern that the throne was bought and sold in the praetorian camp. In the Senate, however, it was debated to appoint a new emperor, but it was cut short by the guards and forced them to put him on the throne. After a brief resistance, the Senate yielded in and conferred imperial power upon Claudius.

Until his accession at the age of fifty, he hadn't taken any offices in public. The emperor was handicapped by a congenital infirmity, clumsy gait, uncouth appearance, and slow and distracted state in his mind. As he got older, he became dependent even more on his mentors and advisors. He was inappropriately scruffy for his position as the emperor.

Claudius found his confidants or aides within his household for guidance on policies and personnel appointments. In his later years, a small group of freedmen (emancipated slaves) performed the roles of administrator and accountant and wielded great influence. Offices and favors were trafficked, and bribery and corruption became rampant.

The resentment of the Roman elites was aggrieved by the two wives of Claudius. The older, Messalina, was a licentious woman, while the younger, Agrippina, was lustful for power. The unscrupulous empresses influenced the emperor, and a great sense of insecurity prevailed, as dissenters were tried behind closed doors, booted out or executed out of hand.

The two wives fought a battle for succession: Messalina had a daughter, Octavia, and a son, Tiberius Claudius Britannicus, who was considered Claudius's heir, but he was challenged by his stepmother Agrippina's son, Domitius, from her previous marriage. Agrippina induced Claudius to adopt Domitius (renamed Nero Claudius Caesar) and to betroth him to Octavia.

When Claudius died in 54, the throne wasn't promptly transferred to Britannicus. Seeing this, Agrippina arranged for Nero to present himself to the praetorian guards, who were offered a bounty in exchange for their allegiance. The Senate confirmed the choice of the praetorian guard. The whole affair of prompt enthronement was orchestrated by Agrippina.

The tangled succession exhibited multifaceted factors that influenced the transfer of emperorship: the praetorian guards backing specific candidates in return for bounty, the emperor's senility, and the path-dependence of the Senate were to blame for the inordinate succession. The Romans were unfortunate to witness a series of undeserving emperors.

Nero (r.54-68, 14 years)

Nero was sixteen years old when he became emperor. He was the antithesis of his power-oriented mother and his paternal ancestors, who were headstrong aristocrats. He was an amiable weakling lacking staying power, and his robust frame concealed a weak will. A dilettante to his fingertips, he amused himself with horse racing, music, painting, and literary composition.

Nero got tired of his mother's attempts to exercise domination in political affairs. Even Seneca, the emperor's tutor, and Burrus, the prefect of the praetorian guard, quarreled with her. In the quest for power, she even developed an affection for her stepson, Britannicus, to rival her emperor son, Nero, who later arranged her death.

During the ministry of Seneca and Burrus, Nero exercised efficient administration, but the death of Burrus and the retirement of Seneca marked a turning point in Nero's reign. Nero banished his wife, Octavia, under the pretense of adultery and later had her put to death. The praetorian prefects, in place of Burrus, led Nero to profligacy, dereliction of duties to attend to public affairs and burning the treasury. His shifting, peremptory and sordid character became apparent.

Accusations of treason against Nero began to surface. Nero reacted harshly to any form of perceived disloyalty, or a drop of criticism spilled onto him. Terror prevailed to stifle dissent, and professional informers were unleashed to watch high-standing officers. Many were given court orders to commit suicide without proper trial, including Seneca, Nero's former minister and tutor.

In 64, a great conflagration swept for six days, destroying more than 70 percent of Rome. It consumed living quarters, and Nero administered the measure of relief for the homeless. He also picked a part of the burnt-out region as a pleasure ground and sumptuous palace. Rumors went around that Nero had set the fire on purpose to obtain his coveted land at low cost.

To deflect blame and assuage growing public anger, Nero shifted responsibility for the fire onto the Christian community. This marked the beginning of a series of persecutions against Christians, who were scapegoated for the disaster. Numerous of them were burned or tortured to death. The Great Fire and its aftermath had a profound impact on Nero's legacy. After the event, Nero's reputation was a lost cause.

After the Great Fire, Nero resumed plans for his planned villa, the Domus Aurea, for which he set about to get it however he pleased. He sold positions in public office to the highest bidder, increased taxes, and took money from the temples. He devalued the currency and reinstituted policies to confiscate property in cases of suspected treason.

In March, 68, the governor Gaius Julius Vindex rebelled against the invidious Nero's tax policies. He recruited another governor, Servius Sulpicius Galba, to join him and declare himself emperor. While these forces were defeated and Galba was declared a public enemy, support for him increased, despite his categorization as a public enemy.

Sensing his imminent demise, Nero fled and planned to head east, where many provinces were still loyal to him, but he returned to his palace because everyone had deserted him. The Senate had condemned him to death, and he committed suicide with the assistance of his secretary. The promising debut of Nero ended up with a fiasco, and it left indelible loss and damage as Caligula did.

Four Emperors Who Appeared During the Civil War Period (68-79)

Galba (r.68-69)

Born into a wealthy family, Galba held the positions of praetor, consul, and governor of the provinces of Gallia Aquitania, Germania Superior, and Africa. He ruled for seven months as the first emperor with the support of the Praetorian Guard during the civil war year of the four emperors following Nero's suicide.

His physical weakness and general apathy made him unable to gain popularity with the people or maintain the support of the Praetorian Guard. Galba was murdered on the orders of Otho, who became emperor in his place.

Otho (r.69)

Otho was a friend of the young emperor Nero until he was banished to the remote province of Lusitania in 58, following his wife Poppaea Sabina's affair with Nero. He allied himself with Galba and joined him on his march to Rome, but later revolted and murdered Galba.

The civil war took place, resulting in 40,000 casualties; Choosing to save the empire from civil war, he uttered his final words, "It is far more just to perish one for all, than many for one," before taking his own life. The title of emperor was given to Vitellius.

Vitellius (r.69)

He was elected consul in 48 and served as proconsular governor of Africa in either 60 or 61. In 68, he was chosen to command the army of Germania Inferior by Emperor Galba. He defeated Otho and was recognized as emperor by the Roman Senate. However, he was soon challenged by legions stationed in the eastern provinces, who proclaimed their commander Vespasian as emperor instead.

War ensued, leading to a crushing defeat for Vitellius in northern Italy. He prepared to abdicate in favor of Vespasian, but he was not allowed to do so by his supporters, resulting in a brutal battle between Vitellius' forces and the armies of Vespasian. He was executed in Rome by Vespasian's soldiers in 69.

Vespasian (r.69-79, 10 years)

Unlike the predecessors of short-lived emperors, who died by murder or suicide, he died a natural death, and his eldest son, Titus, succeeded him. He is noted for his fiscal reforms and consolidation of the empire, which generated political stability and led to a vast Roman building program, including the invasion of Britain in 43 and the Jewish–Roman War in 66. He was an administrator rather than a statesman.

In the civil wars of 69, professional functionaries retained their posts and offered political continuity in the administration. He was industrious, sane, and had a sense of humor. By exercising these policies, as a paragon of virtues, he established his authority and assured the succession of his sons, Titus and Domitian.

In contrast to the debilitating disorder of past emperors, his stable character signaled a new age where reason and rationality led administrative decisions. The organized succession enabled stability with less waste of resources and a greater focus on the common good. This created a virtuous circle in orderly succession and produced better results.

Undoubtedly, this may seem natural and clear, but it was so rare in the early period of the Roman Empire.

Titus (r.79-81, 2 years)

Succeeding his father, Titus assumed the duties of emperor for two years until he died of a fever, which looked like a natural death. He gained renown as a military commander for ending the Jewish rebellion in 70, by which he was awarded a triumph; the Arch of Titus commemorates his victory in Judea.

As emperor, Titus is best known for completing the Colosseum and for his generosity in relieving the suffering caused by two disasters: the eruption of Mount Vesuvius in 79 and a fire in Rome in 80. He was deified by the Roman Senate and succeeded by his younger brother, Domitian.

His reign of two years was too brief to show his talent and capacity to pave the way for future prosperity.

Domitian (r.81-96, 15 years)

He was an enlightened but overbearing despot in guiding the Roman Empire into a new era of brilliance. He created a new judicial system that relieved governors in imperial provinces of their jurisdiction over civilians. In large measure, he completed the restoration work that Vespasian had successfully begun and at any rate, he was an efficient driver of the state.

He fostered a cult of personality in the sphere of religious, military, and cultural propaganda, and he nominated himself as a perpetual censor; he sought to control both public and private morals. Consequently, while Domitian was popular with the people and army, he was considered a tyrant by members of the Roman Senate.

In a court-conspiracy, he was assassinated in 96, and Nerva was appointed as the succeeding emperor by the Senate.

The Five Good Emperors

Nerva (r.96-98, 2 years)

Domitian left no heir, and the vacant throne needed a prompt fill to avoid civil war. The answer was to select a 66-year-old man, Marcus Cocceius Nerva. He ensured his own succession and stabilized the empire by adopting Trajan as his heir, who wasn't part of his biological family.

He introduced a welfare program, the alimenta, which alleviated the burden of taxation on the neediest and provided municipal support to the children of needy families. The alimenta was later expanded by Trajan, Antoninus Pius, and Marcus Aurelius, becoming an integral part of social security in the Roman Empire.

He reduced expenditures by limiting public games and exercising greater oversight over the budget. In January 98, Nerva suffered a stroke and struck by a fever, and died. Trajan succeeded him without incident or opposition. The mode of adoption sets a new precedent for future succession.

The next three rulers, all of whom were providentially childless or had outlived their sons, followed Nerva's example of adopting a man of proven ability and securing the power for the new emperor. Nerva helped establish the foundations for a new golden era for Rome, which his chosen successor, Trajan, would bring to full fruition.

Trajan (r.98-117, 19 years)

Trajan was first and foremost a military man. He expanded the Roman Empire to its largest size ever. He conquered Dacia (now part of Romania), which provided land for Roman settlers and wealth from gold and salt mines. He then attacked the Parthians (now part of Iran) and reached the Persian Gulf.

The Roman Empire stretched from the borders of Scotland, and southern Spain across Europe to the Middle East, encompassing Iran, Iraq, Israel, Türkiye, Lebanon, and Syria. Trajan made good use of the proceeds from the Dacian War to improve the social infrastructure throughout the empire.

He built roads, bridges, aqueducts, and harbors from Spain to the Balkans to North Africa. In Rome itself, a new aqueduct supplied the city with water from the north. With the people, he oversaw the introduction of social welfare policies such as giving out cash, increasing free grain, and reducing taxes for poor citizens.

He treated the Senate with respect and made officials competent to rule the provinces. His tolerance and courtesy formed a vivid contrast with the overbearing manner of the past emperors. The title of Optimus Princeps (Optimus means "the best") was conferred upon him by the Senate as a genuine expression of gratitude and relief.

Trajan was fair but strict, ordering the execution of the Praetorian Guard who had defied Nerva. He stopped the customary persecution of Christians and treated them equally. His civilized rule established a multi-cultural and multi-ethnic melting pot that is still relevant today. Finally, he was discerning in choosing his successor.

Hadrian (r.117-138, 21 years)

Emperor Hadrian was a reformer. He was famed for building monumental architecture, reforming laws, and reinforcing the governance system. He redefined the empire's boundaries and changed the policy from expansion to defense across the vast expanse of the Empire. This led to a withdrawal from the east of the Euphrates, a territory that had been annexed by his predecessor, Trajan.

He identified the critical factor in the situation to stabilize the vast territory of Empire, designed the way of focusing actions to deal with the pivot point of border-restructuring that multiplied the effectiveness of effort to make the Empire sustainable. The border restructuring saved the time and cost to manage the extended borderline if not restructured, and then he could concentrate action and resources on them.

This strategic retreat aligned with Hadrian's vision of making the empire more manageable. The withdrawal from Dacia (now Romania) and Parthia (now Iran) was particularly contentious. The retreat not only contradicted the tradition of the Roman Empire but also demoralized the legions, who saw the relinquishment of hard-won territories as a betrayal of their sacrifices.

At this point, we wonder if Nazi Germany and Imperial Japan had adopted a similar disciplined strategy of concentration. The Nazis stopped expansion after occupying center-eastern Europe (Austria, Czech Republic, Poland, and France) without invading Russia, while Imperial Japan ceased its expansion after occupying parts of Asia without attacking Pearl Harbor.

It shows how it is difficult for leaders to discern the situation from a long-term and wide-range perspective. They adopt disciplined strategies of defense and concentration to sustain their previous achievements in a spree of victories. In that sense, Emperor Hadrian was truly a transformative reformer who attempted to make its future sustainable.

Hadrian was a field-oriented emperor. He visited far-flung provinces within the Empire. His travels were not merely for inspection; he aimed to bring a sense of unity and find solutions tailored to local standards and requirements. For example, the Hadrian Wall in the U.K. was designed for local defense and consolidation.

He also reformed Roman law by compiling a permanent record of edicts and codifying them to make them accessible to all citizens in the empire. This legal reform influenced the legal system in Europe and around the world, notably during the revolutionary changes of the French Revolution. It helped bridge cultural gaps across locality and time.

Hadrian's reign was not without controversy. He centralized power and reduced the influence of the Senate and dissenters. He even executed a prominent senator, contrary to Roman customs. Hadrian's personality stoked controversies. His tendency to be temperamental, secretive, and occasionally harsh made him prone to making enemies.

These traits made him at odds with those around him often. His manner of involvement in provincial affairs and insistence on personal loyalty undermined the established Roman political and social order. For him, his primary goal was to make the empire sustainable, which required effective interpersonal communication.

Thus, the controversies surrounding Hadrian's traits may be viewed from the perspective of the common objective. Namely, it is about whether the traits were effective for achieving his goals. At any rate, the means of achieving a sustainable empire must be distinguished from the methods of effective interaction with the various stakeholders.

Hadrian's last years were marked by chronic illness and his marriage was both unhappy and childless. In 138, he adopted Antoninus Pius (then 52 years old) and nominated him as his successor on the condition that Antoninus adopted Marcus Aurelius (then 17 years old) and Lucius Verus (then 8 years old) as his own heirs.

With the benefit of hindsight, posterity marvels at his perspicacity in appointing his immediate heir, Antoninus Pius, and the next in line, Marcus Aurelius Antonius. The two Antonius governed the Roman world for forty-two years, bringing stability and prosperity.

Antoninus Pius (r.138-161, 23 years)

Born into a senatorial family, Antoninus held various offices during the reign of Emperor Hadrian. He married Hadrian's niece, Faustina, and was adopted by Hadrian as his son, becoming one of four ex-consuls to have jurisdiction over Italy. The Senate awarded him the title "Pius."

Antoninus Pius' reign was a period of unparalleled stability and prosperity in the Roman Empire. With the defense, Antoninus did not engage in expansive military campaigns, which had often drained the imperial treasury and put immense strain on the populace. Instead, his reign focused on dealing with internal concerns and maintaining peace.

After he inherited a stable empire from Hadrian, he emphasized fiscal responsibility. Recognizing the importance of economic stability, he implemented measures to ensure fiscal prudence, economic stability, and the financial health of the empire. Antoninus avoided unnecessary conflicts while rationalizing expenditures.

With the administration, Antoninus focused on the development of infrastructure to sustain the empire's growth and the prosperity of its citizens. He sponsored numerous public works projects, including the construction of roads, bridges, and aqueducts, which facilitated efficient transportation and improved trade across the vast territories.

Through reforms in the Roman legal system, he emphasized fairness, impartiality, and transparency in law enforcement to protect vulnerable populations like slaves and orphaned children. Such reforms reflected his commitment to social justice and equity, which were relatively not yet fully matured in his time.

One of the achievements was the construction of the Antonine Wall in the U.K. This wall extended Hadrian's Wall and served as a defensive structure. Many Roman cities flourished, benefiting from the building and restoration of temples, public buildings, and aqueducts, which enhanced civic life.

With a deep commitment to the welfare of his people, he responded to natural disasters by providing relief to victims of fires and earthquakes. This benevolence extended to cultural and social development as well. Under his patronage, the arts flourished. Poets, historians, and artists received support and encouragement, contributing to a cultural renaissance.

He made a smooth transition of power to Marcus Aurelius and Lucius Verus. His reputation as a singularly gifted speaker and a wise decision-maker made him a respected figure, even beyond the borders of the Roman Empire. Although Pius had two sons, he preferred his adopted heirs.

He died of illness in AD 161 and was succeeded by his adopted sons, Marcus Aurelius and Lucius Verus, as co-emperors.

Marcus Aurelius (r.161-180, 19 years)

He was the last one of the Five Good Emperors, and his demise marked the end of the Pax Romana (27 BC-180), an era of peace and stability in the Roman Empire. He served as Roman consul in 140, 145, and 161, having received an edict from Emperor Hadrian in 138 at the age of 17, designating him as the heir-apparent of Antonius Pius.

While the reign of Antoninus Pius was relatively calm, the reign of Marcus Aurelius, by contrast, was a time of continuous fighting, rebellions, and plague.

The Antonine Plague erupted in 165 AD with common symptoms were fever, diarrhea, vomiting, thirstiness, swollen throat, and coughing. There is wide variance on total casualties of the Roman populace, but it is suggested a quarter to a third of the entire population perished, estimated at 60-70 million throughout the empire.

The wars with Parthia (161–166), the rebellions of the Germanic tribes (166–180), and a devastating plague in 165 had severe impacts on both the frontlines and the population.

Riddled with gruesome wars and plagues, Marcus Aurelius administered governmental affairs, heard court cases, and dispensed justice. He stood out as having an intellectual aptitude with a peaceful nature, and an ardent proponent of Greek Stoic philosophy. His rule is perhaps the closest to that of a true philosopher king in the history of the Western world.

In between shadows of follies, good government had its day. Hastened by cabals and plots, usurpations, assassinations and uprisings, the turnover in emperors after Marcus Aurelius was rapid, none holding the thrones for more than seven years on average in the Western Roman Empire.

The Following Emperors After the Five Good Emperors

Lucius Verus (r.161-169)

As the adoptive brother of Marcus Aurelius, he was co-emperor of Marcus Aurelius, marking the first time that the Roman Empire was ruled by more than one emperor simultaneously. This trend would become increasingly common in the later history of the Empire.

During his reign, he primarily focused on directing the war against Parthia, which ended in a Roman victory and some territorial gains. After initial involvement in the Marcomannic Wars, he fell ill and died in 169, after which Marcus Aurelius became the sole emperor.

Commodus (r.180-192)

Marcus Aurelius and his wife, Faustina, had 14 children, but only one son, Commodus, and four daughters outlived their father.

Commodus's accession was the first hereditary succession in almost a hundred years. After three years as co-emperor with his father, Marcus Aurelius, Commodus started his sole rule in 180 following the death of Aurelius. He is remembered in sharp contrast to his father and the other good emperors, marking the end of the era of the Five Good Emperors.

Though raised by a wise and philosophical father, Commodus shirked intellectual pursuits and instead expressed idleness. You may refer to the historical fiction "Gladiator" by Joaquin Phoenix displaying the character of Emperor Commodus. The decline of the Roman Empire opened with a patchwork of deviant behaviors that happened one after another.

In 176, a rebellion broke out in the Eastern provinces led by Avidius Cassius after rumors of Marcus Aurelius's death, which was initially spread by none other than Marcus's wife, Faustina. In 182, Commodus's sister, Lucilla, conspired with a group of senators to assassinate him. When the plot failed, Commodus administered harsh reprisal by executing several senators.

Commodus was lapsing into insanity. He gave Rome a new name, Colonia Commodiana (Colony of Commodus). On 31 December 192, his subjects had him strangled by a champion wrestler. The grateful Senate proclaimed a new emperor—the city prefect, Publius Helvius Pertinax—but the empire quickly slipped into civil war.

The end of the Five Good Emperors and the beginning of deviant emperors revealed an issue of succession in the Roman Empire. What if Marcus Aurelius had followed the suit of Antonius Pius who appointed the heirs based on competence rather than familial ties? The vice of fostering nepotism in succession planning was to blame.

Pertinax (r.193)

Publius Helvius Pertinax was the son of a freed slave. Pertinax entered the army, commanding units in Syria, the U.K., and on the Danube and the Rhine. He earned distinction during the great invasion by German tribes in 169.

Given senatorial rank and command of a legion, he was soon promoted to the consular commands of Moesia, Dacia, and Syria. However, under Emperor Commodus, he fell out of favor alongside the future emperor Septimius Severus during the ascendancy of the praetorian prefect Perennis.

In the last years of Commodus's life, Pertinax became the prefect of the city of Rome, while Severus commanded the armies of the upper Danube. When Commodus was murdered, the Senate met before dawn and proclaimed Pertinax emperor.

He enforced unpopular economies in both civilian and military expenditure. Less than three months in power, he was murdered by a small group of soldiers. A frenzy of aberrant patterns of succession in the Roman Empire deepened until its downfall.

(7) The flowering of classical civilizations

Within a span of merely six centuries (800-200 BC), all the major civilizations produced incredible people with ideas that laid the foundation for the classical civilizations. Karl Jaspers called it the Axial Age which referred to broad changes in religious and philosophical thought in a variety of locations during the period.

There were notable thinkers and prophets in history such as Confucius (551-479 BC), Mencius (372-289 BC) in China, the Buddha (c.483-c.400 BC) and the writing of the Hindu Upanishads (800-500 BC) in India, and Socrates (470-399 BC), Plato (428-348 BC) and Aristotle (384-322 BC) in Greece, Jewish prophets like Isiah and Ezekiel in the eighth to sixth century BC, Christianity in the first century AD and St. Paul the Apostle (4 BC-62/64 AD), and Islam in the seventh century.

The foundational ideas emerged in Mesopotamia, the Hellenic Empire, the Persian Empire, the Roman Empire, the Indian and Arabic empires, the Judean wilderness, and the Chinese warring states. We are left wondering what caused people to generate such a wave of universal philosophies in various ideologies during that time in the lengthy history of humanity.

Greek philosophy opened the doors to a particular way of thinking, with an explicit preference for reason and rational thought, which provided the roots for the Western intellectual tradition. Thales of Miletus (626-548 BC) broke from the prior use of mythology but instead used natural philosophy to explain the world.

Socrates was born in Athens in 469 BC. Whereas pre-Socratic philosophers examined the natural world, Socrates emphasized human experiences, individual morality, and socio-political questions. His ideas became the foundation of Western philosophy. He died after being sentenced to death in 399 BC with charges of being unreligious and corrupting the city's youth.

With Plato came one of the most creative and flexible ways of doing philosophy, which some have since attempted to imitate by writing philosophical dialogues covering topics in ethics, political thought, metaphysics, and epistemology. Plato's student, Aristotle, was one of the most prolific ancient authors. He wrote treatises on the natural world.

The Platonists, Aristotelians, Epicureans, Cynics, Stoics, and Skeptics in Hellenistic and Roman philosophy developed schools or movements devoted to distinct philosophical lifestyles of various and conflicting methods to attain good spirit or happiness, yet each shared reason and humanity at its core.

In Eastern Asia, specifically, the ideologies of Chinese Confucianism and Japanese Bushido are the products of foundational thoughts. Both set the course of the ideological stream of the people in both countries which also had heavy influence on neighboring countries in the times of peace and war.

For China, Confucius innovated a framework to find a way forward by revisiting the past. Confucianism was based on a strong predisposition for order in society, obligations to discharge duties, respect for traditional culture, and an emphasis on the value of decent behavior.

Propriety was an essential criterion in behavioral patterns; without it, respect for others becomes a laborious bustle or fictitious hypocrisy, cautiousness can appear as sheepish timidity or a vacillating mind, discipline is an expression of rigid formality or excessive perfectionism, and straightforwardness is a camouflage of rudeness and brutality.

Confucianism was successful as many of Confucius's pupils won fame and success even though his teaching deplored the conscious quest for such earthly goals, advocating for gentlemanly self-effacement. The tenet imbued later into moral precepts for Chinese civil servants for thousands of years; loyalty(忠), filial duty(孝), virtue(仁), and righteousness(義).

They became professionally capable and ideologically homogeneous bureaucrats, in principle, and they administered governmental policies to achieve the tenets until the Chinese dynasty was embroiled in chaos and humiliation triggered by the colonial expansion of Western powers in the 19th century.

Confucianism and Taoism are in contrast with concepts of community: Confucius taught that social harmony is based on the dutiful performance of social roles and conformity to external expectations, while Tao valued simplicity and living a natural and unforced life in harmony for peace within oneself and with others. Social behaviors differed following each dogma.

In Japan, its socio-political structure originated from centralized feudalism. It was the governance of the Tokugawa house in the pre-Meiji Revolution that made the feudal lord's vassals of the Tokugawa Shogunate. Society was strictly stratified by hereditary classes and the regime set the structure and made all live in good order.

All the lords, or daimyos, were carefully monitored. The samurais were the warrior rulers who dominated society as did the gentry bureaucrats of China. The creed of Bushido stressed loyalty and obedience to his lord. The other classes were peasants, artisans, and merchants who were the lowest in the social hierarchy.

The self-assertive ethos of merchants that emerged in Europe was unthinkable in Japan, despite the formidable vigor of Japanese trade. The aim of the whole system was harmonious stability, emphasizing duties, knowing one's place, discipline, scrupulous workmanship, stoical endurance, and strict regularity.

The unique system of uniformed masses in the insulated island country steadily accumulated energy and ambition with great intensity. When they reached the level of critical mass, it exhibited a special character. At its best, it became one of the most impressive national achievements; at its worst, it inflicted atrocities on those who stood in its way.

The assessment of the schools of philosophy leads us to ask questions about the philosophical foundations of the West and Asia. The West laid reason and humanity at its core, whereas Confucianism was based on duty and conformity, and Bushido emphasized loyalty and obedience. These differing tenets made their respective mindsets and societies.

(8) Peoples' struggles and protests

Humans sustain life because they can argue and protest. People have argued for their beliefs and staged protests as a way of publicly making their opinions heard to enact desired changes themselves. Empirically, the proportion of protests by the weak and suppressed was predominantly high, while the rate of success was conversely lower.

Merriam-Webster Dictionary defines the types of revolution and rebellion.

"Revolution" applies to a successful rebellion resulting in a major change of authorities and societies. It was the American Revolution in 1765-1783 that overthrew the authority of the U.K. and founded the U.S., the French Revolution in 1789 that transformed Europe, and the Russian Revolution in 1917 which dismantled the Tsarist autocracy.

"Rebellion" involves organized resistance against an established authority or system, driven by long-standing political, social, or economic grievances; it is often unsuccessful. The Servile Rebellions in 135-132 BC and 104-100 BC in the Roman Republic, and the Scottish rebellion led by William Wallace (1273-1305) in 1297-1298 against the U.K.

Many of the rebellions revolved around landed property and structured poverty in pre-Industrial Revolution societies, which were governed by customary rights and obligations rather than by codes of law. Those landowners grew rich through advanced agricultural tools and skills, trade and transportation, and the mass provision of enslaved laborers.

The tenant farmers and poor peasants of smaller landholdings resented the prohibitive rents and dues, as well as the taxes collected in the form of tax farming. In any harvest failure, the farmers and peasants had to pay the rents, dues, and taxes first, and they often fell into debt to the rich, who eventually used this to seize their land and often their very persons as bondslaves.

Courts taken control by the oligarchs gave judgments against the poor. A situation was commonly ruled by the Law of the Fishes with the large and powerful devouring the weak in a sea of chaos. The oligarchic cartel of the extractive economy was sometimes shaken by the upward rebellions of disgruntled farmers and by the downward land reforms initiated by ambitious politicians trying to help people in distress; however, they were not many and often failed to do it, or sometimes descended into tyranny.

The word, democracy, means the rule of the people. It never actually referred to the whole population, as it excluded slaves, women, and non-citizens such as traders and craftsmen. This metric often excluded a large proportion of the populace. Democracy did not challenge the concentration of wealth or the exclusion of the people from the hands of the rich or powerful.

It should come as no surprise that the democratic forces were led by the landed nobility. Not only did they take up some of the poor's demands to further their economic or political goals, but they also severely repressed the poor. The impoverished rebelled against the extortion of powerful landowners and politicians.

The Peloponnesian War (431-405 BC) was fought between Sparta and Athens, arising out of a struggle for influence over other city-states. Sparta built an alliance of states around the Peloponnese in the southern Greek mainland. Athens was dependent on its sea routes for trade and had a sea-based alliance.

The war was about more than just which of the alliances would dominate the land. It involved a rivalry of conceptions of how society should be organized. In Athens and its allied states, many in the upper classes at least half-welcomed Spartan successes in the war as an excuse to overthrow democracy and further their political positions or economic interests.

For some, Spartan extortion was a model of how a privileged minority deprives everyone else of rights in history. In modern times, drastic regimes such as fascist Italy and national socialistic Nazi Germany did the same to the upper class of politics and business, as well as to the middle-class families in the 1930s across Europe.

The Patricians treated the people as slaves, executed and flogged them, and drove them out of their lands. Crushed by these cruel practices, and above all by the load of debt occasioned by the necessity to contribute money and military service for continual wars, the common people armed and took up position against them.

But most uprisings, such as the peasants' revolts, slave rebellions, or citizens' disobedience, failed to dismantle the structure of extortionate abuse and break the hold of the great landowners. The reasons for failure lay in the characteristics of the rebellious mobs in disorder, mistrust, and indiscipline during armed conflicts.

The peasants in rural areas rose against the extortion of the rich and powerful, and they even flocked to rich leaders who seemed to promise to rescue them from their incessant plights. But they could not execute their program to reorganize society in its entirety, which could go beyond demands for land redistribution, debt annulment, or freedom from enslavement.

The urban masses were equally incapable of taking the lead in a revolutionary reorganization of society. They were even less central to production than the small peasants. The most impoverished were dependent on casual labor, while others were artisans in the trades of luxury or convenience products, whose livelihoods depended on supplying the needs of the rich.

The slaves in urban areas, including Rome, lived in dismal conditions; however, they often fared better than those in rural agriculture. Many could hope to join the upper echelon of the capital's population if they succeeded in bringing value or contributing to the political positions or economic interests of the upper classes.

Finally, although rural slaves were central to production, they found it almost impossible to go beyond heroic rebellion and formulate ideas to manage the difference in assembly. They came from everywhere in the Mediterranean, spoke a mass of different languages, and nothing was identical except their enslaved status.

For those who made such uprisings with the idea of establishing a pure community free from internal dissension, ferocious fighting, and inhumane exploitation over a long period, it was far from reality, and such movements couldn't be sustainable even if they temporarily succeeded in establishing a rebellious regime to control their occupied regions.

The riots, revolts, rebellions, and civil wars did not lead to a revolutionary reorganization of society, but they did radically change the political superstructure by which the landed rich dominated the rest of society. The Senate came to depend on generals and their armies to maintain control over the poor.

But the strongest general was then able to dominate the Senate. The civil wars over social issues ended only to be replaced by civil wars between generals: Marius and Cinna against Sulla; Pompey against Julius Caesar; after Caesar's death, Brutus and Cassius against Mark Antony and Octavian (Caesar's nephew); and, finally, Octavian against Mark Antony.

Eventually, the rich—old and new alike—felt that allowing Octavian (now called Augustus) to establish a de facto monarchy was the only way to re-establish political stability. Augustus was able to use the debilitating fatigue of the people over decades of social conflict to ascend to a virtual emperorship.

He offered security to the rich while posing as the friend of Rome's urban poor by providing them with cheap or even free corn, which was paid by the vast tribute flowing in from conquered lands. It could be considerably increased through labor in the fields and mines, supplied by childless slaves.

Slavery had existed for a very long time in ancient civilizations. In ancient times, the slaves were marginal for surplus production because they had to concentrate on providing personal services to rulers while doing agriculture and making crafts were left to semi-free citizens. Then, in Greece and now on a much greater scale in Rome, slavery became a major source of surplus production.

The enslavement of war captives provided precisely such a labor force, representing a cheap way of exploiting other humans. Significantly, Sparta, one of the major Greek city-states that relied upon the exploitation of a serf-like peasantry, was centered on a relatively fertile inland area. It set an example for the enslaving patterns of the Roman Republic and Empire.

Slave revolts do not punctuate the history of Greece in the same way that peasant revolts occur in the history of China. This is because the character of Greek, and later Roman, slavery made it very difficult for slaves to organize collective resistance against their exploiters. They were overwhelmingly captives from wars waged across the Mediterranean, the Balkans, Asia Minor, and even southern Russia who were disparate in origins, and unable to communicate in the same language on the vast expanse of the Roman Empire.

There were slave markets where those from different cultures and speaking different languages could only communicate with difficulty through the Greek dialect of their masters. The masters could usually rely on other Greeks to help punish rebellious slaves and hunt down escapees.

The masters had little interest in improving the conditions of slaves and kept them in their place. Opposition to their exploitation could only take the form of resentment. This resentment was itself an important factor in Greek and, later, Roman history. The slaves were rarely able to intervene in the historical process on their behalf.

3.2. From 601 to 1500 (The Middle Ages)

1) The Rise of Islam and its Expansion of Influence (622-1453)

This is a view on global issues in the 7th century when the Western Roman Empire had long gone, Christianity was in retreat following the demise of the Roman Empire, and China faced division again after the brief unification by the Han Dynasty (207 BC-220 AD), and Islam began to spread and conquer the Middle East and beyond.

In China, the short-lived Sui Dynasty (581-618) was replaced by the Tang Dynasty (618-907), which stretched its territory from Korea in the east to the steppes of Mongolia in the north, present-day Afghanistan in the west, and northern Vietnam in the south. Guangzhou was a seaport connecting the Middle East, East Africa, India, and Southeast Asia.

In Korea, Silla, one of three states in Korea, united the Korean Peninsula in 676 in alliance with Tang. In Japan, the Asuka period (538-710) transformed its arts, society, and politics through the introduction of Buddhism and the establishment of the imperial court of Yamato.

In Arabia, life in the deserts had been dominated by small and bickering nomadic tribes for more than a thousand years. Upon the main caravan routes, Medina and Mecca rose to towns of around thirty thousand inhabitants. Arabia was unified in 622 with the establishment of the first Islamic State, aka State of Medina, by Islamic prophet Muhammad in Medina.

After Muhammad died in 632, Islam spread throughout Asia, Europe, and North Africa beyond the Arabian Peninsula from the 7th through the 18th century in the forms of military conquest, trade, pilgrimage, and missionaries including the downfalls of the Sasanian Empire (224-651) in Iran and the Byzantine Empire (330-1453) in Asia Minor.

In 570, Muhammad, the founder of Islam, was born into a prominent clan of the Quraysh tribe in a Bedouin encampment. He was raised as a merchant and moved to Mecca in his adolescence. By his early 20s, he worked as a trader for a wealthy widow, whom he married some years later.

During his travels, Muhammad encountered adherents of the Christian and Jewish faiths, whose monotheistic ideas significantly influenced his teachings. He spent increasing amounts of time in meditation in the hills and wilderness surrounding Mecca.

In 610 or earlier, Muhammad received the first of many revelations, which his followers believed were transmitted by Allah (the common Arabic word for God) through the angel Gabriel. In a vision in a cave on Mount Hira, Muhammad learned of his destiny as a Prophet of the Lord. Muhammad began to preach against the prevalent idolatry in Mecca.

This made him extremely unpopular with his fellow townsmen, notably the Umayyad merchant family, who viewed Muhammad as a threat to the gods of Kaaba (a stone building considered the holy House of God in Mecca, Saudi Arabia) and to their commercial interests associated with pilgrimages to the site.

In 622, Muhammad escaped from Mecca to Medina with the assistance of Ali ibn Abi Talib, with whom he arranged the marriage of his daughter, Fatima, and swore a pact of brotherhood. The journey to Medina marked a pivotal moment in the Prophet's life, effectively establishing him as the leader of Islam. It was like for St. Paul the Apostle to experience a life-changing event on the road to Damascus that led to his awakening to a divine calling and transformation into a prominent figure in the Christian community, advocating for Christianity and becoming a leader in ecclesiastical missions.

Ali served as Muhammad's secretary and deputy in this period. His role in Muhammad became the bone of contention in the Muslim world after Muhammad's death.

In 628, he rode on a camel into Mecca at the head of 10,000 faithful followers. He struck down the heathen idols in the shrine of the Kaaba and transformed it into the holiest shrine for his followers. After four more years of teaching at Medina, the main body of the Prophet's wisdom was recorded in the Holy Book, the Quran, and he died on 07 June 632.

This has a biblical reference to Jesus Christ, who entered Jerusalem in praise, riding on a donkey, cleansed the Temple, and was crucified and resurrected. A great multitude spread their clothes on the road, and cried out, saying: "Hosanna to the Son of David! 'Blessed is He who comes in the name of the Lord!' Hosanna in the highest!" (Matthew 21:9).

Then Jesus went into the temple of God and drove out all those who bought and sold there. He overturned the tables of the money changers and the seats of those who sold doves. "It is written, He said to them, 'My house shall be called a house of prayer,' but you have made it a den of thieves" (Matthew 21:13).

In a world where religion seems to be the cause of conflict and bloodshed, it is easy to overlook the ways in which the great faiths learnt and borrowed from each other. In the early years of their coexistence relations were not so much pacific as warmly encouraging. The support of Jews in the Middle East was vital for the propagation and spread of the world of Muhammad. Muhammad and his followers went to great lengths to assuage the fears of Jews and Christians as Muslim control expanded.

Islam, meaning submission, holds basic precepts as a religion that all Muslims are brothers and sisters. Muhammad denounced the economic privileges of the ruling elites, insisted on the rights of women, called for social, economic, and political equality, and adhered to a revolutionary creed supported by military power.

A loyal Muslim is required to respect the teachings of the Quran, which consists of 114 chapters that provide a source of law, science, and philosophy, as well as a collection of myths and an ethical textbook. Both Sunnis and Shiites read the Quran, believe that Prophet Muhammad was the messenger of Allah, and follow the five tenets of Islam.

The five tenets of Islam are listed:

Shahada. The confession of faith ("There is no God but Allah, and Muhammad is His Messenger").

Salah. The ritual prayer requires the faithful to wash and touch the ground with their heads turned towards Mecca at daybreak, noon, sunset, and evening.

Zakat. Charitable giving to the poor.

Swam. Fasting during the month of Ramadan. Every sane and healthy Muslim adult must refrain from food, drink, and sexual intercourse from dawn to dusk.

Hajj. The pilgrimage to Mecca at least once in a lifetime.

The Sunni-Shiite split:

After the death of Muhammad in 632, the leadership of the new Muslim community was claimed by the Prophet's old friend Abu Bakr, who had the support of many of Muhammad's followers. Others believed that Muhammad's closest male relative, his son-in-law Ali, should be the Prophet's successor.

Although Ali himself agreed to accept Abu Bakr's headship, a subset of Muslims continued to insist that only Ali and his successors were divinely appointed, and that Abu Bakr and his immediate successors were illegitimate usurpers. They became known as Shiite Muslims (the "party of Ali"), while the supporters of Abu Bakr became known as Sunni Muslims.

Both Sunni and Shia Muslims are committed to the five pillars of Islam and prioritize the Quran. They adhere to Islamic law (sharia) but differ on issues of religious authority and the role of the Prophet's descendants. The Battle of Karbala in 680, between Husayn ibn Ali (Shia), the grandson of Muhammad, and Umayyad caliph Yazid I (Sunni), further galvanized the schism.

Sunni Muslims focus on the life, examples, and traditions of the Prophet Muhammad. As followers of Muhammad (Sunnah), they supported Abu Bakr, and later the Umayyads who took on the religious and political leadership as successor, Caliph. It accounts for 90 percent of the global Muslim population are Sunnis in most Muslim countries.

Shia Muslims focus on Muhammad's family lineage through a series of Imams who were invested with his religious and political authority. They follow Ali who was Muhammad's cousin and son-in-law, and his descendants, Hasan and Hussein as Shia. It accounts for 10 percent of the global Muslim population with the majority in Iran, Bahrain, Azerbaijan, Iraq, and Lebanon.

Islamic influence expanded following the death of Muhammad. The siege of Jerusalem (636–637) resulted in its occupation, leading to immense consequences for both Muslims and Christians, which ultimately contributed to the Crusades beginning in 1099. Christian pilgrims visited Rome because they couldn't reach Jerusalem, and their center of gravity gradually shifted from Constantinople to Rome.

The expanse of Islamic influence created a realm of common language and customs in the Mediterranean and Arabic world, within which trade, ideas, and culture flourished. The expansion cut Europe off from the Indian Ocean. While the Muslim took delight in innovation, progress and new ideas, much of Christian Europe withered in the gloom, crippled by a lack of resources and a dearth of curiosity. The Islamic blockade restricted Europe in trade and intellectual interaction, leading to the Dark Ages of the Middle

Ages in Europe.

The armies of Islam advanced relentlessly. Byzantium was unsuccessfully besieged on two occasions, in 673-678 and 717-718. In the 8th century, Muslims crossed Gibraltar, overwhelmed Spain, breached the Pyrenees, and advanced to Tours on the Loire, deep in the heart of the Frankish kingdom.

From that point on, Islam imprinted a lasting presence in Europe, Asia, and Africa, extending beyond the Middle East. It expanded from the 7th to the 17th centuries, westward into the Mediterranean Sea and Iberia, eastward into the Balkan and Black Sea regions, and further down to the Indian Ocean as far as Indonesia, and northward to Central Asia.

The long-running Islam-Byzantine conflict began when Arab forces besieged Constantinople between 674 and 678. It lasted for 779 years until Constantinople fell in 1453 under the attack of Islamic forces. Its demise brought Islam's influence on the eastern Mediterranean Sea, and it has persisted to this day. As the two great powers of late antiquity flexed their muscles and prepared for the final battle, few could have predicted that it would be a faction of far reaches of the Arabian Peninsula that Islam would rise up to establish the greatest empire that the world has seen.

The history of Asia Minor, the Greek peninsula, and the Balkans was not merely conflicts for regional hegemony at the Eastern tip of Europe, but also clashes of civilizations, religions, and ideologies such as Hellenic and Islamic cultures, and Christianity versus Islam religions. It led to the Battle of Vienna in 1683 by the Polish-Lithuanian Commonwealth and the Holy Roman Empire against the Islamic Ottomans. It was one of the reasons for the outbreak of World War I.

Christians and Muslims have interacted through the vicissitudes of history, producing enduring features of political and cultural life in both Europe and Asia. Over the 8th century, the Bishop of Rome, deprived of support from Byzantium, was forced to turn to the Franks and embark on the enterprise of the Roman Papacy as an absolute papal monarchy.

The Franks saw their chance to support the Pope in protecting Christianity, but it also entailed political interests that justified their monarchical power. In the wider context, Charlemagne, as the overlord of Western Europe and Christianity, emerged partly due to the threats posed by the followers of Prophet Muhammad.

Both Christians and Muslims were taught to regard each other as infidels. Their antagonisms and negative stereotypes were endless. As a result, a strong dichotomy developed between the Christian West and the Islamic East. Many Westerners regarded themselves as bearers of a superior civilization and viewed the Muslim East with disdain.

2) Sui Dynasty (581-618) and Tang Dynasty (618-907)

China assumed the proportions she has today when Han Dynasty (206 BC-220 AD) extended her boundaries to the north, and the Sui and Tang Dynasties spread her civilization to the south and into Central Asia. Throughout the 7th to 9rh centuries, China was certainly the most secure, civilized, and internationalized country in the world.

Specifically, the four centuries from the fall of the Han Dynasty in 220 until the Sui Dynasty unified China in 581 were characterized by chaotic division and discord during the Three Kingdoms (220-280), the

Western and Eastern Jin (265-420), and the Northern and Southern Dynasties (420-588). They all did little to establish security for the people or to foster industry and culture.

The short-lived Sui Dynasty (581-618) was overly fond of extravagant construction projects, such as the Great Wall and the Great Canal, which linked the fertile south to its capital in the west. The harsh taxes, forced labor, and heavy casualties in the Korean Campaign (611-614) triggered widespread revolts, as warlords and provincial governors called themselves sovereign rulers. Bandit gangs and nomadic raiders looted and pillaged at will.

The Sui Dynasty collapsed when the last emperor, Yangdi, indulged in deranged escapes from the rigorous realities of his reign and was finally assassinated in 618.

The first emperor of the Tang Dynasty (618-907), Gaozu (r.618-626), began the task of refilling the imperial treasury, which had been emptied by war and canal-building. As the Tang Dynasty cautiously found its footing toward stability, he abdicated in favor of his second son, Tang Taizong (r.626-649), who laid the foundation for the golden age of the Tang Dynasty.

The Tang Dynasty was a period of expansion, especially in trade with foreign lands. Caravan routes traveled as far as Syria, transporting items ranging from glassware and tapestries to jasmine and other exotic herbs. Between 622 and 676, the Tang Empire battled with Tibet, the Turks, and the Koreans.

The borders of the Tang Dynasty expanded even further than during the Han Dynasty. The Tang Court welcomed numerous dignitaries from foreign lands, exchanging goods and ideas with countries as far west as Persia, the Byzantine Empire, and India through the Silk Road, as well as states in Korea and Japan to the east.

The capital cities, Changan (長安, 618-690) and Luoyang (洛陽, 657-690), became melting pots of many cultures and beliefs, such as Zoroastrianism, Islam, Christianity and Buddhism. Tang Taizong (r.626-649) gave courteous hearing to envoys from Islamic Arabia in 628, a party of Christian missionaries in 635, and representatives from the Byzantine Empire during Heraclius's reign (r.610-641).

The Huaisheng Mosque in Guangzhou, built in 627, is one of the oldest mosques in the world. The culture and civilization of the Tang Dynasty were very different from those of the Han. A new and more vigorous literary school appeared, leading to a great poetic revival; Buddhism revolutionized philosophical and religious thought.

There were great advances in art and literature, renowned for their simplicity and naturalism, technical skill, and quality of life. Tea was first used, paper was manufactured, and woodblock printing began. An orderly life thrived in China while Europe and Eastern Asia experienced squalid cities or grim fortresses.

While the West was mired in theological obsessions, the Chinese were open, inquisitive, and global. But the dynasty declined from the second half of the 9th century as factions feuded internally, leading to political plots and scandals involving assassinations. The dynasty fragmented into ten separate kingdoms as the central government weakened.

Around 880, northern invaders finally destroyed the Tang Dynasty. Its terminal phase showed a historical pattern: the state disintegrates when wealth is concentrated. Its initial land allocation programs had equalized access to land, but it gradually gave way to the concentration of wealth and power among a small number of ruling elites.

Privilege derived from holding high state offices fueled personal enrichment, tempered only by factional struggles or internal betrayals. Wealth accumulation was greatly aided by tax and labor exemptions for relatives of the imperial family and nobility. The extractive system openly favored the powerful and well-connected.

As a result, the concentration of land ownership among the elite expanded at the expense of the peasantry. Attempts to reform the land ownership structure to achieve greater equality were unsuccessful due to political instability. The trade enabled affluent elites to accumulate even greater wealth, which should have been subject to taxation by the state and allocated for the benefit of the peasantry. A corollary to fortune was then corruption and sacrifice.

The Tang Dynasty was characterized by openness to and leadership over foreign states, as well as the cultured and stable lives of its people in the 7th and 8th centuries. When it collapsed in 907, the golden principle of global openness was not fully choked off, but it kept flickering until it revived with the inception of the Song Dynasty (960-1279).

3) European Feudalism and Christendom (330-1453)

The term "Middle Age" was first used by Christians who saw themselves as living in the interval between Christ's First Coming in the 1st century and the Second Coming when it was due. Much later, people indicated it as the interval between the decline of antiquity in the Classic Ages in the 5th century and the revival of classic culture during the Renaissance in the late 15th century.

The ancient world symbolized high civilization, while the Middle Ages represented a descent into barbarism, parochiality, and religious bigotry. During the Enlightenment, when human reason resurfaced and prevailed the religious belief, medievalism became synonymous with obscurantism and backwardness.

The population of Europe had been divided between Romans and barbarians by the fall of the Roman Empire in 476. The chaotic malaise before and after the collapse opened the door to a series of territorial encroachments by Germanic warriors, including the Goths, Franks, Visigoths, and Ostrogoths. They swept across the borders of the Roman Empire, looting and burning Roman legacies.

The first wave of shocks depopulated Roman urban centers, leaving rural societies utterly bereft of control and governance. Civilization degraded progressively, and the people who had paid the price for Roman glories faced an even greater cost with its demise. Disorder from famine and plague ravaged the lands and halved the population.

When the dust of violence and disorder gradually settled in the ensuing centuries, the states of raiders disappeared one after another, for the same reason the Roman Empire fell apart such as the lack of an effective governing system to sustain their occupation and maintain order, and intense internal strife and external threats that obliterated them.

After enduring the havoc wrought by the Roman collapse, the post-Roman world exhibited gradual recovery as the remnant raiders adopted Roman customs, embraced Christianity, and often spoke in Latin dialects. The post-Roman world was inhabited by a more complex mix of semi-barbarized ex-Romans and semi-Romanized ex-barbarians.

In a nutshell, there were great cycles of European history into the Middle Age (476-1500):

- The pre-historic, Bronze Age civilization, came to an end with Minoan and Mycenean cultures in the 1000s BC

- The classical period of Greece and Rome (8th century BC to 5th century AD)

- The collapse of the governing system with the end of the Roman Empire (476 AD) and its repositioning with Carolingian Empire from 800 in the Western and Central Europe and its offshoot states created by the Treaty of Verdun in 843

- The mix of states by race, culture, and ideology on top of city-states rose and fell, integrated and disintegrated, and made peace and wars among themselves by the turn of the 15th century

- After the Middle Age, the New Word opened, and the waves of defiance burst forth with the Reformation, the Renaissance, the Enlightenment and cultural sophistication that culminated in the Industrial Revolution and the imperialism in following centuries.

The Byzantine Empire, also referred to as the Eastern Roman Empire, was the continuation of the Roman Empire centered in Constantinople. The eastern half of the Empire survived the conditions that caused the fall of the West in the 5th century and continued to exist until the fall of Constantinople to the Ottoman Empire in 1453.

The Greek–speaking eastern half of the Roman Empire showed much more political tenacity than the western half. It weathered the disasters of the 5th century, which saw the complete and final breaking up of the original Western Roman power in 476. Attila (r. 434–453) of the Hunnic Empire bullied Emperor Theodosius II (r.408-450) and sacked and raided almost to the walls of Constantinople, but that city remained intact.

The African Nubians from southern Sudan came down the Nile and looted Upper Egypt, but Lower Egypt and Alexandria were left still prosperous. Most of Asia Minor was held against the Sassanid Persians.

The sixth century, which was an age of complete darkness for the West, saw indeed a considerable revival of Greek power. Emperor Justinian I (527–565) was a ruler of great ambition and energy, and he made a partial recovery of the territories of the defunct Western Roman Empire. H was married to Theodora (tenure of empress, 527-548).

Theodora, his wife and empress, was a woman of exceptional intelligence and strength, who not only supported Justinian in his endeavors but also played a crucial role in shaping policies and advocating for the rights of women. These made Emperor Justinian and Empress Theodora the power couple in intrigue, bravery, and political sagacity.

They commissioned the construction of the grand cathedral in Constantinople, Hagia Sophia, and made reforms to codify the Roman laws by creating the Justinian Code for increasing legal consistency and of improving the status of women in Byzantine society. The Eastern Orthodox Church commemorated Theodora the Empress as Saint Theodora on 14 November.

From the third century onwards, the Persian Empire had been the steadfast rival of the Byzantine Empire. The two empires kept Asia Minor, Syria, and Egypt in a state of perpetual unrest and waste. In the first century AD, these lands were still at a high level of civilization, wealthy, and with an abundant population, but the continual coming and going of armies, massacres, looting, and war taxation wore them down steadily until only shattered and ruinous cities remained upon a countryside of scattered peasants.

Following a political reshuffle on the European Continent, King Charlemagne established the Carolingian Empire, which included what is now France, Spain, Italy, and Germany in 800. It helped restore law and order in a land of disorder. History never stood still as the invasion of the Mongols (1220s-1240s) and the deadly Black Death (1346-1353) devastated the late medieval world.

The Middle Ages (476-1500) lasted for longer than one thousand years and were marked by several political states, such as the Holy Roman Empire (800-1806) in Europe, the Byzantine Empire (330-1453) in Asia Minor, Islamic Caliphates (632-1258) in the Middle East, and the Mongol Empire (1206-1368) in Central Asia.

The color of European feudal societies, bound with Christianity, was the white and black that was reflected in medieval life in Europe. It ranged from pious tenderness to inhuman cruelty, from joy in the community to despair in fear, encompassing both hellfire sermons and public executions, from pains to pleasure of living that modern sensibility is barely capable of grasping them in full.

Christian missionaries and Western traders made contact with societies in Asia, the Middle East, and Africa as religion and life were inseparable. The contacts brought agricultural technologies from Asia and knowledge in mathematics, science, and philosophy from the Arabs and Byzantines. The medieval West received more from the infidels or remote friends than it gave something valuable to them.

The medieval manorial system was the economic and political relationship between landlords and their peasant laborers in estates where serfs worked the land of masters in return for protection and the right to work a separate piece of land for their own needs. Regulations and customs varied among estates over time, but the manorial system persisted throughout the Middle Ages.

Serfs were not slaves. They could not be bought or sold, and they retained essential ownership of their houses and lands, passing their property rights through inheritance as long as they fulfilled their obligations. But life was hard, and some serfs escaped landlord control and grouped themselves as rebellious wanderers.

The manorial system was the economic counterpart to feudalism, where land was granted in return for service and loyalty. It flourished in Western Europe but weakened from the 13th century due to social disruptions caused by the Mongolian invasion and the virulent Black Death. In Eastern Europe, however, the manorial system remained solid even after the 15th century. This illustrated the laggard enlightenment and industrial activities of the Slavic states in Central Europe and Russia in the 18th century and onwards.

The center of gravity of Christendom has shifted throughout history. The authority of Christendom was initially founded in Rome, shifted to Byzantium in 330, and formed a new Christendom with the coronation of Charlemagne in 800. The authority persisted in Constantinople until its collapse in 1453, upon which it moved to Moscow.

Even with the shifting gravities across the European continent, Christendom was in providential flux and upheaval. When Constantinople fell in 1453, a two-year-old baby, Christopher Columbus, started toddling to sail his maiden voyage to the New World four decades later, which opened a new paradigm of Christendom in the globe.

There were notable events in the history of Christianity concerning the Christendom.

After Emperor Constantine relocated the capital to Constantinople in 330, Christendom shifted to it, and the bishop of Rome was under the control of the patriarch in Constantinople. After the downfall of the Roman Empire in 476, the leaders of Christianity assumed the mantle of defunct Roman emperors in response to the inroads of Islam and paganism.

There were two turning instances in Christendom: First, the Roman bishop, Stephen II, crossed the Alps in 753 to get urgent support from the Frankish ruler in Western Europe, rather than from the weak and distant emperor in Constantinople. Second, the last Byzantine emperor, Constantine XI Palaiologos, threw himself into combat against the Muslims in 1453 at the instant of the downfall of Constantinople and the Byzantine Empire.

In the West where the Roman Empire had long gone, the Bishop of Rome materialized a new order of papal authority over the Latin Church and Christian emperors. Pope Leo III crowned Charlemagne as Emperor of the Carolingian Empire in 800, and his territory was known as the Holy Roman Empire which revived the title of the defunct Roman Empire in Western Europe.

In the East where the Roman Empire survived far longer in Constantinople (330-1453), the notion of "church-state relationship" often led to the identification of the interests of the church with those of the empire. The downfall of the Byzantine Empire led Ivan III, Grand Duke of Moscow, to succeed the Byzantine Emperor, adopting the title of Tsar in 1453.

When it comes to religion, it reminds us of the historical fact that splits between religions or within it have caused the world's worst and most protracted conflicts. Christianity was riven with deep divisions between the Catholic Church in Rome and the Orthodox Church in Constantinople. It arose from disagreements about something that would be unknowable to many people and unprovable by anybody – the relations between the divine and human natures of Christ.

The doctrine of the Trinity that God exists in three persons: the Father, the Son and the Holy Spirit has been central to Christianity since it began. According to the Bible, Jesus Christ is both God and human, so it became an eternal question what the relation of Jesus Christ to God the Father is, and how Jesus Christ can be both divine and human.

At the First Council of Nicaea in 325, more than a century before the Council of Chalcedon in 451, the church declared that God the Father and Jesus the Son were "consubstantial" (of the same substance), clarifying that Jesus was divine in the same way that God is divine.

The wording of the Nicene Creed specifically condemned Arianism, a heresy that professed that Jesus wasn't "of one substance" with God, and therefore "not fully divine". Another creed suggested that Jesus was "not fully human".

Even church leaders like Nestorius attempted to logically explain the incarnation but failed to do so without presenting new heretical ideas, and the church ruled against these flawed explanations. At the same time, some of these disagreements were sowing discord between the Eastern Christian churches (Constantinople) and the Western Christian churches (Rome).

Specifically, four main events were associated with the dogmatic struggle:

- The "Council of Bishops in Nicaea" in 325.

    Emperor Constantine convened the council to unite the increasingly divided Christian doctrine. It declared that God the Father and God the Son are of one substance and are co-eternal. Christ is both fully human and fully divine, that is, one person in whom two natures – one divine and one human – are united in the hypostatic union ("one person, two natures"). This was incorporated into the Nicene Creed that is still proclaimed today.

    The Nicaean creed defined the boundary of the Christian domain at the approval of Emperor Constantine, and also it allowed the Church authority to punish heresy with the sword of those who believed that Christ has only one nature known as Monophysitism (single nature).

    However, the framework opened a path that real sanctity was sometimes subject to false sanctity, and those who were preaching truth were condemned by those who were preaching falsehood. In mundane look, it could be a blunder that the church has been stricken with the unprovable debate, and it has not tolerated any deviations from the official creed.

- The Council of Bishops in Constantinople in 381 – Emperor Theodosius summoned the second ecumenical council to attain consensus in the church. The council of Constantinople enacted four disciplinary canons including one against the Arian heresy that maintained that although Christ had a human body, the divine character had taken over his human soul and thus Christ had only one nature, a divine nature.

- The Council of Bishops in Ephesus in 431 Emperor Theodosius II convened the third ecumenical council. The Council of Ephesus was primarily concerned with the doctrine of the Nestorianism and it reaffirmed the Nicene Creed.

    The Nesrorianism was named after Nestorius, Archbishop of Constantinople (428-431), who thought that Christ's two natures, human and divine, were separate. He said that the Virgin Mary ought to be referred to as "*Christokos*," meaning "bearer of Christ, or mother of Christ", not "*Theotokos*," meaning "bearer of God, or the mother of God" because God had always existed because *Theotokos* implied a blending divine and human nature of Jesus (For reference, in the late Middle Ages, a thought of mercy as peculiarly maternal had made the Virgin Mary, not Christ, the intercessor in forgiveness).

    The conflict was especially venomous between Nestorius and Cyril of Alexandria, and Cyril who espoused the orthodoxy of *Theotokos* as did the bishop of Rome. In contrast, the bishop of Constantinople, Nestorius, proposed the concept of two natures.

    At the Council of Ephesus Nestorius planned to denounce Cyril for heresy. Ironically, the council's ultimate decision was exactly the opposite: it rejected Nestorianism as heretical and removed Nestorius from office. Emperor Theodosius II himself was a Nestorian, he was forced to pressure and exile Nestorius to an Egyptian monastery.

- The Council of Bishops in Chalcedon in 451 – it was the fourth ecumenical council convoked by Emperor Marcian (r.450-457) in an attempt to re-assert the teachings of the ecumenical Council of Ephesus against the teachings of Nestorius. It declared that although the divine nature and the human nature were united in Christ, they each remained distinct and unaltered, and Christ "is in two natures". The Chalcedonian creed was definite and decisive by announcing Christ as "truly God and truly Man".

The unprovable argument was not just theological hairsplitting, but there had been always political dimensions because this controversy was partly about the power centers of the empire: the two-natures-mixed school of theology was centered in the city of Antioch while the more mystical one-nature school was centered in Alexandria. The influence and importance of these two cities were at stake.

Fear of Persian influence sharpened the argument further. Zoroastrianism, the religion of the Persians, was a monotheistic religion like Christianity; nevertheless, it was the religion of the enemy, and the Christians of Rome and Alexandria were suspicious of any Christian doctrines that sounded a little too Zoroastrian.

Since Zoroastrianism denied that there could ever be any mixing of divine and earthly substances, Nestorius's two-nature theology fit into the Persian schema in a way that the mystical one-nature theology never could. This tainted it further in the eyes of the bishops farther from the border. They suspected that Nestorius had been influenced by Persian philosophies.

Heresy was a deviation from orthodoxy that was believed to place the thinkers outside the domain of the kingdom of God. The framework had been provided by Emperor Constantine in 325 when he had convened all Christian bishops at Nicaea to hammer out a creed and a statement of orthodoxy as the first official document of the Christian faith.

Many of these heresies were the teachings done by charismatic laypeople who gathered believers. Some charismatic preachers were real heretics with different preoccupations, but many of them preached valid points that the organized Church was fallen and corrupt, and the priests and their authority had nothing to do with true spiritual life.

The Latin and the Greek Churches had all their basic beliefs in common in unity, but they often manifested their theological differences like alien each other in the creeds of Christianity, for example, the languages of Latin and Greek, the *Filioque* (triangle format of trinity in the Orthodox that the Father at the apex and the Son and the Holy are at the bottom whereas the reversed triangle in the Catholic that the Father and the Son in the top and the Holy Spirit at the bottom), the use of leavened or unleavened bread in the Eucharist, the role of icons in worship, and the hierarchical structure.

The schism was evident in the stage that the community of Christendom was divided into West and East. The unity and disunity of Christendom have shifted throughout history. In the eyes of ordinary people, however, it may be seen as two variants of the same faith, like the Sunnis and Shiites in the Muslim world. Both variants were more conscious of their differences than their commonalities.

In the first millennium, they kept a facade of unity because of the hegemony held by Byzantium. In the second millennium, they made a watershed event of the East-West Schism in 1054 that precipitated the separation between the Eastern Church by mutual excommunication.

A series of the Crusades took place late 11th to early 13th century (the 1st in 1095-1102, the 2nd in 1147-49, the 3rd in 1190-91, the 4th in 1202-04, the 5th in 1217-21, and the 6th in 1228-29). During the 4th Crusade, there was the sack of Constantinople by the Venetian crusaders in 1204 who inflicted horrendous atrocities, looted hundreds of churches and relics belonging to the churches instead of taking Egypt from the Muslims. The Crusaders in the six Crusades who set off for the east were motivated by faith and by reports of horrors and atrocities in the Holy City, Jerusalem. While the Crusades are chiefly remembered as a war of religion, its most important implications were worldly. They were great struggles between the powers of Europe for position, riches and prestige in faraway lands triggered by the realization of the prizes on offer. They were blend of piety and greed, and things had shifted in such a way that the west was about to come closer to the heart of the world.

The excommunications were not lifted until 1965, when Pope Paul VI and Patriarch Athenagoras I, following their historic meeting in Jerusalem in 1964, presided over simultaneous ceremonies that revoked the excommunication decrees. It marked a dramatic turn from estranged alienation to mutual engagement.

Nothing comes from a vacuum; everything is interconnected and relative. This holds true in the historical development of Christendom as well.

4) Europe Under Invasions (c.800-1270)

Europe in the Middle Age was decimated by multiple invasions from beyond the fringes of Christendom. The adversity of famine, plagues and climate change was constant and ubiquitous as usual in history. But the invasions of the forces from the fringes were unprecedented and pervasive, aggravating the adverse condition of the people.

(1) The Vikings (c.800-11th Century)

The Vikings were not a race linked by common ancestry or national identity ties. Not being Christians, they were not civilized in the eyes of other Europeans and were good at hit-and-run raids. Most were known collectively as Vikings or Norsemen ("Northmen") from Denmark, Norway, and Sweden in Scandinavia.

The Scandinavians burst forth like a swarm of bees from the midst of the remote lands and islands and invaded the land of Europe which was triggered by migration due to overpopulation, lack of farmland, climate change, scarce resources for survival, innovations in long-ship construction, religious beliefs promising an afterlife, and sheer adventure in the Scandinavian regions.

The Vikings began to raid isolated settlements in the British Isles, north of the Netherlands, and Germany from the 8th century. They turned to setting up their establishments to act as local bases for more protracted campaigns of pillage and, in several instances, for permanent settlements from the mid-9th century.

Danish Vikings plundered Paris and created settlements in 845. They sailed off to Portugal (844) and to Provence and Tuscany in the Mediterranean (859-62). In 911, the Vikings created Normandy in France. They invaded England and ran the Danelaw, where Danish laws prevailed from 886 to 1066.

Norwegian Vikings concentrated on the outer islands in various directions for raids, trade, and exploration. Seafaring was vital to them; they voyaged to Iceland, and Greenland and crossed the North

Atlantic to land in North America, which they called Vinland. They sailed as far as Russia and the Byzantine Empire.

Swedish Vikings operated throughout the Baltic Sea. They joined raids on the Seine River alongside Danish Vikings. They struggled against the Anglo-Saxons in England, journeyed to Novgorod, and appeared in the Black Sea and Constantinople.

The adventurous Vikings adopted local culture and created new political entities, such as the principality of the eastern Slavs in Novgorod and Kyiv in 860-80, Canut, King of England from 1016, and Robert Guiscard, the Norman who conquered southern Italy and Sicily in the 11th century. William the Bastard, Duke of Normandy, conquered England in 1066 by defeating the English army led by King Harold II (r. 6 January 1066 to the Battle of Hastings on 14 October 1066).

The Battle of Hastings marked the point at which Anglo-Saxon Britain became Norman Britain from Normandy in France which was the land of the Northmen of the Vikings. Harold's failure to defeat the Normans lay with his fault for engaging the Normans in too much of a hurry with his weary and depleted army without reinforcement.

Before the Battle of Hastings, Harold had his army force-marched 200 miles (320 km) in just five days from Southern England to York to attack the invading Vikings. He won a great victory in the Battle of Stamford Bridge near York on 25 September. Although it had been victorious, Harold's army, too, had suffered considerable losses.

The Normans set sail on 27 September 1066 and, after a night crossing, they first landed at Pevensey Bay in southern England and then moved the fleet and army to Hastings where they built a wooden castle and pillaged the local areas for about two weeks. It was a deliberate ploy to goad Harold into an early battle.

Now came the news that the Normans fleet led by William landed on the south coast of England. Harold's tired army marched south, pausing for a few days in London where he was advised to delay before going into battle in a hurry. The impetuous Harold ignored the advice and had his weary and understrength army march south and arrived on the evening of 13 October.

In the up and down of the battle situation on 14 October, the tiredness of the English troops began to tell. The impatient King Harold lost the battle and his life. He made a critical blunder to push his understrength army too hard to fight the Normans who had been preparing the battle in Hastings. It marked a great turnaround in the history of England.

Vikings engaged in various activities: raiding, trading, conquering, and settling in those lands. The Scandinavians changed the histories of Ireland, England, Russia, and other European countries with the dispersal of the Vikings during the medieval times. They spread Norse culture, influenced regional politics, and sparked urbanization in the areas they settled.

It changed gene pools and altered European art styles. Global trade invigorated industrial activities through conquests, trade links, and settlements. The shipping tycoons in the Scandinavian regions such as AP Moller-Maersk A/S in Denmark, Stena Line in Sweden, and Wallenius Wilhelmsen ASA in Norway, trace their roots back to the legacy of seafaring in high relevance and vibrancy.

(2) The Seljuk Turk (1037-1194)

Seljuk Turks were fierce nomadic warriors descended from the tribe of Oghuz Turkish on the Central Asian steppes. After they accepted Islam in the 10th century, the Seljuk Empire was founded in 1037 by Tughril (990–1063) and his brother Chaghri (989–1060), who co-ruled its territories.

From their homelands near the Aral Sea, the Seljuks advanced first into Khorasan (an eastern region in the Iranian Plateau between West and Central Asia) and into the Iranian mainland, where they became largely based as a Persianate society. Then, the Seljuk ruler, Tughril, moved west to conquer Baghdad in 1055.

The subsequent Seljuk expansion into eastern Anatolia triggered the Byzantine-Seljuk Wars, with the Battle of Manzikert in 1071. This marked a decisive turning point in the conflict in favor of the Seljuks, undermining the authority of the Byzantine Empire in the remaining parts of Anatolia (modern-day Türkiye), and gradually causing the region's Turkification.

Byzantine emperors involved Turkish warriors to help them fight a civil war, but the Seljuk Turks quickly seized cities for themselves. By 1081, Turkish tribes controlled most of the Anatolian plateau, securing grasslands perfect for their pastoralist lifestyle. The Seljuk Empire united the non-Arab eastern parts of the Muslim world.

To retake Anatolia cities from the Seljuks, the Byzantine Empire in Constantinople as a stronghold of Christianity in Asia Minor invited Western Europeans to fight against the Muslims. Pope Urban II in Rome called for the First Crusade (1095-1102) and the Second Crusade (1147-1149), employing fearmongering and racist tropes against the Turks.

Throughout the 12th century, Western crusaders and Byzantine armies fought the Seljuk Turks in hopes of expelling or converting them to Christianity like other tribe members in the Balkans. However, the Muslims fought on and managed to take root in Asia Minor, where they defied Byzantine rule.

The Seljuk Empire brought significant social changes to Asia Minor, which had been under the control of Christianity for 800 years and Hellenistic influence for 1,500 years. The Seljuk Turks started to Islamize Asia Minor and Orientalize the culture that had been saturated with Christian doctrines.

The Seljuk Sultanates were under constant pressure from the Crusaders in the west, the Arabs in the south, and the Mongols in the east. A quarreling and faction-ridden Seljuk dynasty was unable to withstand the ever-increasing onslaughts, leading to its nationhood in obscurity by 1194.

The Seljuk Empire was short-lived but shared ethnic and linguistic stock with the Ottoman Empire (1299–1922), whose Sultan Mehmed II (r. 1444-1446, 1451-1481) conquered Constantinople in 1453, transforming it into the new Ottoman capital, Istanbul. The histories of the Seljuk Turks and Ottoman Turks led to the modern state of Türkiye.

(3) The Mongol Invasions

As the 13th century opened, the nomadic Mongols or Tartars camped at Karakorum in Mongolia on the arid steppes of Central Asia. They were tribal and migrating nomadic. They subsisted chiefly upon meat and mare's milk while living in skin tents, much like their predecessors, the Huns. They were truly mobile, cruel, and ambitious.

At this time, China was in a state of division that the Tang Dynasty had decayed by the 10th century. After a phase of division into warring states, the Northern Song (960-1127) unified China and restored territories of the Han (206 BC–220 AD) and Tang (618-907). The Song Dynasty, comprised mainly of the Han race, was taken over by the Mongolian Yuan Dynasty (1271-1368).

In 1206, after tribal strife for hegemony, all the Mongol tribes gathered to acknowledge Temujin as their Kahn, hailing him as Genghis Khan, meaning Kahn of All Oceans or Universal Kahn. Genghis Khan (r.1206-27) expanded his territory from the Pacific to the Black Sea.

Ögedei Khan (c.1186–1241), the third son of Genghis Khan and the second Great Khan, continued the expansion, reaching the peak of territorial conquest. He launched an invasion of Persia in 1230, initiated a war with Korea (1231-1257, 9 times in total), and skirmished with the Song Dynasty, while also penetrating deep into Europe.

In 1231, the Mongols crossed the Yalu River to enter the Korean Peninsula to conquer the Goryeo Dynasty. Choe-U, the head of the military state, ordered a fierce resistance. The Mongol invasion met resistance from the start at the northwestern city Kuiju. The defenders held out to the end and didn't surrender until it was ravaged by catapults, siege towers, and tunnels.

The Mongol invasion pushed through and got closer to the capital city Kaesong. The military leader, Choe-U, managed to halt the Mongol progress in return for an enormous tribute of horses, silk, and people. The Goryeo leadership escaped the capital, crossing the nearby island of Kanghwa, where they continued their resistance for 39 years (1232-71).

The Mongols demanded their return, but the Goryeo leadership, able to supply themselves, through trade with unconquered lands, refused. The Mongol commanders had no experience in naval warfare and were unable to subdu e the defenders. The defiant resistance brought a second invasion by the Mongol army in the same year.

For the invasion of Europe, the Mongols invaded central Europe with three armies. One advanced to Hungary and Poland, the second crossed the Carpathian Mountains, and the third followed the Danube River. They re-grouped and crushed the Poles and Moravians at the Battle of Legnica on 09 April 1241, and the Hungarian army at the Battle of Mohi on 11 April 1241.

The Polish and Hungarian forces faced the Mongolian assaults without support from Western kingdoms, notably the Holy Roman Empire and the papacy. The Mongol army was further poised to invade Western Europe, but they withdrew upon hearing of Ögödei Khan's death in December 1241, as a new leader needed to be chosen.

The rest of Europe was saved from the savage Mongols by the death of Ogödei Khan, but there were subsequent raids and punitive expeditions continued into the late 13th century. The Mongol invasions displaced populations on a scale never seen before in Eastern Europe and Asia. The violence of the Mongol invasions cascaded into further violence in the affected regions.

The century of peace under Mongolian rule (so-called the Pax Mongolica) made impacts on Europe, such as the reopening of the Silk Road between Europe and China, fostering more intensive and extensive cross-cultural interaction along trade paths. People were allowed to practice Islam, Christianity, Buddhism or Taoism as long as they did not pose problems for Mongolian rule.

Some ideas and scientific technologies such as papermaking, printing, and gunpowder, spread across Europe and Asia during Mongolian rule. The Golden Horde's occupation of Eastern Europe unified Russia. The new weaponry sparked a revolution in European fighting tactics and firearms technology for the following centuries.

The changes after the Mongol invasions accelerated a massive increase of German influence in Poland and Hungary, which were severely depopulated. German settlers moved into Silesia (Poland), Pomerania (the Baltic coastal plain), and Transylvania (Romania). Cities such as Breslau, Buda, and Cracow were governed by German law and filled with German merchants.

Nothing is free in history, and everything is interconnected in causality. The Mongol invasions devastated Europe, but it also opened a new dimension of European civilization through the effects of the Pax Mongolica. This could be one of the root causes of the Great Divergence, leading to Western Europe surpassing the Orient from the 16th century onward, including its imperial expansions.

5) Slavery (750-1600)

When Adam delved and Eve span, who was then the gentleman? It represents the fact that Adam and Eve just worked with their own hands, and there was no class hierarchy.

The slavery system has been universal to all human societies since the Agricultural Revolution when the class distinction settled in. Without ennoblement, there would have been no enslavement or vice versa.

Mostly, slaves were born, bought, captured, or turned into servants in households, industrial sites, or for military purposes. The masters made the slaves dumb and docile – the ideal being of witless, unquestioning, and free laborers.

The tragedy arises, in most cases, from the fact that the slaves were not to blame for their enslavement. They were just subjected to the fate of enslavement, which some Christians may call a providential mystery that decided their fate by birth or luck. Sometimes, slaves protested their unjust fate to redress adversities on their own, but most ended in defeat, with rebellious slaves often facing punishment or execution.

One example is the Viking slave trade, which took place in the Middle East, the Mediterranean, and Northern Europe. Many slaves were destined for Scandinavia, but many others were sent to where good money was paid for fine specimens. As a result of Viking slave raids against the Slavic peoples of Eastern Europe, the word "slave" became the root of the word "Slavic". Slaves taken from the territories were sold in slave markets in Europe and Africa, which proved to be singularly successful when it came to business.

The abolition of slavery was one of the key social products of the European Enlightenment and cultural sophistication. It progressed through three main stages. The outlawry of slave-owning in the home countries was followed by the suppression of the international slave trade and then the abolition of slavery in overseas colonies.

Although circumstances varied in each case, there were four basic ways that humans became slaves:

(1) It is by birth. Humans were not born free. Children of slaves were destined for the same fate as their parents.

(2) It is by capture. Individuals were captured from local populations or as prisoners of war.

(3) It is by default. Some people, overly indebted, exchanged their freedom for the absolution of debts or were penalized with a term of enslavement.

(4) It is by need. Some became slaves voluntarily, as the desperate sold themselves during times of affliction.

The ruling class owed its position to control over lands cultivated mainly by slaves. In 1452, Pope Nicholas V (1397-1455) issued a papal bull called *Dum Diversas* granting approval to Alfonso V of Portugal for the enslavement and sale of Africans, aimed at reducing uprisings among pagans and other unbelievers.

The pope wrote the bull *Romanus Pontifex* in 1455 to the same Alfonso that sanctified the seizure of non-Christian lands and approved the enslavement of native, non-Christian peoples in Africa and the New World with no compunction about human trafficking. This facilitated the Portuguese slave trade from West Africa and legitimized European colonization of the African continent.

6) King Charlemagne (r.768-814) and the Holy Roman Empire (800-1806)

Charlemagne, or Charles the Great, became king of the Franks in 768. He was crowned as emperor in Rome in 800 and became the Father of Europe. He reigned over the vast Carolingian empire for 46 years (r. 768-814). After fifty-three campaigns and a lifetime in the saddle, he succeeded in the expansion of his realm in all directions.

His kingdom reached from the Lombards in the south of the Alps (773-4) to Saxony, a landlocked state of Germany bordering Poland and the Czech Republic (775-804), Bavaria in southeastern Germany (788), Carinthia in southern Austria (799), Brittany in north-west modern France (786), and the Spanish March across the Pyrenees (795-7).

The empire of Charlemagne consummated the alliance between the Roman Papacy and the growing kingdom of the Franks. The Franco-Papal alliance was consummated in 800 when Charlemagne was crowned by Pope Leo III, who had no recognized right to confer the imperial title without the approval of the Petrarch in Constantinople of the Byzantine Empire.

The fact that there was a Catholic Emperor in the West independent of the Byzantine Empire meant that the barbaric Frankish kingdom was upgraded to regular statehood. The king became dependent on the Pope for his new status. This Franco-Papal alliance was a sort of Realpolitik in the 9th century.

Modern people are reminded of King Charlemagne through the title of a column in the weekly newspaper, The Economist. The Nazis called itself the Third Reich, following the Holy Roman Empire (800/962-1806) as the First Reich, and the German Empire (1871-1918), ruled by the Kaiser of Prussia, as the Second Reich.

It is saying that one obedient slave is better than three hundred sons for the latter desire their father's death, but the former his master's glory. When it comes to succession, a great leader achieved a lot during his life, but the achievements humbled him from his demise or collapse.

Charlemagne's posterity disputed the inheritance of his realm and disintegrated it after the death of

Charlemagne in 814. The Treaty of Verdun in 843 split the kingdom: Charles the Bald (roughly modern France), Lothair I (roughly modern Italy), Louis the German (roughly modern Germany). It created the foundations for modern Germany and France, while the Middle Kingdom was left a bone of contention.

Ironically, the Treaty of Verdun laid out Germany and France for peace. More than one thousand years later, however, Germany and France fought at Verdun during World War I, resulting in the bloodiest battle in 1916, with casualties of more than seven hundred thousand soldiers in less than ten months.

Otto the Great (r. 962-973) was crowned Emperor by Pope John XII and he founded the Holy Roman Empire (962-1806). It was not a unitary state, but a confederation of political entities. It lasted nearly a millennium only by the fiction of Roman resurrection and connected marriages. It made the saying that European royal families were cousins three times removed.

Rising from obscure origins, the reign of the House of Habsburg began in 1246, when the family took control of Austria. They were more successful by winning the throne of the Holy Roman Empire for Rudolf I (ruled 1273–1291) and his son Albert I (ruled 1298–1308). The Holy Roman Empire was not a unitary state, but a confederation of small and medium-sized political entities.

"A.E.I.O.U." was a symbolic motto coined by Holy Roman Emperor Frederick III (1415–1493) and used by the Habsburgs. It means *"Erdreich ist Österreich untertan"* (All the world is subject to Austria).

7) Song Dynasty (960-1279)

After decades of invasion following the downfall of the Tang Dynasty in 907, the Song Dynasty unified China again. It consisted of the Northern Song (960-1127) and the Southern Song (1127-1279), each ending with two external invasions: the Jurchen invasion in 1127 and the Mongolian invasion in 1279.

When the period of the Song (960-1279, 319 years) is combined with that of the Tang (618-907, 289 years), skipping the interposed division for 53 years, the 608 years were said to be the golden age of Chinese history in the sense of advanced civilization, commercial industrialization, active globalization, cultural sophistication, and advanced technologies.

The era produced a virtuous circle of population growth, urban development, improved living standards, and progress in art and philosophy. It was well documented by the Venetian merchant, Marco Polo (1254-1324), who recognized this oriental civilization during his travels through Asia, including China, along the Silk Road (1271-1295).

The civilizations of the Tang and Song are contrasted with the adversities faced in the succeeding dynasties: the Yuan (1279-1368), Ming (1368-1644), and Qing (1644-1911). The Western ascendancy in the Great Divergence, including the 19th century imperial expansion, contrasts sharply with the decline of China from the 14th through 19th century.

During the Northern Song (960-1127), tax money went more to roads, buildings, schools, and books, than to the army. The Song emperors, unlike the Tang, maintained a tense relationship with so-called barbarians in Manchuria, Mongolia, and Central Asia. The policies of appeasement and monetary incentives accumulated costs that distracted the Song Dynasty.

As northern borders were breached, the Song relocated to the south, but the underlying problem of insecurity continued to harass them. In response to the threat against their dynasty, Song intellectuals developed a defensive, inward-looking mindset, and narrowed their focus on internal matters rather than military strength.

They set their minds more on defining Chinese canons of proper behavior, arts, and philosophy of Neo-Confucianism, as advocated by the philosopher Zhu Xi. (1130-1200) The Confucian teachings regarded personal morality as the highest goal to achieve through book learning, personal observation, and engagement with wise individuals.

Its antagonistic mind toward foreign ideas like Buddhism made Chinese rulers less receptive to the outside world. Neo-Confucian thinking exerted a great impact on the mentality of common people as well as intellectuals during the Song era and subsequent dynasties.

Specifically, Neo-Confucianism emphasized rank, obligations, deference, and traditional rituals, reinforcing distinctions of class and gender. The emperor was conceived to possess the Mandate of Heaven to control the empire. Most of its ideas have survived to date and they made impacts in other countries like Korea and Japan.

Even in the staid environment of ideas, the Song Dynasty witnessed significant inventions in science and technology, and economic prosperity. Innovations included paper money, porcelain, tea, restaurants, gunpowder, the compass, canals, bridges, seafaring vessels, acupuncture, and movable type printing that spread literacy and knowledge.

This disparity raises questions about the direction of ideas and science. The mind of rank and obligations under Neo-Confucianism restricted the expression of liberal minds, but innovative advancements were driven by liberal minds.

One wonders how different the world might be if philosopher Zhu Xi (1130-1200) and others advocated ethics and morality in the direction of openness, liberality, practicality, and individual aspiration, like figures like John Locke (1632-1704), Adan Smith (1723-1790) and Max Weber (1864-1920) in Europe.

We find a point in the Song Dynasty that a rich state can collapse when its resolve to confront enemies weakens. The Song Dynasty bought time and peace by appeasement but failed to prioritize military strength. The Roman empires in the West and East showed the same problem of appeasing the enemies. Ineffective policies cannot be a lasting solution.

We find the same case in the Munich Crisis in 1939. The U.K. tried to appease Hitler when he drove his expansion across the European continent. Diplomacy was essential to make peace, but the power must stand behind diplomacy in realpolitik. The impudent aggressors can be handled in a dovish or hawkish manner, but it is the power that makes the peace.

The same story goes on in China as well. China was prosperous when it nurtured practicality in thoughts and actions. remained open to outside ideas and kept communal standards in commerce and cross-cultural interactions. On the other hand, China was forced into a problem when it turned mainly inward, too focused on ideological dogma and patriotic zeal, turned to chauvinistic sentiment, and became antagonistic toward outsiders. Recently, similar phenomena have taken place in China and there is a concern about it.

To be clear, it is not intended to convey any particular preference or criticism at all, but rather to evaluate China from the perspective of the paragraph before. China needs to consider the notion of universal and sustainable prosperity in a global society that is founded on freedom of expression, openness in ideas and ideology, and global standards.

8) The Magna Carta, the Great Charter (1215)

The story of the Magna Carta is intimately tied with the story of King John (r.1199-1216). King John cannot be properly portrayed without the crusade of his elder brother King Richard I, the Lionheart, (r.1189-1199), who went on a costly Crusade in 1190, ransacked the treasure, sold state offices to the highest bidder, and collected 10 percent of the kingdom's goods and cash for the Third Crusade (1187-1192).

The First Crusade (1095-1102) was a military campaign to recapture the city of Jerusalem and the Holy Land from Muslim control. It was requested by the Byzantine Emperor Alexios I Komnenos (r.1081-1118) who was struggling with constant warfare with the Seljuk Turks and the decline of Byzantine influence and supported by Pope Urban II (papacy 1088-1099) with the Council of Clermont in 1095. The First Crusade ended with the success of recapturing Jerusalem on 15 July 1099 (Pope Urban II died on 29 July 1099, fourteen days after the recapture of Jerusalem but before news of the event had reached Italy when his successor was Pope Paschal II).

The Third Crusade (1189-1192) was launched to retake Jerusalem after its fall to the Muslim leader Saladin in 1187. The Crusade was led by three European monarchs, Frederick I Barbarossa, King of Germany and Holy Roman Emperor (r.1152-1190), Philip II of France (r.1180-1223), and Richard I, the Lionheart, of England (r. 1189-1199). The rivalry between King Richard and the Muslim ruler Saladin is known as a romantic frenemy that captured the febrile imagination of contemporaries who never actually encountered on the battlegrounds.

His younger brother, King John, was left to rule England and the western parts of France that Henry II, King John's father, had expanded. He was burdened with expenditures for the Crusade and a ransom payment to get King Richard out of captivity in 1192. For Western Christians, the series of Crusades was s sort of poisoned chalice in undertaking the divine missions with mundane tools,

In 1207, King John disagreed with Pope Innocent III over the appointment of the next Archbishop of Canterbury. He seized church lands and expelled the bishops, prompting the Pope to excommunicate him and turn all of Europe against England after which he was forced to submit to the church in the face of a possible Holy War against England by other European monarchs.

The humiliating gesture was said to be an astute decision that induced the support of the Pope against the Magna Carta. To finance a massive land war in France and the ongoing Crusade, King John drained the royal treasury, raised taxes, and increased fees in available ways such as forest use and court proceedings.

As he lost more tax-producing territories in France, the burden of paying taxes fell on the remaining territories and population. This had set his barons on edge. John pushed more for tax income contrary to the customary standard. In 1210, he even ordered Jews in England to be imprisoned to take money from them.

The unprecedented demand drove the feudal economy into turmoil and John became the despotic head of ill-government. Being protective of what was left of their wealth, the nobility began to turn on the king. Resentment piled on to a critical mass and it hit a new height year after year.

In July 1214, King John suffered a disastrous defeat at Bovines in Flanders of France, losing most of the English-held territories except a southern part, Poitou and Gascony. The defeat induced the resentful barons to press King John to govern within the bounds of custom, and they protested excessive taxes.

On 10 June 1215, King John met the rebellious leaders at a neutral place, Runnymede, on the bank of the River Thames. The negotiations were documented as a series of royal concessions toward baronial grievances in the Magna Carta (meaning the Great Charter).

On 19 June 1215, the rebellious barons made a formal peace with King John by renewing their oaths of loyalty to him, and copies of the Magna Carta were formally issued.

The Magna Carta was written from the perspective of the king. Of the 63 clauses, about a third of it dealt directly with turning taxes and fees back to traditional rates. Another third of the clauses attempted to restore feudal customs that John had disregarded during his reign.

The Magna Carta laid the groundwork for the Petition of Right and inspired John Locke's political philosophy during the Age of Enlightenment. This would explain how the Magna Carta eventually contributed to the development of civil liberties and democratic values.

The importance of the Magana Carta in history was an inception of defiance to the kingly rights. In that context, some clauses are introduced.

Clause 2 dealt with the fee that an heir must pay to inherit land following the death of the previous landholder. The Magna Carta fixed this fee, or relief, at £100 for the heir of an earl and a maximum of 100 shillings (£5) for the heir of a knight.

"Clause 2. If any earl, baron, or other people that holds lands directly from the Crown, for military service, shall die, and at his death, his heir shall be of full age and owe a 'relief', the heir shall have his inheritance on payment of the ancient scale of 'relief'. That is to say, the heir or heirs of an earl shall pay £100 for the entire earl's barony, the heir or heirs of a knight 100s, at most for the entire knight's fee, and any man that owes less shall pay less, in accordance with the ancient usage of fees."

Clause 3 prevented the king from exacting any relief from heirs who were minors when they came of age and inherited their lands.

"Clause 3. If the heir of such a person is underage and a ward, when he comes of age he shall have his inheritance without relief or fine."

Clauses 7 and 8 defined the rights of widows.

"Clause 7. After the death of her husband a widow is to have her marriage portion and inheritance immediately and without difficulty, nor is she to give anything for her dower, or for her marriage portion, or for the inheritance which she and her husband jointly held on the day of his death, and she may remain in her husband's house for forty days after his death, during which she is to be assigned her dower.

Clause 8. No widow shall be compelled to marry while she wishes to live without a husband, as long as she gives security that she will not marry without royal consent if she holds of her lands of the Crown, or without the consent of whatever other lord she may hold them of."

Modern readers interestingly encounter the Jewish practice of money-lending business in Clause 10 and 11.

"Clause 10. If anyone has taken a loan from Jews, great or small, and dies before the debt is paid, the debt is not to incur interest for as long as the heir is underage, whoever he may hold from. And if the debt comes into the hands of the Crown, we will take nothing except the principal sum specified in the bond.

Clause 11. And if anyone dies, and owes a debt to Jews, his wife is to have her dower and pay nothing towards that debt. And if there are surviving children of the deceased who are underage, their needs are to be provided for them on a scale appropriate to the size of his holding of lands. The debt is to be paid from the residue, reserving the service owed to the lords. Debts owed to others besides Jews are to be dealt with in like manner."

It went on to deal with the contentious issue of scutage (a tax levied on a vassal or a knight instead of military service) and aid (a tax levied for help or counsel).

"Clause 12. No scutage or aid is to be imposed in our kingdom without its general consent, unless it is for the ransoming of our person, and knighting of our first-born son, and for marrying our eldest daughter. For these purposes, only a reasonable aid may be levied. Aids from the city of London are to be treated in a like manner."

As we see, the City of London is one of the centers of global finance and legal sectors in the 21st century. The same name and town mentioned in the Clause 13 are still valid to this day.

"Clause 13. The city of London shall enjoy all its ancient liberties and free customs, both by land and by water. Moreover, we wish and grant that all other cities, boroughs, towns, and ports shall enjoy all their liberties and free customs."

Clause 31 is especially representative of the technical (rather than ideal or poetic) nature of the Magna Carta. This doesn't mean to guarantee personal property, nor it is at odds with other clauses which reaffirmed the king's right to tax and collect revenue. As the sovereign king, owner of all land in the realm, and keeper of all the forest, King John was obligated by Clause 31 to respect the land appointments he had already made to the barons.

"Clause 31. Neither we ('Crown') nor our bailiffs shall take, for our castles or any other work of ours, wood which is not ours, against the will of the owner of that wood."

The Magna Carta also addressed the barons' legal grievances, in particular, their exposure to the king's arbitrary decisions regarding justices and his use of judicial disputes to extort huge fines from them. These two clauses are still valid under the Charter of 1225.

"Clause 39. No free man shall be seized or imprisoned, or stripped of his rights or possessions, out

outlawed or exiled, or deprived of his standing in any other way, nor will we proceed with force against him, or send others to do so, except by the lawful judgment of his equals or by the law of the land."

Clause 40. To no one will we sell deny or delay right or justice."

The rebellious barons sought consistency from the king in adhering to the established customs of his office. Clause 49 expressed the point that the king provides sureties of the peace of faithful service.

"Clause 49. We ('Crown') will immediately surrender all hostages and charters which have been handed over to us by Englishmen as security for peace or loyal service."

9) Plagues (6th century, 1347-1350)

Humanity has faced deadly diseases in every corner of age. Leprosy peaked in the 13th century, the Black Death swept across Eurasia in the 14th century, syphilis raged in the early modern times, and tuberculosis, cholera, and influenza plagued Europe's industrial cities. More recently, leprosy and AIDS have left their mark, culminating in the global impact of COVID-19.

The Black Death stands out as a devastating pandemic that halted progress across Europe and western Asia, unprecedented in its scale and impact.

(1) Justinian Plague in the 6th Century

During the reign of Emperor Justinian (r.527- 565), a deadly disease with bubonic, pneumonic, or septicemic symptoms struck Byzantium. A large number of people underwent hallucinations, diarrhea, violent delirium or deep coma. Emperor Justinian himself contracted the disease but managed to recover.

It is only estimated that Constantinople lost up to half of its population and more than 10 million deaths were reported throughout the Mediterranean. The sharp drop in population resulted in a shortage of manpower, rising wages, food shortages in the cities, soaring inflation, and a shrinking tax base, while tax income was most needed to maintain public services.

The societal damage was so severe that the population of the Byzantine Empire was rather slow to recover. It sapped the Byzantine Empire's vitality and marked the beginning of its long decline, diminishing the empire's influence and its status as a regional power.

We find here a providential coincidence that the reformers were tormented by plague-ridden adversities as they were seen in the Justinian Plague herein above and the Antonic Plague herein below.

In the days of the last of the Five Good Emperors in the Roman Empire, Marcus Aurelius (r.161-180), the Antonine Plague erupted in 165 AD with common symptoms were fever, diarrhea, vomiting, thirstiness, swollen throat, and coughing. There is wide variance on total casualties of the Roman populace, but it is suggested a quarter to a third of the entire population perished, estimated at 60-70 million throughout the empire.

(2) The Black Death (1347-1350)

In the early 1300s, Europe began to see a temperature drop, accompanied by violent storms, deluges, and harsh winters. Famine came as rains poured in spring, and grains rotted in autumn. The famine left a tenth of human casualties. Survivors suffered from scurvy, stunted growth, and poor dental health, making them more vulnerable to the next plague.

The Black Death began in Central Asia and spread with frightening speed. In 1347, it reached Messina in Sicily and Constantinople. In 1348, it entered Marseilles, Valencia, Venice, Pisa, and Florence. By summer, it reached Paris, and by the end of the year, it hit England. In 1349, it spread to Germany and the Balkans. In 1350, it came to Scotland, Denmark, Sweden and Russia.

Once people felt sick, they felt hopeless and helpless. People died as soon as the disease appeared on their bodies: conspicuous enlargement of lymph nodes in the armpits, groin, or neck, along with coagulating fluids, putrid fever, and swelling. A large quantity of foul-smelling pus would flow from the infected areas.

The lungs sometimes became inflamed, causing sharp chest pains and foul breath. The throat and tongue appeared blackened and congested with blood. Those who fell ill endured unbearable pain and, within days, often died.

Medieval medicine lacked an understanding of pathogens and the mechanisms of disease transmission. People in crowded towns and with poor sanitation were more susceptible to the plague than those living in rural settings. The wealthy often fled the affected areas, but the poor and young people who worked or buried the dead faced a higher risk of infection. Few places were immune to the plague, but Poland and the northern Pyrenees in Europe were relatively lightly touched.

Giovanni Boccaccio's Decameron, written between 1348 and 1353, consists of ten short stories told over ten days by seven women and three men sheltering in a secluded villa in Florence. It became a classic masterpiece that balances grim reality with the resilience of those who continued to live.

The Black Death had profound consequences. It killed about forty percent of the European population by which the feudal system and Christianity notably declined. It was a troubling and consuming factor for priests, who were tasked with caring for the sick, hearing confessions, and administering burials.

Many believed the plague was a divine punishment for humanity's sins. The tasks sacrificed more than 40 percent of priests in Christendom. Popular reactions to the plague turned to social unrest, rising rebellions, manorial dislocation, languishing trade, labor shortages, urban distress, and widespread panic.

In these chaotic and violent conditions, the only state that still existed was the state of nature. Those who could flee fled, while others perished or endured it. The deep psychological trauma increased charity foundations, and people opted to become flagellants in a mind of seeking divine grace through repentance. Scapegoating also emerged, with Jews falsely accused of poisoning water.

In history, we often encounter Jewish issues as we saw them in Clauses 10 and 11 (the Jewish practice of money-lending business) of the Magna Carta in 1215, Jewish persecution in the traumatic insanity of the Black Death, and the horrible Holocaust during World War II. The people in distress tried to find a breakthrough by mobilizing anti-Semitic sentiment.

As demands for able peasants soared, the scarce labor force increased their leverage in the employer-labor relationship. There was widespread violence in the countryside, with peasants attacking the castles and families of the nobility in retaliation for long-standing discrimination and exploitation.

There was a social-leveling effect in the community. The living standards of laborers and granting ordinary people privileges once reserved for the higher class. But the leveling didn't last long as the population grew, and the labor shortage abated proportionately over the one and a half of the next centuries.

The transformation triggered by the Black Death laid foundation for the European economies in the early modern period with the systemic flexibility, the openness to competition, and the sense of awareness that a strong work ethic was required to create a profit. The roots of the Industrial Revolution of the 18th century lay in the industrious revolution of the post-plague people who lifted productivity rose, set the aspirations upwards, and increased the level of disposable income along with opportunities to spend it.

When it comes to airborne infection and infected lungs, modern readers may recall the COVID-19 pandemic, which stirred comprehensive disorder and despair across the world from 2020 to 2022, resulting in significant human casualties until community immunity materialized in the globe. It had symptoms of dry cough, shortness of breath, loss of taste or smell, extreme tiredness, digestive symptoms such as upset stomach and vomiting, headaches and muscle aches, fever or chills, cold-like symptoms such as congestion, runny nose or sore throat.

An epidemic is a disease that spreads rapidly among many people and stays in a specific community. In contrast, the pandemic affects a much broader population. The rapid spread of the Black Death in Eurasia from 1347 to 1350 exemplifies a pandemic's wide-reaching impact.

On 31 December 2019, Chinese health officials reported some pneumonia cases in Wuhan City. They announced that the situation was under control, but, by the end of April 2020, the global economy virtually screeched to a halt. The World Health Organization (WHO) declared COVID-19 over in May 2023, with 7 million deaths among 775 million confirmed cases reported worldwide by May 2024.

The COVID-19 pandemic was not new but just a repetition of human afflictions. As the modern world becomes more interconnected, urbanized, and subject to climate change, new variants of pandemic diseases may pop up anytime and anywhere. A fatal situation that may happen could be beyond our conventional range of recognition.

Seeking scapegoats during times of turmoil was evident in the Great Kanto Earthquake in Japan in 1923, when the Japanese massacred more than thousands of Koreans based on baseless rumors that Koreans were committing arson, robbery, and water poisoning. The anti-Korean sentiment and atrocity followed the Korean independence movement of 1919.

The pattern of seeking a scapegoat during a crisis has become common in modern life, often driven by impulsive reactions or deliberate intentions in a social network society. Lots of people aspire to be viral, earn an audience, and monetize their content. However, lack of discipline to abide by the law or common sense can lead some opportunists to scapegoat others.

The distinction between the freedom to express opinions and the right to protect interests is getting blurred and complex in modern life. When the distinction is disregarded on purpose or inadvertently, and when malpractice is not checked and balanced, anti-social behavior will emerge, destroying on a scale like that of the Black Death.

10) The Collapse of Byzantine Empire (1453)

The rise and fall of the Byzantine Empire from Late Antiquity (an era of transformations in politics, economy, religion between 250 AD and 750 AD with the emergence of Christianity, the establishment of Byzantium, and the Germanic conquest of the Western Roman Empire) to the Late Middle Ages (13th to 14th century) can be well explained by the size of the population that the empire had governed:

Year (AD)	Population (Million)
457 the Roman East	16
565 right after the rule of Emperor Justinian (r.527- 565)	20
668 just before Arab forces besieged Constantinople (674-678)	10
775	7
1025 under the reign of Emperor Basil II (r.976-1025)	12
1320	2

Source L Wikiedia (Population of the Byzantine Empire. Notes were added by the author)

Byzantium retained many old Roman institutions, but its imperial court was run by an emperor and an army of bureaucrats in a centralized administration, unlike the Western Roman system, which included an emperor, a senate, and various executives. The word, Byzantium, became a byword for subservience, secrecy, and intrigue.

As the empire edged to its downfall, it just held Constantinople and a few surrounding towns. From 1261 to its fall in 1453, it was ruled by desperate emperors seeking aid from various quarters. They tried to end the Schism with the Roman Pope in hopes of receiving support. In 1399, Emperor Manuel II (1391-1425) made a vain journey to raise support in Rome, Paris, and London, but the empirical journey turned out to be lonely and blue in the end. Passionate pleas for military support from the royal courts of Europe went unanswered, leaving the city dangerously exposed.

The most sensational development during this period was the appearance of a new Turkish warrior tribe that supplanted the Byzantines in Asia Minor. The Ottomans filled the power vacuum left by the Mongols' defeat of the Seljuks. They chipped away at the Byzantine frontier, launching fleets of pirates into the Aegean Sea, and advancing into the Balkans.

In 1444, Ottoman Sultan Murad II destroyed the last occasion of the Crusade, and, in 1448, he crushed the last Hungarian expedition forces across the Danube in a battle against a Hungarian-led Crusader army. The feeble, friendless, but still defiant Constantinople awaited its destiny.

The final siege of Constantinople began on 2 April 1453, Easter Monday, and lasted for eight weeks. The twenty-year-old Sultan, Mehmet II (r.1451-81) was eager to attack the Walls of Constantinople that had successfully repelled Arab invasions since 673. The bachelor Emperor, Constantine XI Palaiologos (r.

1448-53), awaited the attack without illusions.

On the day that the first Turkish detachments came into view, only 7,000 defenders stood against an onslaught of 80,000 virulent Muslim attackers. The great cannon, firing once every seven minutes from sunrise to sunset, reduced the outer wall to rubble, but the gaps were filled at night with wooden stockades.

But then, in a masterstroke, the Sultan ordered his fleet of galleys to be dragged overland behind Pera and into the Golden Horn. The city lost its harbor. From then on, the defenders had only three options: victory, death, or conversion to Islam.

On 27 April 1453, an ecumenical mass was celebrated in St Sophia, for Greeks and Italians, Orthodox and Catholics. At this moment, there was a union in the Church of Constantinople without any signs of schism. The decisive assault was launched about half-past one in the morning of Tuesday, 29 May 1453, the fifty-third day of the siege.

The Turks swarmed into the city and the last emperor, Constantine XI Palaiologos, dismounted from his white Arabian mare, plunged into the fighting, and disappeared into the melee of battle. Constantinople was sacked, and gross slaughter and rapine ensued. St Sophia was turned into a mosque. The capture of one of the greatest cities of Christendom was a triumph for Islam which leaped for its advancement once again. In Rome, people deeply lamented with crying and beating their chests when news came through that Constantinople had fallen and prayed for those trapped in the city. But Europe had done too little when it mattered; now it was too late.

The strategic shift was signaled by two landmark events: the fall of Christian Constantinople to the Turks in 1453 and the fall of Muslim Granada to the Spaniards in 1492. The consequences were immense. The kingdom of Spain was bathed in Catholic triumphalism whilst the remnants of defiant Christians were slaughtered in Constantinople.

The shift gave rise to the search for a new trade route to India because the overland route was blocked by Islamic occupation. This led to the discovery of the New World in the 1500s. The Turkish overthrow of the Byzantine Empire was a world-shaker because the transformation of Constantinople into Istanbul was the end of the old world and the beginning of a new era.

Book II

PART 4.

4.1. From 1501 to 1800 (The Great Transformation)

1) The 15th century as a build-up period for the next century

It is time to wrap up the history that humans have developed through the evolutionary process of human characteristics as a part of hominization. The historical status and development in the 15th century were the conclusion of human activities from ancient times, and it became a prelude to a new paradigm of human behaviors from the 16th century that transformed humans and the environment across the globe.

Humans transitioned from hunter-gatherers to farmer-cultivators in the period from 11,000 to 4,000 BC. The legacy of human development flourished during the Classical Age, from the inception of the Greece-Macedonian Kingdom in 808 BC to when China was unified in the Chin, Han, Sui, and Tang Dynasties, the fall of the Roman Empire, and the rise of Islam until the 7th century. This era laid the foundations of human civilizations and philosophies.

In the Middle Ages, Europe opened a new environment for the resetting of the geo-political order and the decline of medieval culture. The Tang and Song Dynasties unified China again and prospered until they fell in the 13th century. The multiple invasions and raids of Vikings and Mongols, the climate change of low temperatures, and the onslaught of the Black Death annihilated the people until the 14th century.

The formidable shocks of wars, famine, and disease decreased the population. In 1300, it was approximately 475 million, but it crashed to 380 million in 1400 after the Black Death. It took more than 200 years to recover to its pre-Black Death level until the mid-17th century, which saw it decline again due to the Little Ice Age. It increased to 950 million by 1800 with clement weather and sufficiency from the Industrial Revolution.

The 15th century was a turning point of history that linked the old medieval world and the new world of exploration and exertion. In the century after the calamitous incidents that had devastated Eurasia, the world turned polycentric and became more connected through trade and migration. The networks of connection widened.

In the 15th century, there were two kinds of worlds. Most people lived sedentary and static lives in agricultural societies, while some engaged in trade and commerce, bringing a decisive break with the socio-economic medieval tradition. The old order in the countryside remained unaffected, and the new order, characterized by greater contact and dynamic activities, coexisted.

The part of quickening pace of change gave rise to a more refined system of knowledge, experiences, capital-building, social relationships, and adventurism. Naturally, a variety of relationships were getting remolded, for example, between men and women, between sellers and buyers, between towns and countryside, between the rulers and the ruled, and ultimately between people and the environment.

Thus, the 15th century was a historical point at which the world started to jump the curve from old patterns of behavior to new ones in the 16th century and onwards. People broke with stultifying convention and generated a new mode of acquiring knowledge and exercising adventurism. They circumnavigated the globe, found new lands and oceans, and connected the world.

Christendom was reset with the momentous shift in the Muslim's two pincers toward Christendom. One arm of the pincers was lost in the Iberian Peninsula (the land of Spain and Portugal) when Muslim Granada surrendered its control in 1492 to the forces of Christianity, but another arm was secured in the East as the Byzantine Empire fell to the Ottoman Turks in 1453. It caused Christianity to move westward after the collapse of Constantinople.

The Chinese explorer Zhenghe made seven seafaring expeditions to South and West Asia (1405-1433). China built a network of relationships based on trade and diplomacy but let the chance to sustain the network slip away voluntarily. This raises the question of what if the Chinese had set the navigation course eastward, not westward, and then they would have reached the western coast of America much earlier than the Europeans who made it their colony.

Robert B. Marks offered details on the global network of trade in his book *"The Origins of the Modern World."* He said that there had never been a central controlling or dominating states, but they ran themselves. Furthermore, it was the composite of contingencies, accidents, and conjunctures that made the Industrial Revolution in 1750-1800 in Britain, and the rise of industrial capitalism in the 1800s:

(1) The East Asian loop that linked China and Southeast Asia to India. Later, the British ran the East India Company (1600-1874), and the Dutch East India Company (1602-1795) operated trade routes in Asia, marking the history of extraction and exploitation until the early 20th century. The vestigial colonialism still influences the social-political practices of Southeast Asian states.

(2) The Middle East-Mongolian loop that linked the European continent from the eastern Mediterranean, through the Mongol Empire, all the way to China, along which Marco Polo ventured in the late 1200s. Unfortunately, it was the same route that the pathogens of the Black Death spread across the Eurasian continent, and the nomadic attackers from the steppe stormed westward. Virtue and vice come and go together.

(3) European trade linked Genoa and Venice to the Middle East and the Indian Ocean, and further to North and West Africa, creating intricate trade relationships between Europeans and Middle East countries.

2) Renaissance and Reformation

The Renaissance is the rebirth of old wisdom following the Dark Age. Throughout the 12th century, European intellect pursued the intellectual enterprises of scientific inquiry. The experiences from the expeditions in the series of Crusades helped stimulate people's minds for higher standards of comfort and security.

The 13th and 14th centuries were a period of growing cities with many travelers and traders throughout Europe. The vitality of commercial activity and free mind was contrasted with the constrained mood of medieval societies. The mismatch between freer minds and constrained realities stirred men to question the validity of political leadership and the authority of the church.

The Ottoman conquered Constantinople in May of 1453, bringing an end to the Roman dream ruling the world of Europe and Asia. However, the cultural phenomenon continued well after 1453, as seen in the political philosophies of Machiavelli, the paintings of Michelangelo, the inventions of da Vinci, and the observations of Galileo.

Niccolo Machiavelli himself was a Florentine bureaucrat, diplomat, political adviser, and practical philosopher. H wrote The Prince in 1513, but it was published until 1532, five years after the author's death, as a handbook for rulers and asserted Machiavelli's own qualifications to serve as an adviser at a time of great turbulence and danger in Italian affairs.

He went beyond tolerance for ruses and subterfuge in war. Machiavellian came to describe anyone with a talent for manipulation and an inclination to deceit in the pursuit of personal gain, fascinated with power for its own sake rather than with virtuous and noble things. Machiavelli's amorality was denounced by the Church as an instrument of the devil.

Machiavelli understood that even if power was obtained by force and guile and consolidated with cruelty, it required consent to be secured. The best power was that which had to be exercised least. Although Machiavellianism has become synonymous with strategies based on deceit and manipulation, Machiavelli's approach was far more balanced.

He understood that the more the prince was perceived to rely on devious methods, the less likely it would be that they succeeded. The wise strategist would seek to develop a foundation for the exercise of power that went beyond false impressions and harsh punishments but on real accomplishments and general respect.

The Renaissance began in the late 15th century when medieval customs were mixed with initiatives for change. In the Middle Ages, filled with divination, miracles, witchcraft, fairies, and fears, humanism was revitalized along with scientific inventions, the Reformation, the circumnavigation of the world, and challenges to monarchical and papal order.

As the world became more enlightened by the middle of the 15th century, a new mode of thinking and action distinguished European civilization from medieval Christendom and other non-European civilizations such as Islam and China, further making Europe in the mid-18th century distinct from what it had been in the 15th century.

The causes of the Renaissance were deep and broad. They were related to the growth of cities and trade, to the rise of capitalist patrons, technical progress, the rebirth of interest in classical learning, and the pondering of deviations of the Church. The part and parcel of the movement made people feel free to pursue the ideal of the complete man who mastered the world.

The new learning displayed some features: first, a creative renewal of the Greek and Latin classics that had been pillars of European culture and Christianity, such as Homer, Cicero, Lucretius, and Seneca; second, the intellectual movement of humanism and science. This marked a shift from the theocratic worldview to the anthropocentric view of the Renaissance.

The new learning expanded the scope of knowledge across Europe: the printing made knowledge widely available; a principle that nothing should be taken as true unless it can be evidenced; an emphasis on the individual conscience rather than the restraint of religious collectivity; and the idea of the sovereign nation-state rather than the community of Christendom.

The Reformation wasn't an extension of the Renaissance, but an appeal to the devotional traditions of Christianity. English scholar John Wycliffe and the Bohemian priest Jan Hus challenged the Roman Church, which lacked religiosity, with nepotistic popes, simoniac bishops, promiscuous priests, greedy monks, and a sheer appetite for worldly wealth.

Marsilius of Padua (1270-1342), an Italian scholar, sought to limit the power of the Papacy. A thought was fomented that the true Church was not centered in Rome, but that the true Church is made up of all who worship Christ, all over the world, in any place or community. This community or congregation – the ecclesia – is spiritual, not earthly, so it cannot have an earthly ruler.

The religious revival coincided with the nadir of the Church's reputation during the papacies of Alexander VI (1492-1503) and Julius II (1503-1513). Pope Alexander sought after gold, women, and the careers of his bastard children. Pope Julius II, nicknamed the Warrior Pope, gratified a love of war and conquests. He initiated the construction of Saint Peter's Basilica in Rome.

In 1509, when he was planning to pay for wars and the construction of St Peter's Basilica through the sale of indulgences—paper certificates guaranteeing relief from punishment in purgatory— a young monk from Wittenberg, Martin Luther (1483-1546), made a pilgrimage to Rome in 1510-1511, where he was appalled by the abuses of the papal court and the nadir of depravity.

Pope Leo X (papacy 1513-1521) granted indulgences to those who donated to St. Peter's Basilica, which was soon challenged by Martin Luther, who was a man of courage willing to face injustice. Luther found himself at the head of the Protestant revolt against the papal depravity of selling indulgences, led by a German Dominican friar, Johann Tetzel.

Tetzel had been banned from the territory of the Elector of Saxony, who had no desire to see his subjects pouring large sums into papal coffers. So, by challenging Tetzel's theological credentials, Luther was reinforcing the policy of his prince. This implied the struggle between politics and the papacy in the ensuing centuries of the Protestant Reformation.

On 31 October 1517, All Saints' Eve, he took the fateful step of nailing a sheet of the 95 Theses to the door of Wittenberg's castle church. The Ninety-Five Theses rejected the sale of indulgences as well as the very concept of purgatory, and the religious authority of the pope in the concepts of sola scriptura, by scripture alone, and sola fide, by faith alone.

Pope Leo X (papacy 1513–21) tried to persuade Luther to change his beliefs and brought a case against him for heresy, but Luther only grew more vocal and refused to accept the authority of the pope. In his Papal Bull of 15 June 1520, the Pope denounced Luther's condemnatory position and threatened to excommunicate him unless he recanted the Theses.

Defiant Luther publicly burned a copy of the bull on 10 December 1520. On 3 January 1521, Pope Leo X issued the Papal Bull which excommunicated Martin Luther from the Catholic Church. German politics was split between the advocates and the opponents of Luther's punishment. As a result, various reformers threw their weight behind Luther's central aims to reform the church.

Several different denominations of the Lutheran Church in Germany and Scandinavia, and the Calvinist Reformed Church in Switzerland and France came into being supported by state leaders and institutions anxious to be free of papal political power. Protestantism dominated northern and eastern Europe by the middle of the 17th century, and it made a permanent break from the Catholic Church rejecting the Catholic doctrine.

Papal hegemony over Europe was at an end. In 1650, Pope Innocent X (papacy 1644-1655) responded by declaring the Westphalia Treaty of 1648 null and void. The protests were ignored by the European powers. In summary, the excommunication of Pope Leo X in 1520 was a blunder because the Pope refused to listen or respond to criticism directed at the papacy and the Catholic Church. They didn't reform themselves but asserted their power to suppress the reformers. The anger and greed made them do the blunder.

In 1521, the Holy Roman Emperor Charles V (r.1519-1556) summoned Luther to appear before the Imperial Diet (Highest representative assembly in the Holy Roman Empire), where Luther defended himself with fortitude, stating that he was captive to God's Word and would not revoke anything against his conscience. After that, he fled to the Wartburg Castle in Saxony, Germany.

The ban pronounced by the Imperial Diet against Luther could not be enforced. Religious protest was turning into political revolt. At this point, the impressive statement of Luther in the imperial court to save souls is sadly contrasted with Hitler's court statement in the trial of his failed coup in 1924 in Munich, which elevated him into popularity and later led to the loss of innumerable souls.

Luther's text is formally titled "The Disputation on the Power and Efficacy of Indulgences", or "The Ninety-Five Theses". The Ninety-Five Theses are introduced in contemplation of its significance as a watershed reform in history and a strong wish that contemporary Christianity is reminded of the tenets in the Theses.

Theses 1–4 (The Nature of Repentance)

According to Jesus, we should live a life of repentance; only God, not a priest, can provide

These concentrate on the concepts of repentance and forgiveness for sin. The term "repentance" does not refer to the ritual of penance performed by clergy. Rather, it is an internal process that leads to the transformation of Christians in inner beings and outward acts of penance.

Theses 5–7 (The Pope's Ability to Absolve Sins)

The power to suspend the punishments for sin belongs to God, not the Pope. The validity of the papal claim to jurisdiction over indulgences is called into question by this. However, Luther launches the theses in a way that shows respect for the Church and the Pope.

Theses 8–24 (The Limits of the Church's Power to Reduce Punishment for Sin)

Luther held that only those who are alive can be punished for sin by the Church. As purgatory is an issue that belongs to God and the afterlife, the Pope's authority does not span over it. As a result, it is deemed dishonest and inefficient to sell an indulgence to a person who is in purgatory.

Theses 25–26 (The Power of the Pope Over an Individual's Soul)

This was to mean that Jesus granted the pope the authority to absolve the faithful of their sins, which was extended to issuing indulgences for the souls in purgatory by the pope. Luther holds that the Pope has no authority over the fate of the faithful. This was perceived as a challenge to the authority of the Pope. *Matthew 16:18: "And I also say to you that you are Peter, and on this rock, I will build My church, and the gates of Hades shall not prevail against it."*

Theses 27–31 (The Corrupting Influence of Money on the Church)

he building of Rome's Saint Peter's Basilica was financed by the sale revenues. A large number of potential indulgence buyers were illiterate, economically deprived, prone to superstition, and susceptible to dubious claims and scare tactics. Luther argued that redemption and forgiveness are gifts from God. The act of placing a monetary value on sin forgiveness promotes the growth of immoral business activities, such as fraud, avarice, and personal corruption.

Theses 32–38 (The False Promise of Indulgences and the True Rights of Christians)

Luther criticizes those selling indulgences for preaching unchristian doctrine and states that salvation is achieved through contrition and repentance, not indulgences. He urges people to be vigilant against misleading promises. Nevertheless, he maintains that papal blessings and remissions of sin should not be dismissed entirely. It is not his intention to launch an unbridled attack on the Pope or the authority of the Church.

Theses 39–49 (Dangers of Indulgences and What the Church Should Teach)

Luther argues that by promoting appropriate repentance for sins, indulgences lessen the importance of genuine regret for sin. They might persuade even the most pious person to seek a quick route to salvation. He fervently urges the Church to teach the poor the futility of squandering money on indulgences and to focus their funds on addressing basic necessities or offering humanitarian assistance. He thinks that a careful study of the Bible's teachings ought to be the Church's first priority.

Theses 50–52 (The Pope and Saint Peter's Basilica)

Luther asserts that the Pope is ignorant of the improper practices related to indulgence sales. Pope Leo X would be more willing to see St. Peter's Basilica reduced to ashes than to tolerate such acts if he were made aware of the dishonest methods used by those who sell these indulgences. While voicing his disapproval of the indulgences that the Pope had approved of, Luther remained respectful of the pope.

Theses 53–55 (Condemnation of Priests Promoting Indulgence Sales)

The pope and Christ are opponents of those who preach pardons as the standard and forbid the Luther strongly opposes the custom of local priests calling off church services in order to get parishioners to attend services that promote indulgence sales. He believed that the Pope's and Christ's teachings were at odds with the promotion of indulgences over the teachings of the Bible.

Theses 56–66 (The True Treasures of the Church)

It is obvious that the church's authority is sufficient on its own to pardon sins. God's grace and the gospels should be the church's greatest treasures. Excessive indulgences make the worst things appear unfairly nice. As a result, without repentance or forgiveness, evil appears to be good. The nets that the workers use are the goods that are prized in the Gospels. The wealthy utilize indulgences to generate income. Matthew 20:16, *"So the last will be first, and the first will be last,"*

Theses 67–80 (Criticism of Bad Leaders and False Messages)

Luther praises individuals who raise concerns about the possible dangers of indulgences and exhorts clerics to be open and honest about their nature. He adds that the Pope would denounce any indulgences that would take away from God's actual message. Additionally, he exhorts bishops to defend the Gospel's priority. Luther is cautious while addressing the Pope, pointing out that he has a lot of spiritual power.

1 Cor 12:28, *"And God has placed in the church first of all apostles, second prophets, third teachers, then miracles, then gifts of healing, of helping, of guidance, and of different kinds of tongues"*.

Theses 81–91 (Damage to the Church's Reputation)

Indulgences were sold, and the response was very negative. There was criticism of the behavior of wealthy church leaders who were asking the less wealthy for money to build a church instead. The sale of indulgences is hurting the Church's prestige and people's faith, according to Luther.

"People naturally ask why the Pope doesn't just release souls from purgatory out of compassion instead of charging a fee for this service," Luther remarks. Luther claims that believers have suffered as a result of the indulgence, with some departing from Church doctrine and others doubting the legitimacy of the pope and the clergy.

These 92–95 (A Path Forward for the Pope, the Church, and Christians)

Luther uses scripture to support his conclusions, just as he does at the beginning of the Ninety-Five Theses. He compares the acts of indulgence sellers to those of the false prophets mentioned in the Book of Jeremiah and the Acts, whom he cautions against following. *(Jer 6:14, "They dress the wound of my people as though it were not serious. 'Peace, peace,' they say, when there is no peace"), (Acts 14:22. "where they strengthened the believers. They encouraged them to continue in the faith, reminding them that we must suffer many hardships to enter the Kingdom of God")*.

Protestantism was observed in many countries across the globe. By placing a premium on the importance of Bible reading, it influenced educational practices and, consequently, the general literacy rate. It fostered an entrepreneurial spirit, which in turn gave rise to the capitalist economic system. It created two distinct groups within Europe: those who supported it and those who opposed it. It prompted the Counter-Reformation within the Roman Catholic Church.

Most significantly, it undermined the concept of a unified Christendom. The 1530s represented a pivotal moment in the history of Christendom. Prior to this, the Christian world had been divided into two distinct halves, Orthodox and Catholic. However, following this period, the Christian world was further divided into three distinct groups: Orthodox, Catholic, and Protestant. Furthermore, the Protestant movement itself became increasingly fragmented, giving rise to numerous rival factions.

The religious disunity ultimately led to the outbreak of the Schmalkaldic War (1546-1547) between the imperial forces of the Holy Roman Empire and the Lutheran Schmalkaldic League. The imperial forces were victorious in crushing the Schmalkaldic League, but the ideas of Luther were so pervasive that they could not be contained by military force.

Further conflicts continued until both parties reached an agreement with the Peace of Augsburg in 1555. This recognized the Lutheran Church as a distinct entity while maintaining public order. The agreement was moderately successful in relieving tension by providing the legal basis for the practice of Lutheran confession and allowing local rulers to decide their own religion in their territory.

However, the remaining issues were not fully resolved, and a comprehensive peace agreement was not reached. Western history has seen numerous instances of conflict in the name of religion, spanning from the Wars of Religion from 1517 (the nailing of the 95 Theses by Martin Luther) to the Peace of Augsburg in 1555 and the Peace of Westphalia in 1648.

Specifically, the Peace of Augsburg in 1555 sought to resolve the rift by dividing the Empire into Catholic and Lutheran states. However, over the next 50 years, the expansion of Protestantism beyond these boundaries undermined the settlement, and many Protestant groups faced the risk of being accused of heresy.

Europe was further affected by the Thirty Years' War (1618–1648), which resulted in approximately eight million deaths. The Peace of Westphalia finally established peace regarding religion in the Holy Roman Empire. It recognized the equal rights of the Catholic and Protestant churches and allowed states to choose a religion for their territory.

The treaty guaranteed religious freedom, allowing Catholics in Protestant-majority regions and Protestants in Catholic-majority regions to practice their religion and attend religious services. Furthermore, individuals were permitted to relocate to an alternative region where their religion was observed within a specified timeframe.

The Treaty marked a pivotal shift from the medieval to the modern world, paving the way for the emergence of the sovereign state and international legal order. The Treaty's historical implications were comparable to those of 1815 (the Congress of Vienna that reorganized Europe after the Napoleonic Wars), 1919 (the Treaty of Versailles that ended WWI), and 1945 (the Potsdam Agreement that ended WWII).

The involvement of religion in politics has prompted reflection on the extent to which religion extends beyond the boundaries of reason and science. The war demonstrated that when religion and politics are combined, the resulting conflict is particularly destructive, resulting in significant losses and damage for all parties involved.

Religion and politics were inextricably linked and mutually reinforcing. King Henry VIII (r. 1509–1547) in England rejected the Protestant Reformation. In return for his support, the Pope rewarded Henry with the prestigious title of Defender of the Faith. However, just a decade later, Henry VIII broke away from the Catholic Church and assumed the title of Supreme Head of the Church of England.

British parliamentarism was established with the involvement of religious groups. Queen Mary I (r. 1553–1558), an ardent Catholic, reinstated Roman Catholicism, earning her the epithet "Bloody Mary" due to her persecution of Protestants. Elizabeth I (r. 1558-1603) developed a distinctive synthesis of Anglicanism in the Church of England, integrating elements from both Protestant and Catholic traditions.

From that point forward, Anglicanism demonstrated two distinct theological orientations. Anglo-Catholicism (worship characterized by liturgical readings and rituals, special clothing, and a calendar of religious observances) and Calvinistic-Evangelicals (worship characterized by the involvement of the congregation, a relatively unstructured program, and a focus on evangelical tenets).

Despite the harsh treatment they received under Elizabeth, both recusant Catholics and non-conformist Puritans managed to survive by operating underground. The latter reemerged in the 17th century under Cromwell's Commonwealth (1649-1658), where they exercised control over the state for a brief period. They made a notable contribution to the early history of America during the British Protectorate (1653-1659).

3) Lutheranism, Calvinism, and Huguenots

The spread of Protestantism had consequences in social, political, and geographical terms.

Lutheranism appealed directly to independent-minded princes in Germany. This was due to their loyal faith to the doctrines originating from Martin Luther, but it was also due to the political power and legitimacy that they could obtain by breaking off from the pope and the Roman Catholic Church, which helped maintain the existing social order.

Core beliefs of the Lutherans were *Sola Scriptura* (Only the Bible communicates God's word in contrast to Catholicism where the pope also does), *Sola Gratia* (Humans could be saved only through God; they could not get salvation by indulgences or charitable deeds), and *Sola Fide* (Faith in God alone was enough for humans to achieve salvation).

Jean Calvin (1509-1564) in Switzerland expressed the relationship between Church and State. It was related less to state politics and more to private morality in ethical matters. The code of conduct made his followers stay away from earthly pleasure and frivolity and stick to sobriety, self-restraint, hard work, thrift, and, above all, godliness.

Other than those faithful to the doctrine, it added a new burden of keeping up appearances of serious formality to those who were already burdened with a sense of sin. They avoided direct portrayal of the Deity and all mystical symbols and allegories. They were to find the sole source of joy and guidance in the daily reading of the Bible who were known to be the Puritans.

In France, the Calvinists were derisively nicknamed Huguenots. They spread rapidly in the south and west and among the urban populations of all provinces. The Huguenots were confronted by the dilemma of reconciling two duties of obedience: their duty to obey the Catholic king of France as subjects and their duty to serve God as Protestants.

They reconciled these duties by performing their duty of obedience to governing authorities so that such obedience didn't deter them from serving God. They held the stance as the Bible dictated in the words of Jesus Christ in Matthew 22:21: *""Caesar's," they replied. Then He said to them, "So give back to Caesar what is Caesar's, and to God what is God's."*

The St. Bartholomew's Day Massacre was a widespread slaughter of French Protestants (the Huguenots) by Catholics beginning on 24 August 1572 and lasting over two months, resulting in the deaths of between 5,000 and 25,000 people and mass emigration of the Huguenots from France. The massacre was horrific and had far-reaching consequences for France that helped slow industrialization compared to other European states.

The French Protestants fled to Prussia, the Netherlands, England, and America. They were well-educated and enterprising, contributing their skills to those communities. This meant a drain of brains for France, leading to the Royal Edict of 15 December 1790 during the French Revolution, which awarded French nationality to people who had been exiled for religious reasons to mitigate the damage.

In the Netherlands, the rise of Calvinism provided a basic factor in the split between the Catholic provinces to the south of the modern states of Belgium and Luxemburg and the United Provinces of the Netherlands to the north of the Protestants of the Dutch Reformed Church, which was founded in 1571 during the Protestant Reformation in the Calvinist tradition.

4) The New World economy

European civilization was on the move outward, and its worldwide network of colonies was established by operating seaborne lines of commerce and communication. The decade of 1492-1504 was one of the most striking turning points in history. Europeans made trans-oceanic sailings and came to know the New World.

Upon the return of Columbus from his sailing to America, Pope Alexander VI (papacy 1492-1503) published a bull, *Inter Caetera*, in 1493 to divide the New World between the colonial rivals of Spain and Portugal in the Atlantic Ocean, 370 leagues (roughly 1,100 miles) west of the Portuguese-controlled Cape Verde Islands off the northwest African coastline.

Under this agreement, Spain could claim ownership of all non-Christian lands west of the line, while Portugal alone laid claim to all non-Christian lands east of the line. The line of demarcation was not just a separation of colonial influence between the seafaring countries; it set an example of turf wars over colonial territories among European powers.

Amerigo Vespucci made a transatlantic voyage (1497-1504), following whom the continent was named America. Portugal was quick to exploit the commercial opportunities of the new lands. They claimed Brazil in 1500, Sumatra in 1509, and Malacca and Indonesia in 1511. To protect their trade, they established a chain of fortified stations stretching from India to Macao.

The Spaniards applied military might. With the dream of El Dorado (the gold), they colonized the Aztec Empire of Mexico (1521), the Maya of Central America (1524), and the Inca Empire of Peru (1532). The circumnavigation by Ferdinand Magellan (1519-22) proved that the earth was round, that the Pacific and Atlantic were separate oceans, and that the Americas lay between them.

European colonization in North America began late. France found Montreal, and Spain established Florida in 1565. The Dutch expelled the Portuguese from Indonesia and Malacca in 1641. England settled its colony at Jamestown, Virginia in 1607, and the Mayflower, carrying the Puritan Pilgrim Fathers, landed in the Province of Massachusetts Bay in December 1620.

The presence of another continent in the antipodes was not suspected. In 1605, a Spanish ship out of Peru and a Dutch ship out of Java sailed to northern Australia, and the main outlines of the great Southland, such as Australia and New Zealand, were drawn by the Dutch navigator Abel Tasman in 1642-1643.

At this stage, let's venture to understand what made it possible for Europeans to explore sea routes to reach the New World, establish their colonial presence in the colonies, and develop the colonial economy to extract value from the colonized peoples ahead of those in other continents. The four items below are notable.

- Europeans steadily accumulated knowledge from the experiences of trade over the past centuries. These enabled them to systematize the colonizing process: instituting organizations for profiteering, enslaving and acculturating local people, relocating and localizing home people, establishing colonial establishments, and Europeanizing the colonized lands.

- The transcontinental voyage in the uncharted ocean was challenging because the navigators could not locate the ship at sea. The development of marine chronometer watches in 1761 made it possible to determine longitude by comparing Greenwich Mean Time (GMT), helping to fix the coordinates of their ships at vast sea.

  Compass was essential for the discovery of the world relevant to geomancy that understood geographic features in the energies of earth. Its discovery is known to have taken place in China for pivoting needle compasses in the 9th century, but it was localized in Europe.

- Politics formed the order of the new world economy for exploitation and colonization with two wars that produced a rule of sovereignty as nation-states. The concept of the nation-state was refined later in the French Revolution in 1789. It developed nationalism that advanced the interests of a people or country united by a shared culture and history.

  The Thirty Years' War (1618-1648) was the deadliest European war of religion. The Peace of Westphalia in 1648 eventually shifted the balance of power for France as Spain declined. It set the stage for the Sun King, Louis XIV (r.1643-1715), to influence Europe for the next sixty years. As a result, France and England came to contest in the New World.

  The Seven Years' War (1756-1763) was a global contest for colonial interests, especially between Britain and France in the world. France lost the war and their colonial claims in North America and India. This led to greater British power in both parts of the world, but its jubilation was short-lived as it lost the American War of Independence (1776-1783).

- The European systems of finance and investment protection made it possible for those who are willing to take the risks of offshore investments. The practices of accounting, information disclosure, sharing the risk of investments, insurance coverage and general average for owners of ships and cargoes, and arbitration and legal proceedings were put in place for trans-oceanic businesses.

A typical triangle of trade arose in the 17th century that linked England, Africa, and the New World, through which Europeans and North American colonists accumulated wealth.

- From England to Africa transported finished goods, like weapons for tribal wars in Africa and cotton textiles imported from India.

- From Africa to America, specifically to plantations in the northeastern six states of Connecticut, Maine, Massachusetts, New Hampshire, Rhode Island, and Vermont in the Caribbean and New England, transported slaves.

- From the Americas to England transported commodities such as sugar, timber, and fish.

The new world economy exhibited features of mercantilism. It promoted governmental regulation in the colonial economy to augment home-state power. As the economic counterpart of political absolutism, it viewed wealth as finite and trade as a zero-sum game. It aimed to ensure a trade surplus and accumulate national wealth in billions of gold or silver.

It was Jean-Baptiste Colbert, the minister of finance in France (1665–83), who managed the ailing French economy and its fiscal condition under King Louis XIV of France. He adopted mercantilist policies of strong government based on the financial strength and reserves of precious metals like silver or gold, the so-called Bullionism.

The need for bullion reserves was the background of continuous wars. It was costly to mobilize large numbers of soldiers, supply them with expensive arms, and conduct wars outside the monarchies. Hence, the policies aimed to prevent the outflow of reserves by minimizing imports and maximizing local production using available raw materials inside the country.

The policy of Mercantilism was aimed at preventing current-account deficits or turning current-account deficits into surpluses, implementing measures to beef up monetary reserves by ensuring a positive balance of trade and imposing heavy import tariffs to downsize imports and retain silver or gold bullion to the hilt.

4.2. The 19th Century (Why the West Matters)

1) Minds and thoughts in the flux and upheaval

Those who control the mind control the time. The 19th century exhibited various thoughts and beliefs that represented the forces at play at the time. They often theorized some ideologies that tended to accompany power and violence. The ideologies that influenced the minds of the 19th century were instrumental in shaping the 20th century.

2) Liberalism

It took its name from *liber* in Latin, meaning free. Liberalism was fleshed out during the animating Age of Enlightenment and cultural sophistication in the 17th-18th century, the limited governments in British parliamentarianism, the spirit of liberty in the French Revolution, and the defiant venture of the American Revolution (1765-1783).

It embraced republicanism and appealed to the social constituency stuck between the privileged nobility and the propertyless industrial mass. Liberal humanism sanctifies humans and respects individual personality; however, it did not deny the existence of God and was, in fact, rested on monotheistic beliefs.

Liberal humanism perceives humanity as individualistic rather than collective, and it promotes individual rights, equality of opportunity, and autonomy against threats from the state and private sectors. It holds that minimal government, and unfettered free markets are the best means to achieve personal liberties.

The progressive addressed the problems of poor working conditions, industrial monopolies, and urban squalor in the early 20th century. It aimed to reform socio-economic inequalities through government intervention and the promotion of social welfare programs. Over time, it evolved to emphasize climate change, racial justice, and healthcare as a human right.

John Stuart Mill (1806-1873) stands as the supreme monument of liberalism, endorsing the laissez-faire spirit and the principle of the utilitarians for the greatest happiness of the people. Key themes are that individual human rights can be restricted only if they impinge on the rights of others. In modern times, it diverged into political and economic liberalism.

He indicated a tenet that unrelated people can live together in a place where diverse individuals respect each other's rights and band together voluntarily to help those in need or to change the laws for the common good

Political liberalism stressed the rule of law, individual liberty, constitutional procedures, and religious toleration. It is well illustrated in Great Britain with liberal ideas, the rule of law, free trade, and the absence of revolution. The monarchy and the parliamentary system reigned according to the rules and customs of the Glorious Revolution in 1688.

The correlation between liberal politics and the growth of the bourgeoisie is contrasted between Britain's success and Germany's failure in building a stable parliamentary system and middle classes. Unlike their British counterparts, the new German capitalists shirked their democratic duty and submitted to the enlightened but essentially illiberal system of imperial Prussia.

The tenet of Germany's *Sonderweg* or special path honored legal forms but was subject to the authoritarian traditions of court, army, and bureaucracy. This has given the German imperial government after 1871 the label of a facade democracy, and it was related to the rise of Hitler and the Nazis in the 1930s.

In Russia, a series of reforms in 1815, 1855, and 1906 contained education by the state and the emancipation of the serfs, in order to transform it from a ramshackle, archaic kingdom with agrarian economy into a reformed and ambitious empire, but Tsars were unable to sustain them for long due to force majeure events like the Decembrist revolt of 1825, the Polish rising of 1863-1864, and the outbreak of WW I in 1914. Its autocracy virtually remained intact until the Bolshevik Revolution in 1917.

Economic liberalism focused on the concept of free trade and laissez-faire that opposed protectionist tariffs. It endeared the right to engage in economic activities, demanded the dismantling of economic barriers, and opposed collectivist organizations such as the ancient guilds and the new trade unions.

Karl Marx viewed Western values as a remorseless quest for profit, the extraction of surplus from the exploited, and a series of class struggles that would save the people in a class-divided society. Max Weber, however, saw Western values as built upon rationalism, the work ethic, and Protestantism associated with the rise of capitalism.

The liberalism of the 19th century clamored for lifting high tariff barriers to promote international trade as the World Trade Organization does today. The policies of liberalism have dissolved many of the interposed barriers, but it is also to blame for economic crises and financial market collapses because of inordinate excesses in desires and lack of proper governance.

In modernity, meanwhile, free trade based on economic liberalism has been hampered by protectionism which wrecked the economy, reduced wages, and achieved little in return, The share of employment in manufacturing has fallen mostly because of technology, not trade.

Liberalism and capitalism are two influential ideologies that have shaped much of modern political and economic thought. Liberalism and capitalism often go hand-in-hand because both emphasize individual freedoms—liberalism in the political sphere and capitalism in the economic sphere.

Liberalism	Capitalism
Liberalism is a political and moral philosophy based on the principles of liberty and equality. • It puts emphasis on protecting and expanding personal freedoms and rights. • It supports democratic systems of government where power is derived from the consent of the governed. • It advocates a legal system where laws are clear, public, and applied equally to all citizens. • It supports economic systems that allow for competition and private enterprise, though this can vary with respect to regulation and state intervention. • Various strands of liberalism which advocate for more regulation and state intervention in the economy to address inequalities and provide public goods.	Capitalism is an economic system characterized by private ownership of the means of production and operates on the principles of profit and market competition. • It ensures that individuals and corporations own property and businesses. • It facilitates a market economy where prices and production are determined by competition in a free market. • It upholds the profit motive by which businesses operate to maximize profits, which drives innovation and efficiency. • It ideally limits government intervention to protect property rights and maintain order.

In "The Protestant Ethic and the Spirit of Capitalism (1905)", Max Weber described the capitalism in the concept of devotion to the work of the secular "calling" in the German word Beruf" carrying some religious connotations – namely, those of task set by God, in the highest level possible of moral activity in doing everyday labor. He saw the labor in a secular calling as a form of religious service and outwards expression of Christian charity which was a departure from the monastic lifestyle of Catholic tradition. In contrast, labor.

This moral justification of the worldly activity as a secular calling was a significant shift in mundane life as well as religious thought. The new perspective connecting practical life and religious motives contributed to the "capitalist spirit" that helped to nurture the fabric of the development of our modern material culture. The religious influences on capitalist business have in fact been partially responsible for the quantitative shaping and the quantitative expansion of the "capitalist spirit" across the world.

A comparable case happened in 1998 in the Republic of Korea when the Korean government fell into national default and asked for a bail-out fund from the International Monetary Fund in a solemn promise to restructure itself to reinstate its credit standing and resume debt service in good order. The IMF stepped in with a 58-billion-dollar loan, its largest-ever bailout of a country. By the end of the year, banks stopped loaning or rolling-over of existing loans that resulted in massive bankruptcies of various-sized companies who were unable to afford the 13 to 18 percent monthly interest rates of loan sharks.

The crisis, at first, caused catastrophic confusion and painful disintegration across all sectors of Korea including corporations and families. Responding to the national crisis, most Korean people, voluntarily and collectively, lined up at domestic bank offices where they sold all kinds of gold in their households to let the government hoard the precious metals and help it revive the economy.

The gold was just one of the elements that turned the Korean economy around, but it was a factor that solidified public opinion for resilient recovery. This story in Korea was in stark contrast to the street protests in Europe in response to the policies of austerity of their governments during economic crises.

However, the Korean crisis also called for attention to excessive liberalism. What would happen to the public, when the state and businesses fail to manage risks in their reckless execution of the economic liberalism? It also manifested the value of precious metals when modern financial markets stopped working for whatever reasons.

3) Socialism

It took its name from socius in Latin, meaning companion. As opposed to liberalism, which arises from liberal humanism and regards the freedom of individual humans as sacrosanct, socialism seeks equality between all humans. Socialists seek equality, and inequality is considered blasphemy against the sanctity of humanity.

Socialists adopt policies to pool resources, exercise equitable wealth distribution, and subordinate individual rights to the common good. It often conflicted with liberalism regarding economic laissez-faire and inalienable human rights and objected to oppressors at home and abroad. Its stance toward international solidarity made it an opponent of nationalism.

In the 19th century in Europe, there were Christian socialism, the trade union movement, and utopian socialism.

Christian socialism held the principle that true compassion would result in such actions. Those who believe in justification by faith may still accept brotherly love in fraternity for those in crisis. It decides the eternal fate of believers, whether life in paradise or punishment in fire and brimstone. Matthew 25:31–46 illustrates it: *"Then the King will say to those on his right, 'Come, you who are blessed by my Father, inherit the Kingdom prepared for you from the creation of the world. For I was hungry, and you fed me. I was thirsty, and you gave me a drink. I was a stranger, and you invited me into your home. I was naked, and you gave me clothing. I was sick, and you cared for me. I was in prison, and you visited me."*

The trade union movement originated in the 19th century as a response to the vulnerability of wage laborers in the free-market economy. After a lengthy and arduous process, working men and women were finally granted the right to form unions, stage collective bargaining over salary and working conditions, and engage in strikes. By 1900, most European countries had an active labor movement.

The concept of utopian socialism, derived from the fictional town of Nowheresville, was ultimately unsuccessful. Its core principle was the elimination of social conflict. Given the inherent challenges of implementing this ideal in mundane world affairs, where the desires of each individual or association conflict, and ethical considerations among themselves differ or contradict, it was considered that the ideal of utopian socialism was unlikely to be successful.

In the 20th century, two distinct branches of socialism emerged: revolutionary socialism and democratic socialism.

The revolutionary socialism gave rise to two distinct ideologies: Marxist-Leninism and anarchism. Marxist-Leninism drew upon the tenets of utopian socialism, incorporating the concept of class struggle. It was the driving force behind the Bolshevik Revolution in 1917 and it subsequently evolved into Stalinism. The transitional process resulted in an unparalleled loss of human life on a global scale, which came to an end with the dissolution of the Soviet Union in 1989. A residual element of Marxist-Leninism persists in the 21st century, albeit in a revised or vestigial form, in Russia, China, North Korea, and Vietnam. They differ in the extent of loyalty to orthodox ideology and in the range of revision from the ideology for reform and openness.

The democratic socialism was based on the principles of democratic decision-making, public ownership in a socially owned economy, an emphasis on economic democracy, and a decentralized planned economy. Democratic socialists contend that capitalism is inherently incompatible with freedom and equality. They believe that these values can only be achieved through the establishment of a socialist society.

While the majority of democratic socialists advocate for a phased transition to socialism within the framework of the rule of law, they did occasionally endorse revolutionary strategies to materialize socialism. Democratic socialists opposed the Stalinist political and economic planning system, which was characterized by authoritarian and undemocratic governance under a command-control structure.

A notable historical precedent is the ascent of the Nazis in the 1920s-1930s, which exploited the lawful and rule-based administration of the social democratic Weimar Republic by manipulating public opinion through propaganda, coercion, and bribery. While both Nazi National Socialism and Soviet Stalinism had a similar approach to taking power and exercising it, their different ideological aims led to general hostilities between the two powers on the eastern front of WW II.

The points outlined by Yuval Noah Harari in his book *Sapiens: A Brief History of Humankind* (p. 233) help to gain a deeper understanding of liberalism and socialism in the context of humanism.

Homo sapiens have a unique and sacred nature that is fundamentally different from the nature of all other beings. The supreme good is humanism, but it differs.		
Liberal Humanism	Socialist Humanism	Evolutionary Humanism
Humanity is individualistic and resides within each Homo sapiens.	Humanity is collective and resides within the species Homo sapiens.	Humanity is mutable. Humans might degenerate into sub-humans or evolve into superhumans.
The supreme commandment is to protect the inner core and freedom of each Homo sapiens.	The supreme commandment is to protect equality within the species of Homo sapiens.	The supreme commandment is to protect humankind from degenerating into sub-humans and to encourage its evolution into super-humans.

4) Nationalism

The nation-state is one where the great majority of citizens are conscious of a common identity and share the same culture. Nationalism was related to the emergence of nation-states during the French Revolution, and it was set in place through social and political upheavals in the 19th century in Europe and then spread to the world.

Nationalism was initiated for the propagation or preservation of the culture of a national community and further claimed the right of self-determination to achieve the nation-state. In the 19th century, most European governments strove to strengthen national cohesion through ceremonies, interpretations of history, common language, and education in a common culture.

Popular nationalism mattered to the ethnic community, not artificial frontiers. An extreme example was the Nazis in the 1930s, which justified their occupation of regions inhabited by German-speaking people, even though they belonged to other states. The nationalistic idea was also used as an excuse for the imperial expansion of the Nazis, too.

Racial theories gained weight in conceiving nationality. Some states in Europe were tempted to conceive of themselves as a unique racial kinship group. They studied ethnology to find their racial identity. In some respects, it sounded quizzical to distinguish unique ethnic characteristics among people who had been mixed and migrating for thousands of years.

The growth of nationalism was closely intertwined with the modernization of European states. Civilization was the sum of ideas and traditions inherited from the ancient world, and new ideas and traditions were grafted onto the native civilization by people from outside. All these converged and formed a new civilization in a new environment that also evolved.

Culture, in contrast, grew with the elements of everyday life of the people specific to a particular nation, such as common language, folklore, religious rites, and idiosyncratic practices. In history before the emergence of nationalism, civilization had been extolled and culture tended to be belittled. Nationalism did the opposite. National cultures were extolled, while common civilization was downgraded.

In the case of Europe, the educated, multilingual, cosmopolitan elites grew weaker; while national masses with half-baked beliefs, who thought of themselves only as Frenchmen, Germans, English, or Russians in the intertwined Europe, grew stronger. This is still valid in the modern world, where nationalist politicians gain votes in their campaigns by vocalizing nationalistic policies such as rejecting immigrants.

The nationalism developed from the late 18th century and flourished in an aspiration for national pride, but it subsided with a sense of fin de siècle (social degeneracy, decadence, ennui and pessimism) at the end of the 19th century as the nationalistic mood weakened.

In case of Korean nationalism, Michael Breen, writer of "The New Koreans", had pointed out three standout characteristics of South Korean nationalism. The first is "ethnicity" focusing on the belief in a unique bloodline. The idea of being distinct by virtue of a unique bloodline conveyed an image of being a frog in the well, alone and with no sense of what lies outside of the dank walls, the second is "victimhood". Victimhood is in a sense sweet temptation because it confers righteousness. This was the sentiment after thirty-five years of rule by Japan, and it has been extended all the way back in history, and the third is a "lack of confidence" which comes from the disconnection of the long history with the way they live today that was adopted from the outside after WW II.

5) Imperialism

Colonialism can be traced all the way back to ancient times when the Phoenicians, Greeks, Romans, Turks, and Arabs practiced it. It began to take modern form in Europe during the colonial expansion from 1492 to 1650, while the European powers actively expanded their colonies across different continents. This influenced all aspects of the modern world.

Europeans would stop at nothing to take what they wanted and needed to get closer to the center of where the world's wealth and power lay. In the context of the greedy going on the rampage, they treated the colonized world with abysmal cruelty as virgins were raped and innocent victims impaled.

European colonialism rampaged across the world until the 20th century, interrupted intermittently by decolonization in the Americas from 1770 to 1820, when Britain, France, Spain, and Portugal lost many of their colonial territories, and again from 1945 to 1999 when the end of WW II opened the spree of independence movements in the world.

Colonialism enabled Europe to accumulate astounding fortune at the cost of colonized people, leaving indelible marks on Western supremacy, free-market capitalism, and liberal mindset in modern history. The inveterate legacy is so deeply rooted in the economic and social structures that it is still palpable in the modern world of international economy and politics.

Colonialism and imperialism are distinct but share much in common. Both involve powerful nations asserting control over other territories; however, a difference is that colonialism establishes colonies in foreign lands and exercises direct control over them, while imperialism broadly extends its influence in trade or politics. Imperialism doesn't necessarily entail establishing colonies.

Western imperialism was based on the unbounded self-confidence of the leading imperial powers during the Century of Peace in Europe (1815-1914) when the British Empire held global hegemony. England, France, and Germany led the trends with their superior cultural, economic, and political apparatuses.

Spain had passed its peak in the late 1700s and early 1800s. The Dutch East India Company was established in 1602, and it ruled much of Indonesia with violence and expropriations. Imperial Japan promised Indonesia its independence from Western colonial rule but it exploited millions of workers as forced labor for its war efforts during WW II.

The rich imperial club of Western Europe was marked by its advanced industrial economies and administrative system, in contrast to peasant societies, stateless nations, and coarse autocracy in Eastern Europe. Marxism can be seen as a mirror image of the imperial governing structure of Western powers.

Marx and Engels announced that the imperialist countries of Western Europe would result in decadence and revolution. Their opinions carried little weight in their days but gained currency as the Soviet Empire adopted Marxism-Leninism in 1917, becoming a new imperial power in the 20th century.

Political and economic imperialism was accompanied by a cultural mission to Europeanize the colonies. Christian missionaries were officially detached from politics and businesses, and they did evangelic works in cooperation or tension with the colonial authorities. However, politics and religion were inherently connected in the colonial administration, as they were closely interlinked in their home states.

A different story occurred in Korea. Western missionaries reached the reclusive Joseon Dynasty in the late

19th century while Joseon was subjected to the imperial advances of Europe and Japan. They arrived in an undeveloped and wretched Korea, dedicating themselves to building schools, hospitals, and enlightenment of the illiterate public, as well as conducting evangelical missions.

The type of colonization was distinct. Britain adopted a policy of managing its large colonies with a minimum of military force, relying on its naval strength and local troops. All the large territories under British rule were given self-governing status - Canada in 1867, Australia in 1901, New Zealand and Newfoundland in 1907, and South Africa in 1910.

In 1947, however, India gained her independence somewhat late. Given that Churchill was unwilling to give up colonial control over India during the Atlantic Charter debate in 1941, it is uncertain if India would have gained independence in 1947 had the United States not exerted such pressure on the United Kingdom. India seemed too important to Britain to abandon.

In this sense, the Atlantic Charter is different from the Wilsonian misconception of 1918. Wilson's self-determinism might be a sort of proclamation without his real will to enforce it, while Roosevelt's stance was determined to assure the self-determination of colonized peoples, regardless of Great Britain's underlying passivity.

We see here the double standard of the imperial British, who fought Nazi's imperial expansion in Europe while clinging to their imperial interests in India. It was countered by Japanese officers who wondered, *"Why did the Japanese invasion of China matter to the Westerners while Britain occupied India contrary to the will of the Indians?"*

Germany was later in its industrialization than Britain and France, and its political unification occurred only in 1871. The German colonial empire did not match the proportions of Germany's pride as well as the size of the colonies of Britain and France. German ideas of Lebensraum, or living space, were first voiced in connection with its modest colonial status.

Objectively, Germany's disadvantage was more imagined than real. Its economic penetration of adjacent areas in Eastern Europe offset the lack of distant colonies, yet its psychological resentments ran deep. Apart from the antisemitism that incited Germany to start the war, the desire to balance its colonial status with that of Western powers was another reason for the war.

The period (1871–1914) from the end of the Franco-Prussian War to the outbreak of WW I, La belle époque (the beautiful age), marked a time of peace in Europe with advances in arts, literature, and technology. The beauty of these times in Europe was contrasted with the exploitation and massacres in non-European colonial regions in the same period. They were two sides of the same coin.

Conflicts in Asia and India destabilized the world before WW I, with two significant wars: the Sino-Japanese War in 1894 and the Russo-Japanese War in 1904. Japan won the wars and upped the ante in its imperial expansion by occupying Formosa (modern-day Taiwan) in 1895 and Korea in 1910. These turned Japan into a player in the imperial contests.

The imperial expansion caused great suffering for colonized people, for which the imperialists are undoubtedly responsible. For those colonized, the recuperation from the damage and losses of colonial rule took longer in the process of dissolution or oblivion of the damages and losses.

The lesson from history is that a party should avoid being dominated and use counterforce or diplomacy to prevent them anyhow. After the injury and damage are done, it is always more hurtful and awful for the victim to heal than for the one who caused the harm to pay compensation for them.

Who do you hold responsible for the harm? On the outside, the people who caused the afflictions should definitely be held accountable first. Internally, those who failed to oppose the invasion or resist the coercive attempts are still accountable because their failure left their descendants with a painful recovery process.

In Korea's instance, imperial Japan undoubtedly was to blame for the suffering of the Korean people, but the Joseon Dynasty's governing class were also held accountable at the time of annexation in 1910. They were unable to stop or oppose Japan's annexation, which left their descendants to bear the burden of repairing the harm.

6) Communism

Karl Marx was born on 5 May 1818 in Prussia. He conceived his theory on how society is founded, and the society runs.

According to Marx, the mode of production in a society is founded on modes of production:

The Marxist Conception of Society

- **Superstructure of the Society**: Art, Law, Religion, Ideology, Education, Government, Values, etc.
- **Foundation of the Society**: Relations of Production (Social Classes) | Means of Production (Resources & Technology)

Paul Kleinman, *Philosophy 101*, Adams Media ,2013 (p.211)

(1) The Relations of Production ("A") refers to the relationships of social classes between those who own the means of production, like the bourgeoisie or capitalists, and those who do not, like the workers. Capitalism is based on private ownership, and it relies on the idea of getting the most out of labor for the lowest cost. Workers are paid only enough to keep them alive and able to continue producing.

(2) The Means of Production ("B") is what is used to produce goods (for example, raw materials, factories and machines, and labor).

(3) The Mode of Production evolves as A interacts with B. While "A" continues to evolve productive capacity, "B" is affected by "A," in which conflicts arise between the social classes of capitalists

and workers as the workers become aware of the exploitation of capitalism. This will ultimately lead to the overthrow of capitalism by the working class.

(4) A new Mode of Production is created through the workers' revolution based on collective ownership. It supports the superstructure of a communist society that governs art, law, religion, ideology, education, government, and values. It stood on the premise that the history of existing society is the history of class struggle.

The Marxism-Leninism had manifested the five stages of social development:

(1) Primitive communalism

Pro-historic people live as hunters in small groups. Everyone was roughly equal

(2) Slavery

Great warrior-kings in ancient Babylon, Egypt and Rome lived well by exploiting the work of masses as slaves

(3) Feudalism

The monarch (king, Tswar) and a small member of landowning nobles live well by exploiting the peasants who work the land.
In this, middle-class merchants and bourgeoise capitalists want the country to be run to benefit businesses, not agriculture. They seized power from the monarch and nobles (the Bourgeois Revolution).

(4) Capitalism

The means of production (factories, mines, banks, etc) are owned by bourgeoise capitalists and run by private enterprises who invest money in them and want a good profit. They achieve this by exploiting the industrial workers, the proletarians. There is no democratic government, but although lots of people may have the right to vote, the bourgeoisie runs the country.

(5) The workers' state.

This will be the final and perfect state of human history. Everyone is equal and none exploits anyone else. People work according to their capability and the state rewards them according to what they need.
In this, the workers rise up in revolution and throw out their bourgeoise masters in the form of class-struggle. They proclaim "Workers of the world unite! You have nothing to lose but your chains"

The class-struggle theory has been in dispute.

(1) The theory that the history of mankind is based on economic need is argued to be false because it ignores non-economic factors that have shaped history such as ethnic, political, and religious factors. Thus, it cannot explain racial prejudice, political bias, and religious obsession that developed human history. The emergence of Christianity and Buddhism, for example, did not originate from class struggle, but rather from classless and selfless dogmas.

(2) The theory that class is based on production, ownership, and labor is also argued. Economic

and social development has generated many classes that cannot be simply classified into capitalists and laborers. Also, classes may differ in specific political and economic structures, and furthermore, they interchange positions. So, class struggle is unrealistic because the class distinction is getting blurred in modern economic reality.

(3) While Marx was right that economic factors triggered historical changes, it is inappropriate to say that economic factors are the only ones to decide history. Marx recognized that society can be classified by the criteria of wealth and rank, but he didn't consider crucial aspects of human behavior which are influenced by greed, desire, selfishness, honor, sacrifice, abandonment, and so on.

(4) Marx pronounced the idea of distribution, "From each according to his ability, to each according to his needs!" This refers to free access to and distribution of goods, capital, and services. In real life, however, this can't be feasible, as there is not enough of everything for everyone.

The communist revolutions of the 20th century caused dramatic social leveling through a program of confiscation, redistribution, expropriation, and violence. It started with the Bolshevik Revolution in 1917, after which it spilled over to Central Europe, South America, and Asia. History has revealed the fact that enforced equality lasts as long as the revolutionary regime is in power. Once it is lost or slacks, economic liberalization ascends, leading to income disparity.

At the inception of communism, it had the ring of truth that looked compatible with the circumstantial needs of societies. Communism sacrificed a hundred million lives through political upheavals and atrocious wars. The loss and damage were unprecedented, but the ideological value of the proletariat revolution has virtually been lost or gone. It makes us question the losses and damages that communism has inflicted, as well as the ongoing states that still advocate it.

Communism lingers in the 21st century in a compromised, modified, or reformed form. States tinged with communist ideology complicate geopolitical conflicts, as seen in Europe (the Ukraine-Russia War from February 2022 to the present) and Asia for decades (China's One-China assertion to Taiwan, North Korea's perennial threat to South Korea). When it comes to effectiveness and compatibility with contemporary patterns of life in the world, the practices of current communism are well away from the fundamental tenets of the ideology. It leads us to wonder whether the class-struggle theory was weasel words that proved to be a false dawn because the mismatch between the theoreticality and the practicality tends to be a recipe for disaster.

7) Eurocentrism

Unlike physics or economics, we read history not to make predictions, but to widen the horizons of understanding the present situation and the future. Nothing is guaranteed nor inevitable in history. The fact that Europeans dominated the world in the post-Industrial Revolution era was not guaranteed or inevitable; it resulted from a number of historical reasons.

European history was under three cycles: first, the Mycenaean culture (1750-1100 BC) in Greece and the Minoan culture in Palace of Knossos (1900-1350 BC); second, the classical world of Greece (800-500 BC) and Rome (340 BC-475 AD); and third, the emergence of imperial Europe following the Renaissance and imperial expansion (1500-1750) and the Industrial Revolution (1750-1900).

The ideas of democracy from Greece were passed on to the Romans, who dropped the baton with the fall of the Roman Empire, succeeding the Dark Ages of the early Middle Ages. Christianity created a distinctive European culture since feudal times; the ancient Greek heritage was rediscovered during the Renaissance and further elaborated upon during the Enlightenment.

The ideas of the Enlightenment were partly fulfilled in the French Revolution and the American Revolutions of the late 18th century. The rise of the West was founded in the wake of the discovery of the New World in the 16th century and the Industrial Revolution in the 19th century. Eurocentrism began to be dismantled following WW I and WW II.

Over the historical process, the West accumulated unique qualities in race, culture, and environment. This enabled Europeans to build moral authority, secular power, and economic advantage, which allowed Europe to diffuse modernity around the globe and occupy a dominant position.

To better understand the Eurocentrism that dominated the world until the 20th century, some more details are dealt with in the chronological descriptions below:

In the 15th century, there was a resilient transition from the Mongolian invasions and the Black Death in previous centuries toward modern novelty, marked by enlivened cross-country trade, gaining knowledge, experiences, and capital for exploring the unknown world. It was a build-up period for the adventures of the next century.

In the 16th century, the Spanish conquest of the Americas astounded the world that just hundreds of Spanish conquistadors vanquished the American civilizations, in particular, the Aztecs and the Incas. The Reformation was a defiance against breaches of conscience and belief. Westerners ventured on trans-oceanic voyages in uncertainty with faintest sense of what it was about.

In the 17th to 18th century, the Great Dying in Mexico killed nearly 90 percent of the twenty-five million population due to smallpox and influenza. European superiority in knowledge and experience, the evangelistic mission of Christianity, territorial expansion, the secular Greco-Roman heritage, scientific inventions, and the free mind of the bloodless Glorious Revolution characterized this period.

In the 18th century, it was the Industrial Revolution while the rest of the world stagnated. The accumulated knowledge and experiences from past trade generations began to take effect, alongside proximity to required resources, a colonial economy supported by profitable trade, and the French Revolution in 1789, that removed the ancient monarchic regimes in Europe.

In the 19th century, Europeans' universal appeal for reforms in the principles of the French Revolution – equality, liberty, and fraternity. Democracy and republics became established, while political reshuffle occurred across the continent, including Prussia, France, and the Habsburg monarchy. Full-fledged capitalism brought socialism and European imperial expansion across the world.

In conclusion, from the 16th century to the 19th century, Europe acted globally while the rest of the world responded regionally. Europe initiated changes while the rest of the world followed, pursuing imperial expansion across the globe that brought massive wealth at the cost of colonized peoples in Asia, Africa, and Latin America.

Reflecting on some inflection points of change in history, we venture a hypothetical assumption: What if the Greek-Persian War (499-449 BC) had ended with a Persian victory, leaving the Greek peninsular annexed to the Persian Empire? What would have happened to Greek civilization and its legacy for European posterity in political and cultural terms, especially regarding the Eastern campaign of Alexander the Great a century later and the Roman civilization thereafter? Would we then be arguing about Western supremacy?

Everything has its origins; nothing comes from a vacuum, and everything mutates and transforms in history. This applies to Europe as well.

8) Polycentrism

Polycentrism is suggested as a contrast to Eurocentrism for a balanced perspective on history during the same period. Some dissenters regard Eurocentric views as part of capitalist ideology. It overlooks the world's diversity and the features of contingency, accident, and conjuncture that connect it globally (this is based on *The Origins of the Modern World* by Robert B. Marks).

History has shown more similarities than differences between Asia and the West in respect of population, industry, and agricultural productivity until about 1800, when industrial capitalism and nation-states in Europe emerged, leading to the West's rise to preeminence.

Everything is contingent. There is nothing in the past justifying the rise of the West was inevitable. As the rise of the West was contingent, the future is also contingent. If the past could have been different, then so can the future. The past was contingent on events before it, and the future is contingent on the present. Nothing is predetermined in history.

Accidental events happen in history. The distribution of coal deposits is just accidental. The Industrial Revolution was powered by the steam engine, which was fueled by coal. Accidentally, coal was easily mined in England, which affected which countries industrialized and which did not.

Conjunctures matter. A conjuncture happens when several independent developments come together in ways that interact, creating a unique historical moment. The world has had regions that were independent of one another, and thus have their own histories.

Even Columbus's discovery of the Americas and Vasco da Gama's sailing around Africa would not have significantly benefited European fortunes had they not discovered vast quantities of silver in the New World, which they could use to buy Asian goods and a supply of African slaves for New World plantations.

This conjuncture of elements conspired a pattern that enabled the West to establish dominance over the rest of the world.

China pioneered the use of paper currency to avoid carrying unwieldy strings of coins. Merchants in the late Tang Dynasty (618-907) started trading receipts from deposit shops where they left money or goods. In the 1020s, the Song Dynasty (960-1276) produced the world's first government-issued paper money on top of the coins that were already in use.

The public had no faith in paper currency because of its devaluation in the Song and Yuan Dynasties (1271-1368). The Ming Dynasty (1368-1644) initially banned silver and decreed that people should use paper money, but people continued to use silver and bronze coins in defiance of the decree. The Ming Dynasty had to reform its monetary system for normalcy.

Thus, at the very time Europe was starting to experiment with paper money, China ironically decided to abandon it. In 1567, the Ming Dynasty fixed silver as the main currency. The decision had global implications in the 16th and 17th centuries when Europeans discovered huge supplies of silver in the New World and an even larger Chinese demand for it.

As a result, a global trade network was established from which Europe made a huge profit: silver flowed into China and India from the New World, while Asian silks, spices, and porcelain flowed into Europe, and weapons and other industrial products were exported from Europe to Africa, from which a multitude of slaves were shipped to the New World.

Robert Marks argued that the ability of one part of the world (Europe led by Britain) to dominate came about by tapping stored sources of energy (coal and then oil). Western supremacy was just a result of contingency, not inevitability.

The first contingency was China which adopted a silver standard in its economy and abandoned the navigation network in the Indian Ocean, losing a part of global logistics for transporting Asian silks, spices, and porcelain. It goes back to the story of Zhenghe, who sailed westward to West Asia, the Middle East, and Africa from 1405 to 1433.

If he had sailed eastward, he might have discovered the west coast of America. Had his descendants kept sailing along Zhenghe's itinerary, China could have jointly participated in global logistics with Spain and Portugal in the 16th century. It is naturally futile to make such an assumption in history, but China's inaction harmed its future prospects.

The second contingency was the accidental discovery of the New World and its vast silver reserves, coupled with the decimation of the native population by diseases carried by conquistadors and the construction of an African slave-based plantation economy subordinate to European interests.

The third contingency involved rapid military innovation and huge costs due to almost constant warfare in Europe. Spain accumulated huge wealth from global trade networks but failed to establish a Spanish-led Pan-European Empire because the costs of warfare to build the Empire were too much to bear, even with the huge wealth from colonial trade.

In the early 15th century, China had advantageous competencies in the world in terms of technology, culture, agriculture, infrastructure, and social organization in its processes of exceptional developments of the Silk Road, exploration of sea routes, operating commercial entrepots, and establishing diplomatic networks with foreign countries.

It was on the verge of becoming a dominant power when the ruling Ming Dynasty deliberately closed the door on the world. It was a decision that plunged China into centuries of isolation from commercial and intellectual exchange, consequently making it a minor player on the international stage. All these led to its inferior capacity to handle colonial expansion in the era of imperialism in the late 19th century.

Out of its pride, China made a blunder to inflict self-imposed isolation, and its technological innovations ground to a halt while the West accelerated the pace of change. In the 21st century, China emerged as a leading nation in the globe, but we also notice a trend in China replete with the excessive and exclusive mood of nationalism that is hardly able to be compatible with global norms.

History tells us that prosperity is sustained when it is operated in the principles of being both agentic (goal-achievement and task functioning with competence, assertiveness, and decisiveness) and communal (relationship and social functioning with benevolence, trustworthiness, and morality) in all fields of its interactions in the globe.

In summary, Western supremacy dominated the world in the 19th century in all spheres of economy, military power, technology, and political hegemony. The reasons for this dominance are open to debate, but one thing is clear non-European entities (except the USA) failed to build the competence and capability that could resist European hegemony.

Emperor Kangxi (康熙, r.1661-1722) was the second emperor of the Qing Dynasty. He ruled the empire for more than 60 years as one of the longest-reigning emperors in history. During his reign, the empire prospered, dynastic succession was stabilized, and he was benevolent and diligent at work. He was open to Western culture and technology.

He made the Treaty of Nerchinsk with Russia in 1689, establishing a border in the northern regions of Mongolia and the Amur Basin. It helped to keep peace and allowed licensed trade along the borders. It also gave the Qing Empire the freedom to expand westward and conquer Taiwan. During his reign, the economy improved, and the population grew.

When he died, he left a big surplus in the treasury as the Roman emperor, Antoninus Pius (r.138-161), one of the Five Good Emperors, did. By around 1750, the Qing Dynasty reached the peak of its position in Asia, secure against invaders and broadly self-sufficient in terms of agriculture and industry.

Within less than a century, however, the Qing's defeat by Britain in the Opium War (1839-1842) led to China's subjugation to Western imperialism. The decline and collapse of the Qing Dynasty from 1750 to 1912 were much quicker and more dramatic than those of the Roman Empire, which fell from 180 AD, with the death of Marcus Aurelius, the last of the Five Good Emperors, to the time of its downfall in 476 AD.

The Qing Dynasty (1636-1912), the axis of Asian power, was rather short-lived and too weak to dominate imperial invasions. The difference can be attributed to the fact that the West had started the Industrial Revolution in the 1750s, while China devolved into internal conflicts and disorientation after Emperor Kangxi's reign during the same period.

With the powerful executions of pro-reform policies of the Meiji-initiatives, Japan made imperial expansion under the cloak of extending civilization and providing colonial protection of economic and cultural benefits to the colonized.

4.3. The Revolutions that built the modernity

1) People, Nation, and State

The modern world has revolved around the tenet of the nation-state and its sovereignty. It starts with the question of how some states first industrialized since 1750, and how the French Revolution triggered a chain of socio-political changes across Europe. All those processes led to the emergence of nation-states, which are defined as states with sovereignty whose citizens share a homogeneous language, culture, or common descent.

The emergence of the nation-state was accompanied by ideas of freedom from tyranny and stability in administration. Thus, modern democracies materialized integral elements of a multi-house system, constitutional checks and balances, and the rule of law.

A state is an independent, sovereign government exercising absolute control over a certain territory with borders that are set and internationally recognized. It has bureaucracies staffed by personnel in various governmental arms such as administration, legal, educational, and defense authorities. It establishes sovereignty and monopolizes functions that require exclusive activities and by making rules and legitimizing the use of force, such as through citizenship, printing currency, collecting taxes, and maintaining a military. It controls information and produces symbols and national interests.

A nation is a group of people who share a cultural or historical identity and see themselves as a cohesive and coherent unit. It is a socially constructed unit, and its existence, definition, and members can change based on circumstances. It can be thought of as imagined communities based on religion, ethnic identity, language, and cultural practices. It differentiates insiders from outsiders. It often ignores political boundaries, as a nation may spill over into multiple states, or a state may contain multiple nations.

States are not always nations, as not every nation has a state. A nation-state became critical in modern politics.

2) The Glorious Revolution (1685-1689)

The Glorious Revolution was an event in which Parliament asserted its rights over the monarchy and drew up the Bill of Rights in 1689. It secured stability in politics and economics, allowing the English to follow a fundamentally different trajectory from other European countries. Stability laid the foundation for the Industrial Revolution in the next century.

It may be traced back to the tragic incident of King Charles I (r.1625-49) who inherited the kingdoms of England and Scotland upon the death in 1625 upon the death of his father, King James I (r.1603-25). He was determined to govern the country in the principle of royal prerogatives and divine rights whereas Parliament wished to pass a resolution that curbed the unauthorized collection of customs duties.

His religious policies including his marriage to a Roman Catholic (Henrietta Maria of France) in 1625 made the people concerned about a return of Catholicism. In 1629, Charles I dissolved Parliament who were thought to have defied the royal prerogative, and it had lasted for 11 years until 1640 when he had to raise the funds to put down the rebellion of the Scottish. He ruled the country without recourse to or check of Parliament which was perceived as a tyrannical absolute monarch.

The English Parliament was now determined to place limits on the king's power, and the House of Commons passed the law that enabled them to implement their own choice of lieutenants over the military without royal consent. By the fall of 1642, a civil war broke out between the forces of Parliament and Royalists, and they fought for over three and a half years. Charles I was arrested and confined to places and finally was tried, convicted, and executed for high treason in January 1949. It was a blunder that Charles dissolved Parliament and ruled the country, so-called Personal Rule.

King Charles I was addressed on the scaffold in front of the Ax and Block before his execution on 30 January 1649. He confessed that he had a guileless innocence in the confrontation because he didn't begin it with them, and he also pronounced that there must be a distinction between the sovereign and the subjects. He delivered his points even in such a dire state.

"I shall begin first with my innocence. In troth I think it not very needful for me to insist long upon this, for all the world knows that I never did begin a War with the two Houses of Parliament. And I call God to witness, to whom I must shortly make an account, that I never did intend for to encroach upon their privileges...For the people.

And truly I desire their Liberty and Freedom as much as any Body whomsoever. But I must tell you, That their Liberty and Freedom, consists in having of Government; those Laws, by which their Life and their Gods may be most their own. It is not for having share in government, Sir, that is nothing pertaining to them.

A subject and a sovereign are clean different things, and therefore until they do that, I mean, that you do put the people in that liberty as I say, certainly they will never enjoy themselves."

With the monarchy overthrown by the execution of Charles I, England became a republic or Commonwealth for a period from 1649 to 1660. The House of Lords was abolished, and executive power was assumed by a Council of State. The military oppositions from Scotland and Ireland were quelched by the forces of Oliver Cromwell in the Anglo-Scottish War (1650-52) and the Conquest of Ireland (1649-53). Cromwell forcibly ruled as Lord Protector. Upon his death in 1658, he was briefly succeeded by his ineffective son, Richard. Parliament was reinstated, and the monarchy was restored to Charles I's eldest son, Charles II, in 1660.

On 6 February 1685, Charles II (r.1660-1685 as King of England, r.1649-1651 as King of Scotland) died and was succeeded by his brother, James II, at a time when relations between Catholics and Protestants were tense. There was also considerable friction between the monarchy and the British Parliament.

King James II, who was Catholic, supported freedom of worship for Catholics and had close ties with Catholics in France. He further antagonized Parliament by asking for the repeal of the Test Acts, which restricted public offices for Catholics and nonconformist Protestants.

In need of a standing army, he asked Parliament for more money. On 19 November 1685, Parliament declined to repeal the Acts and refused the extra money. On 20 November, James suspended Parliament. James's daughter Mary, a Protestant, was the rightful heir to the throne until 1688 when James had a son, James Stuart, who was seen as a prospect of Catholicism.

The birth of James's son changed the line of succession, and many feared that a Catholic dynasty in England was imminent. On 4 April 1687, the King published a Declaration of Indulgence, which suspended all religious penal laws, allowing for the practice of Catholicism. He reissued a second Declaration of Indulgence on 27 April 1688.

These were brave words, but James's heavy-handed insensitivity to the fears of most of his subjects, combined with his use of royal prerogative without Parliamentary approval, caused deep unease. In an act of gross miscalculation, King James II ordered Anglican clergy to read the Declaration from the pulpit to their congregations on two consecutive Sundays.

On 18 May 1688, the Archbishop of Canterbury and six other bishops ("the Seven Bishops") refused to read it and petitioned against the order because the foundation of his Declaration of Indulgence was illegal, based on his suspending power, which had often been condemned by Parliament.

On 8 June 1688, the Seven Bishops were arrested and sent to the Tower of London to await trial. Two days later, the Queen gave birth to a son who was baptized according to the Roman Catholic rite. On 30 June 1688, the Seven Bishops were acquitted by the jury. Huge crowds celebrated in the streets, burning effigies of the Pope and attacking Catholic churches.

The king's elevation of Catholicism, his close relationship with France, his conflict with Parliament, and the uncertainty over who would succeed James on the English throne led to a revolt. The same day, seven prominent politicians signed a letter inviting William of Orange, the Protestant son-in-law to King James, to intervene to save both Church and State.

William landed at Torbay in Devon with about 15,000 mostly Dutch troops on 5 November 1688. James still had his standing army, but the enthusiasm with which William was welcomed and the defections from James's army strengthened William's hand. He entered London on 19 December, and a few days later, James II was allowed to escape to France.

On 12 February 1689, the Convention Parliament issued a Declaration of Rights, which sharply condemned the actions of James II regarding certain ancient rights and liberties. The declaration was later embodied in the Bill of Rights passed by Parliament and received by Royal Assent on 16 December 1689.

The move towards absolutism, modeled on the French system, was halted, but the new king, William III, had no desire for a weakened monarchy. However, the declaration of the Bill of Rights restricted the King's powers, and it insisted on the rights of a free Parliament. The Glorious Revolution induced William III (r.1689-1702) to establish parliamentary supremacy.

This doctrine holds that absolute power has been transferred from the monarch to the elected Parliament. It gives Parliament the power to rule with the authority previously enjoyed by England's kings. Henceforth, the 'United Kingdom of Great Britain' was to be ruled by Parliament at Westminster, and modern British identity derives from it.

At this stage, we refer to the Magna Carta of 1215, which stated that free men wouldn't be imprisoned or punished except by the law (Clause 39 of the Magna Carta). The Bill of Rights was mostly concerned with powers that could be exercised only by Parliament, not the King. It also included some individual rights, such as the prohibition of cruel punishment.

The political upheavals of the Magna Carta in 1215 and the Glorious Revolution in 1688-1689 uniquely enhanced human rights in a bloodless manner, in contrast to the bloody revolutions of the 18th century in Europe and America. The tradition of parliamentarianism in truculent defiance of despotic monarchy paved the path for liberal humanism.

This formed a mood favorable to the British Enlightenment and the ensuing Industrial Revolution in the 1750s. It also spread an influence to the American Revolution in 1765-1783 and the French Revolution in 1789. The Glorious Revolution showcased checks and balances of power, ensured the rule of law, and promoted proper representation of the ruled in parliament.

3) The Enlightenment

From 500 to 1350 in the Middle Ages, there were no remarkable inventions or innovative breakthroughs in science. In the sector of education, the belief system and teachings were based on the works of the ancient Greeks, which had been incorporated into the doctrine of the Catholic Church.

As the world became more enlightened in the 15th century, a new mode of thinking and action made European civilization distinct from medieval Christendom and other non-European civilizations such as Islam and China. It further differentiated Europe in the mid-18th century from what it had been in the 15th century.

The new mode of thinking and actions renewed interest in the natural world and social phenomenon, ushering in discoveries and findings that did not match the doctrines of the church. Scientific discoveries motivated enlightened thinkers to expand the boundaries of knowledge and deepen their insights about the world around them.

Enlightenment primarily originated in the scientific revolution of the 16th century. It resulted in a fundamental shift in intellectual and philosophical progress in Europe, unbound by time and place, from the 17th century onwards. This movement completely revolutionized the way people viewed the world and helped set the Industrial Revolution in motion.

(1) Political background

Throughout the 17th to 19th centuries, Western politics underwent dramatic changes in a row of conflicts among powers, which resulted in a patchwork of treaties during the period. Each conflict ended with a new phase of changes and developments in all spheres of life for the people.

The Westphalia Treaty (1648) brought the brutalities of the Thirty Years' War (1618-1648) to an end. The Treaty marked the shift from a medieval world of allegiances among monarchies to a modern world with the emergence of sovereign states, freedom of religion, and an international legal order, so-called- the Westphalian System.

The Congress of Vienna (1815) wrapped up the kaleidoscopic developments stemming from the French Revolution and the fall of the French Empire. The changes in society such as the rise of the middle class, a sense of equality, ideas advocating for social reform, and the growth of nationalism spread to the rest of the world.

After the fall of Napoleon, an uneasy peace kicked in as monarchies were restored, but they hung in a precarious balance amidst tension. The unfair privileges and intervention in freedom of thought and assembly were back in fashion, but the suppression in the touch-and-go situation fomented conflicts among the public across Europe. These led to a series of wars from 1853 to 1871.

In the Crimean War (1853-1856), which pitted the Russian Empire against an alliance of the Ottoman Empire, France, and Britain, modern war technologies were first used, such as explosive shells, railways, and telegraphs. The defeat of Russia weakened its influence in Europe, but it triggered reforms in serfdom, the justice system, education, and military service.

The Austro-Prussian War (1866) broke out from rivalry between the Austrian Habsburg Empire and the Kingdom of Prussia. It resulted in Prussian dominance over the German states, forming a new superpower, the unified Germany, at the core of the European Continent.

The Franco-Prussian War (1870-1871) was fought between France and Germany that led to German victory. The German states proclaimed their union as the German Empire under the Prussian King Wilhelm I and Chancellor Bismarck, supplanting France as the dominant land power in Europe. A powerful nation-state arose with its reputation of Realpolitik.

European warfare prompted the rise of the west. The Enlightenment and the Age of Reason saw a coming of age where ideas of absolutism were replaced by notions of freedom, rights and liberty. But it was Europe's entrenched relationship with violence and militarism that allowed it to place itself at the center of the world after the great expeditions of the 1490s.

(2) The development of mental faculty

The tenet of the Enlightenment is boiled down to the power of reason. It tried to shed light on the darkness of the Middle Ages, which was an aberration of the human mind. It viewed society as being bound not only by religion but also by irrational dogma. These attitudes exhibited brutality, bigotry, intolerance, superstition, and fanaticism.

Enlightenment thinkers encouraged people to wake up from the ignorance and malpractices of the Middle Ages and to develop their independent understanding of humanity and materiality. They were weary of being dictated to by the ancient conventions of society and dogmatic religious authority.

The scientific and intellectual achievements of the Muslim world were being actively sought by scholars in the west, such as Adelard of Bath (c.1080-c.1152, English natural philosopher) who scoured the libraries of Antioch and Damascus and introduced algebra, his commentaries of Euclid's Elements, and the symbol for zero to Western Europe that formed the foundation for the study of mathematics in the Christian world. The sanguine sophistication of the east was contrasted with backward society of the Christian west, which was replete with fatuous fights among barbarous princes, bibulous bishops, bribable judges, unreliable patrons, sycophantic clients and lying promisers in full of ambitions.

The requirement to free themselves from the yoke of the Middle Ages inspired Enlightenment thinkers to source energy from the cultures of the Classical Age. They found Greek and Latin thinkers to be a fountain of inspiration, not merely as standards of perfection to emulate, but as stimuli for thought and action that adhered to reason and humanity.

To name a few: Cicero (106 BC-43 BC), Lucretius (99 BC-55 BC), Seneca (4 BC-65 AD), and Marcus Aurelius (r.161-180 AD). Their literature was characterized by moderation, decorum, and a sense of order based on Stoicism and Epicureanism that predated Christianity.

The classics were revisited and used as a foundation on which people founded humanism and reason which led to an enlightened mind. In the modern days of the 21st century, the classics continue to offer insights to help build modern philosophy, science, economics, politics, history, education, and so forth.

The mind controls actions. Thus, it is crucial to free the mind from constraints, focus on change, and move on to create something noble. History shows examples of how ancestors tried something noble in the mindset of reason and courage during the era of the Enlightenment:

- Zhenghe in inland-centric China, made seven westward sailings to West Asia, the Middle East, and Africa from 1405 to 1433. Though they were not continued thereafter, the sailings were a noble attempt to know the world over the sea horizons.

- The Reformation in the 16th century was a protest of the deviant unrestraint of institutionalized vices, and it bravely demanded that transgressors revert to the core of their beliefs.

- The people and the nobles, armed with an enlightened mind, convoluted the world by staging the Glorious Revolution in 1688, the American Revolutionary War from 1775 to 1783, and the French Revolution from 1789 to 1799. They broke down ossified political structures, freed the suppressed masses, and reset the terrains of politics and society.

- The enlightened minds committed a string of missteps by colonizing the world to gratify imperial greed. The imperial West ruled the world in the post-Industrial Revolution era, which led to WWI and WWII in the 20th century.

A constellation of political philosophers shined the light of reason during the age of the Enlightenment. Three great thinkers who shaped modern thought are Samuel Rutherford, John Locke, and Montesquieu.

Samuel Rutherford (1600-1661) was born in Scotland. He earned a degree of Master of Arts at Edinburgh College and became a pastor of a rural parish church in 1627. During the English Civil War (1642-1651), he was chosen as a member of the Scottish commissioners and attended the proceedings of the Westminster Assembly in London.

At this time, in 1644, Rutherford wrote his seminary book, *"Lex, Rex" (The Law and the King)*. Lex Rex means Law is King and if the sequence of the titled words is reversed to, Rex Lex, it becomes King is Law. The title Lex Rex, not Rex Lex, is believed to illustrate the points that the author intended to deliver.

In his book, he asserted that absolute monarchy is the worst form of government, and the people have power over the King, equality under the law including kings, justifications for defensive wars against unjust violence, inalienable human rights, government by consent, and separation of powers, and vindicating the Scriptural duty to resist tyrants as an act of loyalty to God.

After the Restoration in 1660, when the Catholic King Charles II returned from his exile in France, the authorities burned Lex Rex and summoned Rutherford for high treason, but he died before the charge could be tried. Lex Rex is considered one of the greatest books of political philosophy in modern Protestant political theory.

John Locke (1632-1704), a British philosopher, made foundational contributions to modern theories of political science. In his book, *"An Essay Concerning Human Understanding,"* he opposed the rationalist idea that humans are born with innate knowledge. Instead, he believed that humans are *tabula rasa,* or blank slate, that gain knowledge through experience.

He believed that experience is the bedrock of all human knowledge, and this signals Locke's adherence to empiricism over rationalism. There are two routes to knowledge via experience: sensation and reflection. Sensation is about coming into contact with the external world, whereas reflection comes from introspection, or from reflecting on what we have experienced.

His book, *"The Second Treatise on Government"* is a seminal document with core premises of the ultimate sovereignty of the people, the necessity of constraints on the exercise of arbitrary power by the executive or legislature, and the revocability of the social contract by the people when power has been arbitrarily used against them.

The book was written during the period preceding the abdication of King James II, and it was published in 1690, serving as a justification for the Glorious Revolution of 1688. The Revolution established England as a constitutional monarchy under Parliament's control and allowed for religious toleration and freedom of expression, as set out in the Bill of Rights.

The book was an attack on political absolutism and addressed that the government exists for the people's benefit. It claimed that a government can be replaced or overthrown if it ceases to function toward its primary purpose. The U.S. system of government was built on Locke's ideas. The Declaration of Independence and the U.S. Constitution are testaments to Locke's core ideas.

The text on natural liberty and rights, as well as the consent of the governed for legitimate rule, is provided below:

Ch.1-2 (Political Power and State of Nature): Adam was not given absolute authority over the world and his children by God and thus Adam's heirs did not have this absolute authority

Ch.3-4 (State of War and Slavery): a state of war if a common authority fails to act justly in violation of the laws of nature and justice, natural liberty and slavery should be freed from arbitrary, absolute power

Ch.5 (Property): a person in a state of nature can claim land by adding labor to it—building a house on it or farming on it—but only so much as that person can reasonably use without waste and make their world rewarding place to inhabit

Ch.6-7 (Paternal Power and Political-Civil Society): all people are born with an equal right to freedom, civil society as a united body of individuals under the power of an executive that protects their property and well-being.

Ch.8-9 (the Beginning and the Ends of Political Societies and Government): the individual agrees to abide by the rules and decisions of the majority, submitting oneself to the laws of civil society, putting oneself under the protection of the executive power of the society, a law, a judge, and an executive working to no other end, but the peace, safety, and public good of the people.

Ch.10-11 (Forms of a Commonwealth, the Extent of the Legislative Power): The majority choose their form of government, democracy and the legislative powers. The legislative power is to preserve society and the limits to the power of the legislature including taxation on the property without the people's consent.

Montesquieu (1689-1757) was a French lawyer and an influential political philosopher of the Age of Enlightenment.

"The Spirit of the Laws" (1748) is a treatise on political theory. It states the separation of powers (legislative, executive, and judicial) under checks and balances, civil and criminal law to provide greater security for the accused more reasonable procedures for parties in lawsuits, the abolition of slavery, and the freedom of thought, speech, and assembly.

Montesquieu divides governments into three types: republics, monarchies, and despotisms. He associates each of the three types with a primary principle: virtue for republics, honor for monarchies, and fear for despotisms. The type of government is determined not by the form of rule but by how that rule is exercised.

For this reason, he distinguishes between a monarchy, where a complex of institutions, men of politics, and honor lead to the rule of law, and a despotism, where everyone is essentially a slave of the ruler. Montesquieu, using the English government as a model, sees the separation of powers as a guarantor of political liberty.

BOOK 3.3 (Of the Principles of Democracy)

There is no great share of probity necessary to support a monarchical or despotic government: the force of laws, in one, and the prince's arm, in the other, are sufficient to direct and maintain the whole: but, in a popular state, one spring more is necessary, namely, virtue.

When virtue is banished, ambition invades the minds of those who are disposed to receive it, and avarice possesses the whole community...The members of the commonwealth riot on the public spoils, and its strength is only the power of a few, and the license of many.

BOOK 11:4 (In What Liberty Consists)

Democratic and aristocratic states are not in their own nature free. Political liberty is to be found only in moderate governments, and even in these it is not always found. It is there only when there is no abuse of power. But constant experience shows us that every man invested with power is apt to abuse it and to carry his authority as far as it will go.

Is it not strange, though true, to say that virtue itself has a need of limits? To prevent this abuse, it is necessary from the very nature of things that power should be a check to power. A government may be so constituted as no man shall be compelled to do things to which the law does not oblige him, nor forced to abstain from things which the law permits.

From an alternative perspective on the Enlightenment, it is argued that the Enlightenment promoted equality, as evidenced by the assertion that "all men are born equal." However, it is important to recognize that the men in question were primarily slave owners, and that the subsequent centuries witnessed the unchecked proliferation of capitalism, which had both positive and negative consequences. On the one hand, the flourishing of democracy and capitalism contributed to a reduction in famine, poverty, and illnesses. On the other hand, the same forces also led to the emergence of new forms of exploitation and inequality.

4) The French Revolution

In the late 18th century, France was at risk of bankruptcy due to its spending in the American Revolution, the extravagance of King Louis XVI, and the corruption of aristocrats. Social unrest worsened with revolutionary fervor against the privileged elites, the despair of common people in economic hardship, and grievous inequalities.

Under the flag of tricolor, combining the white (France's royal standard) with the red and blue (the ensign of Paris), "chanting liberty, equality, fraternity," the totality of all scenes was called the French Revolution. It fundamentally transformed the world as well as France which later led to the rise of Napoleon Bonaparte.

(1) Developmental Stages of the Revolution

The Revolution Began in 1789

France was a hierarchical and rural society. The Church and nobility wielded spiritual, legal, and material power in the community, while the peasantry performed back-breaking work to meet both their domestic needs and the landlords' requirements for rent and other charges. They were bereft of essential surpluses that could be marketed in the cities.

The medieval conception of social order was to "know one's places." An overlord had the privilege of owning land in return for the obligation to care for the peasantry community. The monarchy got hold of authority over the overlords and the peasantry through the exercise of monarchical authority.

By the last quarter of the 18th century, the Ancient Regime in France had become so decadent and detested that the worn-out regime failed to handle the political paralysis and financial crisis. Every segment of society was sharply at odds with one another in the polarized society. Beneath the mundane life of the people, society was somehow getting out of control.

An air of revolt was fomented among the concentrated industrial workers. Those manufacturing silks, carpets, and porcelains gradually organized to run their operations. This led to collective actions for rights and interests. Meanwhile, the French Revolution was spearheaded by affluent lawyers, not by famished peasants.

It was food shortage that initially triggered violence in the Bastilles and the revolution. The National Assembly abolished feudalism, thwarted attempts to reverse the revolution, terminated the monarchy, executed the king, reigned with irrational terror, and established the French Republic. All these later led to a monarchy under Bonaparte Napoleon.

• The First Phase (1789-1794)

The French Revolution erupted against the incompetent monarchy and proclaimed revolutionary tenets, and the Revolution was turned into sanguinary violence.

20 June 1789 (Estates-General): The Estates-General (a legislative and consultative assembly composed of clergy, nobility, and commoners) collapsed when the Third Estate (commoners) formed their own National Assembly to address their own concerns.

14 July 1789 (Bastille prison-fortress): Paris got embroiled in revolutionary commotion, leading to the storming of the Bastille, a prison fortress that symbolized royal authority. Paris cascaded into turmoil and the King lost control.

26 August 1789 (The Declaration of Human Rights): The Declaration of the Rights of Man and of the Citizen was followed by the abolition of provinces in 1789. Religious toleration was guaranteed in 1790, and slavery was outlawed in 1794.

14 July 1790 (An Oath of Allegiance to the King): On the first anniversary of the fall of the Bastille, the National Assembly and the public celebrated the Grand Festival of Federation in the presence of King Louis XVI, swearing a solemn oath of allegiance to the King. It appeared that stability and consensus might have been achieved.

20-21 June 1791, King Louis XVI, Queen Marie Antoinette, and their immediate family were arrested in their attempt to escape from Paris to Montmédy, where the King wished to initiate a counter-revolution by joining up with royalist troops.

22 September 1792 (French Republic): The King was deposed, and the Republic with National Convention

were declared.

21 January 1793 (The Demise of the King): King Louis XVI was executed as a traitor. On 16 October 1793, Marie Antoinette suffered the same fate. Their son, ten-year-old Dauphin Louis XVII, was handed to plebeian foster parents and subsequently died from neglect and tuberculosis later.

The Revolution accelerated through ever-increasing degrees of radicalism until all the institutions of the previous social and political order had been swept away. The National Assembly abolished all apparatus of serfdom and noble privilege.

June 1793 (Reign of Terror): The execution of the King triggered a war with European powers. Fears of foreign invasion and factional infightings within the National Convention led to the bloody Reign of Terror for a year, in which more than twenty thousand people were executed.

The Revolution turned bloody as the Terror raged, victimizing revolutionaries such as Danton and his associates, as well as Robespierre, who was called a *sanguinocrat* (a ruler in the blood) on 28 July 1794, along with a great number of alleged counterrevolutionaries.

- The Second Phase (1794-1804)

The French Revolution visibly halted to take stock, and outrageous bloodlust stopped, although insecurity lingered.

26 October 1795 (The Directory): The National Convention was dissolved, and yet another two-tier, five-man executive Directory came into being and took power. The French Republic with the Directory lasted until 10 November 1799 when it was replaced by the Consulate.

With the military successes that followed in the wars against the Dutch Republic, the Prussians, and the Spanish, Bonaparte Napoleon inspired enthusiasm among the French people, as he successfully thwarted foreign interventions.

18-19 November 1799: Lucien Bonaparte, the brother of Napoleon Bonaparte and President of the Council of Five Hundred, engineered the coup that brought his brother, Napoleon, to power. It disbanded the Council of Five Hundred, and a three-man Consulate was instituted, confirmed by a nationwide plebiscite. This event brought the four-year Directory to the end and it was said to be the closing of the French Revolution. The Napoleonic era began.

In May 1802: Napoleon Bonaparte raised himself to the status of first Consul for life; in May 1804, he declared himself Emperor.

The Kingdom of France had controlled the Louisiana territory from 1682 until it was ceded to Spain in 1762 in the secret Treaty of Fontainebleau. Following French defeat in the Seven Years' War (1756-63), France ceded to Spain the territory of west of the Mississippi, and to Great Britain the rest of New, the territory to the east of the river.

In 1800, Napoleon Bonaparte, the First Consul of the French Republic, regained ownership of Louisiana with the Third Treaty of San Ildefonso on 1 October 1800 between Spain and the French Republic by which Spain agreed in principle to exchange its North American colony of Louisiana for territories in Tuscany in Italy. For Napoleon, he made the deal in his own strategic vision for rebuilding France's empire in the New World.

The vision was centered on Saint-Dominigue with a mainland base. Napoleon's forces succeeded in regaining the colony in 1802, but a rebellion broke out in opposition to the reintroduction of slavery. The French army, already ravaged by yellow fever, was finally defeated in 1805 and Napoleon abandoned his vision of the French Empire in the west. The revolt of the slaves of Saint-Dominigue was the only rebellion that succeeded, and it led to the establishment of the first independent black state, Haiti, in the New World

It opened a prospect of renewed warfare with the United Kingdom and thus it prompted Napoleon to consider selling to the United States the Louisiana Territories (it contained the whole of present states of Arkansas, Iowa, Kansas, Missouri, Nebraska, and Oklahoma as well as parts of Colorado, Minnesota, Louisiana, Montana, New Mexico, North and South Dakota, Texas, Wyoming, and Canadian provinces of Alberta and Saskatchewan. It was more than 1.3 million square kilometers or 530 million acres occupying almost a quarter of the USA today).

President Thomas Jefferson leveraged this opportunity to take steps to secure US access to the Mississippi River and sent a delegation including diplomat Robert Livingston to Paris to negotiate the purchase of the vast New Orleans with the price limit of ten million dollars. In the meanwhile, a war between Britain and France was imminent and Napoleon needed cash to fund the invasion of Britain.

On 11 April 1803 Napoleon instructed his treasury minister to offer the Louisiana Territories for the sum of fifteen million dollars. With the ceiling of ten million dollars, however, Livingston thought the offer was too good for the US to be true because it meant for the US to pay less than three cents per acre (For reference, Russia sold Alaska to the US in 1867 for about two cents per acre). He accepted the offer which was beyond his authorized level before Napoleon reconsidered the offer. On 30 April 1803, he signed the Louisiana Purchase Treaty with his counterpart Barbe-Marbois, the French Treasury Minister.

Napoleon said about the deal that "I have given England a maritime rival who sooner or later will humble her". Napoleon had good political and financial reasons for ceding the territory to the US, but he made a blunder by misjudging its value and setting the price much lower than it deserved.

The National Assembly in the French Revolution promulgated the Declaration of the Rights of Man and the Citizen in 1789. Inspired by Enlightenment philosophers, the Declaration was a core statement of the values of the French Revolution. It represented essential cores of the French Revolution.

The concept of human rights, if not invented by the French revolutionaries, provided a strong impetus to modern history. It expressed mankind's natural, inalienable, and sacred rights that were reflected in the Magna Carta of 1215, the Bill of Rights of 1689, and the U.S. Declaration of Independence in 1776.

"Declaration of the Rights of Man and of the Citizen:
I. Men are born and remain free and equal in rights. Social distinctions can only be founded on public utility.
II. The purpose of every political association is the preservation of the natural and imprescriptible rights of men. These rights are liberty, property, and safety from, and resistance to, oppression.
III. The principle of all sovereignty resides in the nation. No body of men, and no individual, can exercise authority which does not emanate directly therefrom.

IV. Liberty consists in the ability to do anything which does not harm others.

V. The Law can only forbid actions which are injurious to society...

VI. The Law is the expression of the General Will... It should be the same for all, whether to protect or to punish.

VII. No man can be accused, arrested, or detained except in those instances which are determined by law.

VIII. The Law should only establish punishments which are strictly necessary. No person should be punished by retrospective legislation.

IX. Every man is presumed innocent till found guilty...

X. No person should be troubled for his opinions, even religious ones, so long as their manifestation does not threaten public order.

XI. The free communication of thoughts and opinions is one of men's most precious rights. Every citizen, therefore, can write, speak, and publish freely, saving only the need to account for abuses defined by law.

XII. A public force is required to guarantee the [above] rights. It is instituted for the benefit of all, not for the use of those to whom it is entrusted.

XIII. Public taxation is indispensable for the upkeep of the forces and the administration. It should be divided among all citizens without distinction, according to their abilities.

XIV. Citizens have the right to approve the purposes, levels, and extent of taxation.

XV. Society has the right to hold every public servant to account.

XVI. Any society in which rights are not guaranteed nor powers separated does not have a constitution

XVII. Property being a sacred and inviolable right, no person can be deprived of it, except by public necessity, legal process, and just compensation.

The term "*Men*" in Article I of the Declaration meant males, excluding women. The exclusion infuriated Olympe de Gouges (1748-93), a butcher's daughter who came to Paris, rejecting her married name. She published *The Declaration of the Rights of Woman and of the Female Citizen* in 1791 with the same number of seventeen articles as the *Rights of Man* in 1790.

Her work highlighted women's equal rights to men in society as a counterblast to the Rights of Man. The radical feminist demands evoked little sympathy in leading revolutionary circles. In June 1793, women were expressly excluded from citizenship. De Gouges sided with the moderate Girondins, calling for a plebiscite to allow citizens to choose their form of government.

After the fall of the Girondins in the summer of 1793, she was arrested. On 3 November 1793, she was executed by guillotine. This inferred that the revolutionary motto of Liberty, Equality, and Fraternity was not universal to all, but only to males. Gender equality would take time to become a central agenda in the post-French Revolution era.

"The Declaration of the Rights of Woman and the Female Citizen"

I. Woman is born free and remains equal to man in rights.

II. The aim of all political associations is to preserve the natural and inalienable rights of Woman and Man. These are: liberty, ownership, safety, and resistance to oppression.

III. The principle of sovereignty resides in essence in the Nation, which is nothing other than the conjunction of Woman and Man.

IV. The exercise of Woman's natural rights has no limit other than the tyranny of Man's opposing them.

V. The laws of nature and reason forbid all actions harmful to society.

VI. The law must be the expression of the General Will; all citizens, female and male, should concur in its formation. All citizens, being equal in its eyes, must be equally eligible for all honors, positions, and posts with no distinction other than those of their virtues and talents.

VII. Women obey the rigors of the law as men do.

VIII. No one may be punished except by virtue of a law which was promulgated prior to the crime, and which is applicable to women.

IX. Any woman found guilty will be dealt with in the full rigor of the law.

X. No one should be persecuted for fundamental opinions. Woman has the right to mount the scaffold; she must equally have the right to mount the rostrum.

XI. Any citizen may freely say 'I am the mother of your child' without any barbarous prejudice forcing her to hide the truth.

XII. The guarantee of women's rights entails absolute service.

XIII. The contributions of Woman and Man to the upkeep of public services are equal.

XIV. Female and male citizens have the same right to ascertain the need for taxes.

XV. All women, united by their contributions with all men, have the right to demand an account of their administration from all public officials.

XVI. Any society in which rights are not guaranteed, and powers not separated, has no constitution.

XVII. Property is shared or divided equally by both sexes.

History takes time to make another history.

(2) Effects of the French Revolution

- *First,* during the twenty years from 1792 to 1812, European political geography and living conditions were widely revamped when the French Revolutionary armies made territorial and political adjustments. The territory of France was vastly extended as it annexed large parts of the Netherlands, Germany, Switzerland, and Italy.

    By 1810, the population increased to 44 million, and life expectancy also rose: for women from 28 to 39 years, and for men from 28 to 38 years. The notable changes in territory, population, and life expectancy spread the French characters to more people over a larger area.

    Except for a few countries such as the British Isles, Scandinavia, Russia, and the Ottoman Empire, much of Europe was subject to revolutionary changes. They swept away the traditional order, allowing people to experience an entirely different environment of political structure, economic activities, and social atmospheres.

- *Second,* the French Revolution held a universal quality that was distinct from other convulsions in Europe. It was not merely a political upheaval, but it upended the socio-political system that reverberated around economic and cultural foundations; it changed people's mindsets. The changes were profound and lasting, even after French forces retreated.

    Paris became a center of power and culture based on Enlightenment and the universal appeal of the revolutionary motto: Liberty, Equality, and Fraternity. The swell of changes originating from Paris sent forth formidable shockwaves, pitting people against political tyranny, social inequality, economic disadvantage, and cultural discrepancies.

One common element is that the historic French Revolution ended with the French monarchy in 1802 after many twists and turns. Similarly, the social democratic regime of the Weimar Republic was taken over by the National Socialistic Nazi regime in 1933. The suppressed people's emotions erupted into public enthusiasm, but the outcomes varied because of the terrorful improvisation of impromptu revolutionary elites.

The key distinction between the French Revolution and the Nazi regime lies in the legacies and aftermaths each left behind. The French Revolution left the comprehensive progress of socio-political structure in the occupied states, whereas the aftermath of Nazi occupation resulted in indelible loss and damage to local communities.

- *Third,* the image of the Revolution is mixed. One was noble aspirations for popular sovereignty, freedom of expression, and respect for human rights. Another was the terror that accompanied it; a bloody brutality driven by ideological obsession and revolutionary expedience.

There was a surge in calls for arms to defend the Revolution and homeland from foreign intervention in 1792. It set a precedent of total war in times of national crisis. Innovations in administrative competence and war technology made total war practicable and mandatory. This happened during WW I in 1914, and WW II in 1940.

- *Fourth,* the Revolution was a rich seedbed for ideologies ranging from militant royalism to liberal constitutionalism, social democracy, and communism. The period of Jacobin rule from 1792 to 1794 put its emphasis on democracy, constitutionalism, social equality, and defense of the Revolution, but it was overshadowed by terror and controls on civil liberties.

The Jacobins were advocates of unlimited democracy, revolutionary dictatorship, and violence. They formed a tiny, iron-hard clique of 3,000 people who controlled 20 million. Their leaders were mainly professional lawyers and journalists such as Georges Danton (1759-94), Camille Desmoulins (1760-94), and Jean Marat (1743-93). They all died almost in the same year. The Jacobin Club was initially moderate in their revolutionary aims, but they became increasingly radical as they fought against the rigidity and ineptitude of the ancient regime, as well as the looming threat of counter-revolution.

Most of their ardent supporters were the radical proletarians of the Paris suburbs, known as the "sans-culottes," who exercised power. They were Europe's very first communists, socialists, and feminists.

The regime of Napoleon Bonaparte had an image of a strong man who delivered social order, prosperity, and national glory, but the image was stained by the blood of heavy casualties during continuous wars. The French war against Russia in 1812 alone costed the French army up to 500,000 soldiers out of around 700,000 deployed.

- *Fifth,* the Revolution produced by-products for future revolutions. It showed an example of professional insurrectionists skilled in overturning the existing social order, becoming the hallmark of numerous revolutions that followed in history.

A new epoch of professional revolutionaries emerged, tirelessly plotting to overthrow conservative orders violently. The professionals believed that revolutions could be started deliberately rather than waiting for public antipathy to overwhelm corrupt state structures.

After the Congress of Vienna in 1815, European societies were embroiled in upheavals. Paternalistic monarchies were back in fashion, the liberal middle class was frustrated with barriers to their freedom, peasants despaired at the loss of hope for an egalitarian life, and factory workers faced poor working conditions amid mass production.

The rueful recollection of the defunct French lordship based on liberty, equality, and fraternity made disgruntled people strive for these ideals themselves. Economic recession and harvest failures in the 1840s ripened the mood of struggles. The French Revolution in 1789 made the idea of revolution no longer a fantasy, but a reality everywhere.

Karl Marx appeared in France in 1843, and he provided a theory of revolution that class struggles would lead to a world run by and for the working class.

In 1848, the factors of Enlightenment, the Congress of Vienna's decisions, and the aftermath of the Industrial Revolution were connected with economic hardships, nationalist movements, and political discontent. Revolutions erupted in the mood, and they spread like an epidemic across Europe. All these led to outward imperial expansion and inward conflicts.

5) The Industrial Revolution

The Industrial Revolution was fundamentally a revolution in the use of energy and power, which entailed production efficiency, reduced cost, and improved mobility.

In the late Middle Ages, craftsmen worked mainly from their own houses, organized into guilds, and were mostly self-employed. In early modern days, they were considered middle class, but they were not rich manufacturers or large capitalists; the rich men at the time were great landowners, moneylenders, or merchants.

In the 18th century in Europe, many workers began to produce large quantities of products using machines and division of labor in factories. This laid a foundation for the Industrial Revolution. It was a brainchild of industrial innovations aimed at addressing the inefficiencies of muscle-using labor and the desire to uplift productivity.

The innovative process was convergent, serendipitous, and costly, while its result was divergent, transformative, and economic. Success factors in innovation were the liberal mind, relentless experimentation, the discovery of principles, and their application to real production. In addition, industrialists funded inventions, while governments protected inventors' patents.

Great Britain led mechanical inventions with Watt's steam engine in 1765, which converted chemical energy in coal into thermal one and then into mechanical one to power locomotives. The proximity to coal was an unexpected benefit that facilitated the widespread adoption of machines, which replaced human powers by working faster, diminishing the reliance on human power.

This is called **the First Industrial Revolution.**

In the 17th and 18th centuries, coffeehouses in England served as public social places where men gathered to converse and conduct business. Apart from caffeinated beverages, they offered the latest news and a platform for vibrant debate. The upsurge in information and intelligence cultivated a seedbed conducive to the businesses crucial for the Industrial Revolution.

In the 18th century, China, India, and England were urbanized and commercialized. While China and India developed their industries based on land resources, England leveraged its proximity to coal to power mass production and profit from its colonies. The naval force parliamentary democracy, and advanced technology of England contributed to Pax Britannica (1815-1914).

The Little Ice Age (14th-19th century) affected outdoor production in China and India, while mass production in England was sheltered in indoor factories. The Industrial Revolution developed rapidly and mass education began. The social infrastructure was reinforced by the mechanical revolution.

In the early 19th century, industrial vitality brought mixed consequences: on one hand, it fostered civil and intellectual development and improved living standards; on the other hand, it incited political convulsions of class struggle, flexed muscles for imperial interests, and engendered imperial contention which was one of the causes that triggered WW I and WW II.

The Industrial Revolution in England was not predetermined or inevitable, but rather it was contingent and accidental, shaped by the proximity of coal, climate changes, and a well-established tangible and intangible infrastructure. It may explain the origins, development, and outcomes of the Revolution over 300 years (1500s-1800s).

The English supremacy at sea was made with maritime revolution in the naval architecture, training and organizational competence: the English built heavy and more powerful vessels so that the newly-designed vessels delivered concentrated firepower and resisted it, training naval tactics systematically based on learnings from the past and they were shared and digested to make the navy best in the world, and maximize organizational competence by transparency of meritocratic system without favoritism and partiality in promotion in grades and sharing of spoils in accordance with pre-set regulations. It was not long before the reforms brought rewards dovetailing with build-up of a stronger trading position in Asia, Caribbean and India.

England, the island in the North Atlantic, was inhabited by Britons whose name was speculated to come from the Latin brutus, that is, irrational or stupid. Separated from the rest of Europe by the Channel, it was distant, isolated and peripheral. The maritime power helped them turn the weakness into formidable strength of one of the greatest empires in history.

This is called **the Second Industrial Revolution.**

The Second Industrial Revolution cut both ways: it brought sufficiency and surplus in the living of the people by global competition for industrialization and wealth in full swing, but it also caused polarity and environmental disasters which cast a long shadow over the people. The burned fossil fuels that the industrial revolutions emitted warmed the globe. It caused a variety of effects that created a gap between the benefits accrued by rich emitters and the damages suffered by poorer non-emitters.

There is an argument in inter-governmental negotiations on climate change and it revolves around accountability: should industrialized states, more responsible for emissions, bear the financial burden, or should all countries pay equal amounts, given the global nature of climate change?

Amid the acceleration of industrialization and the industrial activities had been advancing, there were a series of technological innovations in the 1970s-1980s, which brought about profound changes in production organization. These innovations centered on information technology, biotechnology, telecommunications, and energy engineering. The physical aspects of the earlier industrial revolutions were turned into intangible forms.

The changes led to significant societal transformations in the 20th century. Multinational companies emerged, excelling in administration, production, and marketing. Technological development enhanced productivity through automation and information technology.

This is called **the Third Industrial Revolution.**

In the late 20th century, a new industrial revolution emerged, and within a few decades, it introduced a new way of working, living, and interacting. Technological advancements have impacted a number of areas, including human-machine interaction, robotics, humanoids, 3D printing, artificial intelligence (AI), the Internet of Things (IoT), big data, and cloud computing.

These developments present both significant opportunities and potential risks. While technological innovations can lead to enhanced industrial productivity and economic growth, they may also pose risks to employment, human autonomy, and the integrity of transactions in society.

The latest revolution has given rise to the creation of non-human brains that transcend the boundaries of human intelligence. As humans who once controlled the material world now find themselves competing against these non-human intelligences, there are concerns about becoming inferior or subjugated by their own creations.

Amid this revolution, mobility is of the essence, which never allows the hierarchical and static order to prevail in the world as it had done before. Mobility will upend the roles and responsibilities of the established structure. It remains to be seen if humanity will be able to adapt to this new reality and maintain its status as the supreme entity in charge of man-made creatures.

This is called **the Fourth Industrial Revolution.**

6) The Power of Non-Violence

The advancement of democracy in Western capitalist states has blunted the force of resistance by offering constitutional means to redress grievances, making them accessible to those who were denied democratic rights. Such means were established from classic liberal ideals that opposition to arbitrary power is a right of all individuals.

The French Revolution in 1789 imbued with equality, freedom, and fraternity, along with the Chartist movement in Britain from 1838 to 1848, exemplified efforts to redress grievances, even as many other revolts failed to achieve their goals.

The term pacifists emerged in the 19th century to refer to those who renounced violence in response to aggression. They adopted non-violence as a strategy, choosing to endure aggression without retaliation, engage in peaceful disputes, and confront authority without using violence.

There are underlying reasons for embracing non-violence. Underdogs would lose more than victors when violence occurs, and non-violence would be a more effective countermeasure to achieve goals. The non-violent movement urged non-participation in the violent deeds of domineering authorities such as administration, law courts, tax office, or soldiering.

Mohandas Gandhi (1869-1948) was a lawyer and civil rights activist in South Africa for 21 years (1893–1914). Gandhi's Pacifism was shaped by his experiences in South Africa, where he witnessed virulent racism and violence. His attitude, his beliefs, and his ideologies of pacifism were deeply influenced by these encounters.

It was astonishing that more than two hundred million people, morally lofty and historically rich, found themselves subjugated by a small group whose values were alien to them. One might argue that it was not the English who enslaved the Indians, but rather the Indians who permitted their own enslavement.

Gandhi sought to lead his life in ascetic ways and to bring himself closer to the poor. His philosophy involved a combination of courage and discipline to endure the overwhelm of those who relied on violent means. He argued against the notion that the end justifies the means because violent methods could never lead to a peaceful resolution.

All this was combined with a shrewd political sensibility. Gandhi had a gift for putting his opponents on the defensive, not only by claiming the moral high ground but also by framing issues in ways that made it difficult for the British to respond effectively – whether through violent repression of peaceful protests or by forbidding such protests altogether.

At a time of brutality and upheaval across the world, Gandhi stood out as a leader who personified dignity and goodness in the simplicity of his dress and diet. His spiritual message resonated with people in both India and Britain. At the same time, he managed to forge an authentic and successful mass movement.

Gandhi took familiar tactics of the underdogs - marches, strikes, and boycotts - and employed them as part of a grander narrative. His approach appealed to the better instincts of his opponents, encouraging reconciliation. Such a tactic of drawing favorable responses kept the door open for agreement.

In Western contexts, an agreement was customarily reached by stopping the violence. Gandhi's way of seeking resolution through non-violence was noble yet unfamiliar to the British. It was not until after WW II that such methods gained acceptance, leading to remarkably successful campaigns.

He urged his people to see non-violence as another type of weapon, an innovative approach to struggle that allowed for conflict without violence.

PART 5

5.1. The 20th Century (Hope and Horror)

1) Summary

The 20th century began with great fanfare about the inevitability of progress, growing democratization, promised equality, and all-round prosperity. Globalization had become an article of faith. It appeared in the form of the speedy circulation of information, germs, people, and commodities (however if the concept of globalization is taken as the process by which markets, politics, values, and environmental change are integrated across the globe, globalization may be dated back to 1521 with the circumnavigation of the globe. (Robert Marks, *The Origin of Modern World*, p214).

Yet the reality of life for vast sections of humanity was at various points in the century as horrific as any known in history. The forward march of progress gave rise to the bloodletting of World War One ("WWI"), the mass impoverishment of the early 1930s, the spread of Nazism and fascism over most of Europe, the Stalinist Gulag, and his absolute dictatorship.

The Japanese atrocities in Asian countries, the devastation of much of Europe between the 1940s and 1945, the Bengal famine in 1943 with deaths of some three million people; the obliteration of Hiroshima and Nagasaki; the sanguinary Korean War for three years after the World War Two ("WWII") with numerous atrocities and massacres of civilians reaching up to three million.

The 30-year war against Vietnam and the nine-year war against Algeria, the million dead in one Gulf War at the beginning 1990s, tens of thousands killed by death squads in El Salvador, Guatemala, and Argentina, and hundreds of thousands of dead in the bloody civil wars of Croatia, Bosnia, Tajikistan, Angola, Ethiopia, Liberia, Sierra Leone and Afghanistan.

Western European states were dislodged from global dominance in the 1950s. New industries developed in the fields of automobiles, electricity, electronics, media, airplanes, space travel, and home appliances. There was technological change, economic development, population increase, and environmental concerns. New diseases and inoculations changed the world, too.

2) WW I (28 July 1914-11 November 1918)

WW I, also known as the Great War, was an imperial conflict that spanned approximately four years and resulted in approximately 20 million casualties, including military and civilian deaths. The war had a profound impact on the imperialist order of the late nineteenth century, setting in motion a series of events that shaped the course of the twentieth century as a century of conflict and upheaval.

The competition for military strength, driven by imperial rivalry, was a key factor in the outbreak of war in 1914. The Allied forces were formed as a coalition of the Triple Entente, comprising France, the United Kingdom, and Russia. In 1904, the Anglo-French pact addressed issues related to Egypt and Morocco. In 1907, the Anglo-Russian Entente addressed issues related to Persia, Afghanistan, and Tibet.

The Ententes aimed to define their respective spheres of influence, while simultaneously fostering a stronger alliance among the parties involved. The Allied forces were France, the UK, Russia, the United

States, and Japan. The opposing side was the Central Powers, which included Germany, Austria-Hungary, and Italy.

Following the Russian defeat by Japan in the Russo-Japanese War (1904-1905), Russian interests shifted towards relations with the Ottoman Empire in Southeast Europe. The Central Powers were subsequently aligned with Germany, Austria-Hungary, the Ottoman Empire, Italy and Bulgaria.

The First World War was an imperial conflict in which all the states and empires under the respective alliances were involved between 1914 and 1915. The outbreak of hostilities was long feared, but it missed opportunities for peace in the atmosphere that the world slipped towards war not in the gung-ho bravado but of anxiety and misunderstanding. The First World War was characterized by a prolonged stalemate on the Western Front. However, the conflict saw the deployment of new technologies, including machine guns, tanks, aircraft, submarines, poison gas, and trench warfare, which resulted in unprecedented casualties. The war bankrupted the old world and enriched the new world.

The Russian monarchy collapsed in March 1917, leading to the Bolshevik Revolution in November 1917. This was followed by a further military defeat of Russia. On 3 March 1918, the Russian government was forced to accept the Treaty of Brest-Litovsk with the Central Powers. This treaty granted the Germans control of the territory of western Russia, Belarus, the Baltic States, Poland, Ukraine, and the Black Sea.

On 8 January 1918, in a speech on War Aims and Peace Terms, President Wilson set out the 14 points designed to undermine the Central Powers' will to continue the war, to inspire the Allies to victory, and to frame a new international world order after the war. Four focal points were selected from the 14 points:

II. Absolute freedom of navigation upon the seas, outside territorial waters, alike in peace and in war, except as the seas may be closed in whole or in part by international action for the enforcement of international covenants.

III. The removal, as far as possible, of all economic barriers and the establishment of an equality of trade conditions among all the nations consenting to the peace and associating themselves for its maintenance.

V. A free, open-minded, and absolutely impartial adjustment of all colonial claims, based on a strict observance of the principle that in determining such questions of sovereignty the interests of the populations concerned must carry equal weight with the equitable claims of the government whose title is to be determined.

XIV. A general association of nations must be formed under specific covenants for the purpose of providing mutual guarantees of political independence and territorial integrity to both great and small states alike.

Points V and XIV asserted the right to political independence and territorial integrity, which he believed guaranteed that all peoples and nationalities had the right to live in a fair and just manner with one another. While there is no specific description of self-determination in his speech, he deliberately inferred his ideal of national self-determination.

Without the requisite evidence to substantiate his ideal, the statement misled numerous petitions and lobbies from colonial inhabitants who mistakenly understood it as an opportunity to seek their imminent emancipation. The petitions were never satisfied, and the following year saw widespread protests against the imperial rule of the victorious.

Despite his best efforts, President Wilson was unable to gain the support of the Allied powers for his proposals for world peace. At Versailles, the UK, France, and Italy were primarily focused on reclaiming lost territory and securing additional gains through punitive measures against Germany. They swiftly recognized that Wilson's vision for global peace would not apply to them.

The British and French delegations were successful in persuading Woodrow Wilson to remove the reference to self-determination from the draft Covenant of the League of Nations organizations. Instead, a commitment to the territorial integrity and political independence of existing states was included.

On the morning of 11 November 1918, the Allied Powers and the Central Powers agreed to cease hostilities on general terms dictated by the Allies. The Germans were in no position to refuse to sign, and the peace treaty was finalized after more than six months. The British government sought to use Germany as a buffer against Communism, the United States devised a long-lasting peace plan for Europe without American involvement, and France aimed to regain its former status at the expense of Germany.

The parties involved had disparate objectives in the conflicts that were incorporated into the Treaty of Versailles. Two decades later, however, the reality was that an ideology far more frightening than communism surfaced, another atrocious war returned, the US was involved in the war in Europe again, and France had to pay a high price for its revenge on Germany.

The Treaty of Versailles was signed on 28 June 1919. The defeated German Empire was treated punitively. France, Poland, Denmark, Belgium, and Czechoslovakia were all granted territory that they had previously claimed. The industrially important Alsace-Lorraine in Rhineland was demilitarized and occupied by Allied forces for the following fifteen years. Germany's colonies in Asia and Africa were distributed among several Allied countries.

The treaty specifically prohibited Germany from rebuilding its military capabilities. It limited the size of the German army to 100,000, restricted the tonnage of the German navy, and forbade the establishment of an armed air force. It is possible that the terms would have been more severe if Britain had not been in favor of ensuring that Germany remained a strong nation with the capacity to resist the spread of communism from Russia.

Article 231 of the Treaty, otherwise known as the Guilt Clause, stated that Germany was liable for all losses and damages incurred by the Allies. Concerning the level of reparations, the United Kingdom and the United States of America sought to ensure that the burden was not excessive, to avoid the destruction of the German economy and the potential for political and social unrest. Nevertheless, the total amount was set at $53.7 billion, which was subsequently reduced to $31.4 billion two years later. At that time, Germany was unable to repay the amount.

The German population was incensed by the terms of the treaty. The German people were humiliated by the defeat and the punitive nature of the terms in the Treaty, and as a result, they held the German left and others responsible. It was believed that the German Army did not lose WWI on the battlefield but was instead betrayed by a number of factors, including the actions of Jews and socialists who had fomented strikes, republican politicians, and had overthrown the House of Hohenzollern in the German Revolution of 1918–1919. It was perceived as an act of betrayal.

Despite the negative response from the German people, the Weimar Republic was unable to declare the flawed Treaty of Versailles void ab initio, because it lacked the capacity to defy the coercion. The terms of the Treaty inadvertently created the conditions that led to the Second World War. In this regard, the Allies erred in their approach by creating the conditions for further conflict rather than establishing a lasting peace.

3) Consequential loss and damages

The discrepancy between the success on the Eastern Front (the Treaty of Brest-Litovsk on March 3, 1918) and the stab-in-the-back myth regarding the defeat of the war led to contention among the Germans, including Adolf Hitler, who was angered by the conspiratorial German social-democratic revolutionaries and Jews who were perceived as ill-intended schemers.

Concerning the issue of dealing with the colonies, there was a significant discrepancy between the intentions of the Allies (who sought to retain their colonial interests) and the aspirations of the colonized people (who sought emancipation from colonial rule). This resulted in adverse consequences with high casualties among the colonized people.

This provides a clear illustration of how individuals in a desperate situation can misinterpret declarative statements made by a leader of a powerful nation, which may have been made solely for the sake of appearances without any tangible substance or determined will from the powerful nations involved. The misperception resulted in a desperate campaign by the people, and there was no assistance provided.

In 1919, anti-British riots in India resulted in over a thousand fatalities and the exile of numerous individuals. This was followed by the non-violent Egyptian Revolution, which led to the deaths of at least 800 people.

The situation in Korea in 1919 was significantly worse. The nationwide non-violent demonstrations calling for independence were met with a brutal crackdown by Japanese colonial authorities resulting in approximately seven thousand civilian deaths and forty-six thousand arrests, many of which were subjected to torture and died due to harsh conditions during incarceration. The crass actions of the imperial powers were the epitome of the atrocities committed against those seeking self-determination.

The Declaration of Independence, issued on March 1, 1919, took the Wilsonian principles of self-determination by the colonized people in the wrong perception (as specified in bold in the declaration statement below). Despite the noble intentions to pursue self-determination, it proved to be an unattainable ideal. The wrong perception of the desperate desire to get external support helped cause lots of deaths, torture, and exile of the people instead of emancipation from colonial rule and restoration of sovereignty.

The independence movement seized upon the opportune moment in the new beginning of the international environment after WW I, but it was spasmodic brief and ineffective in securing independence. Japanese colonial rule was too powerful for the non-violent resisters in Korea to draw independence from Japan which seized its own opportunity to expand its sphere of influence in China beyond Korea and to gain recognition as a great power in postwar geopolitics as a member of the victorious Allies in the WW I.

The Declaration of Independence on 1 March 1919

We hereby announce that the Republic of Korea is an independent nation-state, and its citizens are sovereign to the state. Furthermore, we proclaim this to all nations of the world in order to demonstrate our commitment to the cause of universal equality of humankind. We also instruct our posterity to retain the sovereign nationhood in perpetuity.

We make this proclamation based on the rich history of our nation, spanning five thousand years. We represent the collective voice of twenty million people, calling for the unhindered growth and advancement of our people. We are taking our rightful place at the table, contributing to the global shift towards a more interconnected and diverse world. These actions align with the global trend of our age and are in line with the righteous drive for the symbiotic existence of all humankind. We are confident that nothing in the world will deter or suppress them.

Over the past decade, we have experienced significant challenges due to external pressures. Our long history of over a thousand years has been marked by foreign domination and aggression, a legacy inherited from previous regimes. To what extent have we been denied our fundamental right to exist? To what extent have we been hindered in our intellectual development? To what extent has our national reputation been damaged? And how many times have we missed the chance to make a valuable contribution to the global landscape by advancing our creativity and expertise?

The primary objective is to ensure our national independence. This will enable us to address past injustices, overcome current challenges, and protect our future interests. It will also allow us to invigorate and elevate the national conscience. Integrity and righteousness are essential for achieving individual development, avoiding a disgraceful inheritance for future generations, and fostering long-lasting joy.

Today, we have a clear vision and a strong commitment to our mission. We are guided by the values of humanity and the conscience of our time, and we are building an army of justice and a weapon of humanism. We have the capability to engage and defeat any formidable opponents, and we may choose to withdraw and regroup, as well as execute any strategic maneuvers.

We do not view Japan as untrustworthy due to their repeated violations of the 1876 treaty. We do not blame Japan for being narrow-minded. Both its scholars and politicians have sought to please the conqueror by viewing our ancestral patrimony through a colonial lens. They have also disparaged our cultured people as primitive savages and disregarded our lasting social foundations and outstanding character.

We are focused on future-oriented initiatives and unable to devote resources to addressing past issues with Japan.

Our primary objective is to enhance our own capabilities, not to undermine those of others. In accordance with the directive of conscience, we must cultivate a new civilization. We do not exclude others on the basis of past resentment and emotion. In light of the unnatural and irrational situation caused by enterprising Japanese politicians who are constrained by outdated ideas and antiquated powers, we are striving to enhance and rectify it so that it aligns with the natural and rational condition of right principles and grand principles.

The initial action of Japan in annexing Korea was contrary to the intentions of the Korean people. This has now resulted in a number of issues, including the use of coercive measures, discriminatory practices, and statistical inaccuracies. It is evident that irreconcilable hatred is gradually deepening between nations with conflicting interests. It is clear that a two-pronged approach is required: firstly, to acknowledge and address past mistakes, and secondly, to initiate a new, conciliatory phase based on mutual understanding and sympathy. This will help to avert potential disasters and foster a positive relationship between the two nations.

It is clear that the current situation, in which twenty million Korean people are confined, and their anger and hatred are intensifying, cannot guarantee lasting peace in the East. Furthermore, it will inevitably intensify apprehension and misgivings towards Japan among the 400 million Chinese people, who are a crucial element in maintaining regional security. The result will be a catastrophic collapse of the entire Eastern region.

The independence of Korea is designed to enable the Korean people to enjoy a prosperous lifestyle, to provide the Japanese with a valuable opportunity to support the Oriental world, to offer the Chinese a path out of their current difficulties, and to establish a foundation for global peace and the happiness of all humans. These factors are not limited to trivial matters or shallow emotions.

Hurrah! We are pleased to announce that we have reached a significant milestone. ***A new era is upon us. The era of power-driven suppression has come to a close, and a new era focused on humanism and justice has begun. The humanitarian mentality that was developed and nurtured over the course of the last century is now beginning to shed light on human history. A new spring is emerging around the world, stimulating a wave of revitalization.***

In the past, we faced significant challenges due to harsh circumstances. ***However, we are now in a position to express our views clearly in a positive and supportive environment. As we respect the global order and navigate the evolving landscape, we have no reason to hesitate or be afraid. We will achieve prosperity by protecting our inalienable right to freedom and by demonstrating our substantial creativity in the favorable atmosphere.*** *We are committed to upholding our principles and advancing together with integrity. All generations and genders are rising to the occasion, leaving behind the challenges of the past and working together to drive our collective revival. The wisdom of our ancestors will guide us internally, while* ***global powers and prevailing global trends will protect us externally.*** *We have reached the midway point and are moving forward with determination towards our goal.*

We hereby pledge the following three points:

1. Our demonstration today is a national demand for justice, humanism, and prosperity. We pledge to demonstrate the spirit of freedom and to never exclude others.

2. Express the just will of the Korean people to all relevant parties until the task is complete.

3. It is essential that we maintain clarity and righteousness in our cause and attitude, and that we conduct the demonstration in an orderly manner.

4) Partitions of Poland

The intent to deal with the partitions of Poland is that they are among the most relevant cases of imperialistic exploitation for such a long period, and it shows the unyielding determination of the Polish people to endure the vicissitudes of fate and to preserve its sovereignty in the face of such virulently hostile neighbors.

In the history of the European Continent, nothing would be more relevant than forced partitions in the strain of imperial powers than the partitions of Poland. Poland has been in Central Europe surrounded by Germany and Russia which have incessantly harassed the Polish in the invasions of the two forces, such as eastward Germanification and westward Russification.

When the scope of suffering is confined to the history since the 18th century, the Polish have struggled against Russia, Prussian, and Austria with three partitions in 1772, 1793, and 1795 that had progressively reduced the size of Poland until, after the final partition in 1795, the State of Poland ceased to exist on the world map for more than one hundred years.

From the Russian perspective, Russia needed to absorb Poland because Russia couldn't allow any capitalistic state that was hostile to Russia. Unless Poland was not occupied by Russia, Poland then must have remained a buffer zone between Russia and the Western powers that was ruled by a pro-Russian state, at least.

The partition from 1939-1944 by the Nazi-Russo Non-Aggression Pact, and the development after WW II placed Poland as one of the pro-Soviet buffer-zone, the so-called Eastern Bloc comprised of Poland, East Germany, Czechoslovakia, Hungary, Romania, Bulgaria, and Albania in the Central and Eastern Europe.

Meanwhile, considering the perennial threat from hostile countries in the neighborhood, the constant afflictions from forced partitions and occupations, and the persistent resistance even in the process of bearing the brunt of invasions, Poland has much in common with Korea although both countries have had little to overlap and interact until modern history.

The Soviet Union asserted that the Korean Peninsula should remain a pro-Soviet buffer zone as it did to Poland, Finland, and Romania. It never allowed for a possibility that a unified capitalistic Korean government posed a threat, or it should become a springboard to attack the Soviets. That was one of the reasons that the Soviets supported the pro-Soviet North Korea to invade South Korea in 1950.

(1) The First Partition in 1772

It was the beginning of the end for the Polish-Lithuanian Commonwealth (1569–1795). The First Partition occurred after Russia became involved in a war against the Ottoman Turks (1768) and won such impressive victories that Austria became alarmed and threatened to enter the war against Russia.

Frederick the Great (1672-1725) of Prussia, however, was determined to calm the Austro-Russian tension by shifting the direction of Russia's expansion from the Turkish provinces to Poland, which had been structurally weak because it had been devastated by civil war and Russian intervention since 1768, and was, therefore, incapable of resisting violent territorial seizures.

As Poland was such an easy target to pillage, so Russia, Prussia, and Austria helped themselves at the expense of Poland by signing the treaty on 5 August 1772 at St. Petersburg to partition Poland. Stanislaw II (r.1764-1795, the last monarch of the Polish–Lithuanian Commonwealth) asked for help from the Western powers, but they ignored him.

Russia took the Polish territory roughly east of the Dvina and Dnieper rivers. Prussia gained the economically valuable northwestern provinces and gained control of the Polish foreign trade. Austria acquired the regions south of the Vistula River and the area that was later known as Galicia. Russia, Prussia, and Austria were busy devouring their ill-gotten gains.

(2) The Second Partition in 1793

After the First Partition, Poland strengthened itself through reforms, for example, the adoption of a liberal constitution in 1791 to level the society between commoners and nobility. That reform formed the conservative Confederation in 1792, and it asked Russia to intervene and stop the reform. Russia did it and Prussia also sent troops to Poland to suppress the reform.

The two powers agreed upon the partition of Poland which was confirmed in 1793 by the Polish Sejm surrounded by Russian troops. The Second Partition transferred to Russia Lithuanian Belorussia and Ukraine, and it also allowed Prussia to grab Gdańsk and Greater Poland. The partition reduced Poland to a fraction of its former self.

(3) The Third Partition on 24 October 1795

After the Second Partition, the Polish officer Tadeusz Kościuszko led a national uprising in 1794, but the Poles were powerless to resist the renewed invasion of Russia without support from the French revolutionary force. In November 1794, Russian troops killed up to 20,000 Polish civilians and military in a single day in Praga near Warsaw (the Praga Massacre).

Russia and Prussia concluded an agreement with Austria that divided the remnants of Poland between themselves. It was the last in a series of partitions of Poland–Lithuania by and among Prussia, Austria, and the Russian Empire which literally and effectively ended Polish–Lithuanian national sovereignty (1569–1795) and erased it off the map.

(4) The Fourth Partition in WW II

These territorial divisions were altered in 1807, when Emperor Napoleon of France created the Duchy of Warsaw from the central provinces of Prussian Poland, and again in 1815 when the Congress of Vienna created the Congress Kingdom of Poland. However, the loss of sovereignty was fully restored on 11 November 1918 after the First World War.

The Polish-Soviet War of 1919-1920 revealed a discrepancy in ideology. The Poles were opposed to the atheist Marxism-Leninism, which called for the abolition of religion, private enterprise, and the bourgeoisie, while the Polish Republic was a parliamentary democracy with the church, private property, and class interests.

It was also a Polish defiance of the Bolsheviks, who were trying to spread the Bolshevik revolution to Europe, specifically marching through Poland to reach Germany. In November 1918, Józef Klemens Piłsudski was appointed Commander-in-Chief of the Polish Armed Forces of the newly established Polish Republic and led six wars that redefined Poland's borders.

On 4 July 1920 the Russian army launched its offensive with phenomenal speed. By August, Russian cavalry had reached the Vistula, just five days' march from Berlin. On the verge of defeat, the Polish forces acquitted itself with distinction by launching a counter-attack on the southern flank, driving back five Russian armies, three of which were destroyed and one of which took refuge in East Prussia.

During the war, the Polish Cavalry Army took part in most of the battles, including a cavalry battle at Komarów in south-eastern Poland on 31 August 1920. It was the last great cavalry battle in European history, with around 20,000 horsemen charging and countercharging in full formation until the Polish Cavalry completely crushed the Soviet 1st Cavalry Army.

After the Red Army lost its first war, Lenin sued for peace and on 18 March 1921 signed the Treaty of Riga. It stipulated that Poland would receive financial compensation for its economic contribution to the Russian Empire during the partition of Poland. Russia was to hand over works of art and other national treasures taken from Polish territories after 1772 (the First Partition).

The Polish victory was a vindication for Poland, and it also dashed the Soviet hope of a communist revolution in Europe after the Bolshevik Revolution of 1917. In terms of protecting Western liberal culture, the Polish victory could be compared to the victory of the Frankish army at the Battle of Tours in 732, which halted the advance of Islam into Western Europe.

For reference, we look at the clash between Europe and the Arabs up to the Battle of Tours. Islam spread rapidly in all directions after the death of Muhammad in 632. Islamic forces reached North Africa in 709, besieged Constantinople in 717, conquered Barcelona in 719, and France was naturally next in line. It was a medieval blitzkrieg that crushed all who stood in its way.

The conflict never ended. The Battle of Vienna in 1683 marked the first joint military action by the Polish-Lithuanian Commonwealth and the Holy Roman Empire against the Islamic invasion of the Ottomans. It was also seen as a point of protection for Western European culture, after which the Ottomans ceased to be a threat to the Christian world. The long-standing confrontation created a destructive habit in the Islamic world of blaming its ills on imperialism, Jews, and various bogeymen, and conversely, an unwarranted suspicion and belittling of Arab Muslims by Westerners.

During the peace and war of the Nazi-Soviet regimes, Poland underwent another round of partition by and between Nazi Germany and Soviet Russia in 1939-1945. The Eastern Question was, from the late 18th to the early 20th century, the question of how to deal with political and economic instability in the situation following the collapse of the Ottoman Empire.

In this unstable situation, the European powers competed according to their own political strategies. The Russian Empire continued to expand its influence in Poland, while Hitler's National Socialists were repulsed by the Treaty of Versailles, which forced Germany to give up its occupied territories in Poland, Belarus, Ukraine, and the Baltic region in 1918.

The sense of loss deepened when they saw the vast colonial territories of France and Britain. Germany had a certain obsession with the East, seeing it as a living space, a Lebensraum, which to some extent compensated for the sense of loss. For Germany, the Soviets advancing into the East, including Poland, were an illegitimate and oppressive enemy.

Poland could not free itself from the existential threat of Nazi-Soviet aggression either on its own or in an effective alliance with other Western powers, nor did it have the military power to repel the attack. The fact that the Soviets and Nazis expanded while Poland was unable to defend itself is crucial to understanding the Eastern Front, which involved Poland, Ukraine, and Russia.

Poland was again divided and even moved: the Nazi-Soviet partition of Poland in 1939, the Teheran Declaration of 1 December 1943 by the Allies (US, UK, and Soviet), which reduced German territory, moved the Polish border northwest, and the Soviet Union took the space that Poland had moved out. The agreement was ratified at the Potsdam Conference on 26 July 1945.

These three countries (Poland, Ukraine, Belarus) are closely related to Russia from different angles: Poland is a bastion of NATO in the face of Russia, Ukraine is currently at war with Russia (as of September 2024), Belarus is under the influence of Russia, while Germany is a backbone of NATO Europe supporting Ukraine in its war with Russia. It is being, as of October 2024. More complicated with the news that North Korea dispatched its military force to Ukraine to support Russia's war with Ukraine.

5.2. 20th century in WW II (Climax of confrontations)

1) WW II Chronology

WW II was the global conflict that involved virtually every part of the world during the years 1939–45 between the Allies—France, Great Britain, the United States, the Soviet Union, and, to a lesser extent, China, and the Axis powers—Germany, Italy, and Japan. The war ended up with 40-50 million of human losses with the collapse of Nazi Germany and Imperial Japan and gave rise to the Cold War between the U.S. and the Soviet Union.

Again, this book is not aimed at historical knowledge, but at taking references for learning, action, and connection of the people, especially young adults. The chronological descriptions are the minimum of knowledge on WW II for practical purposes:

11 November 1918: After the Treaty of Versailles on 28 June 1919, ending the state of war, the armistice was signed to end WW I.

5 January 1919: DAP (*Deutsche Arbeiterpartei*, German Workers' Party) was formed in Munich and Adolf Hitler joined it. DAP was changed to NSDAP (*Nationalsozialistische Deutsche Arbeiterpartei* or Nazi. National Socialist German Workers' Party in English)

28 January 1923: The first Nazi Party rallies (Nuremberg rallies) announced the slogan *Deutschland Erwache* (Germany Awake) in the form of mass gatherings and discipline parades, which became the routine norm of the Nazis.

8 November 1923: Hitler and his aides, Göring, Hess, and Himmler failed to pull off a military coup to overthrow the Weimar Republic (*Munich Putsch*) by which Hitler was convicted and, on 1 April 1924, sentenced to five year-imprisonment.

20 December 1924: Adolf Hitler was released from prison after serving only nine months during which he dictated the first volume of *Mein Kamp* (My Fight).

27 February 1933: Marinus van der Lubbe, a Dutch communist, was executed for allegedly setting fire to

the German *Reichstag* (Parliament). The fire opened the road for Nazis to abolish constitutional protections for people and paved the way for Nazi dictatorship. Lubbe was found not responsible for the fire and was given a posthumous pardon.

30 January 1933: Ex-chancellor Franz von Papen persuaded the President, Paul Von Hindenburg, to appoint Hitler Chancellor of Germany. After President Hindenburg died on 2 August 1934, Hitler wielded dictatorial powers to build the Nazi regime and rearm Germany.

9-10 November 1938: *Kristallnacht* (The Night of Broken Glass), a pogrom against Jews by the *Nazi Sturmabteilung* (SA, Storm Troopers).

23 August 1939: Nazi Germany and the Soviet Union signed the Treaty of Non-Aggression. It agreed to take no military action against each other for the next 10 years, but it was broken within less than two years by partitioning Poland.

1 September 1939: Germany invaded Poland after the failed attempt by Lord Chamberlain of Britain to prevent it. This triggered Britain and France to declare war on Germany on 3 September 1939 and Poland surrendered on 27 September.

10 May 1940: Germany invaded Western Europe, the neutral Belgium, Luxembourg, the Netherlands, and France. France surrendered on 22 June. Hitler set the scene of the armistice at Ferdinand Foch's railway car in Compiègne in northern France. It was a revenge of Germany for its surrender to France after WW I.

22 June 1941: Germany invaded the Soviet Union at its peak. The war ended with its demise on 30 April 1945 on which Hitler killed himself. Germany believed that the Soviet's demise was the sine qua non of the Nazis's lasting survival. It was the life-and-death total war between radical Fascism and Bolshevism leaving 14 million dead and 8 million captured by armed forces, and 20 million dead civilians. Hitler and his advisers blew hot and cold over the thorny questions of making advance to Moscow.

7 December 1941: The Japanese attack on the American Pacific Fleet at Pearl Harbor. It triggered the US to declare war on Japan the next day. The second battlefield of WW II opened in the Asia and Pacific adding to China. Japan provoked the war in a no-win set of conditions in terms of its weaker capacity to meet the needs of war efforts than the U.S..

20 January 1942: The clandestine conference of Nazis (*Wannseekonferenz*) confirmed the *Endlösung der Judenfrage* (Final Solution to the Jewish Problem) to eliminate Jews in Europe. This was the basis of the Holocaust that caused six million Jewish deaths in WW II.

17 July 1942 to 2 February 1943: An event of turning point of WW II. Nazi Germany lost the deadliest Battle of Stalingrad marked by fierce close-quarters combat, direct assaults on civilians, and the epitome of urban warfare leaving about two million casualties. The defeat made the German forces change from offensive operations to defensive ones all the way through to Berlin. With the benefit of hindsight, what if Hitler had started Operation Barbarossa a few months earlier to avoid the inclement winter weather in Russia which had halted the advance of German forces within the striking distance of Moscow? Or what if Hitler bypassed Stalingrad and let his Army Group Center push forward to Moscow in full formation at full speed while a part of the Army Group South kept Stalingrad at bay?

7 August 1942 to 9 February 1943: An event of turning point of WW II. The Battle of Guadalcanal in the southern Solomon Island in which American forces dealt a crushing blow to the Combined Fleet of the

Japanese navy and the pride of the Japanese army. It was a watershed in the Pacific War, allowing the U.S. Navy and Air Force to conduct their island-hopping operations toward mainland Japan.

23 October to 11 November 1942: A turning point in WW II. The Second Battle of El Alamein in Egypt in which the British victory eliminated the Axis threat to the Suez Canal and the Middle Eastern and Persian oil fields.

18 February 1943: German Propaganda Minister Joseph Goebbels gave the speech on Total War in Berlin as the tide of WW II was turning against the Nazis. He mentioned the Holocaust when he began saying *Ausrotten* (extermination), but quickly changed it to *Ausschaltung* (exclusion).

14 January 1944: The Soviet Army lifted the siege of Leningrad after which Soviet forces began in all sectors of the Eastern Front to drive the German forces out of the Soviet homeland.

6 June 1944: Operation Overlord of the Allies was carried out by landing on Normandy which had finally opened two fronts, the Western Front and the Eastern Front. For Germany, it was the least wanted war situation. What if Germany had managed to fight on a single front by subduing Britain or the Soviet Union before the Normandy landing? Then WW II would have developed in a direction much different from reality.

25 August 1944: Paris was liberated as the German forces surrendered Paris to the Allied defying the order of Hitler to demolish the French capital before the surrender.

16 December 1944 to 16 January 1945: The Battle of the Bulge was the last major German offensive campaign on the Western Front, which temporarily pushed back the winter advance of the Allies toward Berlin.

27 January 1945: Auschwitz was liberated by the Red Army rescuing about 7,000 prisoners who were seriously ill due to the inhumane imprisonment conditions.

16 April 16 to 2 May 1945: The Battle of Berlin marked the end of WW II and the Nazis as the Red Army attacked Berlin from all directions. The Nazis made their last ground under the operation of Operation Clausewitz, named after a Prussian general and military theorist who had been well known for his war strategy of total war.

30 April 1945: Hitler and his wife Eva Braun committed suicide after he dictated his last will and appointed Joseph Goebbels Reich Chancellor and Grand Admiral Karl Dönitz as Reich President of the Third Reich.

7 May 1945: Germany surrendered unconditionally to the Allies at the Western Allied Headquarters in Rheims, France, and with orders from Reich President Karl Dönitz, General Alfred Jodl signed for Germany.

6-9 August 1945: The American bombers dropped the world's first atomic bombs on Hiroshima (about 80,000 people dead) and Nagasaki (about 40,000 people dead).

15 August 1945: Japan's Emperor Hirohito announced his country's unconditional surrender in a radio address.

2 September 1945: WW II ended as Japan formalized the surrender of the Empire of Japan to the Allied on the deck of the USS Missouri in Tokyo Bay.

Post-WW II:

The Nuremberg trials, held by the Allies on 1 October 1946, convicted 19 of the defendants and acquitted three. 12 were sentenced to death and 3 to life imprisonment, 4 to imprisonment from 10 to 20 years. On October 16, executions were carried out by hanging. Hermann Göring committed suicide the night before his execution.

The Tokyo War Criminal Court sentenced 7 to death for war crimes and 16 to life imprisonment.

The massive Marshall Plan to rebuild war-torn European countries after the war was put in place. The U.S. aided Europe in the Marshall Plan after the war as it did through the Lend-Lease Act during the war.

2) WW II before the Nazi-Soviet War (22 June 1941)

(1) 1920s

The defeat in Germany in WW I in 1918 led to the overthrowing of the imperial Germany, the *Hohenzollerns*, and brought an end to the German and Prussian monarchy. The social democratic Weimar Republic instead was established on 19 November 1918. The victorious Allies made sure that Germany would never rise again to pose a threat in the post-war years.

The Treaty of Versailles, signed on 28 June 1919 imposed humiliating territorial concessions and reparations of 132 billion gold marks on the Triple Entente, France, the U.K., and Russia. For the Germans, the sense of humiliating victimhood was ingrained deeply from the gruesome experiences of hunger, unemployment, hyperinflation, and the domineering posture of the Western powers.

They blamed their existential crisis on the Western powers, German Jews, Marxists, and social democrat revolutionaries who had stabbed Germany in the back. The forced territorial concession was regarded as unjustified mutilation of the German living space, *Lebensraum*, by the conspiracy of the international Jews behind the Western imperial powers.

They were recognized as archetypes of cosmopolitan evil. The economic catastrophe after 1929 only served to reinforce the need for territory.

The German idea of securing additional territory to dominate with its racial homogeneity and cultural superiority was deemed to be righteous compensation for the heavy and bloody sacrifices of WW I. So, the idea of territorial expansion became a standard trope in the reflection of Germany's imperial future.

The world order stabilized in the mid-1920s by the American-led economic revival and trading and investment boom. It was deemed possible at the time to work in international collaboration, but it was brought to a screeching halt with the Great Depression in 1928-1929, and this helped the Nazis emerge in the 1920s. The Fascistic Nazis arose with the woes and distress of the people.

(2) 1930s

The Great Depression was the greatest and longest economic recession with the stock market crash in 1929, and banking panics in 1930 and 1931. During the Depression from 1929 to 1932, world trade fell by two-thirds and the panic permeated across Europe. The crisis played a part in destroying the global order since WW I and the internationalism that supported it.

The economic crisis was gleefully regarded by communists as the end of capitalism that sustained the Western operating system, and by Nationalists in Germany as the collapse of Western power with equal satisfaction. It spurred the Japanese military to solve the economic problems through expansion by military conquests.

In the early 1930s Britain, France, and the USA were in no better fettle than Germany, and the Soviet Union was seen to be modernizing with remarkable energy. The three new powers (Germany, Italy, and Japan) launched a new wave of violent territorial imperialism as a campaign to redress the balance in the colonial landscape of the globe, and they started to build the dictatorial nation-empires beyond nation-states.

The German federal election on 14 September 1930 marked a turning point for Hitler. The Nazis made a surprising success (Turnout 82%. Social Democratic Party as ruling party 24.5%. Nazi's NSDAP 18.3%, Communist KPD 13.1%). 6.4 million people, including leaders in business and the army, voted for the Nazis, who were expected to rescue Germany from the national predicament.

The upsurge of the Nazis was held that it couldn't be stopped. It revived the old feelings of German patriotism and nationalism which had been muted during the first ten years of the Weimar Republic. It promised to lead the German people away from communism, communism, trade-unionism, and the futile liberal democracy.

On 30 January 1933, Hitler was sworn in as the chancellor of Germany and it signaled the end of the bungling attempts by the Weimar to make social-democracy work during the fourteen years (1919-1933) in power.

The rise of Hitler and the Nazi Party was unquestionably connected to the economic woes from the Great Depression, it is not the only one reason. The Nazis did not march on Berlin at the head of the unemployed, nor was there any coup. Hitler did not topple the weakened Weimar Republic as the Bolsheviks did, nor threaten the head of state as Mussolini did.

He came to power through participation in Germany's democratic process and by the invitation of the lawful authorities. It was the German people who had accepted the bizarre Hitler and his ruffians who were anything but democrats or constitutionalists at heart. The German people realized how they were duped and what they did when WW II was brought to the end.

Within a year of chancellorship, Hitler changed almost everything. He had substituted his personal dictatorship for the social democratic system, defederalized for central control, wiped out labor unions, stamped out democratic associations, driven the Jews out of the public, abolished freedom of speech and press, stifled the court-independence under Nazi rule.

In foreign affairs, Hitler took Germany out of the League of Nations and claimed equal treatment with Western powers, which most Germans gave a roar of applause for. The national reawakening made the German people assert its true strength and dispel the threats of Jews, Marxists and liberals that was believed to turn Germany into a second civilization.

In Japan where the military dominated national politics, it triggered a new imperial age by provoking the Manchurian Incident in 1931. This was encouraged by the global economic crisis, and it also raised national awareness and enthusiasm for territorial expansion, and it stimulated the theme of national honor and sacrifice for the nation.

The leaders of these countries hoped to avoid a general war for the moment while they were working on the imperial projects. There was a sweeping influence of nationalism and frequent criticisms of the attempts to uphold democratic values of checks and balances were molested by the secret police, the censors and the mobs who were loyal to the nationalistic ideologue.

(3) Hitler and Third Reich

Adolf Hitler (1889-1945) was born in Austria as the son of a local customs official and grew up with the stigma of his father's bastardy. His early life had been mediocre in his works. He had some artistic ability but failed and drifted around Vienna's low-cost lodging as a part-time decorator. He was an introverted, resentful, lonely, and poor man.

In 1913, he moved to Munich and voluntarily enlisted in the Bavarian Army in 1914 at the outbreak of WW I. It is argued that it was an error to enlist the Austrian Hitler, not a German. The service was a blessed relief for Hitler who was honored twice with the Iron Cross medals. The humiliating end of the war embittered Hitler profoundly.

Hitler's post-war political career filled the void of the early failures. His party, the NSDAP, had adopted racism and German nationalism which were attractive to drifters like Hitler, and later to millions of voters.

His words were immaterial, but he delivered them effectively by captivating the audience with modulating pitch and tempo and gesticulating and making faces of both smile and fury. His emotional intensity uncannily matched the dismal feelings of the humiliated Germans. He played on people's fears, ranting against the Jewish-Bolshevik conspiracy and the Allies' stab in the back.

His only attempt to seize power illegally was a fiasco. The "Beer-Cellar Putsch" in November 1923 taught him to stick to legal means to take power through mass rallies, electoral procedures, and political blackmail. His trial, where he railed impressively at the judges, made him an impressive national figure.

In his private life, Hitler remained withdrawn, and unmarried until his final hours. He loved animals and children, was well-groomed and polite. Although his heart was filled with hate, he had never committed personal violence. Hitler drew support by personal charisma and expected his supporters to devise policies that corresponded to his rhetoric.

His personality, career, and social interaction had built his thoughts as a drifter and outsider. It suggests an idea that "Had he finished the regular educational programs until university, worked in the formal workplaces, interacted with those in established societies, and built his thought in check and balance, did he then act differently?"

Hitler's rise to power was attributed to chaos of the economy while the insecurity in society was already full to the brim. The street battles of extreme left and right were ever-present. The Weimar Republic was mercilessly squeezed by both the Western powers and the fears of German voters. The Germans were harassed for a decade, first by reparations, and then by hyperinflation.

Like most revolutionaries, Hitler thrived in evil times when the masses were unemployed and hungry, and later they were intoxicated by victories in war. Yet what was unique was that he took the power legally, and then instigated the Nazi revolution. This was the opposite in the sequence of other revolutionaries who made revolutions outside of legal boundaries and then took power.

The Nazi Third Reich was born on 30 January 1933. Hitler boasted that it would endure for a thousand years, but it lasted twelve years and four months. It caused an eruption of violence that raised the German people to heights of power they had not known since the coronation of King Charlemagne in 800.

It became the master of Europe from the Atlantic to the Volga, and then it was plunged to the depths of destruction and desolation at the end of a world war that the Third Reich provoked. It instituted a reign of terror over the conquered peoples through its butchery of human life, and it outdid all the savage oppressions of the previous ages.

Hitler's democratic triumph exposed the true nature of democracy. Democracy is as good, or as bad, as the principles of the people who operate it. In the hands of liberal and tolerant people, it produces a liberal and tolerant government, whereas, in the hands of rogues, it produces a rogue state.

There is no reliable information on Hitler's paranoid antisemitism to stigmatize Jews during his Vienna period (1908-13, age 19-25). Hitler established the image in the early 1920s after the failed coup and his trial in 1923 gave him a platform to express his nationalist sentiments. His unique insights about societies as antisemites were set in a hospital where he was convalescing from blindness from mustard gas in November 1918. The news of Germany's defeat was humiliating, and it smacked of hysteria.

Hitler's word Weltanschauung (a point of view of the world) evolved in his political career fraught with eccentric eclecticism, like racism based on Aryan supremacy and antisemitism. It was formed through contacts with Dietrich Eckart, editor of a harshly anti-Semitic periodical, Alfred Rosenberg, a Baltic German, and Gottfried Feder, an opponent of financial capitalism.

They thought the Jews have no sense of humor and no sense of proportion. The half-baked worldview was woefully out of tune with the normalcy of the 21st century, but the Germans embraced it emphatically and many Germans collaborated with the Nazis and brought ultimate ruins to humanity and the great number of innocent people in Europe and the Germans, themselves.

Reich means realm or empire, and the "Third Reich" refers to Germany under the rule of the National Socialists Party from 1933 to 1945. The Nazis gave historical meaning to their reign not only over Germany but over the vast expanse of European land by emulating the glories of the great German empires that had gone before.

The First Reich was the empire of King Charlemagne in 800, the medieval Holy Roman Empire that unified Central and Western Europe in the Early Middle Ages and ruled for almost 1,000 years until it was dissolved in 1806 during the Napoleonic Wars.

The Second Reich meant the unified German Empire (the Hohenzollerns, the ruling house of Prussia from 1415–1918, including imperial Germany from 1871–1918). King Wilhelm I of Prussia was proclaimed Emperor of Germany at Versailles on 18 January 1871, after Prussia's defeat of France. It was then the greatest power on the Continent, and its only rival was England.

The united Germany became a strong state by means of a disciplined and a trained civil service whose success contained the seed of ruin, for it nourished the arrogance and power-hunger that from 1914 through 1918 was to bring it down.

(4) Nazi and Nazism

Nazi identity. The Nazi was a far-right political party in Germany active between 1920 and 1945. The Nazi Party emerged from the paramilitary culture of extreme nationalists, irredeemable racists, and populists, which fought against communist uprisings after WW I.

Initially, the Nazi's political strategy focused on anti-big business, anti-bourgeois, and anti-capitalist rhetoric, but it was later downplayed to gain the support of business leaders as it entered WW II. By the 1930s, its main focus shifted to anti-Semitic and anti-Marxist themes in its pursuit of intense nationalism, mass appeal, and dictatorial rule.

Nazism shared many elements with Italian fascism. However, Nazism was far more extreme in its ideas and its practice. In almost every respect, it was anti-intellectual and atheocratic, emphasizing the will of the charismatic dictator as the sole source of vision and inspiration for the Aryan people and the nation.

Nazi Germany prosecuted the German culture that the Germans had cultivated and treasured over time. Through the steady diet of calculated and incessant propaganda from the Nazis that falsified its intents and distorted the context, the cultured minds of the Germans were misled and manipulated. Later, they couldn't escape from risking the grim and dreadful consequences.

In the field of coercion and terror, the Nazis were fast learners. Their Brownshirts (the *SA. Sturmabteilung*, Stormtroopers) and the Blackshirts (the *SS. Schutzstaffel*, Protective Echelon) played the roles of coercion and terror on which Hitler built the solid base of common fraud, force and fear (the three Fs). They had no intention of striking a delicate balance between coercion and concession as their homeland ancestors had practiced in the Second Reich under the leadership of King Wilhelm I of Prussia (r.1871-1888) and Otto von Bismarck as Chancellor of German Empire (1871-1890).

Racism and racial purity. The sense of cultural superiority was based on the notion that genetic differences create a natural hierarchy, namely the genetically superior races rule the inferior ones. The contrast was taken for granted and was used to justify racial discrimination and structured exploitation in a permanent state of subjection.

The Nazis believed that the world order wasn't formed by capitalists as the Bolsheviks articulated, but rather by the imperial world-Jewry. The alternative to capitalism and communism was National Socialism. For the Nazis, Western capitalism just exploited colonies, and communism was just a Jewish fairy tale of impossible equality or inevitable inequality.

Hitler's antisemitism had firm pre-war roots. Germany's defeat in WW I was a stab in the back by Jewish defeatists. The Jewish threat was so grisly that the Germans would be destroyed completely. On 30 January 1939 in the German parliament, Hitler stated annihilation (*Vernichtung*) was the fate of the Jews if they plunged Germany again into another war.

Jews were excluded from state employment and German citizenship, Jewish traders were officially boycotted, and marriage and sexual intercourse between Jews and non-Jews were forbidden. From the outset of WW II in September 1939, Hitler conferred the concept of the war against the Jews into the war against the Western powers.

Hitler raised the anti-Semitic issue of the *Endlösung der Judenfrage* (Final Solution to the Jewish Problem) to eliminate the Jews, which deliberated on a systematic genocide on 20 January 1942 at the *Wannsee*

Conference that murdered six million Jews (90% of Polish Jews, and two-thirds of the Jewish population in Europe), the inhumane Holocaust meaning a burnt offering.

World opinion was shocked at the sights of atrocities and revolted by such barbarity in Germany which boasted a civilized culture of centuries-old Christianity and humanism. There were many types of responses among the Germans: some including the leaders of the Christian churches and politics were horrified but kept silence in the face of coercion, some overlooked them in ignorance, some were brainwashed to perpetrate the atrocities, or, the repulsion some felt after WW I for national malaise and deep humiliation was so great that they didn't express their indignation to the inhumanities, to say the least.

In an attempt to deliver the inhumanity per se at the risk of disturbance, the two cases of the Holocaust are drawn from *The Rise and Fall of the Third Reich* by William Shirer which illustrates how the wretched Germans perpetrated these unforgivable atrocities in deadpan and callous manner. Both are patchy and episodic, and they are not enough to tell the truth of the Holocaust, but they illustrate the appalling aspect of it.

First, Hermann Graebe, the manager and engineer of a branch office in the Ukraine of a German construction firm, witnessed the *Einsatz* commandos, supported by Ukrainian militia, execute 5,000 Jews on 5 October 1942 at Dubno in the Ukraine:

"My foreman and I went directly to the pits. I heard rifle shots in quick succession from behind one of the earth mounds. The people who had got off the trucks - men, women, and children of all ages- had to undress upon the order of an SS man, who carried a riding or dog whip. They had to put down their clothes in fixed places, sorted according to shoes, top clothing, and underclothing. I saw a heap of shoes of about 800 to 1,000 pairs, great piles of under-linen and clothing. Without screaming or weeping these people undressed, stood around in family groups, kissed each other, said farewells, and waited for a sign from another SS man, who stood near the pit, also with a whip in his hand. During the fifteen minutes that I stood near the pit, I heard no complaint or plea for mercy. An old woman with snow-white hair was holding a one-year-old child in her arms and singing to it and tickling it. The child was cooing with delight. The parents were looking on with tears in their eyes. The father was holding the hand of a boy about 10 years old and speaking to him softly; the boy was fighting his tears. The father pointed to the sky, stroked his head, and seemed to explain something to him. At that moment the SS man at the pit shouted something to his comrade. The latter counted off about twenty persons and instructed them to go behind the earth mound ... 1 well remember a girl, slim and with black hair, who, as she passed close to me, pointed to herself and said: "Twenty-three years old." I walked around the mound and found myself confronted by a tremendous grave. People were closely wedged together and lying on top of each other so that only their heads were visible. Nearly all had blood running over their shoulders from their heads. Some of the people were still moving. Some were lifting their arms and turning their heads to show that they were still alive. The pit was already two-thirds full. I estimated that it contained about a thousand people. I looked for the man who did the shooting. He was an S.S. man, who sat at the edge of the narrow end of the pit, his feet dangling into the pit. He had a tommy gun on his knees and was smoking a cigarette. The people, completely naked, went down some steps and clambered over the heads of the people lying there to the place to which the SS man directed them. They lay down in front of the dead or wounded people; some caressed those who were still alive and spoke to them in a low voice. Then I heard a series of shots. I looked into the pit and saw that the bodies were twitching or the heads lying already motionless on top of the bodies that lay beneath them. Blood was running from their necks. S The next batch was approaching already. They went down into the pit, lined themselves up against the previous victims, and

were shot. And so it went, batch after batch".

The next morning the German engineer returned to the site. "I saw about thirty naked people lying near the pit. Some of them were still alive. Later the Jews still alive were ordered to throw the corpses into the pit. Then they had to lie down in this to be shot in the neck I swear before God that this is the absolute truth".

Second, all the thirty-odd principal Nazi concentration camps were death camps and millions of tortured, starved inmates perished in them.

The gas chambers themselves and the adjoining crematoria, viewed from a short distance, were not sinister-looking places at all, it was impossible to make them out for what they were. Over them were well-kept lawns with flower borders, the signs at the entrances merely said baths. The unsuspecting Jews thought they were simply being taken to the baths for the delousing which was customary at all camps. And taken to the accompaniment of sweet music!

For there was light music. An orchestra of young and pretty girls all dressed in white blouses and navy-blue skirts had been formed from among the inmates. While the selection was being made for the gas chambers this unique musical ensemble played gay and melodious tunes from 'The Merry Widow and Tales' of Hoffmann. Nothing solemn and somber in Beethoven. The death marches at Auschwitz were sprightly and merry tunes, straight out of Viennese and Parisian operetta.

To such music, recalling as it did happier and more frivolous times, the men, women, and children were led into the bathhouses, where they were told to undress in preparation for taking a shower. Sometimes they were even given towels. Once they were inside the shower room - and perhaps this was the first moment that they may have suspected something was amiss, for as many as two thousands of them were packed into the chamber like sardines, making it difficult to take a bath - the massive door was slid shut, locked and hermetically sealed. Up above where the well-groomed lawn and flower beds almost concealed the mushroom-shaped lids of vents that ran up from the hall of death, orderlies stood ready to drop into them the amethyst-blue crystals of hydrogen cyanide, or Zyklon B, which originally had been commercially manufactured as a strong disinfectant.

Living Space (*Lebensraum*) and Greater Area (*Grossraum*)

The physical gradients of the European Plain slope in two different directions; from south (the Alpine Ridge) to north (the shore of the Northern Seas), and from east (the peak of the Urals, 1,894 m) to west (France's Atlantic coast). The gradients of cultural ascent are undertaken in different directions, from south, through to north and the center, to east.

This cultural ascent was implied in the German nationalism that exerted its force to the West while laying claim to the East. It can be observed in some aspects of French attitudes toward Belgium, the Germans' attitudes toward the Slavs in Poland, Ukraine, and Russia, the Polish attitudes toward Russia and Ukraine, and the Russian attitudes toward Central Asia. (*Europe* by Norman Davies, page 52-54).

In 1897, the German geographer Friedrich Ratchel coined the term *Lebensraum*, that Germany needed more territory to thrive. This became the goal of WW I and WW II. The German political theorist Carl Schmitt

(1888-1985) used the term *Grossraum* during the Nazi era to justify territorial expansion, and an economic and political space dominated by Germany.

The space theories entailed the process of deterritorialization (moving non-Germans, mainly Jews and Slavs) off conquered Eastern lands and then reterritorializing them by settling Germans there. The space theories were combined with the concept of the race (the Final Solution, *die Endlösung*), and they became the foundation of the Nazi war on the Eastern Front.

Japan, Italy, and Germany took risks to achieve the territory; for example, the seizures of Manchuria by Japan in 1931, Ethiopia by Italy in 1936, and Austria, the Sudetenland in Czechoslovakia, and Poland until 1939 by Germany. The risks were regarded as worth taking because the Western powers were preoccupied with their economic crises.

The irony was that the more they seized territory, the more the global order was fragmented. The territorial expansions were supposed to enhance security and enrich populations, but they engendered instead growing insecurity, high costs, and, in the end, destruction. The imperial dreams unsullied by reality to build empires were shattered to pieces within not more than a few years.

Facing the challenges of Western powers toward German expansion, Germany did not give up the territories it had gained through forced treaties and conquests because it couldn't repeat the mistake that it had abandoned the acquired territories after WW I. The issue was serious enough to justify a retributive total war to preserve the new-won territory.

A view that sees 1 September 1939, on which the Nazis invaded Poland as the opening of WW II can be argued to be 13 March 1938, instead, on which the Nazis annexed Austria. From that point on, the Nazis started the expansion spree of the Sudetenland in Bohemia in 1938, Czechoslovakia in March and Poland in September 1939, France in May 1940, and the Soviet in June 1941.

In the expansions, the Germans destroyed and restructured the entire area to reduce the conquered land to an object of exploitation. The special action units (*Einsatzgruppen*, Deployment Groups) were tasked not only to police the rear areas behind the front but to execute the national elites as the Italians had done in Ethiopia (1935-1937).

We refer to the address that Haile Selassie (c.1890-1975), the emperor of Ethiopia, delivered to the League of Nations on 30 June 1936 after Italy had invaded Ethiopia on 3 October 1935 and the capital city, Addia Ababa, was occupied by the Italian force on 5 May 1936.

. *"Should it happen that a strong government finds it may with impunity destroy a weak people, then the hour strikes for that weak people to appeal to the League of Nations to give its judgment in all freedom... Faced by numerous violations by the Italian government of all international treaties that prohibit resort to arms, and the use of barbarian methods of warfare, it is my painful duty to note that the initiative had today been taken with a view to raising sanctions. Does this initiative not mean in practice the abandonment of Ethiopia to the aggressor?...I ask the fifty-two nations, who have given the Ethiopian people a promise to help them in their resistance to the aggressor, what are they willing to do for Ethiopia?...Representatives of the world, I have come to Geneva to discharge in your midst the most painful of the duties of the head of a state. What reply shall I have to take back to my people."*

The League of Nations offered little help, and Emperor Selassie spent the next five years in exile in

England (1936-41) before returning to Addis Ababa on 5 May 1941 and resuming the throne.

3) WW II from the Nazi-Soviet War (22 June 1941) to its end

(1) Why the Nazis started the ill-fated war

After the German victories in Poland in 1939 and France in 1940, the relations between Germany and the Soviets soured as they double-crossed each other. Hitler felt helpless to prevent the Russians from grabbing the Baltic States, and oil-rich Rumanian provinces which were crucial for Germany because the British blockade barred the petroleum import by sea.

Until December 1940, the planned campaign against the Soviets had developed with mixed motives for Germany (a) defeat the British Empire who was refusing to make peace with Germany, (b) confront the Jewish Bolshevik menace in the East, and (c) seize the living space in the East for the German people.

Until December 1940, the planned campaign against the Soviets had developed with mixed motives for Germany:

- It was to defeat the British Empire which was refusing to make peace with Germany. Hitler believed that the possibility of a Soviet intervention in the war was sustaining the English, and that the British would stop fighting if this last continental hope from the Soviets were demolished. For the British, losing the war would mean that they no longer had the power to hold together the British Empire.

- It was to reset the fronts and war efforts. Hitler pointed to further advantages for Germany that the army in the east could be substantially reduced in size, allowing greater deployment of the armaments industry for the navy and the air force, and Germany would then be unassailable. The smashing of Russia would also allow Japan to turn with all its might against the USA, hindering American intervention in Europe.

- It was from twin obsessions of removing the Jews, specifically, the Jewish Bolshevik menace, and seizing the living space (Lebensraum). Germany had to dominate it economically and politically, though not annex it, because the gigantic territory of Russia contained immeasurable riches. It would then be able to preside over Europe and it could not be defeated by anyone.

The issue of a single front was common in WW I and WW II. When it invaded Poland in 1939 and France in 1940, it did away with the probable Eastern Front by signing the Non-Aggression Pact with the Soviets. To prepare for the Western Front in 1941 with England and the US, it needed to preclude the Eastern Front with the Soviets before the Western Front opened.

The invasion of the Soviet Union was a roundabout route to defeat Britain and thus aimed to remove threats to Nazi Germany: first from the Soviet Union in the east and second, from Britain in the west. This will accomplish its vision to establish a German empire that controls the Eurasian continents from the Baltic Sea to the Middle East, from the Atlantic Ocean to Soviet Urals.

In the campaigns in Poland and France, the German forces proved to be professional and inherited the authoritarianism of the Prussian Army, the authority of every leader downward and responsibility upward. In the Soviets, however, they were harassed by long supply lines, debilitated by Hitler's mistrust, and the depth of resources, expansiveness, and unyielding spirit of the Soviet forces as showcased in the war against Napoleon, France in 1812, and by the peoples' solidarity to win the acrimonious turf-war.

Considering the massive forces in total war, the Nazi-Russo War from 22 June 1941 (German invasion) to the end of April 1945 (Hitler killed himself) would be a series of the Battle of Gaugamela in 331 BC where two great empires (Alexander for the Greek and Darius for the Persian) fought the historic battle with the life or death of the emperors and empires at stake.

Germany failed to achieve its purpose of subduing England by leveraging a victory over the Soviets, and the Soviets managed to defend its homeland with territorial gains in Europe and Asia. The Nazi-Russo War is worth special consideration because it obviously transcends the scope and scale of wars in history concerning intensity, casualties, and consequential effects.

In conclusion, Hitler made a blunder in the risk assessment of the Soviet Union. He underestimated the strength of the Red Army, the resourcefulness of the Soviet Union, and the patriotic passion of the Russian people that was seemingly and partly attributed to their experiences and lessons from the war with the French forces in their homeland centuries ago.

In addition, Hitler made another blunder by overestimating the military power of the German forces without in-depth knowledge and enough preparations to wage the war in the vast expanse of lands under severe weather conditions.

(2) Non-Aggression Pact

The German-Soviet Pact was signed between German Foreign Minister Joachim von Ribbentrop and Soviet Foreign Minister Vyacheslav Molotov on 23 August 1939, just before the German invasion of Poland. The Pact consisted of two parts: one public and one secret between two bitter enemies, Hitler and Stalin, in the capacity of friends of necessity.

The public part was a non-aggression pact in which each party promised not to attack the other. They also agreed not to aid a third country that attacked either of them. The secret part specified spheres of influence of the signatories who agreed, for example, to divide Poland along the line of the Narev, Vistula, and San rivers.

As per the Pact, the two bullies invaded, partitioned, and put Poland under their spheres of influence. It was the national disaster of Poland, inter alia, the Polish Jews. Both parties pledged non-aggression for mutual prosperity for 10 years, but the pledge was born to die sooner. The two greedy savages scapegoated the Polish to gratify their need for space.

The concept of the Grossraum (Great Area) was not unlike the idea behind the Co-Prosperity Sphere of Imperial Japan in Asia. Both aimed to dominate a greater area of economic and political space. Following the Pact, the Soviets invaded Poland, Lithuania, Latvia, Estonia, and Finland. The Nazi-Soviet dictators were two of a kind, and so they were mutually exclusive teetering between alliance and hostility by their own needs.

(3) Poland, Again

Until the end of 1938, Poland had been a potential ally of the Nazi Germany. Only when the Polish government repeatedly refused the flagrant demands of Nazis for an extra-territorial rail and road link across the Polish Corridor and for taking the Free City of Danzig back into Germany, the relationship grew sour. This refusal led to the German invasion in September 1939.

Hitler might well have accepted a protectorate solution had the Poles simply acquiesced to German threats. In March 1939, Britain and France guaranteed Polish sovereignty. The Nazis invaded under the pretense of protecting the Germans in Poland. A hypothetical question arises: if Poland had acquiesced to the Nazi threats, were the Poles safe in the end? I vote for No.

The Nazis and Soviets divided and subjugated the Poles. More than 20 percent of the Poles, or 6 million, died and over 90% of the deaths were non-military. When WW II ended, the Soviets gained recognition of Polish territory. As compensation for it, a portion of eastern Germany was ceded to Poland by which the Polish borders were shifted westwards.

Britain and France performed their commitments to Poland by declarations of war, but the problem was that they were only in words betraying the desperate Poles. Both did not support the Polish resistance actively which led Hitler to believe that the Allied declarations of war were merely a sham. The sheepish Western powers remained feeble until they were attacked.

Poland was not rescued but victimized again when the Nazis and Soviets played out the fourth partition in the modern world was played out by the Nazis and Soviets.

(4) *Lebensraum* and Racism in the Nazi-Soviet War (22 June 1941-9 May 1945)

Hitler entrusted Himmler and the security apparatuses (*Einsatzgruppen* composed of security police, SS, and SD) to follow the armies into the Soviet and uproot the Communist system by murdering elites, intellectuals, and Jews. The vast regions of Eurasia were to be resettled by the Germans over thirty years in ways of deportation, detention, and mass executions.

A difference existed between Asia and Europe. Japan regarded itself as a superior race and committed atrocities, but it promoted the idea of Asian brotherhood under the rule of Japan. In Europe, Germany placed itself at the apex of a hierarchical order and implemented policies of displacement and mass murder to realize the concepts of *Lebensraum* and the Final Solution.

The Germans treated the Soviets as they had treated the Poles in Poland. For the Soviets, the treatment proved a disappointment, as they had assumed a better life during the first weeks of German occupation after the Stalinist regime disappeared. But, within months, the seizure of food and mass murders suggested that Stalinism might be the lesser of two evils.

For Hitler, there were two impending priorities in the process of constructing the living space; first, economic recovery from the disastrous economic crisis, and second, the re-militarization of Germany to a level that would restore Germany's great power. The actions for priorities were to extract values from the conquered land in the Soviet as much and as soon as possible.

Since the Western powers already possessed land in abundance in the colonies, Germany could only compete by seizing land in the East to fight its mortal enemies, Russia, and Britain. Hitler claimed that the space in the East was for Germany as India was for England. Interestingly, Japanese officers claimed that China was for Japan as India was for England.

(5) Who is to blame for the emergence of the Axis states?

No class or group in Germany could escape its share of responsibility for abandoning democracy and allowing the advent of Adolf Hitler in the 1920s and 1930s.

The German people failed to unite against Nazism. They were too divided, opportunistic, and shortsighted to fight against a common danger. They introduced the Nazi tyranny to themselves and many of them did not quite realize what it meant when Adolf Hitler assumed the chancellorship on 20 January 1933 in a perfectly constitutional manner.

The Communists, at the behest of Moscow, were committed to the actions of destroying the democratic forces of Social Democrats, the trade unions, and the middle class, in a belief that the dictatorship of the proletariat would be established when capitalism died. This tactic weakened the power of Social Democrats to resist the ascendancy of the Nazis.

The Social Democratic Weimar Republic (1919-1933) became weak and sick to control the situation. The surge of the Nazis and the unprecedented economic woes of the Great Depression were attributed to its incompetence. At the beginning of the 1930s, they were too confused and timid to preserve it from the savage attack of the Nazis.

Britain and France failed to subdue the Nazi aggression when it annexed Austria in 1938, even though they assumed that the growing bellicosity and military strength of Germany, Italy, and Japan were ultimately directed at them and three Axis countries deemed war as a necessary means to secure regional domination as new imperial powers.

The impotent Western powers just saw the alliance of Axis states emerge. In October 1936, Italy and Germany reached the Axis pact to dominate Europe. In November 1936, Japan and Germany signed the Anti-Comintern Pact to coordinate resistance to communism. By 1938, Germany and Italy recognized the Japanese puppet state of Manchukuo.

(6) Abortive efforts to prevent the Nazi

The excesses and deficiencies in history are sometimes mitigated or corrected by the checker and balancer. Some people could have done the work as stoppers of the Nazi emergence or as rectifiers who had tried to remove it or reformers who tried to change the policies to be in tune with normalcy.

In the ascendancy of the Nazis and its actions in WW II, there were some inflection points. If the people had done something rectifying or hadn't done something patently wrong, history would have unfolded in different ways.

History tells us that refusal had consequences, but so did acquiescence did. Five incidence are listed that, with the benefit of hindsight, would have ended up with different results if they had acted in some other way.

• Diplomatic Efforts

In the face of the sphere of the international community, the Western powers, especially Britain and

France, were not decisive and resolute, and even flinched at the opportunity to forestall the ascendance of the Nazis and to foil their attempt to assert their unhinged power and unleash the extreme violent actions domestically and internationally on the continent.

When Hitler took power in 1933, his extreme nationalist ideology was well-known to foreign politicians and the press. In his first year of the German chancellorship, he announced its withdrawal from the Disarmament Conference and the League of Nations, in response to the Western powers' refusal to meet his demand for equal treatment.

The Treaty of Versailles, signed after WW I, forbade Germany from developing an offensive military. In 1935, Hitler revealed that Germany had developed an air force and was expanding its army in violation of the Treaty. France and Britain did not take any actions against Germany, but they placed their hopes in the appeasement of Hitler to avoid war. The policy was ineffective and flawed.

• Britain and France

The act of declaring war against the Nazis was grievous and irremediable for Britain and France because it stoked widespread fear of war which should be much deadlier in terrible bloodletting and costlier in massive destruction than those in WW I. The grim reality of the advancements in lethal weaponry and the adoption of the total war concept worried them much.

Both countries struggled with a double whammy: first, they had to defuse the tension and keep regional security to avert the risk of another world war in the era of economic turmoil, and second, they needed to keep the status quo of international order so that they would protect their imperial interests in Asia including India, Africa and America beyond Europe.

England's gain was France's loss. Competition for regional hegemony was intensified by the rivalry which was bound to produce one of two actions: tension would either escalate, resulting in violent fragmentation, or there would be consolidation within and between the competitors. The choice was to fight or cooperate. Their history has been mingled with the fight and cooperation.

The Anglo-French strategy in the 1930s was never simply an imprudent abdication of responsibility or subservient kowtow toward brutality, but rather delicate modulation or sometimes inconsistent efforts to square the circle of averting a war by moderating the hard-charging Axis states and protecting their imperial interests that were hanging in the balance of the status quo.

The policies to contain the Nazis were as follows: maintain alliances like the Anglo-Polish Alliance in 1939, enact laws on economic support, concessions, or sanctions like the Lend-Lease Act of the U.S. on 11 March 1941 to support the other Allies, and appeasement to win over new friends in necessity like the Non-Aggression Pact in 1941.

When stuck in a stalemate with no hope of an immediate solution to avert the imposing risk of a great catastrophe, the parties are tempted to seek a grand settlement in appeasement as the British Prime Minister, Neville Chamberlain, did. He got the relevant parties to sit together to rewrite the Versailles Treaty to appease the Nazi regime.

The diplomatic efforts turned out to be ineffective because it was almost impossible to bend the will of determined opponents who were impudent to renege on treaties or who were skilled at double-minded tactics to achieve their objectives under the table or behind the scenes. The ambition to contain the crisis in the way of appeasement in the 1930s proved illusory.

• The Rhineland Coup

Following the Versailles Treaty in 1919, the Rhineland, an area of Western Germany along the Rhine, had been ceded and was supposed to remain a demilitarized buffer zone between Germany and France, Belgium, and the Netherlands against future German aggression. This area of Germany was also important for coal, steel, and iron production.

There were preceding events that had violated international law and the inability of the League of Nations to cope with them, for example, the Manchurian Incident on 18 September 1931 and the public announcement of Germany in 1935 of its rearmament. The League of Nations should have been policing Japan as well as Germany, but it failed to do so.

On 7 March 1936, Adolf Hitler deployed German troops into the Rhineland to occupy it. This move was the first of many violations of the Treaty of Versailles. Great Britain and France did nothing substantial in reaction to this breach of the treaty. Due in part to this lack of reaction, Adolf Hitler was emboldened to take over other lands throughout Western Europe.

The occasion in March 1936 was the last chance for the Western democracies to halt the rise of totalitarian Germany without the risk of a serious war. Faced with compelling evidence that peaceful methods were impotent to prevent the disturbances of peace, the democratic nations remained stubbornly hypnotized by the allure of peace.

Britain and France, the major states in the League of Nations, wouldn't obstruct the path of Germany in its empire-building. Each successful step taken by Germany invited the belief that the League was no longer effective with its raison d'etre. The Axis states finally left the League; Japan in March 1933, Germany in September 1933, and Italy in December 1937.

• The Munich Crisis

Hitler annexed Austria on 12 October 1938 and vowed to invade Czechoslovakia on 1 October 1938 to occupy the German-speaking Sudetenland region in a move for a greater Germany. The Munich Crisis unfolded in September 1938 when Nazi Germany met the delegations of the U.K., France, and the Fascist Italy. Czechoslovakia wasn't included.

The negotiations were to draw a line against German expansion to the East. Yet the Western negotiators weren't as hard as nails to stop Hitler from achieving his vision of *Lebensraum*. Neville Chamberlain represented the war-averse British public, and his underlying gullibility masked by a hardened face led him to muse that perfidious Hitler who was firebrand who lacked the willingness to compromise was a man of words who could be relied upon.

Chamberlain's three rounds of discussion with Hitler can be seen as degrading capitulations under the pressure of the ruthless Hitler. The Munich Agreement said that the German army was to complete the occupation of the Sudetenland by 10 October 1938, and an international commission would decide the future of other disputed areas.

Chamberlain conceded that Germany annexed the Sudetenland without consideration for Czechoslovakia's security. Edvard Beneš (December 1935-October 1938, April 1945-June 1948 in office), the Czechoslovak President, had no option but to accept it. Churchill chided him that Britain suffered a defeat without a war, and Britain would get war because of that.

On his return from Munich on 30 September 1938, Chamberlain held aloft the flimsy paper of the Anglo-German Declaration that was inked by him and Hitler only hours before, and told to the excited crowd at Heston Airport, *"It is peace for our time, the desire of our two peoples never to go to war with one another again."* This was the climax of the appeasement policy.

The Munich Agreement didn't make war inevitable, but it made Hitler confident that he would get more cost-free gains. The West came to terms with the idea that they could deter a war with negotiations. Chamberlain's concession strengthened Hitler's position in Germany, and it also added to the power of the Third Reich vis-à-vis the Western powers and the Soviet Union.

Six months later, in March 1939, Hitler reneged on his promises and ordered his armies to march into Prague and bullied the Czech into surrender. On 15 March 1939, Hitler excitedly received Dr. Hacha, the Czech President, in Berlin, where he was given a stark choice, either to accept becoming a protectorate or face destruction. After Hácha reluctantly agreed to give up his country's independence, the German army started moving in. It was the beginning of six long years of occupation.

After the Nazis crossed into Poland on 1 September 1939, Prime Minister Chamberlain again spoke to the nation, but this time solemnly, calling for the declaration of war against Germany and the launch of WW II. On 10 May 1940, Chamberlain was forced to resign, and he was replaced by Winston Churchill.

The Anglo-French diplomacy had faltered and retreated step by step when Hitler made moves of declaring conscription in 1935, occupying the Rhineland in 1936, taking Austria and the Sudetenland in 1938, taking over Czechoslovakia, and invading Poland in 1939. The threshold of the diplomatic bankruptcy was the Munich Crisis in September 1938. Lord Chamberlian who was noble and conscientious but not sagacious enough to detect the brazen impudence and not determined enough to deter the rapacious ambition of Hiter had a full share of his misfortune.

Hitler was not free of anxiety about major conflicts with Western powers in his adventurism, the deluded and feeble appeasement and deterrence from the Western powers turned the anxiety into reaffirmation that Britain and France had no definite red line of war or peace. The containment policy could be deactivated by letting the fear of war abound in the countries.

With the Soviet Union on their side, the Western powers could defy the brinkmanship of Hitler or, if that failed, they could challenge him in armed conflict. But they allowed all opportunities to slip out of their hands. The last opportunity to challenge Hitler was washed away by breaching the commitment to come to the aid of Poland when she was attacked.

It was the point of sensibility. After the German invasion of Poland on 1 September 1939, Chamberlain offered Hitler the opportunity to withdraw his forces from Poland rather than a clear and strict warning of facing another WW I. His action made us wonder if Chamberlain thought that the withdrawal from Poland was a viable and realistic option for Hitler.

- The Valkyrie

As early as 1938, German military officers had plotted to overthrow Hitler, but indecisive headmen in the military and the lack of corresponding support from Western powers had stymied the plan. Plotters gained momentum in the sense of urgency in 1943 after Germany lost the Battle of Stalingrad and Soviet forces turned the table to push back towards Germany.

General Guderian recalled that Hitler was rapidly deteriorating in his condition of body and mind. His usual hardness became cruel, he believed no one as he assumed others lied to him, he frequently lost self-control, and his language grew increasingly violent. The condition went steadily from bad to worse. In his intimate circle, he rejected any restraining influence.

The once mighty German Army and the Germans were being slaughtered mercilessly on the fronts and in the homeland, but military leaders were too timid to stop the doomed process and remove Hitler, but a handful of conspirators in the Army raised their hands to rid themselves of Hitler who was leading the entire German people and the fatherland to total annihilation.

Under the leadership of Major General Tresckow and Colonel Claus von Stauffenberg, plotters missed the chance to assassinate Hitler five times in 1943 and 1944. Some generals and officers were aware of the plots, but neither supported them nor reported them to the Gestapo. As the Gestapo closed in on them, anyhow, a final attempt was set on 20 July 1944.

On the day, Stauffenberg personally took a briefcase full of explosives to a conference in the Wolf's Lair, Adolf Hitler's war headquarters located in Poland. The explosives were armed and placed next to Hitler in the conference room, but it was moved unwittingly at the last moment behind a table leg by an officer, Heinz Brandt. All the plotters were executed or killed themselves.

When the bomb detonated, it killed Heinz Brandt and two others and injured the rest in the room. Hitler suffered a perforated eardrum and conjunctivitis but was generally unharmed. The failed attempt, including the other lost chances, were attributed mainly to a lack of courage as well as to inexplicable fortunes that plagued the plotters at every turn of their actions.

The occasion rather strengthened the belief of many Germans who accepted Adolf Hitler as their savior and supported National Socialism despite the bleak prospect of defeat. Hitler had held the allegiance and trust of the Germans to the real last of the Third Reich. They followed him as if gregarious, dumb cattle proceeded with a march to the cliff of downfall.

(7) The Total War

In *"On War"*, Carl Von Clausewitz mentioned the character of total war.

"War therefore is an act of violence intended to compel our opponent to fulfill our will. Violence, that is to say, physical force (for there is no moral force without the conception of States and Law), is therefore the MEANS; the compulsory submission of the enemy to our will is the ultimate object. In order to attain this

object fully, the enemy must be disarmed, and disarmament becomes therefore the immediate OBJECT of hostilities in theory."

On 9 March 1945, the Nazis named its final operation of defending Berlin (16 April to 2 May 1945) as the "Operation Clausewitz" which led to Hitler's suicide on 30 April and the Nazi's capitulation on 8 May. The operation manifested that Berlin would be defended to the last man against the Soviets, who were within two blocks of Hitler's underground bunker.

It is the modern state and nationalism that made total war possible.

First, only modern states could mobilize national resources using statistics and administrative capability. States lacking the modernity to mobilize the resources, like Nationalist China, could sustain warfare only with external aid. None of the combatant states could fight the world wars on the same scale a generation earlier. Again, modernity mattered.

Second, the emergence of modern nationalism shaped the willingness of governments and the people to endure unlimited mobilization of national resources. The modern nation, exceptionally capable of mobilizing resources, made the people perceive total war as a means of securing national existence and survival.

The Darwinian paradigm of the struggle for survival was widely understood to apply to the contest between peoples, empires, and nations. Considering the lessons from WW I that defeat meant national extinction, and the dangers of treaties that imperiled the defeated nation, winning the war was an absolute objective to achieve at all costs and resources.

As the civilian population took part in total war with various missions, it could no longer expect immunity from military action by the enemy. It became impossible to draw a clear line between combatant and non-combatant. So, the ultimate aim of military operations was to destroy the will of the people, and thus civilians became a party to combatants as well as victims.

Of all the imperial powers, Britain was the most successful beneficiary of empire manpower by mobilizing 2.6 million from Canada, Australia, New Zealand, and South Africa, and 2.7 million from India. The Japanese began recruiting Korean and Taiwanese volunteers in 1937 and conscripted from 1942 onwards. Around 220,000 Koreans served with the Japanese forces.

The Battle of Britain in World War II was between Britain's Royal Air Force and the Luftwaffe, Nazi Germany's air force from 10 July through 31 October 1940 for the control of airspace over Great Britain and the English Channe. It was the first battle in history fought solely in the air. The life and death of the British hinged upon the result of the battle because the German army would have landed on the English soil if the Luftwaffe won the air battle. Then, Britain would not only be skinned but flayed to the bone by the German occupiers if they lost the battle. It was a total war for life in the sky.

The total war entailed significant economic challenges. Ordinary men and women caught up in the coils of total war. A large deficit and runaway inflation happened along with the massive mobilization of resources.

Actions to the problems were to pay more taxes, encourage saving, and buy war bonds. So, with no nation, there was no repayment. Under the total war, there was slight difference between dictatorships and democracies when they ran wartime economies.

Total war was the war of all people, and thus it democratized society. Women joined the war as civil defenders or military personnel as radar plotters, radio operators, transport drivers, or intelligence personnel in places usually remote from the front lines except the Soviet where there was little hesitancy about female enrollment.

The heavy casualties of men in the war made the recruitment of women a necessity that helped advance gender equality after WW II. The home front had to fund the war effort, work long hours on war orders, and accept the priority of the military for food and consumer goods. Total war meant working harder, receiving less, staging no protests, and dying for the homeland.

In the total war, the states had to balance military demands and civilian living-standards, to balance consumption, savings, and taxation without inflation as John Maynard Keynes said. A proportion of fiscal money was deferred but it should not have increased national debt, protected those in substandard condition, and linked wage-pension rates to the cost of ration without raising prices.

The Axis empires had further resources to exploit. They recruited from conquered territories to build roads, railways, and factories. Japan conscripted a large number of workforces as virtual slaves working in poor conditions for little pay.

Workers in the Japanese colony were in high demand for labor to serve Japanese war needs. In the case of Korea, there were more than 7 million people by 1945 who were mostly assigned to menial work in low grades of labor, but there was a growing number of Korean engineers and businessmen who gained profit from the demands of wartime production.

The German war economy was much larger than that of Japan and the need for labor was consequently more acute. By the end of 1944, 8.2 million foreigners worked in Germany and 28 million in the annexed areas. It is said that up to 15 million foreign workers, prisoners of war, and labor camps worked as German manpower which was one-fifth of the civilian workforce by 1944.

The use of the resources to produce war products was not efficient in the productions by reason of waste, corruption or incompetence, and the products were not wholly utilized on battlefields due to air raids, failures in logistics, sudden changes in front situation, or ransacked by enemies.

In the case of Korea under colonial rule (1910-1945) as a part of the total war of Imperial Japan, the history is mixed with various aspects.

First, it was the policy of Japan-Korea homogenization that Japan nationalized the annexed Korea. This policy prioritized the extraction of value from the colonized Koreans, favoring Japanese colonizers. It resembled the pattern of colonial exploitation, but it was different from exploitative colonization that did not nationalize people and lands (like India).

Second, Japan had developed the annexed Korea to serve its imperial interests. They had built sites of social infrastructure and industrial facilities, and modernized systems of education, administration, jurisdiction, land and forests, etc. These developments had cut both ways that were to contribute to the total war and to help rebuild Korea after liberation in 1945.

Korean elites and even pro-Japanese collaborators hadn't been objectively following up on the war situation, as Imperial Japan was losing the battles and the war. There was a Korean government in exile in China and an armed force for independence, but their resistance to Imperial Japan was not capable of waging a total war on their scale and scope of strength.

(8) The Nazi-Russo War

Hitler considered the war with the Soviets inevitable to secure Lebensraum with access to the resources of the Soviets, to remove the twin threat of the Jews and Communism, and to isolate Britain. He expected to gain access to food supplies and oil in the Soviet. More dangerously, assumptions of racial superiority, whether biological or ethical, were used to justify the level of extreme violence that actually underlay the wave of new imperialism.

The war undulated with the peak in supremacy from June 1941 to July 1943 but waned from August 1943 to April 1945. Hitler intended to finish the war promptly with reasons: He dreaded the prospect of two fronts that would drain national resources. He intended to subdue Britain after the Soviet war. Americans were likely to join the war eventually, but not until 1942 at the earliest. Doing away with the Soviets would help prevent a coalition from building up against him.

After the successes in Poland and France, Germany was so confident that the Soviet defeat was granted with a campaign for eight to eleven weeks. Yet the planning took little account of the problems of supplying scattered forces and staging mobile warfare in such a vast and treacherous area. The German intelligence was not competent to prepare for this reality.

Just before the invasion, Hitler gave his generals a fiery speech that the war was the decisive battle between two ideologies and that the practices had to be measured by completely different standards from international laws. He gave clear orders to carry out an unprecedented terror attack in Russia by brutal means.

Stalin of the Soviet Union hoped that the Non-Aggression Pact with Germany would create a new equilibrium of power in Europe around a Soviet-German axis. The two Allied powers began to treat the Soviet Union as a potential enemy and the pact as a virtual alliance. The malaise of uneasiness turned worse after the Soviet invasion and occupation of eastern Poland.

When, on 30 November 1939, the Soviet Union attacked Finland, after the Finnish government had rejected requests to cede bases to Soviet military forces, there was a wave of indignant protest across Britain and France. The two states took the lead in expelling the Soviet Union from the League of Nations.

The Soviet irrecoverable losses of men (dead, missing, or taken prisoner) amounted to an astonishing two million, and the early successes brought a sense of elation to the German side while seeming to confirm the pre-war predictions of Soviet fragility. The expansive plans for the whole campaign at last seemed feasible.

The Soviet forces were determined to fight, even suicidal resistance in the prospect of overwhelming disaster. German forces had shown their professional skill in advancing fast against a disintegrating defense, but the campaign revealed many of the drawbacks and deficiencies. The belief that the Red Army was beaten was, in truth, an optical illusion.

The topography and climate presented problems quite different from those encountered in Poland or France. The infantry and vehicles had to negotiate the unpaved roads on the vast expanse which were changed to a swamp of muddy road with sudden rainfall. The army became exhausted by long marches, low supplies, sudden ambush, and the heat and cold.

The quick victory was a gamble based on a complete misreading of Soviet strengths and the nature of the zone of combat, just as the Japanese had misjudged the war with China in the vast expanse of central China. German forces needed to rest and refit, while the fighting forces of the Soviets were not willing to accept defeat but weakened for the moment to win anything decisive.

The West was not only blind to the inhumanities of the Stalinist regime, but it had little information, since an almost impenetrable veil was drawn over the real treatments meted out to all those deemed to be hostile to or incompatible with the Soviet system, both in the Soviet Union and in the areas occupied in Eastern Europe.

The Soviet repressive apparatus had engaged in crimes against humanity: mass deportations to labor and concentration camps, the operation of camps with a record of abuse and routine death that matched the worst camps in the German Empire, intolerance to all forms of religion, and the absence of liberal freedoms of speech, association or respect for the rule of law.

(9) Watersheds of the war

The year 1942 was extraordinary with watershed victories by the Allies in major battle fields whereby the Axis turned defensive in WW II.

- The Battle of Stalingrad and other battles after it.

    It was the battle (17 July 1942-31 January 1943) along the Volga River around Stalingrad. After the failure at Moscow and Leningrad in 1941, Hitler turned south in 1942 to capture the Caucasus and its oil fields, for which Hitler needed to take Stalingrad. Still, it is questionable whether it had such a corresponding strategic value to risk the fate of the war for Hitler.

    Three gateways in Europe hold great strategic values: the Straits of Gibraltar at the mouth of the Mediterranean leading to the Atlantic, the Dardanelles linking the Mediterranean to the Black Sea, and the Danish Sound, the choke point linking the Baltic Sea to the North Sea.

    Stalingrad wasn't one of them, and Moscow wasn't far, and the offending German force needed balance on the fronts.

    The decision might be equivalent to the decision of Hannibal in the Second Punic War (218-202 BC) that had not attacked Rome when people in Rome slumped into a fog of doom and gloom, but he bypassed it to advance into Southern Italy which made him genuinely remorseful about it later. Hitler's decision to turn south was a matter of his focus, but the Battle of Stalingrad was a decisive turning point in the European war.

    The battles engulfed millions of soldiers and resulted in military casualties greater than those suffered by either Britain or the United States in the entire war. While 22 divisions battled in the desert in the Battle of El Alamein, there were 310 German and Soviet divisions locked in combat in the battle for Stalin's city, Stalingrad.

Meanwhile, it helps us understand the war with some geographical knowledge.

In understanding the war that was fought on the European plain, one of the key factors is the rivers that flow the plain
- to the north: Seine, Rhine, Elbe, Oder, Vistula, Nieman
- to the south: Ebro, Rhoene, Martisa, Dnieper, Volga, Ural
- to the west: Tagus, Loire, Severn (the U.K.)
- to the east: Danube, Po, Dniester, Thames (the U.K.)

The Ural Mountains divide Russia (Europe) and Russia (Asia) and the distance from the Atlantic to the Urals is 2,400 miles (4,000 kilometers).

Operation Uranus of the Soviet army (19-23 November 1942) gathered a force of over 1 million soldiers, 14,000 artillery, 979 tanks, and 1,350 aircraft in utmost secrecy. German intelligence failed to detect the build-up. It started on 19 November in the north and south to trap the German forces, and on 23 November the two pincers met at the village of Sovetsky.

As many as 330,000 men including the Sixth Army of German forces were trapped. The remarkable success of the operation showed the extent to which the Soviet army had learned from its past mistakes. The idea of General Paulus of the Sixth Army to fight his way out of the trap was crushed on 20 November when Hitler ordered him to stand fast in Stalingrad.

The promise of air supply proved ineffective because of poor winter weather and growing intervention from the Soviet air force. When General von Manstein, German commander of the Army Group Don, tried to break through to save the trapped German forces, but his units were repulsed by Soviet armored reserves. Paulus was left to fend for himself.

More than 250,000 German forces were in the pocket. Paulus could muster barely 25,000 men capable of fighting, along with 95 tanks and 310 anti-tank guns. Food and ammunition were reduced dramatically. Resistance was nevertheless surprisingly stout for the first week. By 17 January 1943 only half the pocket remained, and the Sixth Army headquarters was stormed on 31 January 1943.

Operation Mars of the Soviet Army (25 November-20 December 1942), designed to encircle and destroy the powerful German Ninth Army, regarded by Stalin as more essential than Operation Uranus, was a disastrous failure for the Soviet force with the loss of more than 500,000 casualties and 1,700 tanks, but the failure was masked by the success at Stalingrad.

Stalingrad was fought for the most critical weeks amidst the ruins of a large conurbation, some 65 kilometers wide, first in intense heat, later in bitter cold. Dysentery, typhoid fever, and frostbite affected the attackers more, but both parties shared hardships on a major scale in the battleground.

Stalin and the Soviet high command were disappointed that more did not result from the rout in the south, but Stalingrad was nevertheless a remarkable victory, more grandiose than the modest successes on Guadalcanal and at El Alamein. For the German public, the withdrawal from Stalingrad and the loss of the endeared Sixth Army delivered a profound meaning.

The withdrawal after the defeat meant the end of the ambition to use Soviet resources to fight the battle with the West and a possible fatal challenge to the whole imperial project. Strategically, it delivered the Soviet Union from the endless crises during the first fifteen months of the war, though it did not end the German threat entirely.

The Battle of Kursk (5 July 1943 – 23 August 1943) in southwestern Russia, along with the Battle of Stalingrad several months earlier, is the most oft-cited battle that was one of the turning points in WW II. The battle began on 5 July with the launch of the German offensive (Operation Citadel) from north and south to pinch off the Kursk salient held by the Soviets.

After the German offensive stalled on the northern side of the salient, on 12 July, the Soviets commenced its counter-offensive and, on the southern side, the Soviets also launched powerful counterattacks which ended the German offensive because it had failed in its initial aims. The attritional battles of July and August ensued in the Battle of Kursk.

In terms of human casualties, the German side lost more than 200,000 casualties, almost one-third of the starting force. Soviet losses were much higher with more than 700,000 combat casualties. A battery of tanks, aircraft, heavy guns, and anti-aircraft guns were destroyed on both sides, but the Soviets could replace them more easily than Germany.

The support by the Lend-Lease Act of the U.S. to the Soviets helped mass-produce weapons, but the collaboration was almost one-sided and the Soviet's reception of the support was disconcertingly ungrateful.

The Soviet Union exacted the harsh maximum from its population during the war. The consistent improvement in war efforts changed Soviet forces from the clumsy and inept entity of 1941 into a formidable fighting machine in 1943. German forces had been truly disciplined and professional with tactical ingenuity, but they were hardly able to subdue the Soviets with affluent resources and sharpening expertise.

- The Battle of Guadalcanal

Guadalcanal was a small island, 145 kilometers long and 40 kilometers wide, covered by a dense jungle filled with lives and the dangers of malaria, dysentery, and dengue. Nearly all the soldiers of both sides who fought on Guadalcanal succumbed to one or more insects and diseases.

The Solomon Islands were occupied in May 1942 by Japanese forces. In June, Korean laborers and Japanese engineers were sent to Guadalcanal to construct a strategic airbase, to be finished by mid-August. It was not only to be a threat to Allied shipping, but it would also protect the

Japanese navy's main base at Rabaul on New Britain, further to the north.

The seventy-six ships of the U.S. force landed on the shore of Guadalcanal on 6 August without being detected. They were fortunate to make the surprise landing, helped by dark, heavy rain and mist. As there was little the Japanese could have done against the overwhelming enemy force, the Korean laborers and garrison soldiers fled into the surrounding jungles.

The Battle of Guadalcanal centered on the island airfield. The Japanese Supreme Headquarters gave Guadalcanal priority over all other operations while the Japanese navy continued to raid the navy task forces of the U.S., bombarded the airfield regularly, and the army operations against the American forces, armed with heavy artillery in a small enclave around the airfield.

The size of the forces in the battle was modest, but the intensity of the fighting was enormous. The U.S. deployed more than 60,000 troops, with casualties of 15,000, while Japan sent 36,000 with 20,000 men killed in combat. The U.S. lost 29 ships and 615 aircraft while Japan lost 38 ships and 683 aircraft including hundreds of experienced pilots.

The losses of the United States were significant but resupplied, but, for the Japanese forces, their losses were disastrous absorbing men, ships, and aircraft for a single distant airbase that was hardly able to be replenished, especially the naval force. The disproportion revealed a moment of truth, as shown in Stalingrad, that the Axis powers reached the limit of their war efforts.

On 31 December 1942, Emperor Hirohito approved the withdrawal, and, on 20 January 1943, more than 10,000 men were boarded off Guadalcanal. Along with the U.S. Navy's decisive victory in the Battle of Midway on 3-6 June 1942, the defeat of the Japanese army and the naval Combined Fleet in the Battle of Guadalcanal marked a turning point in WW II in Asia.

- The Second Battle of El Alamein

This battle of El Alamein waged as an air and tank battle (23 October -11 November 1942) pales in comparison to the great battles on the Eastern Front, but it made a big difference in the war situation in southern Europe, the Middle East, and North Africa including its implication with Suez Canal.

El Alamein was fought in the barren desert over distances of hundreds of kilometers from supply bases. In Rommel's case, by July 1942, it was over 1,450 kilometers from the main port of Tripoli.

The Allied plan of El Alamein was to attack with Italian infantry to the north of the line and to stave off the expected counterattack for which an elaborate deception plan showed a mass of armor in the south that compelled Rommel to keep the well-organized German Panzer Division and the Italian armored division in opposite positions.

Rommel was absent from El Alamein to recover his health. By the time Rommel arrived on 25 October, the British Empire had pushed for a critical breakthrough in the north. Axis tank and anti-tank forces held off British armor for two days, but, by 26 October, the German forces had only 39 tanks left. The Axis forces crumbled in an unwinnable war of attrition.

The Allies captured 40,000 Axis soldiers, adding to more than ten thousand dead and wounded. The Allies had 14,000 casualties, including those captured. The Italian war effort was virtually over, while the German forces lost a large quantity of manpower and equipment to secure the Middle East and the Suez Canal which was critical for oil and for blocking the route to and from India.

Rommel wasn't sufficiently supplied by Hitler to make victory possible. The Allied victory eliminated the Axis threat to Egypt, the Suez Canal, and the Middle Eastern oil fields. The battle revived the morale of the Allies, and it coincided with the Allied invasion of French North Africa which opened a second front in North Africa.

In addition to this point, we need to think about the fate of Arabic states and their people.in the battles who had been caught in the double whammy of British imperialism and Nazi expansionism. For them, it was difficult to distinguish the perfidious wickedness in between them.

All three battles—Stalingrad, Guadalcanal, and El Alamein—demonstrated the perils of imperial overstretch. The Allies won the battles not simply because of Japanese, German, and Italian strategic and tactical failures or poorer resources, but because the Allies learned to fight more effectively. The result changed the course of the war.

(10) The Eastern Front

An adage remarks that there is a difference between the sun and Hitler. The sun rose in the east; Hitler went down in the east.

The Eastern Front (22 June 1941-8 May 1945) was of great attrition in the vacillating range between northeastern Baltics and southeastern Balkans. The outcome eventually served as the reason for the defeat of Nazi Germany. More than 80 percent of all combats during WW II took place on the Eastern Front. The truly decisive fixed the fate of the Allies and the Axis.

Historically, it could be similar to the Battle of Gaugamela (331 BC) in which Macedon Alexander and Persian Darius fought the battle for the life or death of their empires and his lives. Conservative estimates of Soviet military casualties indicate 11 million on the Eastern Front, and those of Germans were 4 million, around 80 percent of military casualties of 5 million.

This meant the losses on the Eastern Front were heavily preponderant. A hypothetical question arises that if there were no Eastern Front, the mighty German forces would have been much more dangerous, and they would have inflicted much heavier losses and damages to the Western Allies and the fate of WW II was much different from the reality.

As the Eastern Front moved westward to Berlin, the Soviet loss rates declined and the German losses progressively increased. It was mainly because the competence of war efforts of the Soviets was growing higher and deeper while Germany was steadily weakened by fighting two fronts including incessant air raids of the U.S. and Britain.

As a benefit of hindsight, WW II might have developed in a far different direction if Hitler stopped its advance at the line of Baltic-Poland-Ukraine-Romania in 1941 and stabilized the Eastern Front by seeking another round of international recognition. By then, Hitler had already secured the vast expanse of *Lebensraum* in the East, and he achieved the aim.

It might mean a different feature of the war situation: a stable line of supply to the full formations of a strong German army and air force, securing leverage to negotiate with the Allied either for war or peace, mitigating a serious concern about all-Germanized Europe, and even to the Middle East while it secured its aspired the vast territory in the Central and Eastern Europe.

(11) Hitler's folly and blunders

This mistake was down almost entirely to Hitler's own ideologies and racist beliefs. Hitler chose to ally closely with Italy due to his and Mussolini's shared beliefs, but this ended up being disastrous to his war effort. Germany had to step in to clean up Italy's mess in North Africa, Greece and Yugoslavia. If Hitler had been able to disregard his racist beliefs he would have fared better to ally closely with Japan and take full advantage of their advanced military might.

Hitler had become a prisoner of his oversized ambitions infected by the virus of folly. Events were proceeding outside of all reasons.

A greater inducement to folly and danger is excess power because no one is able to resist the temptation of arbitrary power. In the first stage, mental confidence of Hitler succeeded in gambling on territorial expansion in European states (Austria, the Sudetenland in Czechoslovakia, and Poland until 1939, Belgium, Luxembourg, the Netherlands, and France in 1940. In the second stage, when failures in the air warfare with Great Britain in 1940 and the defeat at the Battle of Stalingrad in 1942-43, the initial principles of confidence were changed to obsession and rigidity. In the third stage, when the German forces turned to defensive war all the way to Berlin in the two fronts of East and West, the failures enlarged the damages until it causes the fall of the Third Reich.

Hitler's capabilities as a military strategist had been effective only while the lightning offensives of German forces had been possible. Once it was forced int defensive strategy, Hitler's inadequacies as supreme warlord was fully exposed even though his decisions not always counted for nothing in the desperate war condition.. In many cases in the state, he forced his generals into compliance with the lunatic orders. Hitler's tactics were frequently absurd and stood in crass contradiction to the military advice he was receiving.

- The Uprising in Serbia was initiated on 27 March 1941 by the Communist Party of Yugoslavia against the German occupation forces. The uprising soon reached mass proportions. Partisans and national guerillas captured towns that weak German garrisons had abandoned, and the armed uprising soon engulfed great parts of the occupied territory.

    The coup in Belgrade threw Adolf Hitler into one of the wildest rages of his life. He took it as a personal affront and in his fury, he decided to invade Yugoslavia by issuing Directive No. 2581 with an order that the beginning of the Operation Barbarossa to invade the Soviet Union will have to be postponed for up to four weeks.

    It was Hitler's spite that was vented upon a small Balkan country. It bungled the last-ditch attempt to pursue routing Soviet forces. This decision put the German forces in a state of deep bitterness in the striking distance of Moscow when the deep snow and subzero temperature of Russia hit them. They were three or four weeks short of achieving final victory.

- On 19 July 1941, Hitler sent out Directive No. 33, which brought to a halt the advance of the Army Group Centre towards Moscow. Some of its resources were diverted north to help with the encirclement of Leningrad, and south to help envelop Kyiv and further drive down towards the Donets Basin and the Caucasus oil fields beyond it.

  The advance on Moscow was to resume only in early September when the supply improved. Army leaders vigorously objected to the Directive because the defeat of the Soviet forces around Moscow would bring the final decisive result. Throughout late July and early August, the strategic initiative was lost as arguments continued over priorities.

  Hitler viewed that economic resources in Ukraine and Caucasus oils were more critical than in Moscow. He said that his generals knew nothing of the economic aspects of war when he rebuffed a proposal of General Guderian, the commander of the Second Panzer Army, on 24 August who insisted that his forces drive to Moscow rather than move south to Ukraine.

  Hitler was frustrated over a month of inconclusive argument. He got his way. General Guderian led his forces south with less than half the necessary tanks, and after bitter fighting in poor weather in a joint operation with the Northern Army, finally trapped five Soviet armies that Stalin had ordered to stay and fight for the Ukrainian capital.

  On 19 September, Kyiv fell, and Soviet armies capitulated after fighting a savage combat for six days. The Kyiv operation captured 665,000 Soviet prisoners and it suggested that the final victory was close at hand. But the reality turned opposite when Hitler stoutly ordered the German forces to stay and fight instead during the horrible winter in Russia that year.

- Hitler finally allowed the Army Group Centre to rebuild its forces to destroy what he believed to be the last reserves of the Red Army before Moscow was assembled on the Soviet Western and Reserve Fronts. Directive No. 35, issued on 6 September, focused principally on defeating the armies to the west of Moscow, rather than seizing Moscow itself.

  Army commanders and the rank and file saw the city itself as their goal after endless campaigns through the battered and abandoned countryside. Historically, a similar sort of blunder took place in the Second Punic War (219-213 BC) between Carthage (Hannibal) and Rome when Hannibal's army swept across the Italian Peninsula.

  He didn't attack Rome but bypassed it to occupy the lands in the south of it. This gave Rome an opportunity to regroup and it later invaded Carthage. Hannibal later cursed on his own head for not having led his armies straight to Rome.

  Another case was the Battle of Dunkirk from 26 May to 4 June 1940, when some 338,000 British Expeditionary Force (BEF) and other Allied troops were evacuated from Dunkirk to England as German forces closed in on them. The ex-corporal Hitler made the same mistake.

  Contrary to the wishes of officers in the field, he ordered a halt to the advance of German panzer divisions bearing down on Dunkirk out of worry about an Allied counterattack, and the German air force could prevent any evacuation attempt at Dunkirk. His decision saved the souls of the Allied, many of whom waded the beaches of Normandy four years later.

- The German decision to declare war on the United States on December 11, 1941, was a deadly strategic blunder. In a state where Germany was already engaging in costly campaigns against the Soviet Union and the British Empire, the addition of war with the world's largest economy was scarcely a rational choice.

  Hitler held derogatory views of the capacity or willingness of the United States to wage a major war given its relative military unpreparedness and its isolationism. Upon the declaration, Hitler asserted that American officers were merely businessmen in uniform, not real soldiers and that American industry was terribly overestimated.

  In the National Socialist version of the world, Roosevelt was a Jewish lackey who drove the Jews in Moscow and London to continue the war and thus the war with the U.S. was engineered by the Jews. The Jewish complicity made the declaration of war a rational reckoning for Hitler, rather than the irrational gamble it otherwise appeared to be.

  This is a vivid illustration in history of how irrationality overwhelms rationality in the form of biased conviction and deep-rooted prejudice and expediency.

- Hitler lost what little sense of reality he still retained in his final weeks leading up to the end of April 1945. He sometimes lost himself in his own thoughts, and floated away, as if in a mist. He sacked senior officers who failed to stand fast. He failed to allow the German armies trapped on the Courland Peninsula or cut off in East Prussia to leave by sea, when it was still possible, to strengthen the defense of the German heartland.

  Finally, on 19 March, he published a decree usually known as the *Nerobefehl* (Nero Order) for a scorched-earth policy in the remaining German territory to leave nothing intact, from bridges to food stocks that the Allied military could use. By this stage, local military and Party authorities refused to implement the decree.

  When the collapse came, it usually came suddenly.

(12) The scene of the Hitler's real end

Over the time until that Soviet troops had forced their way into Potsdamer Platz and streets in the immediate vicinity of the Reich Chancellery, Hitler had been caught in the Hitler's bunker where he was sometimes in catatonic state in the frenzy of despair and disorder. When they were no more than a few hundred yards away from Hitler's bunker in a breakdown in communications for most of the day, it was time to prepare for real end of it.

As long as Hitler had had a future, he had ruled out marriage because his life, he had said, was devoted to Germany. Eva Braun had chosen to come to the bunker, and she had refused Hitler's own entreaties to leave. She had committed herself to him once and for all, when others were deserting. The marriage now cost him nothing, but he did it simply to please Eva Braun, to give her what she had wanted more than anything at a moment when marrying him was the most dramatic quirk of fate.

After the midnight of 29 April 1945, Hitler and Eva Braun exchanged married vows in the most macabre surroundings with the bunker shaking from nearby explosions as Goebbels and Bormann were witnesses, and the rest of the staff waited outside to congratulate the newly wedded couple. Champagne, sandwiches, and reminiscences – with somewhat forced joviality – of happier days followed.

At 11:30 pm, just before the wedding ceremony on the day of reckoning for the moment of truth, Hitler had asked his secretary, Traudl Junge, to take down some dictation of his last will and testament. He began with a brief Private Testament. He referred first to his marriage to Eva Braun, and her decision to come to Berlin and die at his side. He disposed of his possessions to the party.

His last words for posterity were a piece of pure self-justification. The rhetoric is instantly recognizable, redolent of *Mein Kampf* and countless speeches; the central idea of the responsibility of international Jewry for the death, suffering, and destruction in the war remained unchanged, even as he now looked death in the face. The conspiracy theory continued unabated.

He attributed the rejection of his proposal on the eve of the attack on Poland partly to the business interests of 'leading circles in English politics', partly to the 'influence of propaganda organized by international Jewry. He came to a key passage – an oblique reference to the 'Final Solution' relating it once more to the fulfilment of the prophecy of 1939.

'It is untrue that I or anyone else in Germany wanted the war in 1939,' he dictated. 'It was desired and instigated exclusively by those international statesmen who were either of Jewish descent or who worked for Jewish interests … Centuries will pass away, but out of the ruins of our towns and cultural monuments the hatred against those ultimately responsible ..international Jewry and its helpers.'

He could not forsake Berlin. The forces there were too small to hold out against the enemy and he said his resistance was gradually devalued by deluded and characterless subjects who had betrayed him. He would choose death at the appropriate moment. Again, he indicated his own fear of what he saw as the still dominant power of the Jews.

He avowed that a renaissance of National Socialism would eventually emerge from the sacrifice of the soldiers and his own death. He ended with an exhortation to continue the struggle. He begged the heads of the armed forces to instill the spirit of National Socialism in the troops and fulfill their duty unto death. The Political Testament concluded by charging the merciless resistance to the international Jewry.

(13) Japanese imperial war

Japan's leaders thought that war with the U.S. was far from ideal, but the situation in which the U.S. restricted Japanese access to key industrial resources had provoked them. The decision had much in common with Hitler's claim that the British enemy could only be defeated by attacking a larger, and more powerful opponent. For Japan, fighting the U.S. was a similar predicament.

It was evident that further warfare could not be conducted successfully without access to additional material resources, whether in Ukraine or Southeast Asia. After ten years of imperial expansion, Japan saw Eastern Asia in much the way the United States viewed the Western Hemisphere as its area of domination which other powers have to respect.

Japanese leaders found it hard to understand why the status should not be accepted as a fait accompli, and negotiations with the U.S. had begun on the basis that Japan had a legitimate claim as the leader of Asia, that its expansion couldn't be a violation of international norms, and the stance of the U.S. to reject Japan's role to build a just peace was unacceptable.

American intransigence was interpreted as an international conspiracy to stifle Japan's national existence. Unsurprisingly, there was almost no common ground between the two sides in 1941 to find a modus vivendi with the U.S. that would allow them to resolve the China war on their terms and gain secure access to the strategic resources for its empire.

As early as 1938, Roosevelt had called for an embargo of oil, steel, aircraft, and finance for Japan. In January 1940, the 1911 Commercial Treaty with Japan was abrogated. Following Japanese entry into northern French Indochina in the summer of 1940, the U.S. introduced formal restrictions on aviation fuel, scrap iron and steel, iron ore, copper, and oil-refining equipment.

Japan was expected to be cowed by the economic crisis provoked by American sanctions, but the complete dislocation of Japan's economic situation indeed accelerated the shift to more radical solutions. The pressure that the U.S. had put on Japan deflected the direction of energy that Japan erupted, not in the way of obeying the order of the U.S. but in the creation of its own order.

During 1941 the Japanese political and military leadership arrived incrementally at the point where war seemed both necessary and unavoidable as Hitler had. American politicians failed to understand the impact the four years of the China war had had on Japan. Japanese society was now geared for total war with shrinking supplies of food for the civilians although there were some circumspect advisors who assuaged the hatred and tempered the boldness of those belligerent but blasé warmongers..

In the final phase of negotiation before the attack on Pearl Harbor on 7 December 1941, on 22 November, the Americans intercepted a message to Japanese negotiators in the U.S. that 29 November 1941 was the final deadline for an agreement. *'This time we mean it, that the deadline absolutely cannot be changed. After that, things are automatically going to happen.'*

A key breaking point in the deal was the issue of China that the U.S. was resolutely against any agreement that left any part of China in Japan's hands which was unacceptable for Japan. The U.S. delivered a note to the Japanese negotiators on 26 November 1941, making clear that an agreement could only be made only when the occupation of Manchuria was reinstated.

Japanese leaders regarded the note as an ultimatum, the government discussed their choices and, on 29 November, it concluded that the war option prevailed. Few Japanese leaders seemed to have favored war with the U.S. and the British Empire, but the decision was taken with a fatalistic acceptance that fighting was preferable to humiliation and dishonor.

The day the Hull Note was delivered to Ambassador Nomura, the Japanese Navy's Mobile Striking Force was sailing from its base in the Kuril Islands to attack, if ordered, the American Pacific fleet at Pearl Harbor. On 2 December, Nomura received the coded message *"Climb Mount Niitaka 0812"* authorizing the attack to go ahead on 8 December, Japanese time.

Troop convoys were also on the move south from China and Indochina towards the Philippines and Malaya. The latter movement was reported in Washington, where it was assumed that Japanese forces aimed to occupy Malaya and the Dutch East Indies, but the fleet of Mobile Striking Force remained sealed in secrecy until the hour of the attack on Pearl Harbor.

The surprise attack of Pearl Harbor was completed on the morning of 7 December by a Japanese force that consisted of 6 aircraft carriers with 432 aircraft, 2 battleships, 2 cruisers, and 9 destroyers from which a total of 181 aircraft were launched in the first wave and 167 in the second. Despite the intensive training, the operation was fraught with difficulty and mistakes.

The success was the destruction and damage of the 309 American aircraft. The attack on the American naval ships met with less success. Out of forty torpedo bombers, only thirteen hits were scored and just damaged two of the eight cruisers. The second wave found the targets obscured by smoke. Not only was the hit ratio poor, but many bombs failed to explode.

The American carriers were all at sea. Four battleships were sunk, two cruisers and three destroyers were seriously damaged, and two auxiliaries were sunk. A total of 2,403 were killed and 1,178 were injured. The attack could have achieved much more including aircraft carriers if the Japanese raiders were armed with more experience, better tactics, and intelligence.

The Japanese attack electrified the American public and ended the debate between isolationists and interventionists for years. Defeating Japan at all costs united Americans. Following the attack, President Roosevelt delivered the address to Congress asking that a state of war be declared between the United States and Japan on 8 December 1941.

Japan made a blunder to trigger the war with the US by attacking the Pearl Harbor. It would be understood in the same context of invading the Soviet Union by Hitler in 1941 who underestimated the strength of the Soviet forces and people in the wake of Germany's victories in neighboring countries such as Poland and France from 1939. The successes in its military campaign in Southeast Asia, Pacific and China made the Japanese forces did the same blunder in their war with the US.

5.3. The 20th century in WW II (Beyond WW II)

1) WW II Closing Stage

(1) The Finale

By early 1945, the power of the Allies was overwhelming, and resistance against it was close to suicide. The Axis states exerted a final effort to preserve the homelands. The German army ran the order of fanatical struggle for every meter of their homeland soil. On Iwo Jima, the first homeland territory of Japan to be invaded, the troops were said to kill ten GIs before dying.

The U.S. Air Forces in Europe had 5,000 bombers which bombed military and transport targets in Germany to a point where the social and psychological damage would make it impossible to continue the war. The knockout blow was delivered through the cumulative damage to the Germans. The bombing of Dresden on 13/14 February 1945 allegedly killed 25,000 people in the city.

Japan's final struggle could materialize beyond the German scale because their home island had never been conquered by foreign enemies in history. The military was determined to fight the life-and-death battles should their homeland be invaded. The possible U.S. casualties would be too great to endure as had been experienced in Iwo Jima, 26,000, and Okinawa, 84,000.

The onset of heavy bombing inflicted substantial damage on Japan, but the bombings in daylight at high altitudes in the fierce winds proved ineffective. U.S. Air Force changed its tactics upside down by bombing at night-time from low altitude with incendiary napalms. The air raid by 325 B-29s on the night of 9/10 March 1945 killed more than eighty thousand.

The Allies and Germany had been struggling with the surrender terms in Europe, but it paled in comparison to the difficulty of forcing a Japanese surrender, since for the Japanese military the concept of SURRENDER was unthinkable. They would be left in surrender only after they all died in combat as they had done in Iwo Jima, Okinawa, and other islands.

The U.S. was divided over the surrender terms for Japan: (i) the soft peace retaining the imperial system because the longer the war, the greater the Soviet intervention, and (ii) the hard peace refusing any conditions of surrender. The Potsdam Declaration by the U.S., U.K., and China on 26 July demanded that Japan be destroyed unless it surrendered unconditionally.

The notion of utter destruction was literal because the U.S. just succeeded in testing an atomic bomb at the time. If Germany had not surrendered in May 1945 and fought on as the Japanese did, the first atomic bomb might have been dropped in Europe. Japan dismissed the Potsdam Declaration that required unconditional surrender.

Whatever the moral scruples might be, U.S. President Truman granted approval to go ahead with the nuclear attacks. From the list of cities including Hiroshima, Kokura, Niigata, Nagasaki, and Kyoto, the first atomic bomb was dropped on Hiroshima on 6 August which killed around more or less hundreds of thousands of people. (*Blood and Ruins* by Richard Overy, p.370)

On 9 August, an Imperial Conference had a long argument. The military persisted with the four conditions of surrender (the Allies abandon occupying Japan, the Japanese disarm, punish war criminals, and keep the imperial system intact), and the civil officers just one condition of the imperial system, but none of them presented an unconditional surrender.

A second atomic bomb killed hundreds of thousands of people in Nagasaki, which was chosen because Kokura, the first chosen city, was obscured by clouds on the day. Emperor Hirohito approved the Potsdam Declaration if the imperial system was retained. Other factors of anti-war feelings, a widespread food crisis, and the dreading Soviet occupation mattered, too.

On 14 August, a second Imperial Conference was called at which Hirohito insisted the surrender against army objections, and all military leaders were now bound by the imperial decision. That day Hirohito recorded an imperial rescript to be broadcast at noon on the following day and it was notified to the Allies later in the day. The wider Japanese public heard the emperor's voice for the first time at noon on 15 August informing them of the Japanese defeat. Hirohito did not say the word 'surrender', but merely that he would accept the Potsdam Declaration and bear the unbearable with his people.

Following the demises of Italy, Germany, and finally Japan, the Allies were busy framing the post-WWII structure that led to the Cold War.

(2) The process to end the war.

This was how World War II was ended, and the post-war geopolitical structure of the world was mapped out. The purpose of outlining the agreements reached at the Allies' summits is to show the global political process that underlies the lofty rhetoric of political leaders. Each agreement includes some remarks regarding controversial relevance to Korea, and, in particular, Poland, which had been in a situation much similar to Korea's.

• Atlantic Charter on 14 August 1941. U.S.(Roosevelt) and Great Britain (Churchill)

First, their countries seek no aggrandizement, territorial or other.

Second, they desire to see no territorial changes that do not accord with the freely expressed wishes of the people concerned.

Third, they respect the right of all peoples to choose the form of government under which they will live; and they wish to see sovereign rights and self-government restored to those who have been forcibly deprived of them.

Fourth, they will endeavor, with due respect for their existing obligations, to further the enjoyment by all States, great or small, victor or vanquished, of access, on equal terms, to the trade and to the raw materials of the world which are needed for their economic prosperity.

Fifth, they desire to bring about the fullest collaboration between all nations in the economic field with the object of securing, for all, improved labor standards, economic advancement, and social security.

Sixth, after the final destruction of the Nazi tyranny, they hope to see established a peace that will afford to all nations the means of dwelling in safety within their own boundaries, and which will afford assurance that all the men in all lands may live out their lives in freedom from fear and want.

Seventh, such a peace should enable all men to traverse the high seas and oceans without hindrance.

Eighth, they believe that all of the nations of the world, for realistic as well as spiritual reasons must come to the abandonment of the use of force. Since no future peace can be maintained if land, sea or air armaments continue to be employed by nations which threaten, or may threaten, aggression outside of their frontiers, they believe, pending the establishment of a wider and permanent system of general security, that the disarmament of such nations is essential. They will likewise aid and encourage all other practicable measure which will lighten for peace-loving peoples the crushing burden of armaments.

--

The Charter framed the post-war world structure: to avoid territorial expansion, seek the liberalization of international trade, and establish freedom of the sea. Most importantly, both committed to supporting the restoration of self-government for all countries that had been occupied during the war and allowing all peoples to choose their own form of government.

The Charter dealt with the situation and framed the post-war picture. Great Britain had been spared from the German invasions, the U.S. Lend-Lease Act of March 1941 supported Britain, Germany inflicted humiliating defeats upon Britain and France threatening to block the Suez Canal and British access to its possession of India.

Moreover, after it invaded the Soviet Union on 22 June 1941, suspecting that the Soviets would collapse within a few months, Japan was about to advance to seize British, French, and Dutch territories in Southeast Asia. Public opinion in the U.S. was adamantly opposed to U.S. intervention in the European war.

In the negotiations, Churchill was not able to get Roosevelt into the war, to make a secret treaty for the division of enemy territory, and to recognize the colonial interests of Britain in India and Asia. But, Churchill just felt satisfied with the assurance of Roosevelt that Europe remained the US's priority. The joint declaration raised the morale of the desperate British.

Roosevelt was highly determined to support the self-determination of the colonized people, freeing them from vestigial European imperialism, and for freedom of trade and collective security under the U.S. influence. These helped build the new order of Pax-Americana. The Charter differed from the Wilsonian misconception of self-determination in 1918 which misled the colonized.

Contrary to the principle of the Atlantic Charter, Britain didn't give up its colonial interests, especially in India. In 1942, the Indians were indignant with frustration that Britain was not compliant with the Atlantic Charter. American opinion hardened against the British even though this did not inhibit collaborative war efforts with Great Britain.

In China, Chiang Kai-shek regarded the Atlantic Charter as focused on Europe in its intent, although he decided to interpret the "Nazi tyranny" in the Clause No.6 loosely included Japan. In January 1942, Chiang asked Roosevelt to apply the Charter to the peoples of Asia, and he asked the same to Roosevelt and Churchill in Cairo in November 1943, but without success.

It is the power that rules the decision. This shows in the cases that the U.S. rebuffed the British intent of colonial interests in India and Asia and demanded self-determination which was tuned with Pax-Americana. China had futilely attempted to insert Asia into the Atlantic Charter, but it failed as the U.S. and Britain took no heed of it.,

- Cairo Declaration on 27 November 1943: U.S.(Roosevelt), Great Britain (Churchill), China (Chiang Kai-shek).

It was timed when the war turned in favor of the Allies. Italy had surrendered, Germany was fighting on two fronts, the Soviet forces were pushing the German forces all the way to Berlin, the Allies were battling air warfare with Germany in the Western front, the stalemate in China and Southeast Asia, and the U.S. offensives on the Solomon Islands against Japan.

The declaration developed the ideas from the Atlantic Charter on August 14, 1941, to set goals for the post-war order.

The following general statement was issued:

"The several military missions have agreed upon future military operations against Japan. The Three Great Allies expressed their resolve to bring unrelenting pressure against their brutal enemies by sea, land, and air. This pressure is already rising.

The Three Great Allies are fighting this war to restrain and punish the aggression of Japan. They covet no gain for themselves and have no thought of territorial expansion. It is their purpose that Japan shall be stripped of all the islands in the Pacific which she has seized or occupied since the beginning of the first World War in 1914, and that all the territories Japan has stolen from the Chinese, such as Manchuria, Formosa(Taiwan), and The Pescadores, shall be restored to the Republic of China. Japan will also be expelled from all other territories which she has taken by violence and greed. ***The aforesaid three great powers, mindful of the enslavement of the people of Korea, are determined that <u>in due course</u> Korea shall become free and independent."***

"With these objects in view the three Allies, in harmony with those of the united nations at war with Japan, will continue to persevere in the serious and prolonged operations necessary to procure the unconditional surrender of Japan."

Controversy as to Korea.

The Cairo Declaration pledged independence for Korea *"in due course."*

Many prominent Koreans including Kim Gu and Syngman Rhee were initially delighted by the declaration, but later noticed and became infuriated by the phrase "in due course". This vague phrase aroused confusion and doubt over the intent of the Allied, and Korean leaders requested an interpretation from the United States, but they received no answer.

They took it to be an affirmation of Allied intent to place Korea into a trusteeship, rather than granting it immediate independence. There was significant concern that the trusteeship could be indefinite or last for decades, making Korea again a colony under a great power. It crudely jolted the Korean community which had never dreamed of it.

The phrase "in due course" was allegedly not present in the first draft as it originally read "at the earliest possible moment after the downfall of Japan." The U.S. suggested "at the proper moment", and finally the British "in due time". The exact motivations for these changes are unclear. Again, it is the power that rules the decision following its interests.

- Tehran Declaration on 1 December 1943. U.S.(Roosevelt), Great Britain (Churchill), and the Soviet (Stalin).

The Statement reads:

The common understanding that we have here reached guarantees that victory will be ours.

--

And as to peace—we are sure that our concord will win an enduring peace. We recognize fully the supreme responsibility resting upon us and all the United Nations to make a peace which will command the good will of the overwhelming mass of the peoples of the world and banish the scourge and terror of war for many generations.

With our diplomatic advisers we have surveyed the problems of the future. We shall seek the cooperation and active participation of all nations, large and small, whose peoples in heart and mind are dedicated, as are our own peoples, to the elimination of tyranny and slavery, oppression and intolerance. We will welcome them, as they may choose to come, into a world family of democratic nations.

--

In the underlying meeting for the Statement, the parties agreed that:

1) the British and Americans finally committed to launching Operation Overlord, an invasion of northern France, to be executed by May of 1944 for which the Soviets had long been pushing the Allies to open a second front.

2) Stalin also agreed in principle that the Soviet Union would declare war against Japan following an Allied victory over Germany. In exchange for a Soviet declaration of war against Japan, Roosevelt conceded to Stalin's demands for the Kuril Islands and the southern half of Sakhalin, and access to the ice-free ports of Dairen (Dalian) and Port Arthur (Lüshun Port) located on the Liaodong Peninsula in northern China. The exact details concerning this deal were not finalized, however, until the Yalta Conference of 1945.

3) Stalin pressed for a revision of Poland's eastern border with the Soviet Union to match the 1944. In order to compensate Poland for the resulting loss of territory, the three leaders agreed to move the German-Polish border to the Oder and Neisse rivers. This decision was not formally ratified, however, until the Potsdam Conference of 1945.

It is known that there was no explicit description of Korea in it.

In the talks during the meeting, Stalin addressed his position to secure a Soviet postwar buffer zone by reincorporating the Baltic states (Lithuania, Latvia, and Estonia) into the Soviet Union while Roosevelt advocated that the citizens of each republic vote in a referendum. Stalin stressed it to be resolved by the Soviet constitution implying that the interest of the Soviets should prevail.

Roosevelt sided with Stalin on the issue of a Soviet postwar buffer zone at a high point in US-Soviet relations. It cooled and turned conflicting when both were stuck in the stalemate in 1948 in Korea. The Soviets wanted the Korean peninsula to be a Soviet buffer state while the U.S. pushed for a unified Korean government that wouldn't orient itself against American interests.

• The Yalta Conference on 4-11 February 1945. Roosevelt, Churchill, and Stalin, again.

The Allies launched successful Normandy landings on 6 June 1944. The Battle of the Bulge in December-January 1945 was the last major German offensive on the Western Front. Soviet forces reached less than 50 miles from Berlin, and the U.S. was ending the Pacific War. WW II was not over yet, but it was apparent for the Allies to win the war.

The Statements reads.

--

DECLARATION ON LIBERATED EUROPE

--

The establishment of order in Europe and the rebuilding of national economic life must be achieved by processes which will enable the liberated peoples to destroy the last vestiges of Nazism and Fascism and to create democratic institutions of their own choice. This is a principle of the Atlantic Charter - the right of all peoples to choose the form of government under which they will live- the restoration of sovereign rights and self-government to those peoples who have been forcibly deprived of them by the aggressor Nations.

--

POLAND

A new situation has been created in Poland as a result of her complete liberation by the Red Army. This calls for the establishment of a Polish provisional government which can be more broadly based than was possible before the recent liberation of western Poland. The provisional government which is now functioning in Poland should therefore be reorganized on a broader democratic basis with the inclusion of democratic leaders from Poland itself and from Poles abroad. This new government should then be called the Polish Provisional Government of National Unity.

M. Molotov, Mr. Harriman, and Sir A. Clark Kerr are authorized as a commission to consult in the first instance in Moscow with members of the present provisional government and with other Polish democratic leaders from within Poland and from abroad, with a view to the reorganization of the present government along the above lines. This Polish Provisional Government of National Unity shall be pledged to the holding of free and unfettered elections as soon as possible on the basis of universal suffrage and secret ballot. In these elections all democratic and anti-Nazi parties shall have the right to take part and to put forward candidates.

When a Polish Provisional Government of National Unity has been properly formed in conformity with the above, the Government of the USSR., which now maintains diplomatic relations with the present provisional government of Poland, and the Government of the United Kingdom and the Government of the USA will establish diplomatic relations with the new Polish Provisional Government of National Unity, and will exchange ambassadors by whose reports the respective Governments will be kept informed about the situation in Poland.

The three heads of government consider that the eastern frontier of Poland should follow the Curzon line with digressions from it in some regions of five to eight kilometers in favor of Poland. They recognized that Poland must receive substantial accessions of territory in the North and West. They feel that the opinion of the new Polish Provisional Government of National Unity should be sought in due course on the extent of these accessions and that the final delimitation of the western frontier of Poland should thereafter await the peace conference.

--

The stumbling block was the future of Poland, all of which was now under Soviet occupation. Roosevelt and Churchill reluctantly agreed that the Soviet Union should keep the areas occupied in 1939, but there was no firm agreement on where Poland's compensating frontier in the West, carved out of eastern Germany, was to be fixed.

The new Poland was already under the provisional rule of a committee of communists set up by Stalin in 1944 as a government-in-waiting. Stalin insisted that he wanted a democratic and independent Poland, but in practice, there was no means available to the Western Allies for a different outcome since the Soviet was determined not to give way to Poland for Soviet security.

A temporary compromise was reached when Stalin agreed to allow a commission, composed of Molotov and the British and American ambassadors, to meet in Moscow and work out a formula for a democratic Poland, but the commission soon reached a stalemate when the three men met, and Poland, the initial cause of the war in 1939, was left to its communist fate.

Controversy as to Korea.

Korea was not recorded in the demands and concessions. However, Roosevelt brought up the idea of putting Korea into a trusteeship divided among the Soviets, the Americans, and the Chinese for a period of 20 to 30 years. He expressed reluctance to invite the British to the trusteeship, but Stalin reportedly replied that the British would most certainly be offended.

They both agreed on it and navigated the issue of Korea themselves. Stalin suggested the trusteeship be as short as possible. The two quickly agreed that their troops should not be stationed in Korea. Korea was not discussed again throughout the conference, and they did not document any formal agreement on the future status of Korea.

It was the first occasion on which the trusteeship in Korea was tabled and agreed upon. The partitioning of territory and establishing a satellite state in Poland was seemingly referenced to partition the Korean peninsula and set up a regime favorable to the interests of the Americans or the Soviets, which was, in their ideological nature, hardly able to co-exist and get along.

The two quickly agreed that their troops should not be stationed in Korea. Korea was not discussed again throughout the conference. After the Yalta meeting, there was a growing uneasiness between the Anglo-American allies and the Soviets with issues of European and Asian countries.

When it comes to the effects on pertinent nations, Poland and Korea have a historical similarity in that they were both frequently invaded and harmed by their aggressive neighbors. They were also not fairly represented or treated during the period of imperialism and nationalism, even as they were establishing their own states following WW II.

We understand their remarks in light of Korea and Poland.

   i) They confirmed the principle of the Atlantic Charter pledging the self-determination of all people and nations, but the details were contrary to it. The Statement was heavily weighted on the issues in Europe and those of Asian countries were not handled equally. They professed to discard imperialism, but the reality in the Statement didn't reflect it.

   ii) They agreed to partition Poland as the United States and Great Britain accepted the Soviet demands that cut away a part of eastern Poland that was compensated with a part of north-eastern German territory. They didn't listen to the leaders from Poland and abroad, nor did they try to reflect their interests in the agreements.

   iii) The Polish partition and setting up a Polish provisional government were schemed in the concept that the Soviets took the land and established a buffer state favorable to the Soviets. The reality went against the big and good words of "reorganizing Poland on a broader democratic basis" which gave an impression that the independent sovereignty of Poland could be established and lasting.

Again, national power rules the decisions in international politics. A maltreated party may protest an unfavorable decision with good reasons, but the cold reality, in essence, is the lack of power that is to blame, not the superpowers who place a priority on their interests in the uneven political terrain in the guise of common interests, so-called the clichés of stability and prosperity.

• Potsdam Conference on 26 July 1945. Winston Churchill, Harry S. Truman and Joseph Stalin

The Nazis are gone, and imperial Japan is at death's throes. The members of the Allies, except the Soviet, defined the terms for the Japanese surrender. The Proclamation was issued at Potsdam in Germany after the Nazis categorically collapsed a few months ago, and the last offensive in the Pacific War was sounding the death knell for imperial Japan.

The Statement reads:

--

4. The time has come for Japan to decide whether she will continue to be controlled by those self-willed militaristic advisers whose unintelligent calculations have brought the Empire of Japan to the threshold of annihilation, or whether she will follow the path of reason.

5. Following are our terms. We will not deviate from them. There are no alternatives. We shall brook no delay.

8. The terms of the Cairo Declaration shall be carried out and Japanese sovereignty shall be limited to the islands of Honshu, Hokkaido, Kyushu, Shikoku and such minor islands as we determine.

10. We do not intend that the Japanese shall be enslaved as a race or destroyed as a nation, but stern justice shall be meted out to all war criminals, including those who have visited cruelties upon our prisoners. The Japanese Government shall remove all obstacles to the revival and strengthening of democratic tendencies among the Japanese people. Freedom of speech, of religion, and of thought, as well as respect for the fundamental human rights shall be established.

12. The occupying forces of the Allies shall be withdrawn from Japan as soon as these objectives have been accomplished and there has been established in accordance with the freely expressed will of the Japanese people a peacefully inclined and responsible government.

13. We call upon the government of Japan to proclaim now the unconditional surrender of all Japanese armed forces, and to provide proper and adequate assurances of their good faith in such action. The alternative for Japan is prompt and utter destruction.

Controversy as to Korea.

Throughout the Potsdam Conference in July 1945, the U.S. insisted on encouraging the Soviet entry into the war against Japan. The Soviets asked their U.S. counterparts about invading Korea, and the Americans replied that such an expedition would not be practicable until after a successful landing had taken place on the Japanese mainland.

The ensuing Potsdam Conference included the statement that "the terms of the Cairo Declaration," which promised Korea its independence, "shall be carried out." In the terms of its entry into the war against Japan on August 8, the Soviets pledged to support the independence of Korea.

General Order No. 1 on 11 August by the United States provided for Japanese forces north of latitude 38° N (the 38th parallel) to surrender to the Soviets and those south of that line to the Americans. Stalin did not object to the contents of the order. Troops of the U.S. and the Soviets entered the Korean peninsula to receive the Japanese surrender in September.

The concept of Korean independence "*in due course*" as stated in the Cairo Declaration, and the partitioning of the Korean peninsula and "the trusteeship" as agreed in the Yalta Conference was getting fleshed out. The local protests of the partitioning and the trusteeship couldn't reverse or change the ongoing directives.

The process was gravitated into the general hostilities of the Korean War which was provoked by Communist North Korea under the support of its big brothers, the Soviet and the Communist China. Nothing is firm and lasting in international politics, but it is the power and needs of each party that motivate certain actions.

2) What WW II was

After WW II, the frame of understanding WW II has been set primarily from the perspective of the victorious Allies. We need to redress the balance to understand WW II, which inflicted considerable damage and losses to humankind. A well-rounded understanding of the war is valid for dealing with the problems in the contemporary world.

(1) The Allies and the Axis.

The new wave of regional imperialism of the Axis was challenged by the Western powers to protect their colonial interests, and then the Axis reconfigured themselves to justify their global total war. WW II, in its nature, was a conflict of imperial interests by and between those who wanted to protect their vested interests and take them.

The decades-long process of decolonization after WW II involved the liquidation of the British Empire and other colonial states which dismantled the vested interests of imperialistic legacies.

The incompatibility and fantasy of an alliance of the Allies between the two capitalist states (the U.S. and Great Britain) and the one communist state (the Soviet Union) were destined to fall apart as they just set aside the profound political and moral differences between them during the duration of the conflict.

Until the outbreak of the Nazi-Soviet War in 1941, the Western powers treated the Soviet Union as nothing better than Hitler's Nazis, took it quite beyond the pale of acceptable human behavior, and regarded communism as a profound threat to democratic values and the way of life.

Soviet leaders were also equally harsh in their judgment of the capitalist world. Capitalism was the principal threat to peace and bourgeois leaders were perceived as the agents of immoral class repression. The Non-Aggression Pact with Hitler in August 1939 could be justified as the means to frustrate bourgeois plans to turn Germany against the Soviet Union.

During the period of the Non-Aggression Pact, the Soviets consistently maintained a position that its major enemy was imperialist Britain, and Germany was regarded as a cause for peace which was forced into a defensive fight by the imperialist powers. The moral condemnation evaporated as Germany invaded the Soviet Union on 22 June 1941.

The recapture of Stalingrad and the defeat of the German forces in February 1943 were treated as if it had been a Western victory with rapturous admiration for the Soviet Army and fervent Sovietophilia with no consideration of the moral gloss placed on it. By the last year of the war, the pre-war view of communism and capitalism as morally incompatible began to resurface.

For Soviet leaders, the alliance was deemed a marriage of necessity. In Moscow, they couldn't see a moral distinction between the fascist and democratic states since both were tarred with the same capitalist brush. Around the end of the war, the popular Western honeymoon with the Soviet Union collapsed as they saw how difficult it was to sustain a marriage of necessity.

(2) Moral supremacy in relativity

Waging war against immoral enemies provided a powerful justification for total war. The Axis (Germany, Italy, and Japan) viewed the global order in the 1930s as illegitimate, which limited their claims for just shares. In China, Japanese officers complained, "Britain dominated India. Why not then for Japan to dominate China?".

The apparent hypocrisy or moral ambiguity motivated the imperial conquests of Manchuria in 1931 and Poland in 1939 to seize territory. The Three Power Pact in September 1940 assigned them tasks of establishing new imperial orders in Europe, the Mediterranean basin, and East Asia.

In Germany, the invasion of Poland was met with declarations of war by Britain and France which were seen as a conspiracy to encircle Germany and stifle its legitimate claims to imperial parity. It inverted the invasion to a just war for national survival, and the moral inversion became common to all Axis states until the end of the war.

In Japan, the Western support for China after the Sino-Japanese War in 1937 was a conspiracy to foil Japan's rightful claim to empire. The aggression was inverted into a war of self-defense against encirclement by the white powers. They took on a moral obligation to overthrow the autocracy of the white man and bring the Asian people under the Japanese imperial protection.

For the Allies, the justice of the Allied cause was taken for granted because the wars were self-defense against the aggressions of the Axis, who aimed at territorial ambitions. The violence of the Third Reich and Imperial Japan had to be stopped before their expansion challenged the core interests of Western powers.

For the U.S., the attack on Pearl Harbor in December 1941 resolved the division between isolationists and interventionists. It united the country to defend against the attack of the unjust enemies who were bent on enslaving humanity. Self-defense became a norm that was consistent with the just war tradition.

For Great Britain, they believed that their fight was just against the moral degradation of brute force and oppression of Nazi Germany. However, they were stuck in the double standard that Great Britain was defending democratic values, but it desired to keep controlling colonial empires with no intention of instituting democratic values.

For the Soviets, the Russo-Nazi War was a liberation war. The defense against the unjust fascist aggression of Nazi Germany was the just war of liberating the people in the conquered Eastern Europe as well as the homeland. It was a political gain for Stalin because the war made the unpopular Stalin before the war the center of power to save the country.

The decades-long processes of decolonization after WW II have shown a fact that the vested interests of imperialism were long in dying. The deep-rooted and die-hard legacy of the imperial occupation of the Allies and the Axis has exhibited moral ambiguity or even moral absurdity. Britain and France had retained colonial rule as long as they could.

The term of moral supremacy is relative depending on who is the narrator, but one clear thing is that there have been less privileged people who were colonized and persecuted by the imperial powers, either the Allies or the Axis. The colonial actions were immoral and atrocious to those who were colonized, and they deprecated the colonial rule.

Nonetheless, the cold reality of history reminds us that the best way is to become powerful enough to conquer others or, at least, avert the risk of getting colonized. It was always too late to undo the wrongdoing, or it was always insufficient to make the recovery from the damage. Peace comes and stays when one is powerful and ready for war to protect the peace, not by appeasement or luck for the peace.

(3) Violence and non-violence

There is a wide range of anti-war sentiment in liberal democratic cultures, from militant pacifists to moderate ones. According to radical nonviolent resistance, Christian pacifists' ethical rejection of violence or total pacifism was the most effective way to oppose total war.

Among those who desire peace, however, some did not exclude the possibility of war for a just cause. Participation in total war became a moral imperative transcending the conscientious rejection of violence, even by pacifists or churchmen who before the war condemned the drift to renewed conflict.

In the 1920s, the rejection of war was an endorsement of the new wave of international idealism embodied in the creation of the League of Nations. The anti-war movement embraced Christian pacifists who argued that war was incompatible with the teachings of Christ, as well as socialists and communists, for whom peace was an ideal aspiration.

In the 1930s, popular anti-war sentiment expanded in reaction to the international crisis and the political campaigns for isolation and neutrality. However, the pro-war sentiment surged in September 1939. There was an absolute majority of votes for war in the British Parliament after the German invasion of Poland, and in the U.S. Congress after the attack on Pearl Harbor.

In the 1940s, most of the warring populations endorsed the war effort willingly by their silence, complicity, enthusiasm, or indifference. The states exerted strategies of control, surveillance, and morale-building to ensure that their war efforts were regarded as legitimate and just, even in those many cases where they were not.

(4) Post-WW II World

At midnight on May 8-9, 1945, a strange but welcome silence settled over the Continent for the first time since September 1, 1939. The Thousand-Year Third Reich simply ceased to exist and there were no traces of German authority. It was bizarre and far different from the case of WWI in 1918 where the government had continued to function.

In the vacuum of central power, there was a vast humanitarian crisis. More than millions of prisoners, defectors, exiles, and innumerable civilians were on the move without a government. Moreover, the rift between the former wartime Allies (the U.S. and the U.K. vs. the Soviet Union) became explicit and the Cold War looked unavoidable.

Among all the upheavals after 1945 that helped to shape the new post-war global order, there were four significant factors.

First, it was the radical adjustment of Germany. Not only were the Allies restricted in Germany to the territory following the Versailles Treaty of 1919, but in the agreement with Stalin at the Yalta Conference, Poland was to be compensated for the loss of the eastern territories to the Soviet Union by a large slice of eastern Germany.

Second, it was the emergence of the PRC (People's Republic of China). The Communist Party won the civil war, and it created a unitary nation-state of socialism after driving Chiang Kai-shek to the island of Taiwan. The emergence of was one of the historic events in the 20th century and it made significant impacts to politics, economy, and society of the world.

Third, the international political structure was radically altered with the retreat of the imperial powers whereby the imperial system was replaced by nationalism and anti-colonial sentiment. It ended the centuries of empire-networks in eight years (1946-1954), stimulated emancipation from colonial rule, ended racial discrimination, and encouraged self-determination. It cornered Britain to rely on the U.S. for financial assistance in the condition that economy collapsed, and value of Sterling plummeted. In barely four decades, the Great Britain had gone from world mastery to holding out their caps and begging for help in the Pax-American era.

Fourth, it was the onset of the Cold War. The U.S. and the Soviet Union became hegemonic in the post-war world in massive military superiority and global political ambitions. The Cold War persisted until the end of the Soviet bloc in 1990 after which the American uni-polar system was set in place and governed the globe.

5.4. The 20th Century (Korean modern history and war)

1) Understanding the Colonization by Japan (1910-1945)

(1) The 1800s and 1900s

Over the history of East Asia, the peoples of the Han race, Mongolians, Manchurians, Koreans, and Japanese had been in contact and mingled through migrations in peaceful or hostile terms. The idea of a purely separate national identity is virtually a fantasy for each of them because the web of perennial interactions has blurred the distinction of separate identities between them.

The 19th century was the era of Western imperialism when social Darwinism saw inferior countries as naturally selected entities to be controlled. The imperialistic way of thinking in the West spilled over into Japan when it developed the Western systems of society and industry on a national level.

Located on the peninsula, Korea was a land bridge linking continental China and island Japan whereby Korea has been exposed to a multitude of foreign invasions into or through it as well as playing its roles of cross-cultural experiences between the two regions. An empirical view is that all of them had invaded Korea when they unified their land.

In the 19th century, East Asia faced Western imperial expansion, and their responses were not identical. China was humiliated by its incompetence to engage with foreign interference, Korea was puzzled to find its answer to the riddle of foreign threats, and Japan proactively reformed itself to adopt Western systems. It was their strategy that made the differences in each state.

(2) Japan

Facing the Pacific Ocean in the back with continental China through Korea, Japan had been a backwater feudal society until the 1850s. It was also forced into unequal treaties to open the ports and make trade with Western powers. A part of the ruling elites crafted a strategy to reform themselves in their response to the Western imperialists and propelled the Meiji Restoration in 1868 (the term "Meiji" means "enlightened rule").

The Meiji Period (1868-1912) was an era of the execution of a strategy to modernize its governing systems by blending modern advances with traditional values. It overthrew the Tokugawa Shogunate which had governed for more than 250 years and restored the imperial reign that placed the emperor in the center of power with ultimate responsibility.

The transformative change empowered hybrid reforms that westernized its economy and culture but maintained its sovereignty and national identity. The strategy led Japan to the state of emulating Western imperialists and then it flexed its muscle in Asia and the Pacific to pursue its imperial aspirations as a regional hegemon in the beginning of the 20th century.

For Japan, the sea wasn't merely a route of trade, but a source of learning about modern systems, and expanding its conquests. It was the political leadership that activated the revolution for future generations, not by retreating to the past. This was strikingly different from the way that Korea had responded aimlessly to its challenges during the same period.

Japan has advanced en route from Korea to China. It used the same tactic of forcing Asian nations to accept unequal treaties in humiliation as it had once accepted unequal treaties from Western powers decades ago. Japan had been virtually unchecked in driving its imperial expansion in Asia all the way down the line until the war in the Pacific with the U.S.

The disparity of modernization process in late 19th century to the beginning 20th century between the monarchic Joseon in Korea and the Meiji-Japan is illustrated:

	The monarchic Joseon in Korea	The Meiji Restoration in Japan
Political system	Joseon maintained its self-imposing containment policy. In 1897, it declared itself Empire in 1897 to keep its sovereignty, but it was too late to reverse the trend of decline	Japan made its own the Meiji Restoration which was far different from the restoration of Taewongun in Joseon in that introduced the constitutional monarchy
Neo-Confucianism, led by the Chinese philosopher Zhu Xi. (1130-1200) in the Song Dynasty that advocated rank, obligations, deference, and traditional rituals, reinforcing distinctions of social class and gender	Josen held fast to Sino-centric culture and kept Neo-Confucianism. The ruling elites adopted policies of restoration of monarchic order and expulsion of Western influence. The meagre reform attempts were suppressed. Joseon massacred the Christian missionaries and learned nothing from them.	Japan adopted Japan-centric belief system and challenged the Neo-Confucianism. Japan learned the Western culture from its contacts with the Western Christian missionaries
Reform	After the unequal Ganghwa Island Treaty in 1876, Joseon lost opportunities to reform itself. There was a revolt of some elites to reform the country in 1894, but it was crushed very shortly. After annexation with Japan 1910, Joseon made fundamental socio-economic reforms, but they were forced and involuntary reforms.	After the unequal US-Japan Treaty in 1858, a group of reformers in the final decades of Tokugawa period staged proactive reforms to transform its socio-political systems They took the initiative in the reforms in the manner of proactive and voluntary actions. This is one of the reasons that it spared the colonialism of European imperialistic powers.

(3) Korea

The modern history of Korea begins with the Joseon Dynasty (1392-1910), which had established a unique governing system as a client state of China from its inception but stayed independent. The two characters in the statehood of the Joseon Dynasty had been working properly as far as China was powerful and solid and Joseon was competent to manage the intra-Korean affairs.

King's father, Taewongun, had administered the restoration to stiffen the monarchy (1864-1873) instead of Some adventurous Korean elites initiated some quixotic reforms in the 1880s. The pursuit of enlightenment and Westernization was not comparable to the Meiji Restoration, let alone the Enlightenment in Europe, and was constantly thwarted by reactionary people. King Gojong and his aides were unable to restructure the nation, reset the political structure, and execute reforms.

Joseon ended up in a situation where it helplessly had to see Japan, China, and Russia fight in the Sino-Japanese War (1894-1895) and the Russo-Japanese War (1904-1905) for their benefit in Joseon. Although the wars were closely related to the national interests of Joseon in the Korean Peninsula, it had no power at all to address its concerns to the warring powers.

The watershed was the treaty with Japan in 1876 in Ganghwa Island (which is famous for the resistance against the Mongol occupiers in the 13th century). It was unequal to Joseon who was not proactive nor dominating the negotiation. If it was so, then the history would have been much different.

Many other countries had undergone the stages of Restoration – Reform – Revolution – Regression – Renewal of statehood, but Joseon skipped the stage of Reform – Revolution until the Korean peninsula was divided and there were two states in 1948.

Theodore Roosevelt, President of the USA, received the Nobel Peace Prize in 1906 for the first time as a statesman after the Russo-Japanese War for his role in ending the bloody war between the great powers of Japan and Russia. In the awarding ceremony on 10 December 1906, Roosevelt delivered the message by his proxy on his behalf:

"I am profoundly moved and touched by the signal honor shown me through your body in conferring upon me the Nobel Peace Prize. There is no gift I could appreciate more, and I wish it were in my power fully to express my gratitude. I thank you for it, and I thank you on behalf of the United States; for what I did, I was able to accomplish only as the representative of the nation of which, for the time being, I am president."

For Koreans, the award should be understood in the context of the Taft–Katsura Agreement between Japanese Prime Minister Katsura and U.S. Secretary of War Taft held in Tokyo on 27 July 1905 before Roosevelt became a Nobel laureate in 1906.

It reads:

"Katsura's views on peace in East Asia formed, according to him, the fundamental principle of Japan's foreign policy and were best accomplished by a good understanding among Japan, the United States, and Great Britain.

On the Philippines, Taft observed that it was in Japan's best interests to have the Philippines governed by a strong and friendly nation like the United States. Katsura claimed that Japan had no aggressive designs on the Philippines.

On Korea, Katsura observed that Japanese colonization of Korea was a matter of absolute importance, as he considered Korea to have been a direct cause of the recently concluded Russo-Japanese War. Katsura stated that a comprehensive solution of the Korean problem would be the war's logical outcome. Katsura further stated that if left alone, Korea would continue to join improvident agreements and treaties with other powers, which he said to have created the original problem. Therefore, he stated that Japan must take steps to prevent Korea from again creating conditions that would force Japan into fighting another foreign war."

It was the bold face of international politics that the West recognized Japan as the regional hegemon in their realistic view and the special interest of Japan in Korea. The national interests of the hegemons were traded under the table in the name of peace and stability by imperialists whose actions were applauded, prized, and boasted about on the public stage.

The honor and fame of the Nobel laureate entailed tons of tears and pain for the Koreans as the Taft–Katsura Agreement completed the American conquest of the Philippines which was traded for Japanese special interests in Korea. This again affirms the point that power ruled the decision that played with the issues relevant to Korea and the Philippines.

The Agreement motivated Japan to colonize Korea in 1910 and then to perform its imperial ambition in China. It later advanced into South Asia and culminated in Pearl Harbor. The Nobel Award opened the can of worms of imperial Japan. U.S. President Theodore Roosevelt (1901-1909) served a causal effect of the Pacific War for U.S. President Franklin Roosevelt (1933-1945). Nothing is independent and static, but everything is connected and fluid in history.

Japanese colonial rule shifted its policies to govern Korea from 1910 to 1945:

1910s in coercive policies, 1920s with the policies of appeasement and assimiliation, 1930s in the policies of industrialization and building extortion systems, and 1940s in extraction-extraction policies. Specifically, the period from 1937 to 1945 was the time of the Korean industrial revolution.

On 15 August 1945, the unconditional surrender of Japan was a joyous announcement for tens of millions of Koreans under the decades-long colonial servitude, but the liberation carried a heavy price. Korea was not liberated by the Koreans, and so it was subjugated to the will and wishes of its liberators.

During the colonial period, there had been violence and non-violence protests. However, the Allies didn't perceive the Korean independence army in China and Russia as a military party eligible for joint operations in scale and scope against Japan in China, Southeast Asia, or the Pacific. The lack of military operation with the Allies made the post-WWII history unfavorable to Korea.

Colonizers extracted values from the colonized. For the colonized, the pains were too severe to recuperate from them. For the colonizers, the gains from them were too sweet to give them up. Thus, the colonizers justified their double standards by preaching peace but promoting servitude in the colonies and suppressing them brutally when the colonized people revolted.

From the perspective of international law, Japan was solely responsible for the colonial rule over Korea. From a historical point of view while witnessing a variety of violence at the state levels, however, the ineptitude of the Korean elites was also to blame, as they failed to reform themselves, protect their people, keep their statehood, and do justice against Japan when it was violated, and stage an independence war in good scale and scope worthy of internation recognition. All nations wished for complete independence in the decolonization period, but the real world evidenced that complete independence was never given, but always taken.

The cruel administration under colonial rule had left a variety of legacies that were needed to reestablish the political structure, recover Korean culture, and rebuild the economy. In the process, the systems of education, administration, judiciary, and educated human resources were utilized to rebuild the nation of Korea both in the south and the north in different conditions of natural resources and character of industries (agricultural industries in the south, and rich natural resources and heavy chemical industries in the north).

In South Korea, the conflicting reality was that colonial-trained human resources helped rebuild the country. This has become the bone of contention over the purity of sovereignty in the post-colonial period. Interestingly, the colonial assets of infrastructure and industrial facilities also contributed to the national rebuilding, but the colonial assets were not as contentious as humans.

Again, it was national power that ruled the decisions in international politics.

2) The lead-in process for the Korean War

Two Korean governments were established, the democratic South (the Republic of Korea, ROK) in August 1948, and the communist North (the Democratic People's Republic of Korea in September 1948). In the state that the economies of both regimes were heavily dependent on tenant-farming, both executed the land reforms.

In the North, it was radical and violent, involving the expropriation of lands and free distribution to peasants, which triggered a mass migration of the deprived landlords to the South. In the South, it was modest and rational, involving the purchase of lands from landlords and renting them out to peasants based on rent-purchase.

Specifically, the ROK enacted the Land-Reform Act in June 1949 the government imposed a three-hectare cap on landlords to retain the land, it purchased the excess by issuing bonds to the landlords, and it rented the land to peasants at 30% of harvests in kind for 5 years, after which it issued to the peasants the land-ownership certificates.

The reforms leveled the chronic land inequality in the Korean Peninsula. As to the compensation to landlords and the rents payable by peasants, the inflation around the Korean War (1950-1953) caused different real values for unhappy landlords and happy peasants. It further helped the egalitarian society to emerge.

If the land reform wasn't processed by the ROK in a timely and proper manner, it would have triggered a mass revolt of disaffected peasants in the South during the Korean War because the invader, the DPRK in the North, had already completed its land reform by free distribution to peasants. If so, the War would have ended up with a far different result: a communized Korean Peninsula.

The Soviet Union is primarily responsible for the division of the Korean Peninsula: it was concerned about a case that Korea became an equivalent of Poland in Europe that may be a springboard to attack Russia by the Western powers. So, it asserted that the government in Korea should be loyal to the Soviet Union, or the peninsula should be divided if not.

The Soviets rejected the plan to establish a single government under the guidance of the United Nations and it fomented an environment for two Korean governments on the peninsula, one in South Korea under the recognition of the United Nations and another in the north under the direction of the Soviet Union.

The 38th parallel wasn't set along the natural boundary that was formed by natural features such as rivers or mountains, but it was a geometric boundary that was created using straight lines without considering any physical or cultural features. Henceforth, it has demarcated the homogeneous Koreans in all spheres of life that remain well into the 21st century.

The Moscow Conference of Foreign Ministers of the Allies in December 1945 agreed to organize a joint commission to form a trusteeship of the Allies for five years for one Korean government. The political parties from the right to the left of Korean Communists were strongly opposed to the trusteeship.

The Joint Commission convened in Seoul on 20 March 1946 failed to agree on the details. The Soviets proclaimed that Korea should become independent but loyal to the Soviet Union. On the contrary, the U.S. opposed the Soviet dominance in Korea and insisted that Koreans have a democratic government with rights of free expression. It ended up in a permanent deadlock.

On 14 November 1947, the UN General Assembly adopted a resolution drafted by the United States to establish a unified Korean government through an election under UN supervision. The Soviet Union stood firm against this UN resolution on Korea, making impossible the establishment of one Korean government in Korea.

The Soviet military command in North Korea refused to hold the election and boycotted it. Unable to proceed with the election, the first universal suffrage election was held on 10 May 1948 in South Korea. The National Assembly was formed on 31 May 1948 and the ROK was formally established on 15 August 1945, with Syngman Rhee as its first president.

On 25 August 1948, the North Korean People's Council adopted its own version of the constitution. Kim Il-sung as premier of the DPRK was appointed on 9 September 1948. In this way, the two Korean governments were formally and separately established which has been lasting till now with no immediate prospect of a single Korean government.

On 17 March 1949, the Soviets decided to arm the North Koreans. Korean soldiers in the Soviet army were released to the 105th Armored Brigade, the 3rd and 4th Infantry Divisions that undertook the main attack on Seoul in 1950. The Soviets also induced Communist China to do the same of well-seasoned Korean soldiers to DPRK, which formed the main forces of the 5th, 6th, and 12th Divisions.

After the United States completed its troop withdrawal from South Korea on 30 June 1949, and following the Soviets' successful A-bomb explosion in August 1949, Kim Il-sung asked for the permission of the Soviets to attack South Korea on September 3, 1949. The Soviets opposed the idea because the North Korean forces were not overwhelmingly superior to those of the South.

Kim Il-sung and Park Hon-young, visited Moscow (30 March - 25 April 1950) and discussed with Stalin the situation in South Korea: The Communist victory in China, the Soviet possession of the atomic bomb, and the absence of US soldiers in South Korea. Stalin cautioned about American intervention and the necessity to obtain the support of Communist China as a prerequisite to the war.

Stalin instructed that the war should have three stages: troop concentration, another fresh peace proposal to deceive South Korea, and after the proposal is rejected, the attack. He also instructed them to consult with China. He made clear that the Soviets wouldn't join the war because it was tied up in Europe. Kim Il-sung showed confidence to win the war within a few weeks.

As directed, both Kim and Park visited Mao (13-15 May 1950) and secured his promise to help North Korea in case of American intervention. Stalin's conditions for support and guidance for the war in Korea were met and cleared, and the North Korean army became far superior to those of South Korea in all categories of fighting capabilities.

On the other hand, the U.S. did not want to arm the South Korean forces. The strength of the Korean army was suitable to an extent for maintaining internal order, border security, and coastguard service. The U.S. flatly rejected providing advanced weapons and artillery in its admonition that South Korea should develop its economy rather than amassing a military force.

The difference in policy and strategy between the U.S. and the Soviets created an imbalance in military power between North and South Korea. Kim Il-sung, of course, with permission from Stalin and the guidance of the Soviet military advisers, ordered an attack on South Korea on Sunday 25 June 1950.

North Korea has been a stage country. Everything is pre-planned and controlled by the Party's rules. The people are the victims of megalomaniacal propaganda and dictatorial controllership. Information on the outside world has been blocked and the breachers have been harshly punished. The tradition started from the secrecy and outrageous acts of war against the same race. The Korean War was the result of official policy of the Soviets and the China to provoke the war, not merely nods, nudges and winks to do it.

3) Poor competence of military intelligence

The U.S. withdrew its troops from South Korea on 30 June 1949. It rejected three proposals of South Korea: the expansion of the Korean army from 65,000 to 100,000, public assurance to assist the ROK in case of an armed attack, and a Pacific Pact like NATO. Americans stressed the importance of developing the economy rather than amassing a large military force.

In the meanwhile, the Soviet Union strengthened the North Korean forces with 10 army divisions (including 242 T-34 tanks and 122 mm heavy guns), 200 aircraft, a navy with amphibious and battleships, and military advisers. The Soviets and Communist China released the Korean soldiers who had fought in the Stalingrad and the Chinese Civil War.

The intelligence authorities in Korea and the U.S. failed to gather the correct information on the movement in the communist bloc in 1949-1950 that was arming the North Korean forces and developing the plan to invade South Korea. Lacking intelligence and unpreparedness for the war made the morning of 25 June 1950 chaotic and surprising for the ROK and the U.S. alike.

A similar sort of intelligence failure was found in the German forces about the power of the Soviet forces before it invaded the Soviet, and about the timing and place of the landing in France in 1944, the Japanese navy lost the intelligence war that led to the defeat of Midway Sea battle. The loss of intelligence and counterintelligence wars was catastrophic.

4) The Korean War (1950-1953)

On 25 June 1950, North Korea started the Korean War at an unexpected time against an unprepared South Korea resulting in stunning victories in the first three months. The swift intervention of American and the UN forces turned the tide, the Chinese intervention stalled the war, and the end of the war in July 1953 after a lengthy war of attrition for more than two years.

The legacy of the war was deep and bitter, and it cast a long shadow on the peninsula. It was just suspended with a cease-fire, and it set in motion another confrontation in the peninsula for seven decades. North Korea had failed to communize Korea by military means but it has persistently tried to overthrow the South Korean government in all cunning ways.

The numerous occasions of provocation have produced casualties such as the sinking of a patrol ship of the South Korean navy on 26 March 2010. North Korea has been advancing its nuclear weapons and, from the end of 2023, the North Korean regime has publicly proclaimed that it would abandon its policy of peaceful reunification and annihilate South Korea.

The strength of U.S. forces when the North invaded, was undermanned, poorly trained with faulty and, often, outmoded equipment and surprisingly poor high-level command leadership, were an embarrassment to both the ROK and the U.S. government. The drop-off between the strength of the U.S. Army they had known at the height of WW II, its sheer professionalism and muscularity, and the shabbiness of American forces as they existed at the beginning of the Korean War was nothing less than shocking to all.

The Korean War momentarily turned the Cold War hot, heightening the already considerable tensions between the U.S. and Communist world. When the war was all over and an armed truce ensued, both sides claimed victory, though the final division of Korean Peninsula was no different from the one that one had existed when the war began.

Sitting in the fault lines of the Cold War, the ROK could not build resources to become self-sufficient. The US aid programs from 1951 to 1959, apart from the cost of the U.S. forces in Korea, amounted to 12 billion dollars. For twenty years from 1945 to 1965, it was USD 600 million per year, equivalent to USD 30 per head for 20 million people in the ROK.

The decades-long expenditures in waging the war and maintaining the post-war ROK economy was a hefty burden for the U.S. taxpayers, while South Korea had taken the role of containing the expansion of the communist bloc (North Korea, the Soviet Union, and communist China) for the disarmed Japan and the influence of the U.S. in Asia.

President Rhee was 65 years old when the Korean War broke out, he stood indefensible, but he had hard-fought to preserve the statehood, and finally concluded the Mutual Defense Treaty between the ROK and the U.S. when the Korean Armistice Agreement was signed in July 1953. The CIA (Central Intelligence Agency) labeled him senile, indomitably strong-willed and obstinate.

On one hand, some blame his autocracy and corruption in his regime. On the other hand, he was 75 years old in 1960, much older than the present standard. The threats of North Korea, the burden to rebuild the war-torn country, the industry that couldn't feed the population, and the low levels of civility amidst absolute poverty made it difficult for him to establish a full-fledged democracy.

We must not miss the points that the first President of the ROK had laid the foundation of a liberal democratic country, he withstood the storm of the Korean War that had threatened the ROK to extinction, and he squeezed the Americans to sign the Mutual Defense Treaty that has been crucial for rebuilding the economy as well as the security since the Korean War.

5) Comments on *"Korea's Place in the Sun"*

Reading *Korea's Place in the Sun: A Modern History* by Bruce Cummings, I felt a necessity to make the following comments.

(1) Chapter Four. *The Passions, 1945-1948*. p192

Once the American occupation chose to bolster the status quo and resist a thorough reform of colonial legacies, it immediately ran into monumental opposition from the mass of South Koreans. Most of the first year of the occupation, 1945-46, was given over to suppression of many people's committees that had emerged in the provinces. This provoked a massive rebellion that spread over four provinces in the fall of 1946; after it was suppressed, radical activists developed a significant guerrilla movement in 1948 and 1949. They also touched off another major uprising at the port of Yo su in October 1948. Much of this disorder was owing to the unresolved land problem, as conservative landed elements used their bureaucratic power to block redistribution of land to peasant tenants. The North Koreans, of course, sought to take advantage of this discontent, but unimpeachable internal evidence shows that nearly all the dissidents and guerrillas were southerners, upset about southern policies. Indeed, the strength of the left wing was in those provinces most removed from the thirty-eighth parallel, in the southwestern Chollas, which had historically been rebellious, and in the southeastern Kyongsang provinces, which had felt Japanese colonialism the most.

Comments.

Bruce Cummings just wrote that the rebellion in Yeosu (19-27 October 1948) was owing to the unresolved land problem. He did not specify the points on who had triggered the mutiny in the army unit, what the rebels of communists and collaborators had perpetrated toward the innocent people in the town, and what occasions it had affected.

There was a rebellion of the leftists on Jeju Island, and the ROK Army headquarters was to transfer one battalion of the 14th Regiment to the island to quell the rebellion. Some leftist soldiers inside the army unit disobeyed the transfer because it was fratricidal warfare and incited a mutiny of killing officers and colleague soldiers.

They proclaimed that they made the uprising in the cause of the people's army to protect the same race. They also demanded to stop the fratricidal killing and to get the U.S. Army to withdraw from town. They said they had 'liberated' the regions and ruled the people in the direction of being favorable to the North Korean regime.

It provoked civil rebellion from those who favored the ideas of communism and organized a death squad that massacred innocent civilians of landowners, government officials, police, and Christians including their families. The military mutiny was changed to civil war that needs prompt action to stabilize the fragile geo-political condition.

The ROK government made its decision to suppress the rebellion promptly and strictly. In the ensuing process of battles and clean-up campaigns, there were thousands of casualties, including civilians, in the disorder that made it difficult to distinguish the leftist collaborators from the innocent people.

The occasion rendered a cause to remove the leftists in the military units. The Korean War would have been much riskier for the ROK government if the leftists had remained in the military units when the war broke out in June 1950. The leftists who incited the mutiny purged the military of leftist traitors, but the civil casualties became a matter of clarification.

The leftist soldiers proclaimed to be "people's army" and they wouldn't involve themselves in fratricidal battles. If it was so, would they also reject the DPRK in the Korean War in June 1950, which was a real killing spree on a massive scale against the same race in South Korea? If there was a rebellion of the rightists in Cheju Island, by chance, would they also take the same stance?

Bruce Cummings also highlighted the rebellious Jeolla and pro-Japanese Gyeongsang provinces. Each locale has its own distinctive features, which have undergone a series of changes and adaptations. Historically, and in the modern era, Jeolla province has been distinguished by a higher rate of evangelization of Christianity than other regions. During the Korean War, the North Korean communists caused significant damage to the region's religious infrastructure, by destroying about 900 churches, and around 360 pastors and their families were martyred.

When identifying the specific character of a region, it is essential to consider it in a holistic manner, taking into account historical and socio-political perspectives. Similarly, Gyeongsang province has a long history of independence movements from Japanese colonial rule. The definition of "rebellious Jeolla and pro-Japanese Gyeongsang provinces" is too simplistic and binary and does not reflect the full complexity of the situation. It is not a simple matter of black and white. Such a dichotomous approach to causality in Korean history is inadequate.

(2) Chapter Five. Collision, 1948-1953. p251

When we now look at both sides of the parallel with the help of some new (if scattered and selective) Soviet materials, we learn that Kim Il Sung's basic conception of a Korean War was quite similar to Rhee's, and was influenced deeply by the August 1949 fighting: namely, attack the cul de sac of Ongjin, move eastward and grab Kaesong, and then see what happens. At a minimum, this would establish a much more secure defense of P'yongyang, which was quite vulnerable from Ongjin and Kaesong. At a maximum, it might open Seoul to his forces. That is, if the southern army collapses, move on to Seoul and occupy it in a few days. And here we see the significance of the collapse of the ROK Second and Seventh divisions, June 25-27, 1950, which opened the historic invasion corridor and placed the Korean People's Army in Seoul on the twenty-seventh, and why some people with intimate knowledge of the Korean civil conflict have speculated that these divisions may have harbored a fifth column.

Comments.

Regarding the ROK 2nd and 7th divisions during the three days after the War, Bruce Cummings indicated a possibility of the fifth column in the army that was attributed to the collapse of the divisions. It is unclear how he got such an idea, but I wish to see the bloody battles in the eyes of my father (Myungshik, Min) who had fought the battles as a member of the 2nd Division.

Born in 1932 in a rural village near Cheongju, a mid-western part of Korea, he volunteered for the ROK Army in January 1948. He was a sergeant in the 25th Regiment of the 2nd Division stationed in Onyang, a mid-western town, 200 km away from the 38th Parallel when the war broke out on 25 June 1950.

On 25 June, Sunday, in Onyang. some soldiers were routinely on leave and the available ones in the camp were ordered to support farmers to plant rice on the rice paddy in the villages nearby. While they were in the work not for long, a trumpet blew, and a desperate tone of shouts followed, "*All soldiers, get out of the rice paddies immediately, and run to the campsite as fast as you can!*"

Perplexed, they, including my father, stampeded in a hurry even barefoot, and when they rushed in through the guardhouse of the campsite, they found that the armory was fully opened and officers were ordering "Carry all weapons and ammunition, unlimited!". That was the scene of the morning of 25 June at the campsite of a regular ROK army unit, when North Korea provoked the Korean War.

On 26 June in and outside Seoul, the northbound train in which the ROK army unit of my father was aboard stopped at the Yeongdeungpo Station in Seoul for signal-waiting. When a southbound train was stopping at the rail track beside him, he glanced at the scene where the red blood of wounded ROK soldiers gushed through leaks of carriage doors, and he told himself, "This is real war".

The train went north to Dongducheon Station, north of Seoul near the 38th Parallel. When it was approaching the Station in the afternoon, the North Korean army machine-gunned at the train, and the ROK soldiers instantly jumped out of the moving carriages and started to fire back. That moment was the start of his battle to defend Seoul for three days until 28 June.

Meanwhile, the other two regiments (16th in Cheongju, 5th in Daejeon) of the 2nd Division arrived at the places of battles at different times and places. It meant the 2nd Division headquarters could not control its forces in good order from the beginning. The collaboration with the ROK 7th Division which had been stationed in the front region was also in confusion and disorder.

27 June at midnight in Miari Ridge, northern Seoul: It was the last defense line for Seoul. His regiment had fought ferociously in Dongducheon and Uijeongbu, suffering huge casualties. The mood of confusion and urgency was enormous at the desperate defense lines. The communication line of report and order got gradually disconnected, and the supply was broken down.

The group of disparate groups of soldiers from various army units, policies, and even students of ROK Army Academy were naturally gathered in the last defense line. Exhausted in disarray, however, the ROK soldiers were highly determined to stand the ridge to the last, not to open the gate for the northern army to downtown Seoul.

The ferocious fighting went on throughout the day as my father's foxhole was flooded with piling empty shells of his rifle to his thighs. He alternated rifles of the deceased ROK soldiers beside him when his rifle became too hot to grab and fire. It was the day and night of desperation, determination, ferocity, and anger.

The commander of the battalion gathered surviving ROK soldiers, randomly picked a dozen of them, and ordered them to jump into the enemy tanks with activated mortar shells and self-detonate. My father said that he coincidentally sat behind a tree and was not pointed at the random selection. Very sadly, they were killed one by one even before they reached the tanks.

The fighting ROK soldiers dwindled, waves of the North infantry never ceased, and their tanks dissected and ironed out the defense lines of the ROK Army. The defense of the Miari Ridge was crumbling and finally breached. The heroic survivors had to retreat leaving their dead fellow soldiers there toward the Han River which divides the capital city into north and south.

In the pitch-black night under heavy rainfall, it was a life-or-death scene of hide and seek, escape or capture until the dawn of the next morning. Many of the rain-soaked and exhausted ROK Army soldiers were captured as they retreated, and some of them managed to cross the Han River, which separates Seoul into two parts.

A few ROK soldiers, including my father, were making their way through the rain toward the Yongsan ferry dock on the Han River, which connected the northern and southern parts of the city. As they were making their way through Seoul Station, they happened to merge with a big group of soldiers who were heading into my father's group from a different direction. My father initially thought they were another group of ROK soldiers retreating. As you might expect, they all ended up marching together in a group, shoulder to shoulder, towards the Han River.

My father quickly noticed that their rifles were different, and he realized that he was surrounded by North Korean soldiers. He quickly but silently broke away from the group and ran for his life toward Namsan Mountain opposite Seoul Station. He said it was less than a second that saved his life. By the time dawn broke, he was dressed in civilian clothes only carrying a pistol in his back. He saw that many of the ROK soldiers, though disguised in civilian clothes, were being captured by the North Korean military police at ferry docks along the Han River.

He diverted the course and was unexpectedly guided to the route of escape with the help of a middle-aged woman who introduced herself as the wife of a ROK Army Major and was also escaping the city. She hired a small boat from Nowheresville, and both crossed the river. My father parted away from the woman in gratitude and joined the ROK Army in the south of Seoul.

His impression of the three-day battles was that the North Korean army was professional, and morale was high, their firearms were much more powerful than those of the ROK Army, and they had planned the war very well. However, the battles made him feel that a fight between uniformed soldiers was matchable, but it was their tanks that made the difference.

It was like chicks were slaughtered by wolves. He tearfully recollected the scenes in which the ROK soldiers were hopelessly crushed, machine-gunned, and killed in cannon fires from the roaring tanks. He witnessed the same happening later to the North Korean army when the thunderous fighters and bombers of the UN air force mercilessly strafed and bombed them throughout the war period.

Bruce Cummings alluded to the fifth column, namely sabotage or mutiny, inside the 2nd Division and the 7th Division during the battle (25-27 June). As far as my father experienced, there had never been any sign of sabotage or mutiny, but a mix of determination and confusion in the desperate conditions.

My father was discharged from his service just before the end of the war in 1953, and he died a natural death in 2018 at the age of 86. It may be a little bit funny, but not a joke at all. He would break open his coffin in honor of his fellow soldiers who had fought with him and were killed in the three-day battles if or when he heard that there was likely to be a fifth column that contributed to the collapse of the 2nd Division.

It is an honor of life-and-death for some veterans as well as those who were killed in the battles including their families and descendants. Without solid evidence, such claims should not be simply alluded to or insinuated.

(3) Chapter Five. Collision, 1948-1953. p263-4

Kim Il Sung bears the grave responsibility for raising the civil conflict in Korea to the level of general war, with intended and unintended consequences that no one could have predicted. To say that this was the culmination of previous struggles, and that Rhee wanted to do the same thing is true but does not gainsay Kim's responsibility for the horrible consequences.

Scattered Soviet materials have shown that Soviet involvement in preparing and planning an invasion after Stalin gave his reluctant endorsement in January 1950 was higher than previous writers had thought, but we still know too little to determine the respective North Korean, Soviet, and Chinese roles in initiating the June fighting. Even when we have every document the Soviets ever produced, we will still need the South Korean archives, the North Korean archives, the Chinese archives on both sides of the Taiwan Strait, and the American intelligence, signals, and cryptography archives before we will be able to argue on truly solid ground the question we ought all try to forget, namely, "Who started the Korean civil war?" Whatever happened on or before June 25, it was immediately clear that this war was a matter of "Koreans invading Korea"; it was not aggression across generally accepted international lines. Nor was this the point at which the civil conflict began. The question pregnant with ideological dynamite "Who started the Korean War?" is the wrong question. It is not a civil war question; it only holds the viscera in its grasp for the generations immediately afflicted by fratricidal conflict. Americans do not care anymore that the South fired first on Fort Sumter; they do still care about slavery and secession. No one wants to know who started the Vietnam War. Someday Koreans in North and South will reconcile as Americans eventually did, with the wisdom that civil wars have no single authors. It took Americans about a century to do so; it is therefore not surprising that Korean reconciliation is still pending after fifty years.

Comments.

Bruce Cummings confirmed that North Korea bears grave responsibility for the horrible consequences of the Korean War, but he opened a space for further study to find an answer to the question of "Who started the Korean civil war?" He implied that both parties might have rendered reasons respectively for the Korean War.

It needs some reinforcements to answer the question:

Iron sharpens iron; brother shines brother, or iron dulls iron; brother outshines brother. The existential shape of the two Koreas was the latter that made them mutually repulsive and exclusive.

The front-line skirmishes between the two Koreas before the war were far different from the full-scale invasion by North Korea on 25 June 1950. The Soviets orchestrated the invasion in their East Asia policy to expand the Communist bloc and remove any potential threat that would attack the Soviets in the future. It was the same in Poland, where they sought to set up a Soviet-friendly buffer zone.

When the invasion developed into an international war as part of the Cold War, the Allies of US, the Soviets, and China during WW II were transfigured into the antagonistic confrontation between the United States and the communists of the Soviets and China. The Korean Peninsula naturally became subject to tension and conflict therefrom.

As history does not come out of a vacuum, so the causes and effects of the Korean War were interconnected, and it takes time to become clearer on the causality. From the perspective of South Korea, however, it is patently clear that the South Korean government was not responsible for the all-out provocation on 25 June 1950.

Considering the all-out invasion mobilizing entire regular armies, the ROK did not do anything that any attacker should have done, and it did many things that any defender shouldn't have done before and even on the day of 25 June. It was unanticipated chaos for the ROK. The incompetent intelligence unit of the ROK Army was to blame, but not the ROK government.

The ROK Army allowed its soldiers to have normal weekend leave, and the others in the camps had gone to their beds to sleep away the Saturday night. They were unaware that the North Korean Army amassed in the 38th Parallel in preparation to shell at the ROK Army and cross the frontline at the dawn of next morning in accordance with its war plan.

My father's story illustrates that the army of the 2nd Division was leisurely spending the weekend vacationing and planting rice. It should be out of the question that the ROK army did such things intentionally to shirk the responsibility of starting the war because it was the ROK military leadership who fell into chaotic confusion when the Korean War broke out.

(4) Chapter Five. Collision, 1948-1953. p269

Throughout the rest of southern Korea, local people's committees reemerged, but not in the spontaneous fashion of 1945. The North Koreans exercised sharp procedural controls to assure that committee membership would conform to North Korean practice and discipline. Amid the massive push toward Pusan, thousands of Korean cadres, from North and South, set about restoring the people's committees disbanded in 1945-46 and redistributing land on a revolutionary basis. (p269).

Comments.

When it comes to the people's committee in South Korea under North Korean rule, the perception of South Koreans is the assembly of rabbles seeking revenge, arresting the landowners and officials, announcing the crimes of the persons in arrest, sentencing the death in the applause of the rabble, and execution by make-shift weapons such as bamboo poles.

It was like the organizations of the rural communist party in the Soviet and it also shared the character of the Einsatzgruppen during the German invasion of Russia which killed Jews and Russian elites to eradicate those likely to be hostile to the Nazis. It was from the dogma of National Socialism, and it lacked proper legal process. The people's committee had the same feature of violence from socialist class struggle and eradication of probable dissenters.

As to the issue of land, the ROK government had already been executing the land reform to level the land inequality since before the war. The land redistribution of the people's committee was the version of the draconian North Korean land reform that confiscated the lands without compensation and distributed them to peasants without rents.

It forced an unfair distribution to make the peasants equal in land ownership. The process was violent to coerce the dispossession of lands from the landowners without any compensation for them. It took place in the same manner as in North Korea when they implemented its land reform which had driven off the dispossessed landowners to South Korea.

Bruce Cummings needed to balance the topic of land distribution by touching upon the land reform that the ROK government had been executing before the war, and by delineating the difference of land reforms between South Korea and North Korea, and the atrocities that the cadres of the people's committee perpetrated.

(5) Chapter Five. Collision, 1948-1953. p271

Collier's began an article by saying, "Our Red foe scorns ah rules of civilized warfare, hid[ing] behind women's skirts," and then quoted the following colloquy between American soldiers: The young pilot drained his cup of coffee and said, "Hell's fire, you can't shoot people when they stand there waving at you." "Shoot 'em," he was told firmly. "They're troops." "But, hell, they've all got on those white pajama things and they're straggling down the road." ... "See any women or children?" "Women? I would not know. The women wear pants, too, don't they?" "But no kids, no, sir." "They're troops. Shoot.

Reginald Thompson, a sensitive British war correspondent, wrote in his book Cry Korea that "there were few who dared to write the truth of things as they saw them." Journalists found the campaign for the South "strangely disturbing," very different from World War II in its guerrilla and popular aspect. Thompson witnessed an American Marine kill an elderly civilian as if in a fit of absentmindedness, showing no sign of remorse, and remarked that GIs "never spoke of the enemy as though they were people, but as one might speak of apes." Even among correspondents, "every man's dearest wish was to kill a Korean. Today, ... I'll get me a gook.'" Americans called Koreans gooks, he thought, because "otherwise these essentially kind and generous Americans would not have been able to kill them indiscriminately or smash up their homes and poor belongings."

Comments.

The collateral damage of civilians has been constant in all wars of humans. Death came in many guises and for many reasons, a remorseless companion of war. We can still see it in the ongoing Ukraine-Russian war as the Russian forces bombard the residential areas whereby lots of Ukrainian civilians have been killed and injured. The modern culture and conscience couldn't prevent the attacks or save the civilians from the dangers.

In the case of the Korean War, it had its unique features. The soldiers on both sides were of the same blood, language, culture, and history. The homogeneous people had lived in the same country for thousands of years including the Japanese colonial rule (1910-1945), but they were just forced to split in two under different ideologies.

There have been many causes that triggered bloody wars, for example, geographical expansion, economic gains, and religious motivations. The experience from the Korean War offers a reason that the war for ideological dominance would be so bloodthirsty that both thought symbiotic coexistence was impossible in the abounding atrocities during the war.

It was the North Korean army that initiated a bout of atrocities from the beginning of the war. An example was that they massacred around one thousand people of wounded ROK soldiers and civilian patients including medical staff in the Seoul National University Hospital when they entered downtown Seoul on 28 June 1950.

As the war continued and bilateral atrocities were committed, all civilians were left perplexed about what was right and wrong, who were friends and foes, and they had to save themselves. Such indiscriminate arrest and execution of blacklisted individuals became common, which led to corresponding actions against communists and collaborators, willing, resigned, or coerced, by the ROK army.

Guileless innocent civilians became stuck in the Catch-22 situation that coerced them to side with either of the two parties which may end up with their death when the tide of war situation turned between them. As the war expanded and extended, the desperate situation made the civilians use all means to survive. There was a slender difference between being a resister and turning traitor for the people in Korea, the South and the North alike.

The homogeneous people and soldiers, in their appearance, were impossible to distinguish between ROK and DPRK, which added confusion to the chaotic situation. The frontlines were mobile across the peninsula, and civilians desperately migrated to survive the sandpapering of time, prisoners were turned into enemies when freed, and foreign soldiers of the UN and China added to the chaos.

There was a sad scene in which a senile old man in a rural village waved the North Korean flag in an absent-minded manner toward the ROK Army soldiers who were pursuing the retreating DPRK forces. At the loss of wit and sense, one ROK Army soldier took the flag away from his hand and let him get into his humble house.

One thing to note was the operation of camouflage and deception by the DPRK army who wore plain clothes and mingled themselves in the throng of civilians. When they were let past the checking points of UN forces, they attacked them from behind, causing the further retreat of the defending forces of ROK and UN forces.

For clarity, this part is not to justify the collateral damages and there must have been some cases of inhumane treatment by the soldiers of ROK and the UN. However, we need to balance our thoughts in a holistic view to understand the collateral damage in the ROK and DPRK regions under specific battle conditions.

Both sides inflicted collateral damage on each other. Bruce Cummings highlighted the perpetrations of American soldiers. As he pointed to the GIs for the collateral damage, he should have described the same practices of the DPRK soldiers for fair and balanced understanding. All deceased souls deserve a fair assessment. For him, it seems selective.

(6) Chapter Six. *Korean Sun Rising: Industrialization*, 1953-Present. p326

Park's one great mistake (completely predictable, given his political coalition) was to festoon his home region with all these new industrial complexes and to shortchange the Chollas. Of the six target industries, only one went to the southwest—the petrochemical factory in Yosu and Yoch'on, and this was only one part of the chemical complex; most of it was at Ulsan. Development means growth, no development means the status quo, but underdevelopment means a structural condition in which prospective development is retarded, or in which something happening elsewhere (cotton sales in England) deepens an obsolescent social formation (slavery in the American Deep South). In the Korean case the steel mills, auto plants, shipbuilding facilities, free-export zones, the capital to pay for them, the jobs they created, the new highways and sprouting cities they needed were all going with clockwork regularity to Korea's southeast, home to Park and just about everyone associated with him.

An industrial belt extended north and west from Busan, linking the free export zones in Masan and Ch'angwon with new industries in cities like Taegu and Ulsan. Tittle towns like Kumi and ports erased in the Korean War like P'ohang were transformed overnight into industrial cities because they were near Park's birthplace (next to Kumi) or were hometowns of one of his close associates (P'ohang). Tile roofs and television antennas sprouted on homes all over the Kyongsangs, while in southwest Cholla peasants living in thatched-roof huts continued their backbreaking agrarian toil at near-subsistence levels or sent children off to Seoul in search of a job in a tearoom or a massage parlor. Park paid the price at Kwangju, as we will see.

Comments.

Bruce Cummings commented on the unequal treatment of southwest Jeolla Province by President Park Chung Hee in favor of his home region, Gyeongsang Province by locating only one industry (Petro-Chemical) in Jeolla while the rest five industries went to Gyeongsang (Steel Mill, Shipbuilding, Non-ferrous metal, Machinery, Electronics and Chemical).

This view has been ingrained in the mentality of the people in Jeolla Province as a story of wrongful victimization or unrighteous persecution and has become the basis of their deep-seated grievances and anger toward the right-wing liberal democratic party and its politicians to which President Park had belonged.

This issue of fixing the location of industrial sites should be viewed from the perspective of maximizing the industrial efficiency of procurement, production, and logistics of on-land and maritime. This was very crucial for Korea which had been struggling with lack of funds to develop the economy. The sole criteria in the investments were to run the industrial sites with maximum efficiency.

Before fixing the industrial sites, the artery of transportation in Korea had been the railway of Busan (southeastern port city) to Seoul, built in 1901-1904 by Japan. The same question arose as to why Japan had built the railway in the Busan-Seoul line, not Mokpo (southwestern port city)-Seoul line, for its purpose to extract values from Korea and advance into China.

For the Japanese, the reason for its investment in the Busan-Seoul line should be attributed to the cost-operational efficiency for its purposes. Japanese colonial authority had also built the Jeolla Province line in 1914 linking Mokpo and Daejeon (a midwestern inland city) where the Jeolla Province line was connected to the main Seoul-Busan line.

The six industries were specially selected to develop the Korean economy, led by exports for which they were required to be in the most suitable places for that purpose. So, the key success factors were geographical advantages that meet the requirements of maximized efficiencies in procurement, production, and logistics within the limited budget for the investments.

The location of the sites depended on gaining an appreciation for how the sea works – its currents, tide, winds, depth, sea-miles, capacities of ports and terminals, and proximity to affiliated production and networks of logistics counted for everything.

Specifically, the points in the decision were sea miles for vessels to navigate, port condition with its depth, berth length, vessel turn-around space, and tide. In addition, loading and discharging facilities, provision of stevedoring labor, secured storage capacity in bonded areas in hinterlands to prevent hoarders, smugglers, and black marketeers, inter-modal networks from port-entry to final destinations, and vice versa.

Considering the factors, Busan and Gyeongsang Province were much more advantageous than Mokpo and Jeolla Province in the context of the criteria of operational efficiency and investment effectiveness. It consequently made the level of regional development disparate such as the dynamic and upbeat southeast (Gyeongsang Province) and static and backward southwest (Jeolla Province).

As to the allegation that President Park Chung Hee fixed the sites in favor of his home region, southeast Gyeongsang Province, it would be counter-rational because the idea of Busan and Gyeongsang Province was more sensible and suitable for the export-led growth of the national economy that had to be carefully nurtured and successfully operated.

Just out of a figment of imagination, if, by chance, President Park was born in Mokpo, not in Gyeongsang Province, what would his decision then be, either Mokpo or Busan? It should be up to the advantages of geography for production, export, and logistics. Would he establish them in Gyeongsang Province following the reason, or Jeolla Province because he was born there regardless of geographical disadvantage?

There is nothing personal nor any prejudice of being positive or negative to a specific region but just follow the reason. I throw my vote for the former because of the same reason of the decision that was made in the inception of the industrial sites decades ago.

We may refer to a historical case in 1592. Toyotomi Hideyoshi in Japan had set the course of invading the Joseon Dynasty on the route of Nagoya-Kyushu-Busan-Seoul, not on the route of Nagoya-Kyushu-Mokpo-Seoul. One of the reasons for the decision would be geographical distance and logistics for procurement to support the war.

Busan and Gyeongsang Province had just sat there when they had borne the brunt of the invading Japanese force in 1592, they were there when the railway was constructed in the 1900s, and they were there as the last stronghold for fighting the communists in 1950, and they just sat there as the industrial places for exports in the 1960s with more suitable localities.

Mokpo has had its special features of geography with calm sea and high tide in the port. If new technologies or climate change can induce more cost-operational efficiency into Mokpo and Jeolla Province, for example, tidal power generation, developing value-added industry on muddy flats or salt paddies along the beaches, and environmentally friendly sea-farming.

This does not intend to stimulate regional discrepancy, but this just attempts to understand the underlying reasons behind the decision of the industrial sites in the 1960s in Korea from the perspective of economy and efficiency when it was struggling out of absolute poverty. Again, it was not personal favor nor regional disfavor but an issue of cost-operation efficiency.

The geographical advantage of Gyeongsang Province and the port of Busan were just accidental to contingent circumstances as it has frequently applied to historical occasions. For example, the coincidental proximity of coal to the site of the Industrial Revolution in Britain. No one is to unduly blame for the rational decision, and nothing is granted undue recognition and praise.

Bruce Cummings may need to check and find the geographical relative advantages and disadvantages of the industrial facilities that were specially designed for export from Korea, which has been heavily dependent on ocean-going shipping and inland logistics for importing raw materials, assembling or producing products, and exporting finished products.

Book III

PART 6

6.1. The 21st Century (Issues)

1) Ten Critical Issues

The period of peace for more than seventy years (1953-2024) after the Korean War has been the time of the generations of and after the war. A new world emerges with quadruple changes in demography (extended life expectancy, aging population), climate (global warming, natural disasters), technology (AI, IoT, hyper-connection), and locality (urbanization, rural desertion).

The people get polarized and entrenched (divisive in ideology, wealth, and opportunities); they get sensual (indulging in physical pleasures and visceral responses); they become smart and opinionated (knowledgeable and judging matters on their authority); and they connect in diverse and competitive ways (hyper-connected, diverse, competing in a winner-take-all mentality).

This new world may be caused by the changes that can parallel the one in the 16th-17th centuries when people across the continents of Europe and America came to know each other. A similar realization took place when the primitive people in Papua New Guinea encountered white people for the first time in the 1930s.

The conventional establishments of modern life will be challenged by these changes. The pace of change is so rapid and comprehensive that it becomes irreconcilable and irreversible. The winners who lead the change will help themselves in harvesting the crop of successes whereby the society will be polarized, and the new social hierarchy will get entrenched.

Specifically, the society that the young adults will live in will force them to make a Manichean decision: sheep or goat. In every decision-making situation, the root is the cause of the situation, and the fruit is the effect of it.

The thing is, young adults need to distinguish between root and fruit and to avoid making a choice that is perishable and unproductive, at least, in the waves of ten factors of critical changes. Their best approach is to establish their stance in pursuit of goals that will yield lasting advantages for both individual benefit and the common good.

Group of more global factors:

(1) Climate Change

Burning hydrocarbons releases not only energy but also carbon dioxide, a compound that traps the sun's heat and pushes up global temperatures. If left unchecked, the greenhouse effect will keep warming the earth until polar ice caps melt, oceans rise, ecological changes occur, and our lives become impossible. The only way to slow global warming is to cease emitting carbon dioxide which will require us to overhaul the way we produce and consume energy.

Some parties have presented counterarguments to the premise of man-made climate change. Some parties have stated that it is challenging to delineate causes and effects in the complex interrelationship between climate and human activity. Nevertheless, it is difficult to refute the evidence mined from a morass of obfuscation and denial that human activities are responsible for climate change on a global scale.

Climate change is irreversible, and the weather will become increasingly unpredictable. Generally, temperatures rise, and spring and autumn get shorter while winter and summer elongate. This change reduces species and genera of flora and fauna, and sea-level rises to inundate the coastline. It may also trigger certain variations or the creation of viral diseases while effective vaccines are not yet ready.

The cost of fighting climate change will depend not only on how quickly we transition away from fossil fuels but also on how well we adapt our social and economic systems to the warming we have in store. A proactive stance toward adaptation and resilience may be useful for homeowners or heads of global corporations alike. It may also be vital for ensuring that the ladders of economic opportunity are not fraying for those attempting to climb its lower rungs.

In a pivotal speech on World Environment Day on 5 June 2024, the UN Secretary-General, Antonio Guterres, set out hard-hitting truths about the state of the climate, the grotesque risk the world is facing, and what companies and countries need to do over the next eighteen months to salvage humanity's chances of a livable future.

He presented data on the dire state of the climate and called for key actions to limit global warming to 1.5 degrees, including national climate action plans and a massive expansion of affordable public and private finance. He also called for a ban on fossil fuel advertising and urged companies to stop taking fossil fuel ads.

If the unrestrained emission continues, there will be tragic, or even genocidal consequences for those who will follow us. Remember the chaos in 2020 when COVID-19 inflicted people who lacked resources (face masks, disinfectants, hospital beds, and medical crews) and knowledge of the disease. Climate change won't be much different.

Individuals may feel a moral obligation to do their part to mitigate the harm by curbing their emissions of greenhouse gases. In personal life, one can select a site for residence in a hilly region to be free from the risk of seawater and hot temperatures.

It is to take four contrasting socio-economic scenarios in the actions for the climate change:

- Markets first, in which most of the world adopts the values and expectations prevailing in the markets of today's industrialized countries
- Policy first, where governments take decisive initiatives in their attempts to reach specific social and environmental goals
- Security first, in which there is a world of striking disparities, where inequality and conflict prevails among the parties who are affected with the climate change
- Sustainability first, in which a new environment and development paradigm emerges in response to the challenge of sustainability

(2) Technology and Innovation

Although many people who lived through the second half of the 20th century saw small changes every decade, they will witness a century of development in technology.

Many of those who lived through the second half of the 20th century had noticed somewhat incremental changes every year, but the immediate prospects for the next few decades are completely different from anything that has ever been witnessed. The sea of changes shall be formidable, unprecedented, and irreversible, and it will engulf all people no matter where they are in the hyper-connected world.

In this trend, an era of revolutionary innovation based on and convergence of big data and algorithms will bring a new future in the fields of computation, networks, virtual reality, AI (Artificial Intelligence), 3-D printing, IoT (Internet of Things), and autonomous cars, aerial taxis, smart cities, and floating cities, etc..

Products made by 3-D printing and nanotechnologies are composed of programmable materials and universal spare parts. 3-D printing is additive manufacturing by printing ultra-thin sheets in sequence and stacking them on top of each other to form a three-dimensional object. This is different from subtractive manufacturing which traditional industries have done.

This makes everything from plastic parts to dental pieces or human replacement tissue for transplants. It is ideal for customized parts by accelerating the mini-mills and flexible production methods. Manufacturers produce to meet real-time demands rather than to stock their warehouses to be ready for future demands.

It reduces waste, gives off less smoke and toxic fumes, downsizes carbon emissions from the less frequent and shortened distance of transport, and helps protect the environment. It urges workers and customers to think laterally, to abandon old assumptions, and to imagine new possibilities with greater freedom to design in a waste-free process.

The panoply of benefits from 3-D printing is matched with downside factors that endanger the employment of skilled and blue-collar workers, or firearms made using 3-D printers. Automation by robots redefines the relationship between people and work, AI replaces human mental activity with machine learning. The change affects buyer-supplier interactions.

The boundaries between the digital and the physical are beginning to blur and fade. The world around us is gaining layers of information. They are accumulated and reborn in a new form through the process of big data application. The data, which is invisible but rich, personalized and interactive, converge to make the world vastly different.

The Web 1.0 was characterized by static documents and read-only interactions with consumers through banners,

The Web 2.0 was an upgrade that introduced multimedia content, interactive Web ads, and particularly social media,

The Web 3.0 is a new digital environment of the spatial web that blurs the lines between the physical world and the digital world through the convergence of high bandwidth 5G connections, augmented reality eyewear, the emerging trillion-sensors economy, and the powerful generative AI without human intervention.

We superimpose digital information atop physical environments, and it enables interaction between people, places, and things. The digital information brings us technological disruption. People are displaced into the sea of technological innovations in the next decades, and they must survive in the sea of innovations, let alone navigate safely. The dynamic, or diabolical to some people, of creative destruction ensues in which some people who say to themselves "I'm a complete ignoramus where computers are concerned" are dislocated, careers are derailed, and communities are shattered. It is more relevant to the old who may suffer from geriatric disorders, awkwardness, and cognition lapse.

In their response to them, there must be a program to train the less prepared people for innovation, and they also need to accept the reality of technological disruption and adapt themselves to it so that they are not left behind.

Do start small to be successful since big changes arise from incremental adaptation. Take uncertainty with optimism because every problem presents an opportunity. Believe in the human capacity to innovate and find solutions for problems. Never feel ashamed of the effort to adapt to the new world of digital revolution.

Around the world, a new breed of digital eyes is keeping watch over citizens. Although mass surveillance isn't new, AI-powered systems are providing governments with more efficient ways of keeping tabs on the public. The spread of AI-powered surveillance systems has empowered governments seeking greater control with tools that entrench non-democracy.

To counter the decay of democracies, the international community should establish ethical frameworks for control. In China, the state security apparatus uses AI-enabled face recognition technology to monitor people across the country and calculate a score for each citizen based on their actual behavior. It eerily reminisces of George Orwell's Big Brother in 1984.

Global efforts should focus on developing AI technologies to uphold democratic values like privacy and human rights, rather than being used for surveillance and control. The ethical standard to determine right or wrong can be viewed from deontological (ethics focuses on rules and principles) and teleological (ethics focuses on the consequence of actions) perspectives:

Deontological ethics considers an action morally good based on duty or adherence to given rules, regardless of the consequences. It focuses on duty, rules, and the intrinsic nature of actions, rather than their outcomes. From this perspective, civil surveillance is good because it was alleged to promote civil safety at first, without concern for the outcomes of civil surveillance.

Teleological ethics is known as consequentialism, bases moral judgment on the outcomes or consequences of actions. In this view, actions are right if they lead to desirable outcomes. In its perspective, civil surveillance is judged good (it helped increase the rate of arresting criminals) or bad (it was used for overall civil surveillance rather than detecting criminals)

For thousands of years, humans evaluated everything according to its functions and they regarded themselves as the apex of creation in pride and prejudice. In the 18th century, humanism sidelined God by shifting from the deo-centric to a homo-centric worldview that instructed them to listen to reason and be honest to emotion.

In the 21st century, the Data Revolution sidelines humans by shifting from a homo-centric to a data-centric view. Algorithms armed with unprecedented computing power and giant databases direct humans in their actions. A story arose during the Full Moon Festival in September 2024 in Korea, where the algorithm of car navigation led a multitude of drivers to an inappropriate place.

The data revolution consists of the data-rulers (produce and utilize data), and the data-ruled (sourced for, consumed, and controlled by the data). The key elements are data literacy (understanding and distributing the data), data ethics (moral application in collecting and distributing data), and data commoditization (making the data marketable and monetizing it).

Data processing makes new inventions and disruptions that turn data into information, information into knowledge, and knowledge into decisions. Humans cannot control the data, and an individual becomes just a piece of a giant data system. They initially developed the algorithm that listens for pleasure or aversion in your vocal tone or text messages. When it is combined with big data under the control of AI, it rules humans.

For some people, an event of being disconnected from the SNS is like losing the meaning of life. They find little meaning in doing anything that nobody knows about, and they cross-recognize, cross-pollinate, and cross-feed themselves. They are religious to ubiquity, connectivity, and ingenuity by expressing themselves, and going viral is a divine admiration for them.

As cognitive authority shifts from humans to algorithms, there is tension between human conscience and data ingenuity. The human conscience is a personal sense of the moral content of one's own conduct and it is somewhat indiscernible and indescribable hidden in the heart and soul of man whereas data ingenuity analyses the sequential datasets and visualizes contextual implications that overpower human brains in processing capability, but it cannot express the minds from the deep well of human conscience, at least for now.

The disparity in data accessibility among people can be a seed of contention because the variant level of data availability between the advanced system and the retarded system ends up in ignorance, misunderstanding, and conflict.

All in all, the future society with the technologies and innovation will be a lot more personalized and intrusive.

Recently, we heard some news about K-Pop, K-Cinema, K-Drama, K-Food, etc, which are topics related to South Korea. The sustainability of K-Culture elements is subject to their competence to maintain creative uniqueness and universal application.

Consider South Korea and North Korea which share the same cultural background, but there is a great data disparity. South Korea, in the free market in liberal capitalism, is vividly contrasted with the closed market of the state-controlled communism of North Korea. The data backwardness of North Korea will worsen as the world expedites the data revolution.

An example of data-led efficiency which is common in liberal-capitalist states. Policies based on big data applications are monitored by the markets, authorities are given feedback from the market, and they are corrected by rules and customs. This data-processing system reduces waste and enlarges benefits, and the data in the entire process is reprocessed for other policies.

North Korea has an ideal of communism where people work according to their abilities and receive according to their needs. The central authority takes all products and is supposed to distribute them to the people. However, the system hasn't run properly because the authority hasn't supplied the resources for production or the products to the people.

In a state where the NK regime is unable to control the economy, the people opened the markets themselves in local towns run by capitalistic principles that invisible hands control supplies and demands. Data in economic activities are not systematically collected, processed, or disclosed. There is no data literacy, data ethics, and data commoditization in the country.

(3) Energy security

We live today in a world completely dominated by energy. It is the bedrock of our wealth, our comfort, and our unquestioned faith in the inexorability of progress, implicit in every act and artifact of modern existence. Energy has become the currency of political and economic power, the determinant of the hierarchy of nations. Access to energy has thus emerged as the overriding imperative of the 21st century.

Energy has become the currency of political and economic power, the determinant of the hierarchy of nations for success and advancement in international politics. Access to energy has thus emerged as the overriding imperative of the 21st century which has become a geopolitical principle for all governments and global energy industry to find, produce, and distribute of coal, oil, and natural gas, and their common by-product, electricity.

Yet our energy economy is inherently flawed. The oil industry is vulnerable to haphazard price swings and dependent on despotic petrostates with uncertainty in murky governance featuring ethnic conflict, virulent nationalism, anti-Western resentment, and religious obsession. Natural gas, though relatively cleaner than oil, is complicated in processing from gas field to end users and expensive for transportation at sea and on land. Coal, though abundant and easy to get at, produce huge pollutants that kill people and nature everywhere. Worse is the steadily increasing reliance on fossil fuels, which is connected to subtle but significant changes in climate.

The fossil fuels are followed by a variety of alternative sources of advanced technologies ranging from nuclear to renewable energies such as solar, wind, tide and biofuels which drag the industrializing world into a new set of fundamental and irrevocable transformation reordering human lives at every level.

Electric power is generated from various sources in 2021 (Korea in 2022): oil 31% (0.3%), coal 27% (33%), LNG 25% (28%), renewable 13% (10%), nuclear 4% (30%). The portions of fossil fuels are preponderant: the world 83% (Korea 61%) portion of fossil fuels. For reference Japan's fossil fuels portion in 2022 was 72%, China's in 2021 76%.

When it comes to demand and supply of the energy economy, the modern world has two concerns:

First, it is our steadily increasing reliance on fossil fuels is connected to significant changes in our climate. The burning hydrocarbon releases carbon dioxide leads to greenhouse effect that make our life impossible with melting polar ice, rising of sea-level, more frequent droughts and floods, global warming and ecological anomalies. It becomes crystal clear that the long-term future is hardly sustainable unless the climate change is turned to climate restoration within next three decades (2025-2055), that is, reducing the emission of carbon dioxide from energy production and consumption.

CO_2 emissions, the detritus of incinerated coal, oil, and natural gas, are the principal drivers of global warming. The greenhouse gas emissions can be reduced significantly when fossil-fuel using companies like powerplants change it to cleaner energy. For these reasons, switching to clean energy tops every list of what we can do to stop climate change in energy generation, energy storage, and green transformation.

For the sake of climate-friendly energy, the quest for less problematic technologies of energy production in the next energy economy focuses on renewable energy sourced from wind, sun, geothermal resources, hydropower, and ocean energy adding biomass, and atomic energy; and energy efficiency by development of smart city using less energy with higher efficiency, cars using hydrogen fuel cells or hybrid engines, and refineries that turn coal into clean-burning gasoline.

Renewables emit lower pollution and generate more jobs than fossil fuels, while the upstream and downstream stakeholders in the energy market end up with caveats of predictability, constancy, and contingency in one aspect, and costs in producing and distributing them in another.

Second, it concerns whether humans can produce enough energy to satisfy the world's present and future needs for industrial success and continued economic vitality. Demand will be especially acute in emerging economies where economic successes require a corresponding level of energy consumption. Today's boom in technology and information has made electricity the fastest growing segment of the energy market which is a crucial resource for emerging economies.

As coal dies, renewable energies take its place. Solar and wind technologies converge and have huge upsides. The winds tend to blow when the sun does not shine, and vice versa. Combining wind and solar on the same energy grid is a bit like adding one plus one and getting three. Sunlight and wind are free and abundant. However, power generation from the renewable sources is inherently vulnerable to natural conditions which is growingly subject to climate change and the cost of generating the power varies and not economical enough to rely on it entirely

The factors of geopolitical instability, price volatility and competition for reserves have always been at the heart of many of the most important socio-political-economic events since the 20th century. The global oil and gas systems are so vulnerable that the smallest political perturbations may throw the oil sector into chaos which may lead to global recession, worldwide unemployment, economic disruption, and escalating competition over the remaining reserves in the oil and gas producing regions.

The answer to the question of supplying cost-efficient energy to meet the demand in the state of fixing the problems of climate change would be sought in the parts of "effective energy production" compatible with the countermeasures for climate change, that is, nuclear and renewable, and "efficient distribution and consumption of energy" by advancing technologies, that is, thermal dynamics and smart city.

(4) Economy and people

Markets are globalized. A local corporation is connected with foreign counterparts in the supply chain of resources and sales & marketing activities. The existing multinational corporation that operates in a number of countries and adjusts its production and sales following local market changes is becoming a global corporation that operates in constancy as if the markets in the globe were the single market and sells the same things in the same way everywhere, for example, the cell-phone sets of Samsung and Apple across the world. In other words, global homogenization in production and operation is gaining currency in the global business environment that triggers corresponding changes in the demands of human resources in businesses.

In the rapid change of technological advances and operational modes, workers have been on the fast track to obsolescence since the Luddites wielded sledgehammers to industrial looms in the early 1800s. The agrarian economy morphed first into the industrial economy, and now into the information economy. Automation invokes job substitution as well as job obliteration.

Make no mistake. Certain jobs are heading for extinction as technology develops, but it is worth pointing out that every time technology goes viral and exponential. we find an opportunity tucked inside. The twin pillars of the industrial structure—location and proximity— are set to fall before this decade is done.

As artificial intelligence becomes a user-friendly interface with technology, we are going to see a shift in the skills required for retaining competitiveness. Digital fluency and agility will replace the skills and mastery of conventional technology. A "robopocalypse" may be just around the corner. Taking advantage of these opportunities will require adaptation.

The global economy and the very fabric of society are changing at a fast pace. The nature and velocity of these changes require new leadership mindsets and behaviors to address the challenges of leading in the digital age. The mindset and behavior of responsive and responsible leadership are crucial for young adults to keep pace with the speed of change and to lead that change.

Some individuals have made their organizations or societies sustainable in their time, at great personal cost and even at the risk of their own fates. They have been often censured, condemned, or rendered insignificant. But they are supposed to remain known in history whereas their critics are long forgotten. The sustainability-creators tended to miss the outcome of their efforts, and the posterity enjoyed it instead.

Leadership has taken its roots in its culture, economy, and politics, and it has branched out from the trunk of universality and creativity in dealing with ever-present challenges. It bears the fruits and flowers of dynamic activity, powerful execution, flexible application, and converging disparate elements. All these boiled down to make the organization sustainable.

Under any leadership of the leaders, whether good or bad, individual pathways diverged in the disruptions of technology and society. In the absence of effective policies to reskill the workforce and to provide fair opportunities for competition, the disruptions caught the workforce off guard, the blue- and white-collar workers alike.

Those who had the competencies and resources to adapt to the disruptions had a better chance to maintain career stability and capture high wages, but those who didn't have them were forced into less stable employment. The jobs that were taken over by machines and artificial intelligence became more vulnerable to the obsolescence and atrophy of human work.

The hidden barriers of socioeconomic class and age limitations hindered social mobility, and it entrenched inequalities in career development and income. In a condition that an adequate system to protect employment is not in place, displaced workers had to struggle to reenter the employment market.

For those who were subject to economic displacement, many have been migrating in search of jobs that would fend off insecurity in their livelihood. The costs of housing, living, and healthcare amid inflation made some of them poor and desolate. When they were restricted to necessities for living, they were pushed into radicalization or crime.

Many of these consequences had been felt more acutely in developing economies which had weaker fiscal resources to ease the workers' malaise. The disruptions in technology and society have spread and deepened; meanwhile, they have become prevalent in advanced economies as the disruptions have advanced, too.

For example, workers displaced from the closure of mining towns could become stranded in the local economy which has been dependent on fossil fuel with few alternatives to replace it. Unless otherwise reskilled and get new jobs, the displaced workers will have to rely on social security systems creating a poor regionality.

The disruptions will bring a world where knowledge, technology, income, and wealth are to be concentrated which will perpetuate the polarity of wealth and poverty. An individual born into a less privileged background is likely to face higher barriers in reaching their full potential. This will undermine meritocracy and fairness in society.

By the 1990s, under the influence of the free market system, many emerging nations started to open to outside trade and capital flows, and some nations had borrowed too heavily from foreign creditors. Debt-induced currency crises struck Asia in 1997-98 and then spread to Russia, Turkey, and Brazil. The crisis gave birth to a swell of reforms in pain and confusion.

In Korea, the financial crisis of 1997-1998 revealed a problem with corporate governance. The fast-growing economies of the past decades did not accompany a sense of transparency and accountability. The norm that transparency was the gauge of probity was not established.

Politics had been instrumental in organizing economic development, but the politicians morphed into a power group that took advantage of the economies.

So, when the economy crashed, many big corporations and banks went bankrupt. The wealth of society became polarized even more deeply: The workers lost jobs on a massive scale without safety nets. Those rich in cash, especially foreign currencies, made huge profits by swallowing up stocks and real estate that were heavily devalued in the aftermath of the crisis.

The stock market crashed on Black Monday in 1987, the dot-com bubble burst in 2000, and it was dislodged by the 9/11 disaster in the U.S., but the damage was recovered by 2004. The prices of houses and stocks skyrocketed until both crashed in 2008. The COVID-19 made the economy screech to a halt in 2020-2021. The fiscal money of governments helped them stay solvent.

The vicissitude of business fortunes has been constant, and it will be so in the future. But we must learn from the crisis of 1998 (so-called, IMF Crisis in Korea) what had caused it and why we couldn't avoid it. We must remember those who were unemployed or went bankrupt across Korea and who were so desperate to feed their families in such a dismal situation.

The IMF Crisis removed 19 business groups among 30, and many commercial banks disappeared. The Korean economy in 2024 is ranked as one of the top ten global economies. It has been built on trials and errors of the past. For the sake of a sustainable future, I list some factors focusing on negativity from my experiences from 1989 to 2020 in Korean ocean-going shipping companies.

(a)   It was the lack of corporate governance that made some of them go belly up. They didn't uphold accountability in decision-making. The companies were owned by cross-shareholding and the board was just a stamp-duty vehicle for the best interests of the founder-owner who held only a small percentage of the company shares.

(b)   The executives were not transparent in their disclosure of accounting data and transactional records, and intra-group companies had helped one another with cross-guarantees and cross-subsidies in the name of vertical integration. The profits from the businesses were funneled into the pocket of the founder-owner or his family.

(c)   Managerial ethics and behavioral discipline were illusory, hypothetical, and applicable to workers in lower ranks. They were loyal to the egregious historic norm that "everything that is tasty and good goes to nobles and clergy".

Nepotism had been prevalent, and the familial members mixed the company interests with the founder-families' benefits. The codes in the commercial law were evaded, and the authority overlooked the misbehaviors.

(d)   Hierarchical culture sapped the energy of corporate vitality. In the beginning stages of corporate development, the hierarchy was a necessary evil for rapid growth. When it reached a certain level of maturity in size and growth, it limited the feedback control system, and it sometimes became an agent of organizational malfunction.

There have been many positive factors such as proactivity in decisions of investment and divestment, a never-give-up spirit to overcome limited resources, and persistent pursuit to achieve the targets of revenue, market share, and profits.

But my experiences tell me two factors:

   A bitterly cold winter was often followed by heavy snowfall or torrential cold rains. A bad news brought a worse tidings as if they were coming in a row

   Factors of positive and negative had juxtaposed and mutated over the time, and cross-fed each other.

The economy is volatile; crises are constant, excesses or deficiencies are inevitable; transformative changes are required. Unless the problems are detected and balanced in time, they will at last erupt in the form of implosion (financial crisis) or explosion (threat of competitors). The market does justice to its historical correctness. That is a pattern that transcends time and locality.

So, as conclusion, the cold reality is that the economy and the people will get more polarizing because the followers will find it much harder to catch up with the leaders in all segments of industries and economies. The winners will grab the primes of opportunities and profits in the value chains, and they will solidify their supremacy to make the extorting structure permanent.

The change is impending and inevitable. For young adults, there is no one-size-fits-all solution to the problem but be creative and persistent to make themselves compatible to win the cut-throat competition, and manage the risks embedded in the markets.

Being creative means that they should approach things in a new way of thinking and actions, and being persistent indicates a pattern of behavior that they never give up their pursuit to make them creative. Being creative only gives them advantages to outcompete the established interests.

To manage the risks, they should take the initiative in setting a vision and seizing opportunities and take measured steps in the intricate and drawn-out process of making decisions. Again, they should never overreach themselves beyond the means of risk management. Once a decision is made, execute it relentlessly, assess the risks regularly, and change policies whenever necessary. Again, take time to set targets, make decisions, execute them relentlessly, and adapt to changes in the market to manage the risks in it.

(5) Sharing Economy

The era of no-possessions opens. The sharing economy will grow exponentially as the number of things that we continue to share—homes, cars, jobs, meals, and fashion—will continue to grow. By 2030, it is expected to account for over a third of total work and consumption. Millennials are blurring the lines between home, work, and play, and collaborative consumption is on the rise.

Global surveys indicate that over two-thirds of individuals are willing to share resources to save money. The rise of ride-hailing apps like Uber, Lyft, or Airbnb points to an increasing tendency to leverage the gig economy to share resources. Most of the suppliers of this service are rich and they supplement their incomes, hence increasing the inequalities in society.

The things we share —homes, cars, and jobs— may well be almost endless, establishing a form of collaborative economy. The industries that will grow are crowdfunding, online staffing through employment platforms, peer-to-peer accommodations, ridesharing, and music and video streaming. The collaborative economy will prevail in the service market of the future.

Today, young people are turning away from owning property or products, preferring instead to use someone else's belongings for a fee. They collaboratively view property or products and share them for the mutual advantage of added convenience and lower cost, whereby the form of collaborative or shared consumption will be established.

The sharing economy is based on an upgraded experience economy and top-to-bottom transformation. The internet is a game-changing tool that has changed classified ads to social media marketing within one generation.

These platforms do not produce or deliver services themselves but play a nexus, linking demand with supply, whereby they reduce transaction costs, making it more convenient and affordable to engage in collaboration. Humans can now operate on a person-to-person basis, sharing ideas and conducting business without intermediaries.

The sharing economy operates its resources in the form of a gig economy. On the part of employers, they adopt a system to employ temporary or freelance workers for those who are not core or essential functionaries, and on the part of employees, they select the employers following their own interests rather than organizational loyalty.

Many businesses benefit from so-called network effects on which the entire sharing economy is interconnected and cross-functions for a bigger business scale and scope. The network effect is a phenomenon whereby increased numbers of people or participants improve the value of a good or service.

The internet is an example of the network effect. As more users gained access to the internet, they produced more content, information, and services. The development and improvement of websites attracted more users to connect and do business with each other. As the internet experienced traffic increases, it offered more value, leading to a network effect.

The rise of the sharing economy is a double-edged sword with positive and negative effects.

On the positive side, it helps those at the bottom of the income distribution because it has the potential to help the poor both as consumers (the demand side) and as workers (the supply side). Many young gig economy workers use the platform earnings to reduce their debt or continue their studies. They are monetizing their downtime.

The invisible hand of the free market provides the best possible arrangement for consumers and producers, with the former securing everything they need by shopping for the best deal and the latter making a profit catering to those needs through business platforms. It manifests direct economy on a one-on-one scale, not through the impersonal and inefficient channels of the state

On the negative side, it results in income inequality. The better-educated people obtain supplemental income whereas the jobs of the unskilled are demeaning and underpaid as the companies turn to temp workers, on-call workers, independent contractors, and freelancers. The growth of the gig economy comes hand in hand with an increase in non-standard jobs.

The advent of platform capitalism which enables the likes of Airbnb and, in Korea, home-delivery services from restaurants called "Baemin", fleece the profit of the home-renters and restaurant keepers. All too often, the sharing economy turns out to be more like a shearing economy – we all get fleeced as Ruther Bregman said in his book "Humankind, p317".

It also poses a challenge to individuals dependent on traditional ways, for example, hotels and taxis. They find it difficult to join the sharing economy that runs in rating-based marketplaces and in-app payment systems. The new way to use data, apps, and algorithms through digital platforms has become the prevailing norm, but it dispels the digital illiterate from the market.

The sharing economy upends socioeconomic roles and relationships. It seizes on several distinct societal trends and puts everything together through lateral thinking. It is an economy that monetizes everything it can. Property starts to lose its meaning as people share and use property in lithe and supple manners at lower costs, rather than owning it.

In the sharing economy, the underlying culture is no longer one of owning but of enjoying and experiencing it. This change dovetails with a massive shift in demographics and technology, potentially creating a wholesale transformation of the social order. It is not a matter of option or preference but of prevalence and imperative to join it.

Group of more domestic factors in Korea

(6) Demographic Change

• Status

The pace of population growth is terrifying. In 1820 in the wake of the Industrial Revolution, it was 1 billion people, it became 2 billion a century later. After a brief hiatus due to the Great Depression and two world wars, it grew at breathtaking speed: 3 billion in 1960, 4 billion in 1975, 5 billion in 1987, 6 billion in 2000, and 7 billion in 2010, and 8.1 billion in 2024.

The U.N. indicated in 2022 that it will be 8.8 billion in 2034, 9.7 billion in 2050, and 10.4 billion in 2100. It means the population increased by more than 4 billion during this century. In general, more babies, lower rates of mortality and morbidity, and longer life expectancy are attributed to the exponential growth of the population.

In the meanwhile, the population will grow at uneven rates depending on the regions and income groups. In some developed countries, East Asia, Europe, and the Americas, the birth rate declines, and population decreases in contrast to increases in Africa, the Middle East, and South Asia. This structure will unsettle the global balance of economic and geopolitical power.

For women in the modern world, the issue of childbearing is not merely a choice between their family and their career. They marry later and have less children at a much later age than past generations. They run out of time to have babies before their childbearing year ends. The issue of time is not a matter that money-related governmental offerings can resolve.

In the days of high fertility, social conventions, and practices formed a prevailing mood that many women took their level of wealth granted, married earlier and delivered more babies at an earlier age. The present women however marry later or remain unmarried. When they marry, they have fewer babies at a later age or no babies in marriage, and wealth matters in marriage.

Most women in the past had regarded marriage as a social virtue or familial duty, and non-marriage or marriage with no children was exceptional. Virtually, it was not always a matter of personal choice per se, but it was conceived as a granted code of conduct to comply with that they marry when the age is up, and they bear children when they marry.

It is now turned to a situation where women have been expressive to address their concerns and assert their innate right to determine their lives. Most of them tend to study longer in higher-level educational institutions and develop careers as they wish. The priority has shifted from social convention or familial duty to independent decisions or individual rights.

Women's roles change with the factors of education, urbanization, and job opportunities. It is said that economic development is the best contraceptive, they now enjoy more opportunities outside the household and, to seize those opportunities, they remain in school longer, marry late and postpone childbearing. Therefore, the fertility rate declines.

A correlation is set in terms of income and fertility. When income rises, people tend to replace their clunkers, have a smaller number of children, and invest more in each child, giving them better opportunities in life. Thus, parents make trade-off actions between the quantity and the quality of children they desire to have (Gary Becker, An Economic Analysis of Fertility, 1960)

Some traditional societies that were caught in too harsh environments to feed all generations were forced to neglect, abandon, or even kill their elderly, some others afforded their elderly far more satisfying and productive lives. Factors that decided a case in the variation were the living conditions, the utility and power of the elderly, and the social norms.

The increased lifespans enlarged the portion of the old and decreased the utilities of the elderly. An issue that concerns is whether the elderly can contribute to social sustainability or become a burden of it. Demographic crisis of age stratification in reverse triangle form will require more immigrants and will create a new ethnic composition. A diverse society is inevitable.

Health costs soared due to longer life expectancy, advanced medical technology, and over-consciousness of health conditions. People will die more of non-communicable diseases such as diabetes, hypertension, stroke, heart-attacks, and cancers. Many individuals have changed their lifestyle such as regular exercise, and stopping smoking, to improve their quality of life.

Shrinking populations mean less growth. The decision to deliver a baby is a personal one and should stay that way. But the society of rapid shift to aging and shrinking population will lose social dynamism and individual vitality. In the not-distant future, they will certainly face a fiscal crisis as taxpayers struggle to finance the pensions and the health costs of the oldies.

Many pro-natalism policies come with positive effects. Child benefits reduce child poverty, and mothers who can afford childcare are more likely to both work and bear children. But governments are wrong to think they can boost fertility rates with policies, such as tax breaks and subsidized childcare, that are diagnosed as immediate causes of the demographic decline.

In South Korea, where the fertility rate is 0.7, the population is projected to fall by 60% by the end of the century. Fertility ratio by country varies: South Korea is stunningly 0.7 (2023) while Japan 1.3 (2021), China 1.2 (2021), USA 1.7 (2021), and North Korea is 1.8 (Estimate in 2021).

Specifically, the population composition in the Korean Peninsula is 78 million (South 52 and North 21) which shall decrease to 72 million in 2050 (South 46 and North 26). The trend that the steeper decline in the South, and the moderate increase in the North implies a variety of geo-social political consequences in the peninsula.

This holds the potential to devise mutually beneficial solutions to the problems of political conflict and economic disparity between them. One of the prerequisites for the development of North Korea is to build global standards in all fields, tangible and intangible, of its society. It must transform itself to be compatible with the requirement before it is transformed.

There is an issue of gender equality. It advocates the equal treatment of genders, but there is innate inequality such as childbearing of women and compulsory conscription of men. In the future, women may be required to get enlisted because the number of males for enlistment dwindles, but males cannot bear the children.

- Analysis

Malthus underestimated the potential of invention and innovation which has led to the phenomenal increase in agricultural production, and the international trade that has expanded the supply of food through cheaper transoceanic transportation, and he also missed a point that technology reduced the desire for sex. The greater the available entertainment, the less frequently people engage in sex.

We may segment the issue of low fertility into two-by-two compositions. There may be other criteria that may segment the issue such as level of education, regions of residence, or gender-perception index among which the criteria of age and wealth are chosen because they are believed to be most effective with the issue of low fertility rate.

The four quadrants are self-explanatory among which the Quadrant D is the most promising case to increase fertility In all these efforts of governments to enhance fertility, it should focus on baby-boosting policies that are effective for the Case D. In addition to them, the government needs to broaden the gate for immigration to slow down the decline of the population. However, the cold reality is that the sheer size of the population is unlikely to increase, and the rate of decline is not to turn around within this generation.

`Millennials are the generation born from 1981 to 1996 who are the children of baby boomers. By 2040, the first millennials will retire. They were born in the era when information and communication technology underwent a quantum leap that transformed the world. They were raised digital in the networked digital age not limited by geography.

Few of them ever experienced the routines of the baby boomers: copied papers using a mimeograph, listened to music with a cassette tape, developed photographic film, drove with the help of a driving-map, exchanged documents by fax, used a rotary phone, and mailed written letters for communication, caught up with the news in the papers or radio.

The world of 2040 will be an age in which baby boomers and the millennials are commonly situated and thus it shall not be shaped not by one monolithic generation but by the interplay among the various generational units in the mix of education, income, and ethnicity in which the portion of retired people shall be preponderant.

Millennials will live longer than previous generations. Henceforth their longevity requires lifelong commitment to stay healthy and active. The hyper-connected society will help them overcome the challenges. They often vent their anger at the baby boomers for problems from the financial crisis and climate change to an unsustainable pension scheme.

A new intergenerational dynamic needs to be settled. 2.3 billion millennials in the world are the backbone of economic activity, but, in fact, it is the baby boomers who own half of the world's net worth. By 2030, the sixty-plus-year population will reach 38 percent in Japan, 34 in Germany, 26 in the United States, and 25 percent in Korea and China.

The healthcare and pension scheme will have to be reset to cope with the new demographic realities. The modern senior people enjoy a life of tech-savvy, good disposable income, extended retirement years, and more geriatric care. Gerontocracy will be a contentious issue in the context of job-sharing and wealth distribution between the young and old generations.

The prospect prewarns of the intergenerational gaps: the social safety net (the young pay more and get less), the geographical regions (urban congestion, rural desertion), the uneven opportunities (they get fewer and concentrated), the unnatural proportion (fewer young, more old people), and national security (tax income dwindles, fewer resource of national defense).

Mortality is the life clock that tells the aging, and longevity is the time to fight mortality. Aging is not just a running down of the human system, but it shows an evolutionary truth that the lifespan doesn't go on forever. The old folks must exit so that the young could come in, for which human evolution devised obsolescence and a redundant plan for the exit.

Genomic instability has lived with evolution. Genetic engineering doesn't always replicate according to its plan, and the broken genetic copier produces diseases such as cancer, muscular dystrophy, and ALS (Amyotrophic Lateral Sclerosis, Lu Gehrig's disease). Genetic equilibrium maintains a genotype from generation to generation, but it is subject to variation.

Our lifespan was thirty years to the Industrial Revolution. During the 20th century, marvelous inventions such as antibiotics and sanitation extended it to forty-eight by 1950, then seventy-two by 2014. Science extends it by a year for every year we live. It means humans may stay ahead of death if longevity escapes the velocity of aging (as said by Ray Kurzweil).

• Actions

There are two tracks of action for the people and their government.

First, it is to tell the people as it is. Fertility is falling globally, and it looks irreversible. Population ages and retirees are not replenished by local successors or replacement migration. A small scale of immigration of the high-skilled is a stop-gap measure, but the trend is irreversible. It is a matter of choice for people, but it is an inevitable future that their descendants must struggle with or adapt to.

   a. Governments are doing their utmost to increase fertility and broaden the window of immigration. Hopefully, the policies will take effect to achieve this purpose, but they also must present to the public the inevitable problems from the inevitable demographic crisis and induce the public to be aware of it and adapt to it.

   b. It is recommended that the legal age of seniority be increased in less competitive positions to reduce the financial burden on the government and encourage older individuals to remain in the workforce longer. The new demographic landscape calls for a shift in the labor paradigm, not merely for the benefit of individuals, but for the long-term sustainability of society.

   c. People should embrace multicultural diversity in all fields of society honoring their individual quirks and interests. They should redefine the conventional norm of nationality and national homogeneity, and national policies and social practices must meet the needs of diversity. The tolerance for diversity in gender, race, age, and others is not optional, but mandatory.

d. Men and women should reinterpret the gender roles as women now take a greater share of education and assume the professional posts as males do. The change triggers two factors: the fertility rate naturally declines causing the demographic crisis, but it has diversity rooted in society as well as in workplaces.

c. In history, the human population has decreased due to disorders such as wars, plagues, famine, or conflicts like revolutions, but it has never decreased on a massive scale in times of peace without such population-decreasing disorders. The demographic crisis in the 21st century is unprecedented and thus needs unconventional responses.

Specifically, the issue of immigration needs special attention contemplating the urgency in Korea. First and foremost, there should be a new social consensus on immigration. The National Assembly should pass laws to open a wider window of immigration, the Government should execute policies for that purpose, and the media should help support it.

It is of importance for Koreans to tackle the problems properly because there is a risk of some breakdowns in society, for example, some industrial sites of agriculture and construction that need foreign workers greatly. The issue cuts both ways: If successful, it may be a boon to society; if unsuccessful, it could lead to a doom that might contribute to national extinction.

Some positive effects of immigration may arise not only from their ability to do the work, but from their strong will to settle and achieve their goals in Korea. Immigration can be controversial because people tend to highlight the downside rather than the upside. After all, people tend to be risk-averse or focus on short-term stability.

On the contrary, there are plenty of reasons to focus on the upside of immigration: the rising wave of young immigrants helps rebuild society. It enlivens local schools and communities with new entrants, revitalizes entrepreneurial activity, replenishes the aging workforce in industrial sites, and makes the pension scheme more sustainable.

If we think laterally, we can turn a problem into a huge opportunity. Korean society must be multi-ethnic soon and a second or even a third language would help all establish a new culture. It is not a matter of option or preference, but a reality that it has to establish unless it opts for suicidal extinction on a national scale.

In Four Horsemen of the Apocalypse, a painting by Viktor Vasnetsov in 1887, there is a death squad of Death, Famine, War, and Conquest under the Lamb at the top. Considering the desperate condition in modern Korea, one more horseman should be added, namely the Demography. The new horseman is moving slowly and relatively silent, but it is mightiest.

The conclusion for young adults is that they cannot keep ignoring the elephant of the demographic crisis in their daily living environment. They should respect diversity in all arenas of social interactions by balancing their thoughts and actions in the social revamping process toward diversity.

(7) Urbanization

Cities cover one percent of the world's land area but are home to 55% of the world's population. 68% of this is expected to be urbanized by 2050 (The 2018 Revision of the World Urbanization Prospects). In 2017, there were 29 megacities with more than 10 million inhabitants. By 2030, the world is projected to have 43 megacities, 14 of which will be home to more than 20 million people.

About 90% of urban areas are located near coasts, and these areas are vulnerable to rising sea levels due to climate change. The urban center is a microcosm of the future, with a creative class and knowledge-intensive workers, but with concomitant challenges of pollution, congestion, and security. This brings both opportunities and threats.

On the positive side, cities are good for business because they bring people together and increase productivity. Population density stimulates economic output. As cities grow, they use fewer resources. Bigger, denser cities are more sustainable than smaller ones because cities reduce waste, save energy, and emit less carbon dioxide. The transition to smart cities is helping to sustain the world.

On the negative side, it is fraught with crime, disease, environmental degradation, and prohibitive property prices. Big cities have been dehumanized into lifeless and alienating environments of traffic jams, high-rise buildings, glass windows, and bland walls. The skyscrapers block views and contribute to pollution, noise, and waste.

Big cities create wealth and opportunity but deepen poverty and inequality. While the poor urban middle-class toil and struggle, the rich live in luxury. In the rarefied world, the rich compete with one another for social esteem. As wealth accumulates, class distinctions become entrenched under the polarity and hyper-connected urbanity. The urban rich is also contrasted with the poverty of the rural people who had undergone the shades of growth of towns and trade.

Global cities play a role in globalization that attracts talent and creates breakthroughs. Cities are melting pots of diverse people and technologies for efficiency. This takes the form of secularism, rationality, self-expression, and post-materialism, along with increasing acceptance of divorce, abortion, euthanasia, suicide, diverse sexual orientations, and gender equality.

The urban agglomeration will be dualistic in nature: there will be a vibrant, creative, and knowledge-intensive workforce, but it will also face challenges related to pollution, congestion, and safety. Meanwhile, climate change will make urban life more dangerous or uncomfortable, with more frequent changes in heat, cold, and flooding.

(8) Migration

Our species is a migratory one. Over the past seventy thousand years, we wandered out of Africa and kept on wandering in the influx of innovation. While we left the old for the new, we brought our ideas, technologies, and cultures along for the ride which played as the engines of social progress as well as social disruption in peace or conflicts.

Any migration is accompanied by desperateness.

The movement of people across cultural frontiers has brought about the globalization and integrated world we inhabit today, and it compelled them to adapt and innovate their ways of thinking and doing. The migrants allowed the people on their way to experience the spread of new crops, skills, and products. In that sense, migration was an innovation accelerant.

The mass migration in peace in the modern world happened during the first era of globalization (1850-1913) which became visible in three economic markets: labor, capital, and goods. The latter two markets were relatively more important during the late 20th and the 21st centuries than during the late 19th century, whereas integration in labor markets was of primary importance during the first era of globalization, which occurred before WW I. Migration from the Old World to the New World reached levels of more than one million people per year, considering only transatlantic migration.

Another feature of mass migration has occurred to avoid threats and seek opportunities, or by being enslaved, or displaced by coercion. By the numbers, the big relocations in history were the bifurcation of Pakistan and India by which 18 million people migrated, the slave trade that uprooted 12 million Africans, and the diaspora that rearranged 20 million Europeans during WW II.

In modernity, migration takes various forms.

- Migration is combined with diversity in new forms that racism is just skin deep, nationality is just a distinction of origin, and borderlines exist to be crossed. All of them congregate and produce a new trend of social interaction conducive to more vibrant migration.

- When the weather shifts, people move with it, and the weather will be changing us. Global warming causes not only the rise of sea levels but also drought that makes the lands hotter and more arid. Global reshuffling will take place through the displacement of 130 million people when the temperature rises by two degrees.

- Urbanization will cause people to migrate to urban areas because of better living conditions of education, medical services, job opportunities, and amenities. When this is associated with demographic changes, i.e. less populace in rural villages, the rural places will be deserted, and the bad conditions will be getting worse.

- A new mode of mobility will change the pattern of migration. The emergence of autonomous automobiles, unmanned or manned flying vehicles in the air, and unmanned or manned flying boats on the surface of seawater will change the pattern of migrations on the land and sea, The geographical remoteness and physical disconnection will be redefined in the proximity that the modern technologies will connect and bridge.

- Another one is an unheard-of migration in human history. Currently, people are migrating to virtual reality as they are addicted to gaming, internet surfing, social media, texting, sexting, and porn without physical migration. At the root of this addiction is the thrill ride known as dopamine. We feel dopamine released to arouse excitement and desire. It's released whenever we take a risk, expect a reward, or encounter novelty.

- Once we are hardwired into the reward loop of the link between an activity and dopamine, the desire to get more of this becomes our overarching preoccupation that gives people temporary pleasure. It often causes people to become psychiatrically ill due to mental illness, psychedelic drugs, or an overactive imagination.

- Modern space exploration is reaching areas once only dreamed about unsullied by reality. Many countries are in the race for the work of space exploration. More than 80 countries now have a presence in space. It is believed that the Moon contains deposits of metal oxides. silicon, titanium, rare earth metals, and aluminum. Many countries have the incentive to go after them.

Mars is the focal point of modern space exploration and manned Mars exploration is a long-term goal of the United States. NASA is on a journey to Mars, to send humans to Mars in the 2030s. NASA and its partners have sent orbiters, landers, and rovers, increasing our knowledge about the planet. Space migration is not a topic of virtual reality.

(9) Sustainability

People shared with other people and helped each other. There were no rulers and the ruled, no rich and no poor. The so-called primitive communism in the hunter-gatherer tribal societies prevailed until the agricultural and hierarchical societal structure kicked in. A group of people displaced another one through economic, political, and ideological conflicts.

The human species has evolved over 100,000 years, and, for 95 percent of this time, it has not been characterized by many of the forms of behavior ascribed to human nature today. There is nothing built into the human species that makes present-day societies the way they are, but a variety of human relationships with the external environment has made society what it is.

Environments have conditioned human societies, and humans in turn changed the environments to meet their needs, and the cycle of interaction caused a set of new environmental concerns for both humans and the environment. Climate change entails mass extinction of biodiversity, deforestation, and global warming, and they jeopardize human sustainability.

In 2018, there were an estimated 1.73 trillion barrels of oil in the world. There is enough oil to last another 50 years with an average global oil consumption of 95 million barrels per day ("mbpd"). The real consumption steadily increased from 2019's 100 mbpd to approximately 105 mbpd in 2024, which signals the possibility that global oil reserves may dry up earlier than 2068.

The time of no-oil reserve in the 2060s coincides with a period in Korea when the national pension fund will deplete, and drastic demographic change will lead to a sharp reduction of production-age people from 37 million in 2022 to 17 mil in 2072. When it rains then, it will pour.

The time of the remaining four decades (2024-2064) is fundamentally crucial for Koreans to cut the Gordian knots of energy, pension, and population failing which the statehood will be in grave danger. In the case of climate change, Korea will surely be affected by the change too, but it is not alone in the frenzy of disorders in weather.

The cost of unsubsidized renewable energy continues to plummet, while both high-speed digital connectivity and the availability of cheap, capable devices are exploding to increase the total sum of the world's available information. The digital revolution will increase the use of electricity which poses a further challenge to produce it in an environmentally friendly manner.

A series of environmental, economic, and existential risks threaten sustainability, but it is the destiny of the human species to find solutions to make their history sustainable.

(10) Role of the middle class

In history, golden mean or golden middle is the desirable middle between two extremes, one of excess and the other of deficiency. For example, in the Aristotelian view, courage is a virtue, but if taken to excess it would manifest as recklessness, and, in deficiency, cowardice.

The development since the Reformation and Renaissance has been starting the process of broadening the middle ground in the social hierarchy. With the rising inequality of income after the Industrial Revolution, the middle class emerged. As capitalism flourished, it further widened the income disparities.

High-class individuals tend to feel confident in their social position and therefore have little reason to conform to the rules and practices whereas low-class people feel free to defy accepted practices because they have little to lose. The middle feels pressured to conform to them so that they might move up the ladder and out of fear that they might slide downward.

A middle-class upbringing emphasizes individual choice and independence under individualism, while the classic ethos of the working class is all about solidarity and interdependence under communitarianism. Middle-class parents have been forced to invest more in their children while being guaranteed less by employers and the government.

The future spotlights the growth of the middle class in Asia and Africa. The perfect political community is the one in which the middle class is in control. Even as late as the turn of the millennium in 2000, two-thirds of the world's middle class resided in the European Union, the United States, or Japan.

By 2030, these three entities will account for just 25 percent of this class. China, India, and the rest of Asia will account for half of the global middle class by this time. Cumulatively, middle-class consumers in emerging markets will outnumber those in the United States, Europe, and Japan.

The growth of the middle class across the world means the continuous fall of the people below the poverty line. That's a welcome development, but it also raises a staggering question about scarce resources that should meet the needs of the emerging middle class, for example, water, minerals, and energy in the future.

The conflicting paths of the middle classes in the advanced world and the developing markets will be defining economic and political reality by 2030. Millennials are unable to get steady jobs and are hence being kept out of the middle class. The demographic composition that the old preponderates will give the millennials hurdles to pass over. The thing is, the hurdle gets higher.

Some programs to reduce poverty may increase inequality because wealthier households reinvest the dividend while poorer ones spend it. Replacing anti-poverty programs with a universal basic income would be highly regressive because it just triggers inflation and passes the burden to the next generations.

We have a tendency to assume the worst when in doubt. In Europe (Ukraine and Russia are staging the trench of warfare in the age of drones) and the Middle East (Israel and Arab states including Iran are fighting with air raids and missiles), conflicts including terrorism, dictatorships, and wars occur. In 2024, the world becomes unstable, yet the peace is controlled. We would assume that the world will be hanging in the balance of tension and power unless it is drastically knocked off-balance. We need to give the benefit of the doubt.

People will be living in an age of competition and conflict which hampers their ascent to the middle class or their ability to remain in the rung of the social ladder. Organize yourselves to engage the situation of inflexible social hierarchy and deepening social distinction in the saturated society. Unluckily, it looks more difficult for young adults to get over it as the past people did.

2) Moral Intensity

Being fraught with the ten Critical Issues, young adults will be caught in confusion when they witness conflicts replete in society. Without having a sound sense of morality, they may be swept into chaos of turf war of ideologies.

To prevent this, they need to better understand how contemporary people reason the conflicts following their moral propensity, how people overlook the moral deviations in their relative view of morality, and finally how they make moral choices that are not always balanced and objective.

This part is devoted to building a sound sense of morality of the young adults.

(1) Conflicts abound in divisiveness.

Across the globe, people become more connected with and dependent on one another than ever before, and thus they come into contact more frequently with various topics. In the meanwhile, it seems that we are born with a button for exclusive tribalism in our brains. People are divided in their thoughts on vexing topics, for example, politics, religion, and culture. They often turn on other people out of heat and anger that get them to be divided in their frequent social engagements.

The factors of morality and intuition are involved in the process: morality is the belief that a behavior is right and acceptable and that another is wrong. Intuition is a rapid and effortless process to make moral judgments. The involvement of the two factors often slips into an automatic mental process of forming a visceral and lower-level of cognition. Conflicts arise first individually and later collectively whereby the divided people become subject to herd instinct and attack the opponents recklessly.

In the state of social polarity and entrenchment, young adults shall be pushed into a social milieu that tries to induce them to a specific ideological bias. A theoretical response that the young adults would do to take a stance of acceptance or rejection of it, being aware of it but withholding their judgment on it, simply sitting on a fence nonchalantly, or showing sheer indifference to the issues at stake.

In all cases, however, they should build their own judgment following their belief system in order to be responsible for their own future, and they should manifest their demands to make their future sustainable by casting their votes to reformers. No vote, no complaint.

- First, it is about morality.
  Human nature is intrinsically a combination of moral righteousness and moralistic judgment. Self-righteousness is the state in which a person is so convinced of their own righteousness that they become moralistic or even exclusive or intolerant. The innate cognitive algorithm in the mind fixes the moralistic perception before reason and impartiality in the mind do the work. It takes the form of positive and negative characters.

  In positive terms, a certain degree of conflict roles in making a society healthy even when society is fraught with the malaise of morality. Humans are not always selfish hypocrites, and they can shut down our petty selves and become like cells in a larger body, or like bees in a hive, working for the good of the group.

It changes conflict & defeatism to conflict & resilience whereby it runs a system of check and balance that manages biased morality, and it also builds civility that makes people serene and sagacious to get out of high conflict. Dissidents may splinter off, but they are confined within the ken of common sense and tolerance. The conflict & resilient society produces cooperative and cohesive groups that usually outperform the groups of selfish individualists.

In negative terms, it is viewed that humans are indeed self-righteous hypocrites and so skilled at putting on a show of fictitious virtues that make fools of themselves. The self-righteous end justifies violent means, and it binds the people into political factions composed of a coterie of ideological comrades that share moral narratives. While individuals compete for personal reputation and profits nip and tuck, they band together to fight their ideological foes when it comes to factional confrontation.

- Second, it is about intuition.

When people encounter a situation in which a judgment hangs in balance, intuition comes first to determine our judgment before reason takes a chance to fix it. A rash of intuitive judgments is often based on outrageous lies and conspiracy theories with no intention to find facts and reason causality of an issue at stake. People with rash intuition have a thin thread of fact and a strong tribal bent. They get biased and illogical, especially when they disagree or feel resentment toward their opponent.

Moral argument about truth is mostly post-hoc construction that is crafted to justify past behavior. Reasoning, on the other hand, doesn't take people's moral arguments only with intuition but it undertakes conscious mental processes based on facts, data, and causality.

People should make a fair intuitive judgment by first taking the plank out of our own eyes, and escaping from ceaseless, petty, and divisive judgment.

Once they get trapped in a conflict, they must undergo grinding and painful experiences. It is hard for them to reverse it or get out of it. So, the best way is to stay away from high conflict, but, in reality, it seems virtually impossible for many of the polarized and entrenched people.

Despite the gloomy prospect of debunking the people in bias, it is strongly suggested that they transcend the binaries of partisanship and turn the destructive high conflict into an occasion for mutual recognition and form a symbiotic mood of dialogue and compromise.

(2) Moral reasoning

Moral reasoning is perceived from three angles.

- It is nativism that moral consciousness is native and innate in our minds and forms the basis for acquiring knowledge and moral judgment.
- It is empiricism that derives from observation or experience. It is based on the notion that

children are blank slates at birth as John Locke said, and the experiences set the tone of moral sense of the persons.

- It is rationalism, which asserts that rationality rules the person's nature. Children go through cognitive social learning. It is the reason that dictates a direction of moral propensity.

A balanced view on moral reasoning is that morality is innate in humans as a set of evolved intuitions (nativism), and it is learned as children learn to apply those intuitions within a particular culture (empiricism). People are born to be righteous (native), but we must learn what exactly people should be righteous about and how we should do something righteous (empirical).

The moral domain varies by culture.

It can be unusually narrow in educated and individualistic cultures where moral reasoning tends to be not in search of truth, but it is used to support their emotional reactions or intuitional responses. People become visceral, particularly when their feeling of disgust and disrespect drive out their reasoning. In the heat of emotion, moral reasoning serves as a post hoc justification.

When reasoning (rationalism) is missing, then a combination of innateness (nativism) and social learning (empiricism) emerges and persists.

Emotion and reason are in tension with each other, and they are pulling people in their own direction. People are ruled by intuitions and are in thrall to emotions from the heart, or they reflect and reason in their head by going through the mental-cognitive process. Humans can decide their perception and stance between these points.

- Plato believed that "reason could be the master" over intuition and emotion with the perfectibility of reason. Passions often corrupt reason, but if humans control those passions, our God-given rationality guides us to do the right thing. Seeing the bias in the modern world in politics, religion, and culture, the Platonian notion looks ineffective.

- Thomas Jefferson took the "dual-process model". The head and heart in the process are equal parties. The head processes information with reason and the brain, but it gets overruled by a stronger response from the emotional areas of the heart. The tension of reason and emotion are set in place in the beginning, but they may fall apart in the end.

- David Hum represented the partisan brain work model. The "intuition and emotions" are the leaders, and "reason and reflection" are the servants. First, they have strong gut feelings ("intuition and emotions") and make rapid intuitive judgments about what is right and wrong, and then they make moral judgments.

The intuition launches the reasoning. They, then, construct post hoc justifications about the result that the intuition had brought forth. Even when the servant (reasoning) comes back empty-handed in the post-hoc justification, the master (intuition and emotion) doesn't change his judgment.

Jonathan Haidt has insightfully illustrated the moral reasoning in his book, *The Righteous Mind. (p.35. My early Jeffersonian dual-process model*. Emotion and reasoning are separate paths to moral judgment, although moral judgment can sometimes lead to post hoc reasoning as well)

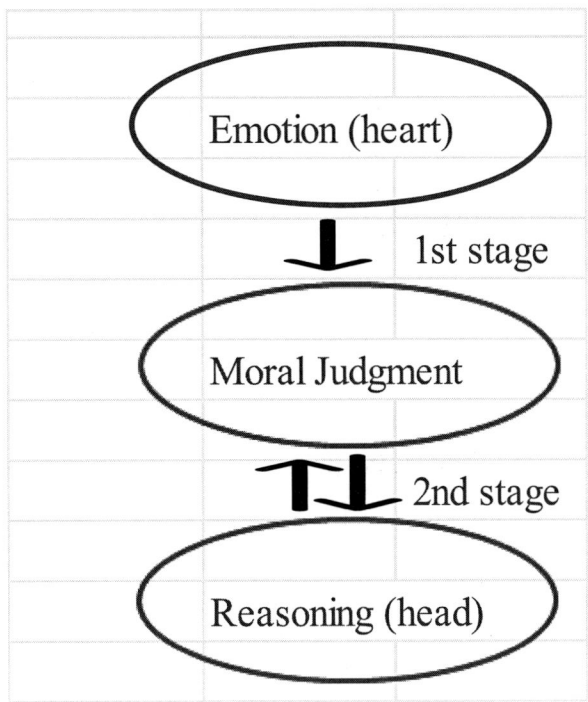

The first stage is the automatic process that drives our perceptions based on "emotion and intuition, seeing that, and lower cognition". We are all intuitive humans and intuitive nature matters in moral judgments. People see what they want to see or reject what they don't want to see.

Affect or feeling is the first process, and this phenomenon is called affective priming because the first word triggers a flash of affect that primes the mind to go one way or the other. We don't feel much conversational pressure to offer reasons, even though we mostly care a lot about what others think of us.

The second stage is the process based on "conscious reflection, reasoning that, and higher cognition". It can occur only for creatures that use language and explain to other creatures. In many cases, reason doesn't rule the process, but it is designed to seek justification, not truth. People may reason a moral conclusion that contradicts the initial intuitive judgment, but it is uncommon.

In this paradigm of forming a moral judgment, we may extend our thoughts that moral judgment is a process of two diverse kinds of cognition: emotion (intuition, desire, heart) and reasoning (reflection, cognition, head). We reason and make our moral decisions in either direction.

- If individuals are put together in the right way, they can use their reasoning powers to judge the claims of others. When individuals feel some common bond or shared fate that allows them to interact civilly, they can create a group that produces good reasoning as a beneficial party of the social system.
- If individuals are put together in the wrong way, we cannot expect people to produce good reasoning, to stay open-minded, and to maintain an attitude of truth-seeking reasoning, particularly when self-interest or reputational concerns are in play.

This is why it is so important to have intellectual and ideological diversity within any group or institution whose goal is to find the truth, such as an intelligence agency or a community of scientists, or to produce good public policy, such as a legislature or advisory board.

(3) Moral deviations

A righteous mind is like a tongue with six taste receptors: Fairness, Justice, Liberty, Loyalty, Authority, and Sanctity. It is healthy for a nation to have a constant tug-of-war, a constant debate between the ideological factions over how and when to nurture and foster, or limit and regulate the individuals, markets, corporations, and government.

- The social-conservative people are the party of order and stability and are sensitive to threats to moral capital. They value the preservation of institutions and traditions that sustain society as a moral community. However, they do not oppose some elements in the six taste receptors. They have the broadest set of moral concerns and put equal priority on Justice/harm, Liberty/oppression, Fairness/cheating, Loyalty/betrayal, Authority/subversion, and Sanctity/degradation.

- The liberal-minded people regard caring for victims as one of their most sacred values. They believe that a major function of government is to stand up for the public interest against corporations and their tendency to distort markets as well as to protect those who are least able to stand up for themselves such as the poor, immigrants, and farm animals. However, they often go too far by being reflexively anti-business. They prioritize Justice/harm, Liberty/oppression, and Fairness/cheating more than Loyalty/betrayal, Authority/subversion, and Sanctity/degradation.

- The libertarian-minded people take individual liberty as the most sacred value. They put priority heavily on Liberty/oppression. They are direct descendants of the 18th and 19th-century Enlightenment reformers who fought to free people and markets from the control of kings and clergy. They split into two camps in the 19th century: one was left-liberals, who viewed government as the only force capable of protecting the public and rescuing victims of early industrial capitalism, while the other was right-liberals (or libertarians), who continued to fear government as the chief threat to liberty.

Confirmation bias is the tendency to seek out and interpret new evidence in ways that confirm what you already think. People are quite good at challenging statements made by other people, but if it's your belief, then it's your possession or child, you want to protect it, not challenge it and risk losing it.

Reasoning has evolved not to help us find the truth but to help us engage in arguments, persuasion, and manipulation in the context of discussions with other people. Skilled arguers are not after the truth but after arguments supporting their views. They fight until their side, the good side, wins. This explains why the confirmation bias is so powerful and so ineradicable.

Confirmation bias is a built-in feature of an argumentative mind, not a bug that can be removed from a Platonic mind. If our goal is to produce good behavior, not simply good thinking, then it's even more important to reject skilled rationalism and embrace insightful intuitionism.

In all these situations, you do not have to be upset or annoyed with any seemingly illogical bias because anyone in the group is just loyal to his or her bias.

The reasoning fallacy is found in moral, political, religious, and cultural matters. This is based on the notion that we are often groupish with hive mind to share ideas and opinions among a group of people in one's community.

People see the right way and approve it instantly but follow the wrong. It is the "emotion and heart" that first leads to moral judgment, and it then interacts with "reasoning and head".

Here is the common misperception that people's moral judgment comes from "reason and head", but **it actually comes from intuition, namely "emotion and heart"**. When the ability to reflect and reason is combined with a lack of moral emotions, it can be dangerous and anti-social, for example, psychopaths who reason but do not feel and have no sociometer.

Another aspect of moral choice is that people are forced to see the world only in two dimensions. In real life, people have complex, ambivalent feelings about things like fiscal spending of government, reforms of imminent national issues of pension, education, medical affairs, labor-employer relations, or immigration. Their knowledge is different and their opinions are manifold, but they are forced to see the world and make a decision only with two dimensions which are pointless or dangerous.

The delicate difference between "can" and "must" is the key to understanding the profound effects of self-interest on reasoning. It's also the key to understanding many of the strangest beliefs in numerous conspiracy theories. When we want to believe something, we ask ourselves, "Can I believe it? When we do not want to do that, we ask ourselves, "Must I believe it?"

Saying "Because I don't want to" is a perfectly acceptable justification for one's subjective preferences. Yet moral judgments are not subjective statements, but rather point to something outside of a person's own preferences, and that pointing is our moral reasoning. We can make minor tweaks in our behavior, but it can cause big changes in ethical behavior.

Egalitarian relationships, such as with peers, invite a bigger window of action, but stratified relationships in hierarchical order narrow their window of maneuverability. In the 21st century, however, humans will notice that human interactional relationships will get egalitarian to the extent that it will blur socio-cultural distinctions.

It will also lessen the conventional disparity prevalent in the hierarchical mode of the past century. The motto of the French Revolution, liberty, equality, fraternity, will be materialized more fully. The reconfiguration process can be discordant or even mutually exclusive as the new mode of interactional relationship settles in.

Personality or self-identity matters so much across cultures. All societies must resolve questions about how to order their society, and how to balance the needs of individuals and groups. There are two primary ways of answering this question:

First, the sociocentric answer places the needs of groups and institutions first and subordinates the needs of individuals (social personality). Second, the individualistic answer places individuals at the center and makes society a servant of the individual (individual personality).

The socio-centric answer dominated most of the ancient world, but the individualistic answer became powerful during the Enlightenment. The individualistic answer largely vanquished the sociocentric approach in the 21st century as individual rights expanded rapidly, and consumer culture spread. The trend will accelerate and dominate social interaction.

If you are not happy with someone's remarks and behaviors about a moral, political, religious or cultural issue, you don't have to feel angry, irritated, or agitated with such seemingly insane actions of others. They are fizzy and just led by intuitive emotion, not by reasoning, and that cannot be an object of criticism from reasoning.

Rather, you start to talk to their heart-emotion first, not their head-reasoning, to win friends, influence each other by osmosis, and change minds. Most ineffective and futile arguments arise from the wrong start that you start an argument by jumping into the head-reasoning first and judging it from that perspective. It is a sort of apple-to-orange application in moral reasoning.

(4) Moral Choice

Contemporarily, many states fail to provide security for people and protect their property. Various social infrastructures are often out of order, resources for rehabilitation are exhausted, corruption and propaganda abound, and social integrity crumbles.

As the signs of collapse accumulate and become severe, there will be a comprehensive process of social unraveling that will show a shrinking population, a regression of the economy to unsophisticated levels, civil disobedience on a massive and sustained scale, and the stalling or collapse of politics in its role of solving problems or diverting them to defuse tensions.

Economic failure, political misery, and social division are rampant. Loss of legitimacy is the hallmark of state failure.

Politics has been morally degraded because it springs from the base human instinct to grab and win for one's own interests, but there have been exceptions in history, for example, the five good Roman emperors (96-180 AD). People, in general, have become more civilized and cultured in a democratic and interconnected world, while politics in particular has remained base and perverse.

The gap between low politics and high civility arises, and the anger or hatred of those who are stuck in the gap emerges. Modern politics becomes acrimonious and direct in addressing a certain bias or prejudice. It is hardly able to resolve conflicting issues in society in a civil or civilized way.

Moral agents are those who have a notion of right and wrong, an enduring self with free will, and who are held accountable for those actions in meeting the demands of morality and, , Not all agents are moral agents because those who have no cognitive capacity, for instance, young children and animals, are agents that are not automatically considered moral agents.

Although society is stuck in an ideological impasse with conflicts impasse, it continues to function at the expense of compliance and tolerance of some moral agents who have generous moral palates. Such acts of social cohesion come from a willingness to contribute to the common good and are the common good, and they are compatible with the title of this book, which is to "redress the balance, respect diversity and remove the elephants".

There are many examples of such moral agents: taxpayers willingly pay taxes even though they know some of it is wasted; ordinary citizens dutifully obey rules and regulations even though some, especially the ruling elites, seek exceptions; the public responds to calls for help in emergencies even though some in the upper echelons plot preferential treatment.

The purposeful actions are not superficial niceties, and they don't focus only on perishable things that fade quickly, but they hold fast to the fundamentals with the intention of preserving the virtue of the imperishable in their society according to their belief or innate nature. Thus, they show a pattern of spreading social cohesion through tolerance, concession, and sacrifice.

It refers to Matthew 25:31-33 in the Bible, which, in the final stage, is to separate the righteous sheep who have sacrificed for the least (the one who receives a new nature, sows the imperishable seed, and then exercises sacrificial love for others, especially the least) from the unrighteous goats who have acted in hypocrisy (the disingenuous hypocrites who betray trust).

Sheep-type people are sociable by nature and tend to converge on the interests of the common good and to calm disputes. A virtuous cycle of interaction is set in motion, producing beneficial results. But Goat types prioritize their interests in conflicts. They instigate arguments without offering viable alternatives.

The conclusion for young adults, then, is that **they should transform themselves to build their moral agency amid degrading politics, abysmal economic conditions, and endangered civility**. They should not only take sides in a civilized and sophisticated way but also avoid being biased and partisan. They should choose to be sheep-like people and live their lives according to the principles of redressing the balance, respecting diversity, and removing the elephants. The established institutions and the people should *say mea culpa*, and improve the conditions of work and lives of young adults by providing tender care and intimate concern.

6.2. The 21st Century (Society)

1) Society in the 21st Century

This is an effort to trace the evolution of social changes to understand how far we have come. The onslaught of constant connectivity and fast-paced activity in societies can feel like utter chaos at times.

(1) Social conflicts

We are all connected and when a human fixes a moral direction, meanwhile, the person more often than not gets mired in the mishmash of conflicts where opinions are asserted and collide, names are called or some of them are blacklisted against one another. In a state of chaotic confusion, we need to see them through and understand the two intrinsic capacities of the people in conflict.

First, it is an instinct for solidarity. People are connected and wired to cooperate with themselves. They are willing to understand others through active listening and empathy. Civility gets them elected to conceive a sense of stewardship by constraining their egos. They undergo conflict without dehumanizing one another. The conflicts are converted to social cohesion.

Second, it is an adversariness that is ingrained in their nature. People become mutually exclusive when they pursue their interests. They are opinionated and assertive in addressing their demands. Conflict bursts into a flame of anger, and every attempt to assuage the conflict fuels more conflicts. Most rational people flee the scene of egregious confrontation.

Once people are attached to an ideological argument, they regard it as a provocation and tend to repel it in a convicted belief that they are just and ethical. Being adamant in their conviction, they do not mind foregoing a system of social cohesion such as tolerance, civility, empathy, and resilience. They are only immersed in their ideological war of attrition.

Hatred is different from anger. Anger suggests that the counterpart changes for a better future, and its underlying goal is to correct the other person's behavior, whereas hatred considers the enemy a party to annihilate. In the adversarial world, anger mutates into hatred, and people slip into grim trench warfare with their ideological bête noire.

The tolerable range of the opinion spectrum gets narrow and shallow. The mind of the people who are stuck to a specific ideological bent become so biased that the people are willing to choose a side blindly. So, they become more favorable to in-groups than to out-groups, they coerce others to accept it, or they take violence against the people who stand in their way.

An example of political junkies in high-conflict situations: the English media, The Guardian, reported the real scenes of physical fights in the Taiwanese Parliament over a domestic issue in the parliament and administration on 17 May 2024. https://www.youtube.com/watch?v=NfYlL_r5xKk.

"A scuffle broke out in the Taiwanese parliament days before the president-elect, Lai Ching-te, takes office without a legislative majority. The opposition wants to give parliament greater scrutiny powers over the government, including a controversial proposal to criminalize officials who are deemed to make false statements in parliament. The ruling Democratic Progressive party has accused the opposition of improperly trying to force through the proposals without the customary consultation process in what they call 'an unconstitutional abuse of power."

People left comments: *"If my country were like this, I would never stop watching the sessions on the congress channel. For Taiwanese parliament this is pretty common, just another day at the office. This is MADNESS!. This is politics. Democracy?."*

In watching the scenes in the video footage, they were disorderly and rancorous. People found that ideological divisiveness can develop into real tussle in the ruckus at the venue of the people's representatives. It figuratively means that the fight among the representatives signifies the physical melee of the people who are in conflict over the legal bill.

But it suggests us to see it in a different view. Taiwan has been caught in a decades-long tension with communist China amid the remarkable development of its economy and democracy. For the Taiwanese, mainland China is a being that cannot be separated due to its proximity of geography, culture and geopolitical interests, but it is not combinable in terms of ideology and political structure.

Both sides won't renounce political ideology. As China won't adopt liberal democracy, most Taiwanese won't accept dictatorial communism. Coercion to compel one another's ideology leads to a total war. The desperate reality of the decades-long situation may have compelled the Taiwanese Parliament to walk a tightrope of tension that has restricted civility and tolerance.

It is not much different from the scenes in the National Assembly of Korea in the last decade in which the lawmakers of the ruling party and the opposition party clashed in a mass melee in noisy scuffling. The public couldn't do anything but just frown at the disorder or turn a blind eye to it. https://www.youtube.com/watch?v=1s7dXFuN6A8

Since its foundation in 1948, democratic South Korea has conflicted with communist North Korea, which invaded the South in 1950 and has made innumerable provocations after the cease-fire in 1953 up to the present. The ideological schism between the two states in the Korean Peninsula is the same as that between the two states in the Taiwan Straits.

In South Korea, there has been a split of opinion in the National Assembly as well as in the public on how to respond to the North in either a firm stance against it with caveats of worsening inter-Korean relationship or a malleable appeasement toward the North to defuse the tension at the risk of being duped or played with continually by the North Korean regime.

It was a very risky game of striking a delicate balance of policies between carrot and stick: *carrot* (appeasement by offering benefits) at one end, *a hybrid of carrot and stick* (some mixed policies of appeasement and tough stance) in the middle, and *stick* (tough stance by power) at the other end. Each policy has its pros and cons, and the pendulum of policies has swung back and forth.

As it was in Taiwan, South Korea has been under the grievous risk of security. The authoritative administrations in the 1960s to 1980s were successful in achieving rapid economic development, but they were not able to make it fully democratic. The thorny question of how to deal with North Korea has caused tension and sometimes conflict among the people.

South Korea has a façade of prosperity in modern civility, but it is riddled with the ideological divide that directs some far different policies when it concerns North Korea. This poses a great risk of inconsistency in its interaction with North Korea which is conversely controlled by the same family for almost 80 years.

The edgy mood of division for decades has probably made the political parties to which the lawmakers belong as well as the people less inclusive and more divisive in their thoughts and actions. The shallow margin of tolerance has had them sometimes locked horns with each other in many of the legal bills that were tinged with ideological propensity or political hue. The standoff frequently developed into physical clashes.

There are a number of cultural factors that decide a specific pattern of behavior in a given society. What I am trying to point out is the desperate acuteness of the situation that tends to make people confrontative or even go extreme when they are exposed to the stark reality of life or death for a long time in the lack of an ultimate solution or effective alternatives.

Meanwhile, please find the hefty mood in the silence of the members of the Chinese Communist Party Congress and the North Korean Parliament.

https://www.youtube.com/watch?v=HzPoIXXbiO8 for China,
https://www.youtube.com/watch?v=hGncMhmgIDI for North Korea (30-48 seconds)

We wonder which one is true to the underlying thoughts or unexpressed voice of the people and what would efficiently reflect the reality of the issues at stake, either the rancorous brawl in the Taiwanese Parliament, the modesty in the Chinese Congress, or the disorder in the South Korean National Assembly, or the unified motion of the North Korean Parliament.

Living in the complicatedness of modernity, conflict is universal and inevitable. In bad conflict, the process stagnates, and conflict is its destination whereas there is movement in good conflict.

Literally, the ideological middle class refers to the class of people who position themselves in the middle of the ideological spectrum which becomes growingly polarized and entrenched. They refuse to be blindly swept away into a specific ideology or belief, but they take neutral ground and decide their stance in their own independent criteria and standards.

They differ in the criteria and standards themselves, but a common notion that may bind them is a universal common sense following which they normally judge a specific point and decide their stance on it. They play the roles of lubricants to reduce ideological abrasion, of buffers to absorb shocks, or of counterweight that balances the bias or prejudice.

The ideological middle class is composed of various classes of people in the social hierarchy, and so they take stances in various angles on the topics of gender, race, religion, age, wealth or other social issues. They are not always identical to the economic middle class who show a certain class consciousness and idiosyncratic pattern of behavior in a society.

They get fewer and are hanging in the balance in the polarized people. It resembles the phenomenon that moderate weather in spring and autumn gets shorter while inclement weather in summer and winter gets longer. It means that the ideological middle class becomes more difficult to play such roles as the lubricant, the shock absorber, and the counterweight.

Typically, a conflict reaches a point of saturation along the toxic interim progress. Once the saturation point is reached, and the loss from the conflict exceeds the gain, people begin to shift their position. At this juncture, the leader should seize the opportunity to facilitate collaboration, rather than further conflict. Failure to do so risks the underlying issues intensifying into another conflict, potentially leading to a spiral of animosity or retribution.

This is the central challenge of our time. We need to change the high conflict to healthy conflict without collapsing into dehumanization by stepping back from the high conflict, recognizing the way it warps our vision, and imagining another way for the change.

We get an insight from *The Righteous Mind* by Jonathan Haidt. It says people place their cherished values on relevant policies that are commonly necessary for society. In the U.S., the Liberals are more sensitive to Care, Fairness, and Liberty, while the Conservatives engage more with Loyalty, Authority, Liberty, and Sanctity without excluding those of the Liberals.

People may disagree on hot-button issues, and they are sure to get riled up. Nonetheless, we don't have to rant and rave with fingers pointing at opponents of policies because all the issues at stake are beneficial to society unless they are illegal. It is a matter of focus and priority, not calling peoples' names in conflict.

(2) Social behavior

The social convention has been established by the toils of ancestors in trials, the occasions of divergence and convergence of social groups, and the accumulated experiences and achievements of those who have lived through those times. Meanwhile, modern society is in confusion where facts and values are confused, core norms are destabilized, and values and biases are jumbled.

So, conventionality in modern society cuts both ways:

First, when the convention is set in place as a beneficent legacy, it helps posterity save costs, keep discipline, improve processes, reduce waste, and engender opportunities. When it is put into the task of performing social roles, it runs in a virtuous circle of social interaction that may contribute to social development and cohesion.

Second, as the convention gains currency, it is set in place as an established convention. Posterity takes them for granted and seeks to gratify their desires. They are explicitly indifferent to formidable changes, or they stick to their vested interests rather than toil for a new norm that makes their future sustainable.

Within the range that social convention maneuvers and effects, we may list the myriads of actions and counteractions of conflicts that the people exhibit in various patterns of behaviors with their own reasons and aspirations.

Pattern	Behavior	Remarks
A	They identify the problems that are deviant from their vision, work out ideas for solutions, carry them out, and complete reform for the future.	This is a virtuous circle for a sustainable future
B	They know what the problems are and what they need to do, but they are irresolute to proceed to fix the action plans, and even lethargic to practice them.	They won't do it anyhow by creating many excuses
C	They project reality in their own way contrary to common sense. It is inordinate and unbalanced, and it causes confusion and conflict among all stakeholders.	There is something progressive, but the direction is wrong
D	They give up doing something constructive in hopeless conditions or they live from day to day. The future is beyond their control, or it is not relevant to them.	This is the least helpful way to make society sustainable

- Conciliatory and constructive actions (Pattern A)

Human beings are born with the capacity to defuse a confrontation and persuade relevant parties to align their actions in a conciliatory manner. They are driven by a desire for conciliatory harmony and benevolent outcomes and are committed to resolving the underlying issues and redirecting high-conflict situations toward constructive collaboration. They reform the structured problems driven by either inspiration or sometimes desperation.

Firstly, they address the complexity and deal with the details. It is often the case that people do not fully comprehend the nuances of an issue unless they have a detailed understanding of the facts and can distinguish between the various elements involved. Individuals who adopt a pragmatic approach to the matter at hand may propose a moderate solution that is more readily acceptable.

Secondly, they practice deep listening. They distinguish between the issue and the speaker and focus on the issue itself by listening carefully. They are tolerant of diverse views and listen to the topics at issue in depth. Deep listening does not imply immediate agreement or passive compliance. It aims to understand the underlying issues and avoid being drawn into a futile power struggle.

Thirdly, they cultivate resilient relationships. Individuals who engage in active listening can identify common ground and establish a foundation for constructive dialogue, even in the context of adversarial conflict. This approach is often referred to as conflict resilience. Resilience enables constructive debate, facilitates adaptation to a range of responses to conflict, and drives forward toward resolution.

Pattern A should be conducted on a long-term basis with consistent standards applied to all parties involved. If this is not done, the effects will gradually diminish over time, and the situation will revert to a state of adversarial echo chambers. The effort invested in these practices will ultimately prove worthwhile. *"The Lord detests differing weights, and dishonest scales do not please Him (Proverbs 20:23).*

- Irresolute or inordinate actions (Pattern B or C)

This is the most toxic pattern, but it is becoming common. Common sense gives in to the pressure of polarity, and the problems become entrenched. No one dares to defy the restrictions or to initiate the right actions at the right time. The irresolute people are slow to volunteer for sacrificial dedication, but they normally are quick for public recognition when a feat of remarkable achievement occurs.

The problems at hand are not resolved but accumulated. The task of resolving them is passed over to the next generations who must settle the bill in addition to the secondary problems of waste of resources or misappropriation of opportunities. Future generations must shoulder the inordinate burdens of their own as well as those of their past generations.

Lack of courage, being self-protective or loss of confidence would be the reasons for irresolute or inordinate actions. The non-action of ex-President Moon in Korea on the reform of the Korean national pension scheme would be a case of Pattern B that had increased the burden for the future generation to shoulder to the extent of the non-action.

Conspiracy theory takes hold and revives when it is called up. Notable socio-political-economic events are frequently cited in that there were schemers who plotted them to reap certain benefits. A case would be the sinking of the Korean Navy battleship, *Cheonan*, in 2010, which was torpedoed by North Korea.

It has been stricken with conspiracies that she got sunk because of its implosion, going aground or attacked by a US submarine, but the investigation revealed the fact that it was the torpedo of North Korea that sunk the ship. Such conspiracies never cease to rise whenever there are some contentious issues irrespective of their credibility. This would be the case with Pattern C.

• Voluntary rejection or resignation into inactivity (Pattern D)

Humans have certain fundamental emotional needs for a sense of belonging, self-esteem, control, and a meaningful existence. These needs are nearly as important to our survival as food and water. When they feel they are not properly heard or represented, or they are rejected with debilitating effects, and then they tend to react with hostility. This leads to their counter-rejection voluntarily and get resigned with no intention to act or cooperate.

The risk of a low fertility ratio of around 0.7 in Korea is catastrophic because it amounts to national suicide unless it turns around or a very active policy of immigration is implemented promptly. The people know it, but they don't act correspondingly because the decision to have a baby is purely a personal matter.

Another example is the excesses and wastes in the National Assembly. There is a large number of bills that they are supposed to review and enact the laws relevant to the living conditions of the national people, but the National Assembly rarely goes through the law-making process, but they just waste time and resources for political confrontations. They are privileged in the entitlements with great perks, but they are most inefficient and backward in the governance themselves.

Another case is the increasing number of university graduates who are in non-economic activity. According to the statistics from the Korean government, there are more than 4 million people who are not capable of working or who are not willing to work. The perception of being hopeless makes some of them give up seeking jobs. This would be the cases of Pattern D.

(3) Social Phenomena in Korea

• Social problems

This cocooning behavior is termed to be "cocoonism," which means choosing to stay inside the established norm in insulation from changes and dangers outside. The vice of cocoonism tends to live off national parochialism, local interests, communal tribalism, and individual selfishness.

It finally nurtures a sense of exclusivity that triggers an action to protect the vested interests of any interest units. A mature society is likely to show such phenomena where opportunities for social recognition, career development, and wealth creation are limited to acquire or advance because of the preponderant focus on short-term benefits.

Usually, this slips into a state of excessive focus on short-term results, mediocrity that justifies the quality of average and ordinary, and even the debasement of the sacred culture that has upheld the society. People are eager for fame and money, and egocentric interests mark the trend of the time. It often thwarts actions aimed to sustain the society in the long-term perspective.

In some cases, people deliberately overlook an opportunity to benefit future generations in its preference for vested interests. Something conventional and mediocre falls short of producing breakthroughs, and they often bring parochialism and cronyism that make matters worse.

Dead fish rots from the head. When the minds of individuals corrupt, society decays, cracks, crumbles, and then collapses. The parts that are supposed to be sound and clean in ethics, and loadstone of morality, such as religion and governmental officials on fame, money, and public recognition. We found some examples in Korea:

• A symptom of hypocrisy

The Protestant churches in Korea had been contributing to the building of Korean society since the late 19th century, firstly by the Western missionaries and then by the local Christian leadership. Their code of conduct, loyal to the Christian doctrines, had enlightened the social backwardness and induced the people to enhance their moral standards in Korean society.

Recently, however, Christian churches in Korea have been said to be weakening in their social influence as well as the intensity of their evangelical mission. The total number of congregations dwindled, and people heard news frequently on the misconduct by some Christian leaders and churches that were violating the social norms or laws, let alone the Christian doctrines.

From the perspective of the public, the decline may be attributed to the reasons below which invoke social apathy or antipathy toward the Protestant churches and the Christians. For clarity, many churches are loyal to their ecclesiastical dogmas, but some bad apples rot all in the basket which foments a mood that helps make the churches seem irrelevant in Korean society.

i) They are accused of having a double standard in being expressive about Christian beliefs and conduct yet allowing their members to renege on them in their lives. They are highly expressive against unorthodoxy outside the churches, but they usually remain silent or take a lukewarm stance toward the misconduct inside them.

ii) The hierarchy in the churches that were supposed to serve the ecclesiastical ministry becomes an organization-like secular stratification that hinders the natural flow of communication and interaction among the congregation. The senior echelon in the stratified hierarchy tends to control, not to serve, and to protect themselves, not the faith.

iii) Nepotism and cronyism in the leadership cause the churches to be governed for the interests of some specific people, not the entire congregation. The practice that the pastor's sons or in-laws inherit the pastorship in some big and affluent churches makes the ecclesiastical ministry an abominable family business to protect familial interests of money and power.

The church leader thinks himself too significant to be challenged in the guise of a representative of divine leadership. So, he controls the church and its wealth by organizing a powerful group of henchmen, and it comes to a stage where he wants the congregation to obey and serve him. All the members of the congregation fall into conflict and division. When the church gets bigger and wealthier, the pastor gets old to consider retirement, then he plots a scheme to inherit the pastorship to his son or in-law. The in-church conflicts get close to boiling point, and it turns into suppression and resistance beyond the divide.

A hypothetical question arises. Would the pastor be determined to do the same hereditary succession when the church is small and poor? Adam and Eve had worked in parity and love, and there was no specific bloodline justifying privilege and supremacy. The inheritance based on nepotism divides churches and conflict in the organization grows geometrically.

Many laities left the church or abandoned their faith. The pastor makes himself a destroyer of the Peace in God and the spirituality of lay people. In medieval Europe, the poor vented a vein of resentment to not just well-to-do knights, but also greedy priests who hogged everything good from the poor. The simoniac legacy lives long, but it gets more prevalent in Korean churches these days.

Surprisingly, the hypocritical pastors who must be reformed ceremoniously observe the anniversary of the Reformation and Martin Luther every October. It is the pastor who makes the church like the trampled salt that lost its saltiness (Matthew 5:13), and they let the lay people derail from the Christian belief.

Such pastors deserve the fate in the Scripture. *"If any of you put a stumbling-block before one of these little ones who believe in me, it would be better for you if a great millstone were fastened around your neck, and you were drowned in the depth of the sea (Matthew 18:6)"*.

This is an example of the impudent practices that occur so frequently in Korean society. It occurs so frequently that it seems not so extraordinary these days. As the insolent action repeats itself and accumulates, the principle that has supported the community as a pillar of strength crumbles, and it finally collapses under its weight. No one is to blame, but the egregious church leaders who are loyal to crony capitalism in their missions contrary to their routine sermons on the pulpit.

• An Elephant in the Room

One of the typical cases of sustainability matters is the reform of the national pension system in Korea. The National Pension Scheme is the public pension created in 1988 in South Korea as a part of Korea's social security programs. The history of the universal pension system in Korea is more than three decades whereas Japan has had it for more than six decades from 1961.

The Korean national pension is in existential threat, as its fund is projected to decrease from 2041 and deplete in 2055 if the current system remains unchanged while the population shrinks and ages. It is like the ailing system got a terminal diagnosis to expire a generation later (say 30 years), after which Koreans are rid of the national pension or the government is at risk of default to cover it.

There have been many talks and discussions to resolve the problem of pension depletion or to litigate the risk among the ruling elites of the Government and National Assembly to no avail. The equation of pension contribution and receiving is not very complicated. It is about time and amount to make the people pension-covered for a longer period than is expected.

> (i) People contribute more (pay a higher amount) now and receive pension benefits following a case from the combination of factors of time (receive longer) and amount (receive less) than the present level.
>
> (ii) People contribute to the pension as it is (pay the same amount) and receive the pension in a lesser

amount for a longer period.

Both cases are affected by the demographic change (low birth rate, longer life expectancy, fewer pension contributors and more pensioners, shrinking population) and the economic situation (lower growth rate and downsizing of the economy). This is most typical in Korea which is in a drastic transition to downsizing population and economy with a lower rate of economic growth.

For clarity, there is no political motivation to address this issue nor is there any bias for or against specific persons or political parties. But this is just to focus on the reforms that would benefit young adults in the future. Again, let me seek the understanding of the readers who may feel favorable or unfavorable to these descriptions.

In August 2018, the committee on national pension reform suggested an idea of reforming the pension system with higher contributions. In November 2018, ex-President Moon Jae In declined the idea because he thought it didn't meet the expectations of the people after which it was left topsy-turvy, procrastinated, and left in limbo until the end of his tenure in 2022.

He decided to leave the problem unresolved whereby the reform initiative was automatically transferred to the next administration together with the burden that future generations would have to bear. The time of four years that had elapsed without progress for the pension reform made the pension reform costlier and procrastinated more to the extent that it was put on ice.

In retrospect, his approval rating was high and the then ruling party dominated the National Assembly. If he was determined to reform the pension, he could have taken the pension reform initiative and proceeded to have it reformed. But he did not do it for an obvious reason of political disadvantage when it was pushed. His passivity in the reform made the people pay for it.

Everyone has their own justification for their decision and action. He did not specify the detailed reasons officially why he did not drive to reform the pension. He chose the way to let the pension reform remain dormant or he lacked the moral fiber to push the reform through the resistance of stakeholders against higher contributions or lower and later receiving.

The incumbency of the presidency counts. The same logic applies to current President Yoon who is also responsible for the same assignment to make the national pension sustainable before his tenure ends in 2027. Seeing the time lag effects of the failed reform, the sooner the reform takes place, the better it will benefit future generations.

The procedures for reforms are discordant because the reform agenda entails resistance from the affected stakeholders. It should start with effective communication with all stakeholders by presenting them with intentions, cogent reasons, and verifiable justifications clearly for the benefit of future generations. In many cases of conflicts, the stakeholders only have a flimsy grasp of reform topics. Ideally, the National Assembly would be the center of discussion and consensus in collaboration with the administrative government.

Political negotiations are to reach a consensus. However, suppose it is indefinitely suspended in the state of stalemate, in that case, there must be someone who shoulders the burden to challenge the status quo, endures the opposition braces for resistance of those who are against the reforms, and denigrates the reformers.

For everyone who has a hammer, everything looks like nails. When salty hearts are associated with immediate odium or long-held hatred among the political tribes, the conclusion through negotiation is out of the picture. If the work fails so, then the costs are passed to future generations. This makes us ponder on the role of political leaders.

Let me suggest an idea to read an article that reported the reform issues by Hyeonjong Min, 2 November 2023. The Paradox of South Korea's Presidential Approval Rating – The Diplomat (https://thediplomat.com/2023/11/the-paradox-of-south-koreas-presidential-approval-rating/)

"There are three critical yet sensitive issues in South Korea, which only strong leadership can address: national pension, public health, and education reforms…These issues are obvious social problems. Yet, like in many countries, these glaring issues are neither addressed nor resolved, because the political costs are high for leaders to even approach these topics… Moon was capable of providing a breakthrough. As he was overwhelmingly popular in his first and second years in office, and enjoyed a majority in the South Korean legislature to boot, he did not even need bipartisan support to make changes. Any opposition to his reforms could be deemed irrational. However, Moon chose to play it safe instead.… Ironically, Moon's unpopular successor, Yoon, is tackling these sensitive issues without hesitation.… Considering the (un)popularity of Yoon, the administration is not in a favorable political position to address these issues. A rational politician in Yoon's situation would choose to promote policies that serve the best interests of core supporters or main stakeholders and prepare for elections. Instead, Yoon chose to tackle hot-button reforms at the risk of endangering his remaining approval rate."

History has unfolded: first, history has developed when someone has done something that was required for the future, second, history has suspended when someone hasn't done something necessary for the future, and third, history made retrograde motion when someone has done something that shouldn't have done. Nothing could be more convincing than a demonstration of actual implementation beyond big and good words.

Other than those reforms of pension, medical, and education, President Yoon's reform initiatives include the digitalization of administrative works, fiscal discipline, and soundness, diplomatic relationships of fostering alliance (Korea-USA-Japan), and maintaining a friendly relationship with China and, to some extent, Russia, and patriot & veterans affairs.

They may for now fall into the first category to remove the elephant for future generations, but it remains to be seen how they will end up. I suggest that young adults be aware of three categories in history that are crucial to understanding the reforms of national pension, public health, and education at work that Mr. Yoon pushes now.

- A holistic approach toward history

We need to see history first in the big picture of events across time, and then in the factual sequence of parties, contents, and duration within a holistic framework. The thing that we should avoid is taking a partial and anachronistic stance in understanding history because anachronism enjoys reaping without the toils of seeding and nurturing. The social phenomenon of the anti-Japanese sentiment in Korea can be an example of pondering history in the context of the holistic view.

When it comes to the history after the 16th century, China and Japan invaded Korea to which Korea fought off bravely or capitulated in humiliation. The history culminated with the annexation of Japan in 1910. Japan had administered colonial rule (1910-1945) during which it pursued its world-turning ambition in Asia, and Korea was managed as a part of it.

The colonial rule was set in place with reasons that the Joseon Dynasty (Korea) could not maintain its statehood in the face of the imperial expansion of Japan. It did not reform itself in the 19th century to be compatible with the global trend, and it was not competent enough to rule the people in the Korean Peninsula to make the dynasty sustainable.

Japan performed the Meiji Restoration in 1868, which restructured its organization and operating system to catch up with the Western powers in mental and material capacities. It grew and developed its competence to run the country, and it established regional hegemony by winning the wars of the Sino-Japanese War (1894-1895) and the Russo-Japanese War (1904-1905).

In its quest for imperial expansion, Japan occupied China, Southeast Asia, and Pacific islands after it did to Taiwan and Korea. From the 1930s. it began the war with the Allies. Imperial Japan tried to establish a Pan-Asian union in the name of the Great East Asia Co-Prosperity Sphere (1942-1945). It committed atrocious crimes against humanity in its war efforts.

In history, nothing comes from a vacuum, and everything happens in its causality. So, we need to understand the flow of events relevant to a specific issue. In real scenes of debates, however, we notice unique behavioral patterns in the media, SNS, and the National Assembly that influence public opinion in Korea.

A vibrant debate on an issue is often sidetracked by emotional, narrow-minded, and parochial topics that are irrelevant and biased rather than objective, comprehensive, and factual. confusion will inevitably arise when intentional bias takes precedence over objective facts. A series of new arguments emerged when some individuals continued to draw upon a well of anti-Japanese sentiment, demonstrating a lack of regard for factual understanding and contextual insights, and instead resorting to a binary, unyielding stance.

Understandably, the debate demonizes colonial rule, but it lacks a holistic approach in understanding it. The debate is defocused, and the momentum in it is lost in despair, and it finally ends up in division. This influences the young adults to have a bias or distortion way that helps form polarity and entrenchment of ideological bent.

Three examples are illustrated.

First, many collaborators had worked for various Japanese institutions for livelihood or career development. Most of them were low-level in the hierarchy as officials, employees of corporations, schoolteachers, police stooges, soldiers, and village-asses in lion's skin. They were not in a position to make meaningful changes in colonial rule.

As the colonial rule went on, people were born in colonized Korea, they grew up under the Japanese education system. The longed-for independence was clueless. The way of earning a living was limited and scarce. Some secured jobs in the Japanese institution and worked at sites in and out of Korea. After liberation in 1945, they were labeled collaborators.

For the sake of clarity, this doesn't mean to overlook some Koreans who played the roles of stooges of imperial Japan motivated by personal aspirations, but we need to discern the facts that some Koreans had earned their living as petty officials, employees and laborers in the works for Imperial Japan.

Anachronism works here in the process of opining on the people only in a contemporary perspective and the causality in the people's stories is downplayed or ignored. The ardent social antipathy against Japanese colonial rule has criticized or blackmailed them and their descendants of grandchildren or great-grandchildren.

Who can blame a person who found out that he or she was a national in colonized Korea due to the work of providential mystery, more exactly, innate destiny of inequality, who had no choice but to be educated by the colonial education system, and who had to earn his living for his family by working in the jobs for Imperial Japan when he could not find employment elsewhere?

The blind criticism toward those who had worked in jobs would be construed that they should have devoted themselves for the independence of Korea, they should have been starving without getting jobs from the colonial authority, or they should have chosen menial works that were less relevant to the Japanese authority, or they should have emigrated to other countries escaping the Japanese rules.

What if the criticasters were born in the times in such conditions? What would be their choices? From a holistic view, the people who are to blame are those who made the people live in such dismal conditions, such as the Japanese authority that scapegoated the Koreans for their imperial interests, the ruling elites of the Joseon Dynasty who didn't reform the country in time, and the public who didn't repel the Japanese colonialists in all available ways.

It's interesting to see the same type of antagonistic approach goes on toward some North Koreans who defected to South Korea. In pro-North Korea bias of sentiment or specific ideological propensity to favor North Korea, some people in South Korea often fall foul of the defectors by expressing hostile sentiment explicitly in their opinions and actions.

The same providential inequality applies to them. They were just born in the impoverished county, they needed food, shelter, medical services, and jobs to survive, and they had no hope of decent human lives under the dictatorial regime. So, they had to cross the border at the risk of their lives and came to South Korea through an arduous journey of escape.

Who is to blame the defectors? What if the antagonistic people were born in North Korea, and they must live lives of absolute poverty in sub-human conditions under strong surveillance and harsh punishments for transgressions, of the fate that their career developments are fixed by birth, and of limitation of freedom to move around, what would be their choice? There is nothing or none to blame, but the providential mystery that some people were merely born in the liberal-democratic South whereas some others were just born in the communist-dictatorial North.

Second, it is the issue of assets that the Japanese government and corporations built. The Japanese authorities built tangible and intangible assets to extract values from Korea and China. Japanese colonial authority funded the cost of building the assets mainly by issuing bonds that were purchased by the Japanese government in Tokyo.

The tangible assets were social infrastructure (roads, ports, railways, dams, power plants), industrial facilities (factories, steel mills), and social facilities (schools, prisons, farmlands), and the intangible ones were systems of administration, jurisdiction, and education. After the liberation in 1945, all of them were confiscated and transferred to Koreans.

On the part of Koreans, the raison d'être of the assets was not for the benefit of Korea. They got them free of charge, regarded them as due recompense for the colonial rule, and utilized them to build the society and economy. Although they were initially used for extracting value from Korea, they later created value when the Koreans used them to build their economy.

On the part of Japan, the Japanese authorities had invested in the assets for their purposes, and they had gained profit from the investments that had enough payback period, but some investments that were made at a time closer to 1945 were surely unable to realize the projected profit. They deemed the free confiscation to cause huge losses to them.

Koreans have been educated with the notion of anti-colonial rule after the liberation in 1945. It demonized it by highlighting atrocities and exploitation of Korean people and resources. For the part that the colonial rule modernized the Korean societies and built assets that contributed to building the Korean economy after 1945, they were sidelined or belittled.

To understand colonial rule, this reconfirms the need for a holistic view that history should be seen in the picture of events across time and then followed by a study of factual sequence. The young adults will require balance in thought, logical evaluation, and a holistic understanding. Once they lose this balance, it will unbalance their cognition and actions.

State	Colony	Year	Investment (USDM)	Investmenr per head (USD)
United States	Philippines	1935	252	15.5
Great Britain	India (including Sri Lanka)	1938	3,050	8.4
Japan	Joseon	1938	869	37.8
France	Vietnam, Laos, Cambodia	1938	295	12.8

Park Seop, "Changes in economy druing colonial period, Korea and India, Moonhak-Jiseong San, 2001. p.150

Third, history enlightens us to understand the present, and well-understood present moves on to create a future. The balanced dual focus is essential in the mutual relationship between Korea and Japan. An unbalance occurs if one is bound with excessive concentration on a part, then the unbalance begets contention and unsettles the motifs of cooperation.

The anti-Japanese sentiment can be traced back to the story from 114 years ago when Japan had annexed, and the year 2025 will mark the 80th year after Korea was freed from colonial rule and the 60th year that Korea made diplomatic relations with Japan. There must be a certain progress to let history develop a new future instead of harping on about bad memories because it does harm young adults more than benefits them. It cannot persist in that way. It is time to remember it, and let young adults do their develop their own history.

A case of cognitive bias in the Korea-Japan relationship is the concerns of the ALPS (Advanced Liquid

Processing System) processed water being released into the Pacific from August 2023, which has been a hot topic in the Asia-Pacific region in the sectors of politics, environment, and economy as well.

Some people in Korea scolded the release because it would contaminate the seawater around Korea. The authorities of Japan and the IAEA (International Atomic Energy Agency) announced that the risk is managed because the water was processed to remove toxic elements before the release. IAEA presented the data and Japan allowed on-site attendance during the release.

The presentation explaining the safety of the released water by Rafael Mariano Grossi, the head of IAEA, in July 2023 in Seoul was given taunt and jeer, boon and heckle from some dissenters. They argued that they do not respect the authority and cannot trust the explanations of the IAEA in their suspicion that there will be radioactive pollution in the sea near Korea.

They also reprimanded the Korean government with inflammatory and pejorative rhetoric with an allegation that the pro-Japanese Korean government had imperiled the health and safety of the Koreans in collaboration with the Japanese government. It brought the issue of released water into anti-Japan sentiment and political polemic.

Meanwhile, when it comes to the release from nuclear power plants, the nuclear power plants in Korea and China also release water that also contains certain contaminants. Some argued that the released water from the Fukushima Power plant is different from others, but the dissenters didn't argue about the release from Korea and China to the same extent as they did for Japan.

For clarity, this is not to handle scientific issues, but this attempts to deal with the issue of balanced thought and holistic approach based on data and reasons. If some people are skeptical about the presentation and announcements of the IAEA and the Japanese authority, then they may take rational actions to ask questions and demand an explanation from them, rather than taunt and jeer.

Unless they believe that the release from the nuclear power plants in Korea and China poses no threat of pollution, they should act in the same manner toward the releases in Korea and China in the same manner as they did toward Japan, for example, to deliver letters of protest to the Japanese embassy in Seoul.

What is intended here is to make a point of universality and consistency. If the dissenters are concerned about the pollution, then they should make contact with all relevant authorities such as Japan, the IAEA, and the nuclear power plants in Korea and China, and tried to break through a crust of their skepticism by communicating with them, rather than focusing selectively on Japan.

As of August 2024, the Korean government has tested 40,000 cases in the seas around Korea for one year. The results haven't shown any sign of atomic contamination, and it cost more than one billion US dollars. We wonder what would have happened if the dissenters had communicated and reached a consensus with the authorities, thus saving costs or using them for other productive purposes.

We also wonder what would have happened if it were not Japan, but Korea or China, that were to release the processed water, or what if the ex-President Moon, who is much favored by the dissenters, had given consent to Japan for releasing the processed water under the surveillance of the IAEA, rather than the less-favored current President Yoon. Would the dissenters resist to the same degree?

(4) Overall assessment of Korean society

Having dealt with specific issues in and around Korea, this is to make an overall assessment of Korean society.

• Facet 1

Korean society is polarized and entrenched so deeply in politics, economy, and culture that the impasse will not improve without a complete motivational switch. The factors of bias, obsessions, and conflicts clog the flow of the consensual approach. Many people lean into the short-term results of fame or wealth rather than balance short-term and long-term rewards.

It is said that South Korea is a society of dissatisfaction with conflicts whereas North Korea is another society of satisfaction in deception and delusion. As to the polarization in politics in the south, it is attributed to the winner-take-all system in the election of offices (in the case of National Assembly members, an element of proportional representation is reflected in a limited level in Korea) of binary parties. The people conflict with one another over tendentious topics in truculent air. Purpose and bias are jumbled and confused. This system creates a much fiercer conflict, and it explains the deeper polarized society than other countries with multi-party systems.

Despite the factors of social instability, society functions in good order due to the compliance, tolerance, concessions, and indifference of some people. They pursue long-term sustainability, perform their duty, and prioritize the common good. However, some others remain indifferent and show a complete lack of interest in the abominable struggles for power.

Among the various patterns of behavior, the actions of social cohesion and national sustainability are of importance. The multitude of ordinary people are taking willing actions to bridge the gap or overcome the polarity by performing duties as usual and they often do more than their duties. The willing compliance and support are pillars of strength in society.

The taxpayers willingly pay taxes even though a part of it would be wasted, the citizens dutifully observe the rules even though some people would evade them; and the public attend to the call for aid or rescue in national emergencies, even though some people seek exceptions or preferential treatment. Many civil servants do the civil services dutifully.

Interestingly, when it comes to the willing contribution or the dutiful observance of social rules and regulations, the young and less affluent people are more contributory and compliant than the old and the rich. This is not based on scientific data, but a facet of social phenomena that is spotted frequently in places where the rules and regulations are supposed to be observed.

My work experiences in the parking lot of Juwang Mountain National Park in Korea in 2021-22 remind me of such cases. The all-day parking charge was 5,000 won (about 4 US dollars) during the weekend. Among the complainers over the charge, the portion of old-aged drivers in luxurious sedans was preponderant over the young genteel ones in small, shabby, and old cars.

Humans tend not to change themselves, but I still hold out hope that society will become more cultured with decent civility and social decorum of the young people which will cause ripple effects of progress in social codes of conduct and strengthen social cohesion. For young adults, the world will be more global, diverse, and competitive which requires their standards of conducts to be compatible with contemporary people in the globe.

• Facet 2

Korean society is getting saturated with apathy and inertia. People become less attentive to the care and kindness of those who do the work of order, safety, and cleanliness in the marginalized corners and limited areas. They are overlooked and unappreciated, and they are constantly accident-prone, often falling victim to undue criticism, and their voices are muted.

In the days of dozens of years ago, at least, the public was often rowdy but good-natured and interconnected in general, but the current people are paying little attention to the willing sacrifices, individually or collectively, and they don't feel beholden to the achievements of bygone generations heartfully. They also often reject communal authority in nihilism. This lack of attention has led to a low degree of social cohesion and solidarity because they are unwilling to make their sacrificial contribution when it is needed.

To be aware of it or not, history makes its moves on its own. Although people are in the flow of the move, they are becoming less interested in history or perverting their understanding of history, especially modern history since the 19th century. The trend of ahistorical approach, unhistorical focus, and wayward interpretation is rampant which scars truth and adds confusion.

The mood of speaking lies in hypocrisy and having their conscience seared with the iron of moral indolence pervades (inferred from 1 Timothy 4:2). Social common sense is blurred in judgment, and social decency is lost in self-absorption or self-justification. It becomes hopeless for ordinary people to expect the return of a prim sense of social propriety.

A sense of indifference prevails when a depressive condition happens to befall a neighbor. People don't necessarily feel like getting involved in such a mishap with the neighbor in the guise of respecting the privacy of the person, or purely out of a simple mind that ignorance is bliss.

People's sensibility gets blunted as they are accustomed to the un-common sense and they find themselves showing no sign of the will to correct or reform the corruption unless they are involved in it, or they are willing to correct or reform it if the actions are likely to bring benefits to them. They opt for expediency over morals.

For the young adults, again, their lives will be global, diverse, inclement, and competitive. Without proper attention and civil participation in the social agenda, society is hardly able to be sustainable let alone socially cohesive. They cannot be independent of one another in the future society, and thus they should break off the apathy and inertia and move on for cohesion.

• Facet 3

Korean society is being harassed by the distortion of truth. Conflicting narratives are repeated and regenerated which makes it difficult for people to distinguish between what is true and false. They could only make judgments following their preferential news, information, and knowledge that are usually controversial, partial, tendentious, or even made up or fabricated.

A first judgment of a social topic, positive or negative, causes individuals to lead their follow-on judgments in the direction as their preference wishes. This truth distortion tends to increase exponentially with a series of repeated or regenerated controversies. Regardless of facts and logic, people maintain their early preference and increasingly distort their evaluation of truth.

The frenzy of those who have engrossed their minds in political antagonism, monetary motivations, or personal aspiration stirs the distortion up. They do not mind bending the truth by using misleading allegations or statistics. They do not feel ashamed of the deliberate concoction and induce others to be insensitive to improper behaviors, too.

Yellow journalism joins the process of truth distortion. It delivers partial, tendentious, and sensational information, not well-rounded facts and substantiated information. Although they proclaim to the public that they represent the truth, they, in actuality, serve their own purposes of enhancing ideological bias, commercial interests, loyal readership, and market reputation.

The delinquent media incites polarity in society by influencing how people come to strongly believe in the claims the media repeatedly delivers over time, while others come to strongly reject the same information in their own judgment. It is uncommon to find media that says "Yes" to what is right in common sense and "No" to what is not. Thus, it is mostly left to all individuals when it comes to making a sensible judgment.

Liberal democracy is sustained by pillars of individual freedom, human rights, and rule of law. It is being attacked by coercion or violence committed by those seeking political gains. monetary profit or group advantages under the umbrella of constitutional rights of assembly and expression. The Constitution is molested by base instincts and undemocratic shams.

People in Korean society frequently have a tendency to use their media appearances as a means of attracting public recognition. Many people in positions of power try to present a public persona that differs from their true behavior or accomplishments. Under the guise of smugness, hypocrisy, or the double standard, they are dishonest in their explanation of the issues at hand and do not directly offer workable solutions. It makes young adults wonder whether only individuals who lack shame can thrive in Korean culture in light of their obnoxious actions.

Putting a priority on the outward appearance, the basics are whitewashed or selectively highlighted. Reality hides behind the showy facade of pretension.

The young adults should be aware of the mechanisms that camouflage, distort, and fabricate the truth. They also need to know the risk that they can be misled or gaslighted by the tactical use of language and signs that manipulate their perception, either positively or negatively. The future is to be more heavily mined with misperception, deception, and manipulation. Watch our and stay alert, and replace them with votes.

• Facet 4

Korean society is being pressured to be equal and egalitarian among the people regardless of their natural abilities or talents. To build the goal of an egalitarian society with equal treatment, some individuals who display exceptional abilities are forced to take handicaps that make their outstanding abilities even with others.

In all segments of society, some superb achievers are destined to appear. Common sense brings a thought of policies to foster talent so that the performer upgrades their competence, but the reality is far from it. A web of rules and regulations encourages the people to be more equal and the society more egalitarian in the name of anti-competition.

This cause of getting rid of competition is intended to reduce the loss of confidence of those who were dropped from the competition. It means that people are getting equal, and society becomes egalitarian by downgrading the performance of the exceptionally gifted talent rather than enhancing the confidence of the dropouts and upgrading the level of all people.

It is said that there are two characteristics of equality in opportunity and outcomes. Equality in opportunity intends to make the opportunity equal to all by getting rid of barriers that block equal opportunity such as economic and geographic hurdles and disadvantages. All people should be given equal opportunities to make a fair competition.

Meanwhile, the notion of equality in outcomes is a sort of compensatory equality for those who are in disadvantageous circumstances. It provides various types of grants and premiums to disadvantaged people to reduce the impacts of the difference in outcomes. The policy from the tenet is selective and exclusive which causes an argument of reverse discrimination.

In the 2024 Summer Olympics in Paris, a Korean lady player of badminton won the Gold Medal with her outstanding performance. Upon winning the final match, she made public comments on the problems of enforced equality. The Badminton Korea Association did not treat her talent properly, exploited her for its benefit, and enforced equality under its rules.

The other examples are the regulation of working 52 hours per week regardless of job characteristics or personal decisions to work longer for their own needs, and, in school, student's performance and grades of their achievements are not evaluated properly to offer appropriate study programs to those students for fear of causing differentiation or an inferior complex among the students. There may be some justifications for the policies, but my challenge is that the reality in the world does not coincide with them. They must be adjusted to make them compatible with the requirements in the real world.

It caused a greater ripple effect in Korean society which is fraught with the problems of forced equality. Any policy has its pros and cons, but the cons of forced equality seem much greater because it is incompatible with the future which will become more global, diverse, and competitive. The young adults shall live in the future, and they will not accept forced equality as much as they will not agree with forced inequality.

The policymakers at present must reform the forced equality in the direction of providing fair opportunities in the process, giving specific solutions compatible with results, and helping all individuals develop their talents and competencies, rather than enforcing equality in the results. This cannot be sustainable, and it does harm the interests of young adults who will be living in the competitive world in the 21st century.

2) Inter-Korean Relationship

The issue of inter-Korean relationships will be one of the most critical issues that will affect the lives of the young adults in the 21st century.

The collapse of North Korea's decades-long national rationing system, including the staple food of rice, in the late 1990s had a profound impact on the country's society. It is reported that a number of people, in the range of five hundred thousand to two million, perished as a result of starvation. The state-controlled market was transformed into a private market, with unofficial public markets emerging where ordinary people could engage in free transactions in line with the dynamics of a free market. On 1 July 2002, North Korea officially allowed the free-market system and began levying taxes on market participants.

For those in capitalistic South Korea ("SK"), the communist NK regime has appeared witless, obstreperous, and macabre in its manner of actions. However, objectively speaking, the NK regime has its own, albeit strange, VSP (Vision-Strategy-Policy) setup. The inter-Korea relationship holds two features of the same coin: first is the threat that the NK regime avows to annihilate the people in the SK, and another one is the opportunity of the peninsula development potential that the capitalistic-unified Korea led by the SK government offers. It so can vary with some cases of co-existence in the mix of tension and appeasement, steady decline of the NK regime that dies a long death, or unification by the collapse of the NK regime in peace or at war.

No one knows the time when the dictatorial regime of North Korea ("NK") is to collapse or it sets the course of reforming itself to open the country or it implodes with a coup or it demises by shocks from the outside, but it looks certain that the closed-dictatorial policy would change within thirty years because Kim Jung Eun turning 70 in 2054 when the world of inside and outside NK won't be so as in 2024

As the gap deepens between the inside issues ("ever-static backwardness and overt violence inside North Korea") and the outside issues ("the rapidly changing exterior world, the swell of outside information that seeps through the borders of the NK"), the inter-Korea situation gets significant. The gap cannot grow for good, and it is destined to be brought to a halt with a certain result. Other than man-made events, an event of global risks such as climate change, epidemics, or natural disasters including the possibility of eruption of the caldera at the summit of Paikdu Mountain at the NK-China border may cause the demise of the self-closed hermit country.

The NK issue is a constant that is closely related to young adults in the 21st century.

(1) Human Rights

Media reported on the memoir of ex-President Moon in which he said that if SK joins the parties who criticize the violations of human rights in NK, it will lead to the worsening of SK-NK relations whereby the living conditions of the NK people get worse. So, SK should not push the NK regime for political freedom and human rights to protect the people in NK.

As to the propaganda leaflets in balloons that were floated to NK over the demarcation line by the civil groups of human rights in SK, he said that the contents were so unreserved and vulgar that they shamed the people in SK. With due respect to it, however, it makes us wonder if his remarks are valid in understanding the issue of human rights in NK.

- Who is responsible for the human rights violation in NK?

It is the NK regime that has caused poverty and substandard living conditions. Specifically, it is NK's political system that has been closed, dictatorial, corrupt, and no check-and-balance. The Corruption Perceptions Index ("CPI") 2023 evidenced its backwardness by ranking NK 172nd among 180 countries in the world (For reference, SK ranked 32nd). It can be explained that the taproot of mass poverty of NK people is their ignorance of the facts and reality about themselves as well as the external world.

The CPI ranks tell how the governing system upholds the law, tackles corruption, and keeps governments in check. The higher the CPI ranking, the lower the risk of trade and foreign direct investment (FDI), and human rights abuse. Hence, the lowest CPI ranking of NK means the NK regime is not fit for the FDI, it is corrupt and not in check, and it abuses human rights.

When it comes to the abuse of human rights, Mr. Moon should have stated the specifics of the human rights abuse: who is abusing human rights, why human rights are abused, and who is responsible for the abuse. Common sense tells us that it is the NK regime that abuses the human rights of those who are at odds with the NK regime. The NK regime is the culprit in the abuse.

The right sequence of raising the issue of human rights balloon would be to state first the specifics about the abuse of human rights clearly that the NK regime is responsible for the abuse, and it is the NK regime who can improve the human rights of its people. Then he may question if the balloon is effective in improving human rights conditions.

In SK, there are a growing number of people who proudly announced that they had fought for democracy and human rights during the period of industrialization and democratization in the past decades. When it comes to human rights in NK, however, they have been surprisingly silent or evaded the issue. It is very hard to understand their double standard when the universal issue is relevant to NK and China.

Humans are humans irrespective of nationality and ideologies, but their inconsistent stance makes people wonder whether nationality and ideologies precede for them because they tend to be much more passionate when an issue arises with Japan (for example, the issue of history and the ALPS issue) and the U.S. (for example, FTA treaty, US forces in Korea).

For them, the virtue of human rights is seemingly selective. They seem to be more concerned about the NK regime than the human rights of the people in NK, who have been suppressed and abused persistently for more than seven decades by the NK regime. Mr. Moon should have been straight and plain to state it based on common sense.

One question arises if SK remains silent or doesn't castigate the problem of the abuse of human rights in NK, will it help improve the human rights in NK? It can be rephrased: will the NK regime change its policy voluntarily to improve the problem of the abuse of rights when no one demands it? Is the NK regime reliable enough to improve human rights themselves?

- Can the SK-NK relationship change human rights violations as well as living conditions in NK?

As the economic system of NK is state-controlled, the system cannot function if the state does not supply resources for production and logistics. In the condition that the state cannot afford to supply them, and domestic consumption cannot sustain the economy either, the economy can only revitalize through investments from external sources.

This is based on my personal experiences in the works for Hyundai Merchant Marine Co., Ltd. (now the company is renamed HMM Company Limited) which pioneered North Korean businesses such as the sightseeing service utilizing a cruise ship between SK and NK ports in the late 1990s and early 2000s, and other various joint-venture businesses until middle of 2010s. The adventurous venture ended up with great losses and damage to the company because of, amongst other things, uncertainty in businesses and lack of legal protection.

Previous cases of FDI into NK by SK parties revealed fundamental problems. The FDIs were not protected: there was no legal protection, it did not compensate for non-compliance of the NK parties, it did not ensure the freedom of capital, and it was too unpredictable to keep the investment as a going concern. NK demolished or confiscated the assets of investment at will.

The lessons from the experiences are that unless NK ensures the protection of investment, further FDI is not possible. Mr. Moon needs to specify that the NK people could exit from poverty and improve human rights by introducing the FDIs, and he also must point out what the NK regime must change to protect the FDIs and how to make the changes sustainable.

He probably wants to specify the need to support the NK regime that will make the SK-NK relations improve, but he should not miss the point if the support benefits the core group of people in the NK regime or the people in NK. NK has been tightly ruled by a single family for over three generations. The FDI cannot be immune to the intervention of the unique regime.

- What is the thing that makes SK people feel shameful?

Objectively, people feel shameful when human rights are violated, and the violation is not properly rectified. Most of the SK people were indignant over the abuses of human rights by imperial Japan during the colonial rule (1910-45), and they were ashamed when some far-right Japanese people distorted the historical truth or even justified their violence.

For some people in SK, they are not universal in their emotions. They feel indignant and shameful about the atrocities of imperial Japan, but they are not so indignant and shameful about the atrocities of the NK regime. They applaud the people who blame Japan, but they stand apart from those who blame both imperial Japan and the dictatorial NK in a universal context.

Mr. Moon said SK people felt shame over the vulgar leaflet in a seeming supposition that mutual respect between SK and NK is important, and the vulgar contents in the leaflet impaired the mutual respect, so he felt ashamed. In this, we wonder what makes us feel shame. Is it the abuse of the human rights of the NK people by the NK regime, or is it the impairment of respect for the NK regime?

The balloons sent to NK were good for the NK people but bad for the NK regime. Mr. Moon is said to have commented on the balloons in negative tones. What if the contents of the balloons are changed to more moderate, not vulgar, texts, but they still express the need for regime change and improvement of human rights clearly—will then he agree with it?

As of September 2024, the NK regime has continually sent its balloons filled with trash to SK. It doesn't contain vulgar expressions, but real trash. Here, there is an unbalance of balloon effectiveness. For SK people know the NK regime and society very well, but NK people are not as knowledgeable about SK as SK people know about them.

The balloons from SK to NK contain information that enlightens the NK people and endangers the NK regime, but the balloons from NK to SK provide nothing but the task of sweeping the trash. The balloon from NK reaffirms that NK has nothing to send but only trash. SK people feel onerous with the trash for months, but Mr. Moon is silent on the trash balloon.

For the sake of clarity, this description is not just judging the stance of ex-President Moon at all because he may have his own view and perception. There is no political motivation or bias in it, either. This is intended to deal with inter-Korea issues for a well-rounded understanding of young adults who need to have universal and consistent common sense. That is the purpose.

In conclusion about the SK-NK relationship, history reminds and directs us that appeasement policy is effective only when the opponent responds appropriately under its pledge to compensate for any loss or harm from occurrences or reasons that are attributed to its fault. It is important to manifest the policy that SK takes measured steps, exercises reciprocity, keeps readiness to develop mutual prosperity, and adopts universality and consistency principles in the relationship.

(2) Future Scenarios of NK

It is impossible to predict the future of the people of North Korea with any certainty, given the notoriously unpredictable and highly reclusive nature of the regime that controls the country. The regime presents an outward appearance of a state with a structured parliament, executive administration, and judiciary. However, the reality is that it is controlled by a single individual. It conceals the disagreeable character of the regime, which is unpopular.

In light of the aforementioned considerations regarding the regime, we proceed to formulate potential scenarios for the future of NK. It is challenging to determine the most probable scenario with certainty. However, it is always beneficial to take stock of the future and to develop a scenario plan for the young adults who will live in the future.

Three scenarios are presented for consideration regarding the future of the NK regime and the NK people. The optimal scenario (Case A) is one in which North Korea transforms a market economy, resulting in the lifting of poverty for its citizens as the reforms take effect. However, it is important to consider the potential impact of the actions of the NK regime on the likelihood of Cases B, C, and D occurring.

Before we proceed with the discussion of NK, it is important to note that the phrase "*E pluribus unum*" (from many, one) is often used figuratively to represent the idea that diverse people can come together to form a unified nation. The process of converting '*pulribus*' into '*unum*' is of great importance in the political sphere. When this process ceases to function, a nation declines or divides.

In the case of NK, however, it can be paraphrased that a successful and sustainable regime can be achieved through the "*E unum pluribus*" (from one, many) process, rather than ""*E pluribus unum*" process.

This is Pot-Scenarios (without considering a case of total war between SK and NK).

Scenario A is that NK implements reforms to its socio-economic systems voluntarily. This would follow the example of Vietnam in 1986, which restructured its operating system to be-come a socialist-led market economy. Once the judicial and administrative systems have been reformed to be more investor-friendly, while maintaining the political system in place, foreign direct investment will be encouraged.

This has positive implications for neighboring countries, as well as for the ruling class and the public. It is possible that the policy will result in a change of political leadership within the political system. Significant changes will not be achieved through coercion or unrequited aid. Instead, they will come about through a process of understanding and change, which is chal-lenging and requires patience.

Scenario B is that the current status quo remains in place. North Korea's economy remains re-liant on a narrow range of resources, with minimal growth and a slow decline. The current system is characterized by inefficiency, corruption and a defunct planned economy with ex-clusive resource distribution. North Korea is unable to defy the inevitable consequences of its economic and social decline. However, it persists by exploiting its own people.

The NK regime is a predator or parasite to the NK people, who are too brainwashed or co-erced to revolt against the regime. It is only possible to assist if the people of NK are willing to help themselves. This is the most unfavorable outcome that could occur, given that the longer this situation persists, the more challenging it will be for the NK people to resume a normal way of life at the same level as those in neighboring countries.

In George Orwell's "1984," the term "crimestop" is a concept related to the control of thought. It is described as the ability to stop oneself from thinking subversive or heretical thoughts. Es-sentially, it leads to form of self-censorship where an individual automatically avoids any thoughts or questions that could lead to dissent against the authority. Orwell describes it as "protective stupidity" - the ability to forget or avoid contradictory ideas and accept the author-ity's propaganda without question. It's a critical element of the totalitarian regime's control over its citizens, ensuring that any potentially rebellious thoughts are nipped in the bud before they can even be fully formed. When outside information was scarce and brainwashing of NK authority was effective toward the insulated NK people, the NK people was in "absolute obe-dience or blind stupidity", but the spread of outside information in 2000s changes it into "pro-tective stupidity".

It's a chilling scenario that the power of ideological control extends to which the oppressive regime maintains their grip on power.

Scenario C means that the suppression of NK regime and the protests of NK people strike a delicate balance which may be unsettled and develop into Scenario B (if the suppressions get stronger) or Scenario D (if the protests get stronger). The NK regime adroitly controls the in-tensity of the suppression so that it doesn't go too strong or weak in so much as unsettle the balance. The ongoing international sanctions are taking some effects, but they are not critical enough to avail themselves to stop NK violating U.N. resolutions in their advancement of nu-clear arsenals.

Scenario D represents an end of the NK regime. The dismal situation saturates, and it finally develops into a case of topple-down of the NK regime because of coup or mass rebellion, or external force instigate the coup or mass rebellion, or the external force advance into NK ter-ritory and occupy it. In this scenario, the SK (Republic of Korea) should involve itself in the process in accordance with its constitution that regards the NK territory and the NK people as a part of the statehood. In this action, the communication is of importance with concerned par-ties i.e. the ROK must say and act speedily to achieve unification for which it bridges the gaps of opinions or stances among the R.O.K (active player for unification), China and Russia (negative fence-sitter for unification who do not always mean what they say), the U.S. and Ja-pan (positive fence-sitter for unification who can say what they mean).

Pot is in good working condition	- Scenario A - Status quo in NK undergoes transformative change in peace - NK regime reforms itself socio-economic structure following the suits of China and Vietnam proactively, and open its markets to foreign investors after overhaul of legal system
Vacuum fire & heat	- Scenario B - $H2O(\ell)$ is present in water but no $H2O(g)$ exists, i.e. a state of vacuum forms (i.e. no expression of protests) because the water can't evaporate. The water degrades under these conditions. - It signifies that the NK regime suppresses protests and removes dissidents among the NK people by strong surveillance and harsh punishment i.e. no-protest in the perennial state of protective stupidity.. - NK people are tightly contained in squalid conditions, and they fall into decay or decline, hardly able to subsist, but the status lingers on and on without being given support from outside.
fire & heat	- Scenario C - Fire boils the pot, and the temperature in the water goes up. - As the temperature continues to rise, $H2O(\ell)$ evaporates which becomes $H2O(g)$ until the moment the pressure of $H2O(\ell)$ equals that of $H2O(g)$ - As the NK regime and the NK people interact, but both maintain the status quo. NK regime continues to press on with suppression and the NK people become growingly indignant, stage protests. The tension escalates but the lid is kept closed and the situation keeps hanging in balance
fire & heat	- Scenario D - Fire keeps heating the pot, the evaporation continues, and finally it reaches a point of simultaneous where the force of pressure from the evaporation equals that from condensation. - When fire keeps heating the pot, and the vapor pressure exceeds the boiling point and breaks the equilibrium, then the pressure makes the lid break open, or an outside force puts the lid open just before it erupts. - The balance of the suppressions and the protests is broken in which peoples' protests overwhelm NK regime or some shocks from outside make the protests grow and overwhelm the regime, or outside force steps in and occupies NK. The NK regime topples down and alternative regime is put in place

H2O(ℓ) : water in liquid (here, it means a natural state of people in figurative terms)

H2O(g) : water in gaseous state (here it means peoples' protest in figurative terms)

Historical examples include the case of Nicolae Ceaușescu, the General Secretary of the Romanian Communist Party from 1965 to 1989, who was executed amid the anti-communist revolution in Romania. Another example is that of Muammar Gaddafi, the Libyan political leader (1979-2011), who was assassinated in 2011 during the Libyan Civil War. It is not possible to predict when this kind of thing will happen in NK.

In the chart, the water boils when the fire heats the pot: an upward curved arrow (evaporation), a downward curved arrow (condensation), two curved arrows (simultaneous equilibrium, water boils), and the lid (it breaks open when vapor is contained). H2O (means water in liter and H2O (g) means water in gas.

Figuratively, it means the pot is NK, the water is the NK people, the fire under the pot is the exploitation of the NK regime, vapor pressure means the protest of the NK people, and the equilibrium and boiling water means the eruption of the suppressed protest. The lid that breaks open represents the downfall of the NK regime.

Another potential scenario is an apocalyptic implosion resulting from a systemic collapse of government due to natural disasters, plague, or drought and famine. The limited capacity and scarce resources of the NK regime may prove inadequate to cope with such an event. In the event of a disaster, there is a risk of further adverse consequences. Such circumstances could result in the uncontrolled decline of governmental functions, ultimately leading to the collapse of the regime.

Specifically, as the last but not least, Scenario D would result in significant uncertainty that may cause great losses and damages for both SK and NK, rather than opportunities or bene-fits, if it is not well-prepared in consensus among the concerned parties inside and outside of Korean Peninsula.

In the meanwhile, NK regime frequently manifests its position to occupy SK by force recently which leads SK people to wonder that NK may think itself it has nothing to lose and therefore it may feel like to have no choice but to provoke the war without a casus belli. An idea of total war is absolutely undesirable, but it is not totally inconceivable when NK goes for the dead-end option.

It is important to note that the future of the dictatorial regime remains uncertain. However, when we consider the future in a broader context, it is evident that the key challenge will be to manage change in a rapidly evolving environment. As Martin Luther King, Jr. observed, the arc of the moral universe bends towards justice. It is important to recognize that change takes time to occur. However, should it occur in a real situation, the impact will be significant.

In holistic assessment of the situation, one thing appears clear that it will up to China to drag NK into the 21st century and finally end the Korean War that was ceased in 1953. The bilateral friendship "forged in blood" doesn't mean that the NK leader, Kim Jung Eun, ceases to make trouble for China wo needs to allow NK regime to showboat its military competence includ-ing nuke arms if it is to avoid collapse. Just how much military power China will tolerate from its recalcitrant neighbor remains to be seen. NK is in dilemma to extricate itself from the perplexing contradiction of instituting economic reforms under the auspice of China and Rus-sia while at the same time preserving its statehood which is so crucial to the legitimacy of the regime.

It is an immutable law of global politics that a lack of strength and vigilant mind to fight war invites aggression, which can naturally result in war.

(3) National Security Act

This is discussed in an article in The Economist on 22 January 2024 by Banyan:

Titled: *"South Korea's ban on praising the North is ridiculous. The government imprisons a dotty fan of Kim Jong Un"*

-- Yet Lee Yoon-seop, a South Korean poet, is currently languishing in prison for just this. The 68-year-old was sentenced to 14 months in November for threatening South Korea's "existence and security". His crime? Writing a poem in praise of the North.

The law used to prosecute Mr Lee, the National Security Act (NSA), is designed to protect South Korea from spies and traitors. But it also bans South Koreans from visiting or contacting the North, reading or watching North Korean media or saying anything good about Kim Jong Un's tyrannical regime. Though South Korea replaced its former military dictatorship with a democracy in 1987, such restrictions on free speech show that some of the generals' autocratic tendencies endure.

Every country has counter-espionage laws. And if South Korea's are rather strict, no wonder. Its capital city is in missile range of a nuclear-armed despot who calls it the "principal enemy". The NSA was modeled on a law designed to quash pro-independence activities during Japan's occupation of Korea from 1910 to 1945. Since 2003 there have on average been more than 60 NSA prosecutions a year, often for clear espionage cases. A businessman and an army officer were arrested for allegedly selling military secrets to North Korea. Soldiers in the South have been prosecuted under the act for endangering morale by distributing pro-North propaganda.

But the NSA is too often used to prosecute satirists and raid the homes and offices of leftists. Some cases have been ridiculous. Kim Myeong-soo, a PHD student, received six months in prison and a two-year suspended sentence for selling books on North Korea that were widely available in public libraries. A South Korean woman was given a two-year sentence, suspended for four years, for owning recordings of 14 North Korean songs.

This is not Mr Lee's first offense. But the claim that the sexagenarian posed a threat to South Korea is absurd. His ode was published on a North Korean website. Access to such sites is banned by the NSA and forbidden from a South Korean IP address. More important, it is hard to imagine Mr Lee's childish verse persuading anyone of the glories of North Korea's leader. It consists of a list of South Korean problems that Mr Kim, in the poet's view, would instantly solve given the chance.

Mr Lee's real offense appears to have been believing his own nonsense. By contrast, police decided not to investigate a man under the draconian law for selling shirts with a smiling Mr Kim and the slogan "Walk a flowery path, comrade". That was OK, officials said, because he was selling them to make a buck.

Worse, the issue points to a broader authoritarian tendency in the South. Its president, Yoon Suk-yeol, often demonizes his political opponents by calling them "anti-state forces", a phrase inspired by the NSA. Unfavorable press coverage is routinely labeled "fake news" and the offices of offending outlets have been raided. The administration and its allies have sued more press outfits for defamation—which in South

Korea can be a crime even when the offending words are manifestly true—in Mr Yoon's first 18 months in office than any of its three predecessors did during their entire five-year terms.

Yet even a more liberal government would be unlikely to remove the NSA's illiberal clauses. No administration has made a serious attempt to reconsider it in 20 years. There is very little political support for scrapping the law, point out Steven Denney and Christopher Green of Leiden University. The current administration at least flirted with allowing South Koreans access to North Korean media, but it recently abandoned the idea. The opposing Democratic Party is no more liberal; it previously tried to pass a similar law criminalizing praise of Japanese colonial rule.

Mr Yoon talks often about South Korea's democratic values. They are at the heart of his pitch for the country to be a strategic link between East and West, developed and developing countries. For that reason alone, he should take them more seriously. South Korea is undoubtedly a democracy, but not a terribly liberal one so long as it locks up old men for their dotty opinions. Reforming the NSA would be a better rebuttal to the sentiment Mr Lee expressed than banning it."

This article indicates an opinion that the National Security Act (the "NSA") is so strict that it suppresses the freedom of conscience and expression in the democratic country of SK in the face of security threats from the NK regime. The topic has been a subject of decades-long argument in SK since the Korean War (1950-53).

Globally, there are many cases of security risk such as Taiwan facing mainland China, Israel dealing with the Arabic states, the real ongoing war in Ukraine against Russia after Russia began a large-scale military attack on Ukraine in February 2022, and borderline conflicts of India with China, India with Pakistan, as well as the civil war in Myanmar.

The security risk of SK-NK is different from the comparable cases in that both sides fought the total war for three years in most of the territory which resulted in huge casualties of 5 million people and the lands were scorched. SK has been under existential threat from NK for more than seven decades during which SK developed its economy and nurtured democracy.

Recently, the nuke-armed NK has manifested its policy that holds SK as its principal enemy and intends to annihilate SK people when war breaks out. NK legitimized the use of nuke attacks in its constitution, it test-launched various types of missiles, showed off fire drills of long-range artillery, and launched a submarine competent for firing ballistic missiles.

Even though they are overwhelmed by the combined forces of SK and the US, the risk is formidable because affluent SK shall be affected far more than destitute NK if armed conflict happens. The demarcation line is 155 miles across the Korean peninsula. The shortest distance to Seoul, the capital city, is merely 23 kilometers, which is too short to defend properly.

Mr. Banyan said, "Its capital city is in missile range of a nuclear-armed despot who calls it the principal enemy." This is not exactly true. Seoul is within the firing range of thousands of artilleries and multi-launch rockets, unmanned aviation vehicles, low-flying aircraft carrying special task force, and chemical/biological WMDs, on top of ballistic missiles and nuke bombs.

A point of triple-nexus of "ensuring security, nurturing democracy and building the economy" is suggested to Mr. Banyan for consideration in his deliberation of the NSA. A balance in the nexus is of importance because if one thread is cut away, then the nexus falls. It is like a hanging balance connected with three threads. If one is gone, then all is gone. It is simple but serious.

All of the tripe-nexus are not mutually exclusive, and they must be hanging in the balance in the face of the NK's provocation. Responding to the provocations, SK people have balanced, become unbalanced, and re-balanced their actions to maintain the status quo. The provocations and the propaganda of NK were so persistent and NK's that SK people often felt gaslighted.

Sitting at the incendiary corner of the Far East, the SK people are noticing the ongoing armed conflicts in Europe (Ukraine's war against Russia), the Middle East (Israel's war against its Arab neighbors), and military tension in the Taiwan Strait. They feel sympathetic toward those who got the short end of the stick in these tensions and conflicts.

The NSA can't be detached from the triple nexus because the NSA originated from the need to ensure the nexus in the confrontation with NK albeit a contention of its involvement in domestic politics. Some people in SK put priority on the part of "nurturing democracy" in the nexus. However, getting the triple nexus in balance is of paramount importance.

First, it needs to describe the qualities of human rights, freedom of conscience, and expression in both SK and NK. SK ensures that the triple-nexus is balanced in which the NSA is executed. Human rights as an integral part of "democracy" in the nexus was fostered or restrained. In the case of the NK regime, there is no balance at all. Mr. Banyan shouldn't miss this.

Second, NK has been very good at executing shrewd propaganda in SK by infiltrating the society. It fomented anti-SK and anti-US sentiment, provoking anti-security incidents, and plotting a conspiracy to make the intra-Korea issues favorable to them, especially since the ROK was democratized in the 1980s. A democratic country is more prone to such propaganda war.

Third, the governance of the NK regime is far different from other socialist countries. NK resists reform of its economy and society. In the view of the people in liberal democratic countries, NK is seen as being at an ideological fin de siècle in social degeneracy, cynicism, and pessimism. It is an unpredictable and self-aggrandizing one-man state with no check-and-balance.

Recently, it is said that Kim Jung-Eun thinks of his eleven-year-old daughter as his successor. If the succession is realized in that way, it means a four-generation inheritance (Kim Il Sung – Kim Jeong Il – Kim Jung Eun – the daughter, Kim Joo Ae) as supreme leader in NK. It looks not certain if NK can sustain its statehood in the serial succession of nepotism.

Mr. Banyan should have described the national governance in both SK and NK that affects the NSA. The basic difference in the national governance between SK and NK is that SK takes a negative system that restricts some but allows the rest of them whereas NK holds a positive system in which it restricts most of the things except some that are specifically allowed.

Fourth, a human has the right to live a life in a way that follows the beliefs of the person. The belief-led life can be perceived as a human right. If the right to the belief is denied, the person protests within the legal boundary or illegally as the person chooses. However, it should be restrained if the right restricts the rights of others.

It would be empathetic to feel pity for the legal sentences, imprisonment, and suspension, of the PhD student, the woman, and the sexagenarian poet in violation of the NSA. Freedom of thought and expression has to be protected by the Constitution of SK, but it can be limited if it purposefully unbalances the triple nexus for the collective common good.

If the sentences are too harsh for the old man, the woman, and the student, should there be limitations on legal sentences by age, gender, and occupation? If so, what are the rational distinctions they would be? If they are relevant to connection with NK, does the propaganda institution of NK approach only those who are within the range of legal sentencing?

A distinction needs to be made between a stance of sympathy for the helpless NK people in dismal conditions and another stance of being collaborative with the dictatorial NK regime without demanding them to make reforms for the benefit of the NK people. It means we need to separate the NK people from the NK regime to take a different approach to them.

In addition, Mr. Banyan should pay attention to the occasions when NK legal authorities sentenced to 12 years of jail and forced labor without suspension onto sixteen-year-old students in charge of watching ROK dramas in January 2022, and another report that the authority is said to have executed 30 teenaged students for the same charge in July 2024.

For those who are charged to have possessed a Bible, they are even more harshly persecuted. For the sake of clarity, this is not intended to advocate a specific political opinion, but this just delivers the point that if there is an imbalance in the view, it needs to be redressed to get a fair understanding of any issue. We hope the NSA issue finds equilibrium in the triple nexus.

In SK, the equilibrium in the tripe nexus should be maintained as long as there is an existential threat from NK. If the equilibrium in the triple nexus is unbalanced arbitrarily in any part of ensuring security, nurturing democracy, and building the economy. Then it should be legally tested and those who are found to have broken the law should be punished.

(4) Mass Migration of NK People

NK has built an asymmetrical structure of politics, economy, and culture that is preponderantly tilted toward one-man leadership, military primacy, closed economy, and isolation. It lacks capacities and resources from within (domestic production and consumption) and from outside (trades, FDI, and loans) to revitalize its economy. It is difficult for NK to turn it around on its own.

As the economy declines, the living standard of the people is degrading. In the age of the 4th Industrial Revolution, geographical isolation cannot block the spread of information and intelligence, and the NK regime is unable to perpetuate its iron-fist rule. Unless the dictatorial leadership reforms itself, it is to collapse by the force of implosion or external shocks.

In this situation, the pressing work is to impose order and let the dust settle in NK. First and foremost, it is SK that should lead the process at the forefront of the international community following its constitution that regards the NK and its people as its territory and nationals. It refuses the intervention of other states because SK has its sovereign right over the Korean Peninsula.

This part is to delineate the process of providing humanitarian aid to help the NK people in disarray other than the other works of politics, economy, culture, military, and others. The aid works shall protect the people from starvation, epidemics, and violence in the safe shelters. The working conditions in and around the aid sites are unstable and vulnerable.

The aid works shall be hampered by a shortage of public utilities such as electricity and clean water, poor social service for sheltering the masses, insufficient amenities, inefficient logistics through improper conditions of roads, railways, and ports, inclement weather such as cold, typhoons, flood or heat, and the threat of security such as violence, revolt, and pillage.

Meanwhile, however, there are a lot of governmental facilities across NK that can be used as bases of aid works such as military facilities including airbases, naval ports, army camps, tunnels, underground storage spaces, equipment and machinery, and military personnel. The civil buildings in towns such as the Museum of Revolutionary History, schools, and collective farms can also serve this purpose.

The deplorable condition of health care in NK looks unable to handle infectious diseases in the stateless condition. Once it cannot be contained, a mass of people shall migrate en masse in search of food, shelter, and safety en route from the affected areas to safe places. As the people amass and get dense, they struggle to afford shelter and finally wind up homeless. When epidemics of such diseases break out, the elderly, the disabled, patients, children, and pregnant women are more vulnerable to the disease.

A special task force of the military needs to protect the humanitarian aid such as aid workers, facilities and supplies, the supply chain linking the aid sites and supply bases, and the sheltered migrants in good order to make the aid work stable and sustainable. When some disorders or breakdowns happen, they must stabilize the regions or the factors as quickly as possible.

Relevant parties and states, such as the United Nations, China, the U.S., Russia, and Japan, should craft, share, and acknowledge an effective operational strategy for humanitarian aid efforts before the aid works start. The strategy should obviate any political motivation or misunderstanding among the nations but seek support for aid materials.

In the cases of mass migration of NK people, the migrants may head south or north. Both tracks shall be blocked by serious impediments such as the DMZ fences and minefields in the south-facing SK and the rivers and borderline security in the north-facing China. One question arises: "In which direction will they head for more—south or north?"

For those who live in the southern parts of NK are supposed to migrate southward where the geographical terrain is plainer, the weather is more clement, and fellow ethnic people who speak the same language whereas the people near the borderline may move northward to China. Ideally, SK needs to induce them to move southward in the principle that Koreans rescue Koreans.

The direction of mass migration may influence the geopolitical development in the Korean peninsula after the NK falls. For the sake of security and efficiency, the SK military troops shall help carry out the aid works by standing guard around the aid sites and providing convoy services for aid-relevant logistics until the aid system functions in good order across NK.

PART 7

Since we started the journey into history in Part 1, we finally reach the point where we need to explore our thoughts on what and how to do.

7.1 of the Four Cases and Three Shifts is the part that shows the possible development of the people in the future and evaluates them in terms of sustainability. As Case C is deemed the most appropriate which is compatible with the sustainability of young adults in the future, the most required shift is Case A to Case C.

7.2 is the conclusion of this book with suggestions to young adults by specifying points of "Be Yourself" and "Do Yourself" with an ultimate mandate to vote for reformers to make the future sustainable. This part is primarily from my experiences including my mistakes and my perceptions on the future, especially the next three decades (2025-2055).

7.1 Four Cases and Three Shifts

Society in the 21st century will undergo transformative changes spurred by the ten Critical Issues in section 6.1.1). The force of transformative change is so pervasive and penetrating that it will upend the social order and norms, and situational complexity will become indisputable and irreversible.

Counteraction is mandatory in the turbulence of social transformation, but the challenge is how to respond to it, especially in light of some specific issues in their real lives. We set two criteria in a two-by-two matrix that distinguish the behavioral patterns in four cases, among which we draw one that looks most appropriate for young adults to live in the transformed world.

I want to deliberate on the suggestions from my personal experiences that hopefully benefit young adults and other readers. This doesn't mean that I have practiced the suggestions at all. The memories have made me painfully conscious of my guilt, especially for those who had been affected by my excesses and deficiencies in the situations.

I want this description to be as real and practicable as possible, to be at least honest about my experiences and effective for the reality that young adults shall face and respond to it.

The key notion in a single statement is that what goes up must come down, and it decides its next step to either rebound or fall flat.

1) The sets of minds to be yourself in the X-Axis:

   (1) Alert, agile and resilient

   People stay alert to changes, are strategic in thinking for a long-term goal, remain resilient in dealing with challenges, and make assertive communication to express their needs until they are met.

   (2) Complacent, inactive and inelastic

   People are crass or complacent with the status quo, they become susceptible to harm, exploitation, or attacks. They resort to spontaneous actions in response to them, and finally, they turn to be inactive.

2) The sets of actions to do yourself in the Y-Axis:

(1) Innovate and flexible (Break the mold and make a breakthrough)

The people who break the mold in their actions are those who innovate or deviate from the usual way of doing things. They put priority on creativity and breakthroughs, and they are good at brainstorming to overcome obstacles and transform the status quo.

(2) Keep status quo (Get stuck in a rut and take no initiative)

The people are used to the pattern from the past. They feel comfortable with conventional code of conduct by perceiving the status quo as fait accompli. Sometimes, they justify it as social harmony or collective security.

3) Four Cases

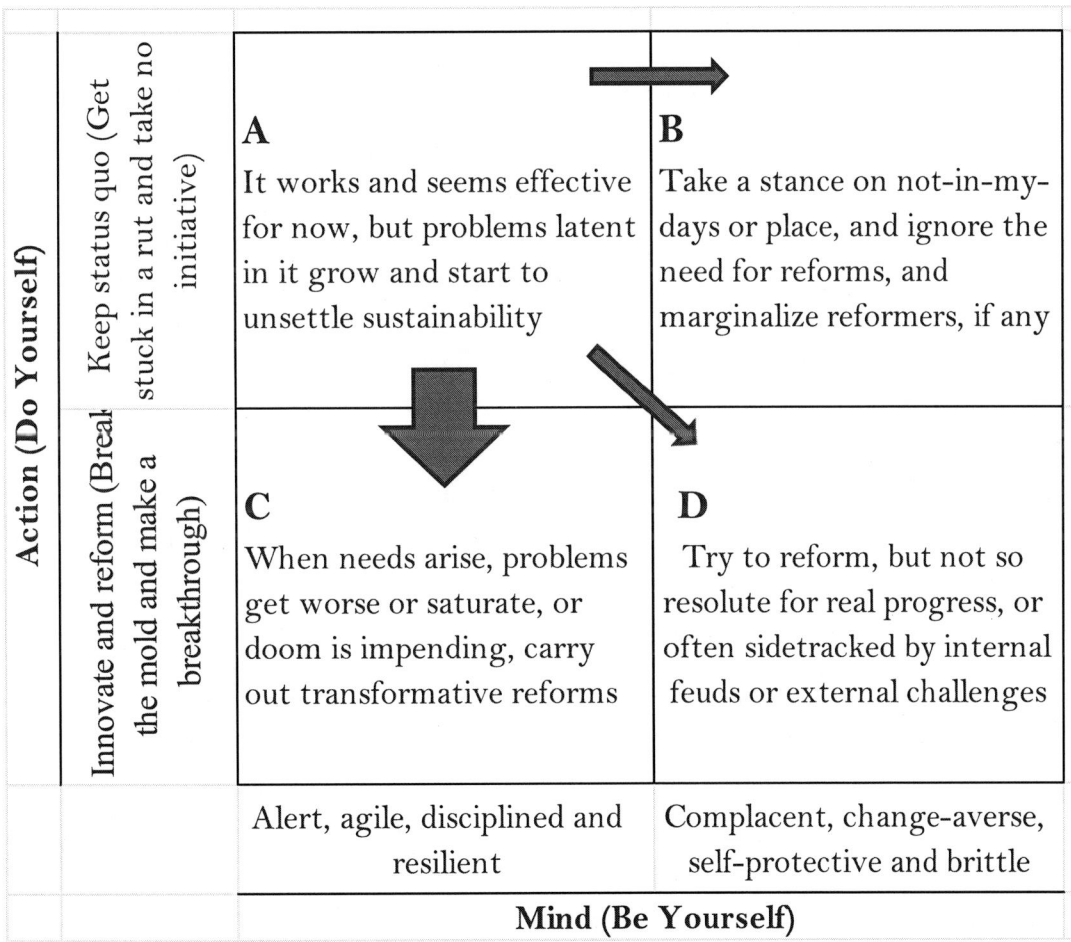

In an endless causality of circumstances, we assume the case that people do not take the courage to break off the rutted pathway. They take the status quo good for now even though they know it won't be sustainable. They say, "Don't worry; be insouciant." We call this Case A as a typical example of the status quo and this is assumed to be a starting point of the possible shifts to Case B, C or D..

Case A may develop into Case B, C or D in which some specific conditions are formed and saturated and, thereafter in each case, a certain result of prosperity or collapse ensues.

We list the probable development of cases in the order of desirability:

4) Case C, the ideal case

Case C should be the most appropriate for young adults to sustain the challenges in the 21st century, and **the shift from Case A to Case C is most desirable**. For example, modern corporations execute the ESG strategy (Environmental, Social, and Governance) to make them sustainable and profitable. The same goes for the young adults who adopt Case C to make themselves sustainable, too.

In the context of mindsets and action sets, we deliberate more on details of how the young adults materialize the Case C

We explore the cases of the shift to the Case C, successful and unsuccessful, in history:

(1) The hunter-gatherers materialized the shift to Case C with innovations as the climate changed with glaciers retreating about 12,000 years ago and temperatures gradually warming. Around 8000 BC, the shift to the agrarian settled lifestyle brought the domestication of plants and animals and the invention of tools for peace and war which were later energized with migrations and trades.

The ancient civilizations engineered by the Agricultural Revolution and socio-political hierarchy made innovations of the Case C in building those great man-made structures such as the pyramids of Egypt, communal sites along the Yellow River Valley in China, the ziggurats of Iraq, the palace of Knossos in Crete, the fortresses at Mycenae in Greece, and the planned cities of Harappa and Mohenjo-Daro in the Indus Valley.

(2) The Gracchus-brothers failed to shift to the Case C with their reform attempts (133 BC, 121 BC) in the Roman Republic: the land reform that a land redistribution program limiting land ownership for the benefit of the plebeians (the common people) and the reform of land-shortage by promoting colonization programs for both Italians and foreigners, specifically in Carthage (an ancient city-state, on the North African coast near present-day Tunis). The failure of timely reforms helped cause the structured problem of polarity to deepen until the collapse of the Roman Empire in 476 AD,

(3) As the Byzantine Empire edged to its downfall from 1261 to its fall in 1453, it was ruled by desperate emperors to shift to the Case C in seeking aid from various quarters. They tried to end the Schism with the Roman Pope in hopes of receiving support. In 1399, Emperor Manuel II (1391-1425) made a vain journey to raise support in Rome, Paris, and London. The failure in the shift ended up with the tragic scene of the collapse in 1453 when the last emperor, Constantine XI Palaiologos, dismounted from his white Arabian mare, plunged into the fighting, and disappeared into the melee of battle.

(4) Defiant Martin Luther rejected the persuasion of Pope Leo X (papacy 1513–21) who tried to change Luther's beliefs and threatened to bring a case against him for heresy, and Luther publicly burned a copy of the papal bull on 10 December 1520 upon which he was excommunicated from the Catholic Church. The temporal and secular popes were not irrational but failed to take notice of the rising dissatisfaction because they were so imbued by rampant greed and lust for power. Human folly and frailties came to the state that passions and desires were stronger than purposes.

Amid the chaotic persecution, conflicts and confusion, Martin Luther made the successful shift to the Case C by the Reformation, and it later prompted the Counter-Reformation within the Catholic Church.

(5) The Glorious Revolution (1685-89) was an event in which the English Parliament was determined to place limits on the king's power, insisted on the rights of a free Parliament, and asserted its rights over the monarchy by drawing up the Bill of Rights in 1689. The absolute power has been transferred from the monarch to the elected Parliament which gave the Parliament the power to rule with the authority previously enjoyed by England's kings. Henceforth, the 'United Kingdom of Great Britain' was to be ruled by Parliament at Westminster, and modern British identity derived from it. It secured stability in politics and economics, allowing the English to follow a fundamentally different trajectory from other European countries. The political entities made a successful shift to the Case C that paved a way to prosperity to the Industrialization in the 18th-19th century, and the Pax-Britanica (1815-1914).

(6) In the Nazi-Soviet War during WW II, the surrender of the General Paulus-led 265,000-strong 6th Army of the German forces signified a representative threshold of the war at the battle of Stalingrad in the harsh winter of January 1943. Just before it was completely surrounded by the pincer-offensives of the Soviet army, General Paulus requested to withdraw and break out of it, but Adolf Hitler prohibited it and ordered it to fight and die when its defense was gradually worn down. General Paulus radioed *"Troops without ammunition or food. Effective command no longer possible. 18,000 wounded without any supplies or dressings or drugs. Further defense senseless. Collapse inevitable. 6th Army requests immediate permission to surrender in order to save lives of remaining troops"*. Hitler answered *"Surrender is forbidden. 6th Army will hold their positions to the last man and the last round and by their heroic endurance will make an unforgettable contribution toward the establishment of a defensive front and the salvation of the Western world"*. On the last evening, 30 January 1943, the hopelessly beleaguered 6th Army by sending its final message to Headquarters of German Army *"The 6th Army, true to their oath and conscious of the lofty importance of their mission, have held their position to the last man and the last round for Fuehrer and Fatherland unto the end"*. At 7:45 p.m. the radio operator at the 6th Army headquarters sent a last message: *"The Russians are at the door of our bunker. We are destroying our equipment"*. He added the letters *"CI"*, the wireless code signifying *"This station will no longer transmit"*. General Paulus failed to shift to the Case C for the 6th Army in the face of impending doom because of senseless Hitler who lost the flower of the German Army which would have been highly essential to defend the homeland against the overwhelming Soviet Red Army until Berlin finally collapsed in 1945, let alone the dismal fate of German prisoners in Russia after the war.

7.2 Suggestions

This is the conclusion of this book that started from the beginning of the human beings through vicissitudes of historical events `that had changed the causality of historical development. I tried to specify the points from my work experiences (Korean shipping companies for thirty-two years and Korea National Parks Service for two years).

There have been many failures as well as some achievements, and I have brought some benefits to the organizations, but I had made cases of grievances and frustrations when I slipped into Case A→Case B or Case A→Case D. I hope my experiences from my excesses, moderacy, and deficiencies will help those who will be proceeding their own shifts to Case B, C or D from Case A.

The part of "Mind (Be Yourself)" searches a set of minds to find what is appropriate to reform to make the future sustainable, and the part of "Action (Do Yourself)" probes a set of actions to reform to build a sustainable future.

The phlegmatically faithful in exercising the "Be Yourself" and "Do Yourself" will be com-patible with the Case C in the 21st century, especially the next three decades (2025-2055), at being all things in all doings.

A man's character is his fate as Heraclitus (c. 535 BC – 475 BC, Greek philosopher) said.

At first glance, this quote by the ancient Greek philosopher Heraclitus may seem simple yet profound. It suggests that a person's character determines their destiny, emphasizing the sig-nificance of one's inner qualities in shaping the course of their life. In a straightforward inter-pretation, it implies that the choices, actions, and virtues of an individual ultimately determine their path and the outcomes they experience.

The quote carries remarkable importance when applied to various aspects of life, from per-sonal relationships to professional endeavors. It implies that the qualities we possess, such as honesty, perseverance, and empathy, can significantly influence the outcomes we encounter. For instance, a person with a high level of integrity is more likely to inspire trust in others, leading to stronger connections and better opportunities. In this way, one's character becomes the very fabric of their existence, intricately woven into the web that determines their path.

However, let us now introduce a philosophical concept that adds an unexpected twist to this matter: determinism. Determinism proposes that every event, including human actions, is pre-determined by preceding causes and the laws of nature. According to this belief, the trajectory of a person's life is predetermined by factors beyond their control, rendering the idea that "a man's character is his fate" somewhat obsolete.

In the realm of determinism, a person's character would merely be the product of their genetic makeup and environmental influences. They would possess no real agency or ability to shape their destiny through their choices and virtues.

This notion challenges the conventional understanding of the quote, prompting us to question whether our character truly determines our fate or if we are mere pawns in a vast cosmic game. However, even in the face of determinism, the concept of character remains significant. If we shift our focus from an individual's impact on their external circumstances and instead contemplate the influence of character on internal experiences and overall well-being, the quote regains its relevance. While our external fate may be shaped by uncontrollable varia-bles, our internal state can still be shaped by the virtues we cultivate. Consider this: regardless of predetermined external events, a person with a compassionate and resilient character will be better equipped to navigate the inevitable challenges and setbacks of life. Developing vir-tues such as patience, kindness, and emotional resilience can fortify our inner world, ulti-mately determining our ability to find meaning, fulfillment, and contentment in spite of exter-nal circumstances.

Additionally, character can significantly impact how we perceive and respond to those predes-tined events.

Two individuals may face similar external challenges, yet their interpretations and reactions can differ immensely based on their character. This suggests that while we may not control the events themselves, we do have agency over how we respond to them, influenc-ing the quality of our experiences and ultimately shaping our perception of fate.

Ultimately, Heraclitus' quote, "A man's character is his fate," carries multi-layered meanings.

On one level, it reminds us of the importance of integrity, virtues, and choices in shaping our external circumstances and forging our path through life.

However, when confronted with the philosophical concept of determinism, the quote calls at-tention to the significance of character in shaping our inner world, influencing our responses to life's inevitable twists and turns, and ultimately contributing to our overall well-being.

In this way, we discover that character's true value lies not solely in its power to dictate exter-nal outcomes but in its ability to shape our internal landscape, guiding us towards a state of greater wisdom, resilience, and fulfillment amidst the unpredictable journey of life.

1) Be Yourself

The wide variance of change in the market produces winners and losers, but it shares common denominators that those who are alert and agile are more prepared to take proactive actions in response to the market changes, and those who are patient are likelier to make a profit.

Conversely, some market players are doing more firefighting than fire-prevention in routine businesses when they are alert or agile enough to do so, and those who lose patience, or cannot wait because of, for example, a lack of capital to endure the slow market, lose money.

When a company undergoes a slow market operating losses accumulate. it signals that a market-change is close because other players are suffering the same problem. This is a challenging period, but it will pass leaving victors and losers.

With this premise, we should be aware of it below:

This industry has no hidden value because the market is too efficient. Everybody is smart and has disparate value drivers to make a deal. The experts with considerable intellectual heft and deep business knowledge are often wrong because they are too confident to make a fair assessment of the market prospects or too cautious to find an upturn in the market. It is inherently unknowable, and some people who ask for your trust usually should not receive it.

The price of a transaction is fixed in the function of supply and demand. All liquidity is searching for value, but money hides when there is danger but pops up whenever it finds value. At the right price, there is liquidity, but a wrong price cannot attract liquidity.

There is no golden rule to make constant successes in constant changes like the ocean mixed with calm summer as a millpond in the northern hemisphere and dangerous winter swell in the southern one. Every decline has its bottom, but you must have a tool to get a purchase on the slippery descent. The only way is to remain alert, agile, and resilient to find an opportunity to make a profit in the circumstance and recover from loss soon.

In business, there is nothing more dangerous for those who have a strong balance sheet and are penchant for loving to show off. They nest in a strong balance and are used to too many distractions such as internal politics, long and sumptuous lunches, luxurious offices, and inordinate perks. They insulate themselves from the ever-changing market that is only noticeable to those who are alert and agile.

There are ups and downs in everything and enjoy the boom while it lasts but remember that the devil lurks in the corner of the boom.

You may question the prospect of the market to others, but please be aware that the answer you get depends on whom you ask the question. To whom you ask depends on what answer you would like to receive.

You must ask for things even when the answer is that they do not know. Ignorance doesn't justify your lack of an action plan. In any case, you must set up your transactional strategy and respond to the changes in the market.

Sometimes things do not change as quickly as you anticipate, but you need to steer toward the point of change.

Again, remain alert to change, agile to cope with the change, and be resilient to any setbacks.

(1) Be lean, agile and principled

I have seen many companies and individuals succeed and fail in the face of market fluctuations. The results were either good or bad, and they were superficially attributed to unexpected changes in the market. For example, there were much earlier slumps or much later recoveries than expected.

From another perspective, however, the changes in the market are likened to the natural ebb and flow in the sea, and there was no room for complaint about the changes. The business result depended entirely on the ability to make a profit and adapt to changes by being lean and staying agile. We are not too big to fail, but too big to be accountable.

In my experiences in the shipping business, the common features of the successes were to pay less for assets with a fund at a low cost of capital and operate them at a low cost by eliminating waste — that is, everything that does not bring value. Debt was essential for running the business, but it had a double-edged sword. It leveraged profit when it was used for profitable investments (ships, terminals). However, it was a fatal mistake to let the debt spiral out of control when negative cash flow accumulated.

- The most virtuous practice was to make the operation lean and simple. They knew certain excesses were inevitable, but they were disciplined enough to keep the pendulum of excesses from swinging too far. They maintained a balance between service quality and profit, between short-term results and long-term objectives. They continuously improved their business operations while strictly paring down their organization to the essentials. There shall be no pyramid of inefficient leadership, and they break down the hierarchy.

  They were quick to identify market trends and highly effective at forecasting them. They were prudent with operational expenses but bold in capital expenditure. The business results in terms of service quality, profit or loss, and market forecast were assessed and announced to all members of the organization regularly. The company's frugal spending and streamlined operations enabled its human resources to focus on the essentials.

The lean and agile mind builds the acuity of vision and trailblazes a niche to explore opportunities. When they are successful in profitability and growth, it often leads to success in other areas. Conversely, the state of not being lean and agile squares the circle of business success and deprives them of flexibility and endurance.

- On the other hand, the most vicious behavior was profligacy in the use of resources, time, and opportunities. They were too distracted by non-essentials and failed to pay sufficient attention to corporate governance. The business operation was conducted haphazardly, with a variety of principles and ad hoc management, which made it unstable and unbalanced.

They loved a showy appearance, building a great office, and promoting social recognition with lapses of reason. They put more emphasis on media management than on executing their strategy for sustainability.

The people never ventured to take risks in the mind that it is better safe than sorry. The long meeting has just listed options to act on, but it did not fix a conclusion. They liked to say, "it is what it is", and they were normally inward-looking rather outward-attentive in their interactive communication and engagement. They worked for the sake of work, cloaked in the veil of hierarchy and systems.

The internal meetings were long, boring, staid, and indecisive, the business results were not open to all members of the organization. The system of operation was archaic, byzantine, and exclusive. All these led to heavy and slow in actions as well as decision-making. Sometimes they took a temporary blip of change in response to longstanding change in marker. The loyalty of employees was taken for granted, and the reward was scanty, uneven, and unprincipled. To put it simply, they were not lean, principled, and agile in ensuring long-term sustainability.

- Adding to the virtue of lean and agile, the measure of being principled matters significantly.

In the early 2000s, I held the position of HR (Human Resources) Manager for a Korean shipping company with its European headquarters in London, UK. This experience reinforces my belief that principles are of greater importance than flexibility.

During my tenure, I received numerous complaints and grievances from local staff as well as Korean expatriate managers who were based in the same office. The disparate work styles of the authoritative Korean managers and the more communal local staff occasionally proved irreconcilable when a toxic dispute escalated into conflict among themselves.

As HR Manager, I was responsible for improving interactional communication and taking disciplinary action when necessary. I was required to find the optimal solution when dealing with staff issues, such as the cultural gap between Koreans and English speakers. It was not a matter of right or wrong, but rather an issue of efficiency in terms of organizational performance.

In some instances, it was necessary to apply principles uniformly to all parties, regardless of nationality. Conversely, in other situations, a more flexible approach was required to address the specific circumstances of each case. Without clear principles to guide decision-making, on-the-spot resolutions were often spontaneous and contentious. Conversely, without sufficient flexibility, many individuals found the decision to be unrealistic and unsustainable. The issue was whether to prioritize flexible principles (giving greater weight to principle) or principled flexibility (giving greater weight to be flexible).

The experiences over the four years in the tasks led me to wonder that the flexible principled approach is both more effective and sustainable in dealing with a variety of HR issues because the flexible principle helps increase work efficiency among employees. I shared this conclusion with my successor when I returned to the Seoul headquarters of the same company. I found here the virtues of lean, agile, principle, and resilient.

In the 21st century, the internet vastly reshapes the world's information landscape, but what's less obvious is how the internet is changing us. The internet is a double-edged sword. Although the Internet has brought many conveniences, it has also burdened us with problems such as information overload and dependency on the virtual world. That means the products of modern science are not in themselves good or bad, but it is the way they are used that determines the value of the information and the content.

Nicholas Carr made the points in his great book "The Shallow, What the Internet is Doing to our Brains". He deliberated the effects of Internet use on our brains, how our thought process is influenced, and what we need to do to adapt to the inevitable reality of internet use.

The internet provides opportunities and problems.

- For the good part, internet enthusiasts celebrate it with good reason and praise the torrent of new content that technology uncorks and see it as signaling a democratization of culture. For them, the internet is the land of abundant Eden heralding a new golden age of access and participation. It enhances their mental flexibility and intellectual litheness so that they adapt to a new situation, learn new skills, and, in general, expand the horizon of cognition.

For the bad part, internet skeptics decry it with equally good reasons and condemn the crassness of the content, viewing it as signaling a degrading of culture. For them, the internet is a vast wasteland bemoaning a dark age of mediocrity and narcissism. Some have suffered from moral afflictions such as depression from a sense of inferiority compared to others, obsessive-compulsive disorder ("OCD") with uncontrollable and recurring thoughts, reflexive bias, blind hatred, or ready obedience to a specific person.

An avid follower of news may be trapped in biased thoughts because the media may skew your view of the world. The news and SNS generalize people into groups, spew hate speech at a distance, amplify, and zoom in on the negativity bias. They make a profit by making people worse.

Our appetite for news and push notifications manifests all the symptoms of addiction. Managers at SNS enterprises limit the time their children spend on the internet and social media. Disengage from your screen and meet real people in the flesh. Think carefully about what information you feed your mind as you do about the food you feed your body. Media-SNS silence for a certain time will help redress the balance in perception, reasoning, and action. Let the wind blow and the leaves are swept away.

In this point, content does matter, but it hinges on personal ideology and taste, and it sometimes goes down a cul-de-sac with extreme views, and it attacks the personality. The popular medium molds what we see and how we see it. It changes who we are, as individuals and as a society. In that sense, the media are not just channels of information that supply the stuff of thought, but they also shape the process of thought.

The digital landscape is inundated with short passages and video clips from many online sources which produce compulsive adopters. The networked thinking process expands our minds together with the old linear thought process. The digital immersion with short and disjointed messages burst open the mentality of the faster, the better. This clashes with a calm, focused, and undistracted linear mind.

The old linear thought process has been at the center of art, science, and society. It ruled the rational mind of Enlightenment, the inventive mind of the Industrial Revolution, and even the subversive mind of Modernism, but it may soon be yesterday's mind. The lives of most Baby Boomers who were born from 1946 to 1964 and the Generation Xers who were born from 1965 to 1980 have unfolded like a two-act play. They lived with Analogue Youth and then after a quick but thorough shuffling of the props, they entered Digital Adulthood.

Human nature seems necessarily fixed and immutable because the brain's plasticity ends with childhood and everything in it may die, and nothing may be regenerated. However, the adult generation should make well-trained and well-directed mental exercises to make their brains adaptable and plastic.

(2) Be steady in mind using alter-ego

In the modern era, the distinction between identity types is becoming increasingly blurred: National identity is evolving as people migrate more widely and societies become increasingly multicultural. Gender identity is also changing, as individuals' innate sense of their gender varies.

Family identity is also transforming itself, as people lose the sense of potency and culture of the home. Family history or legacy is no longer regarded as the supreme value. Generational identity is also getting diluted and diverse. Amid the trend of being in flux of generational consciousness, older individuals tend to feel and act much younger than their biological age. In comparison, younger individuals become less motivated or more apathetic in engagements with mundane affairs in social interactions.

In the context of multiple and sometimes conflicting identities, individuals may find themselves creating inner sanctum for elastic recovery and maintaining dual identities that will take turns responding to external stimuli or confrontation. This can manifest as a distinction between one's authentic self, or true personality, and a second, more protective persona, or alter ego. This latter identity may emerge in situations where the authentic self requires protection from external pressures or confusion.

A well-conceived alter ego can facilitate the alignment between the current reality and the desired future. This does not entail a fictitious mental disorder or maintaining a double standard in judgment and actions.

Rather, it is akin to a mind that comprises two distinct compartments in good order, one representing the real self and the other representing the alter ego.

In the event of an unwarranted attack on your real self, you can call on your alter ego to defend your identity. It is important to ensure that your alter ego is adequately prepared and equipped to play this role, particularly when it needs to be detached from emotion.

(3) Be tough in mind but remain humble and resilient

As business is tough and cruel, businesspersons have to find their own ways to win the market.

In the shipping business, for example, the transaction parties are merciless in exploiting its own market advantage whenever possible, the shipowners charge a high rate of vessel charters onto the charterers (cargo owners) when vessel demand exceeds supply, but the charterers happily lash out at the charter rate when the vessel demand is much lower than supply.

No matter how smart we are, or how much the market analysis is deep and thorough, it is impossible to predict the shipping market so that the player makes a profit in every turn of market change.

The change has produced winners and losers in profitability or existence per se in the market. My experiences tell me that those who were humble and sharp in mind, and persistent and resilient in action found it much more prospective to sustain and prosper.

I have often heard a joke that the possibility of success in the shipping business would be 70% luck by happenstance and 30% managerial capacity in the face of market volatility, e.g. clueless changes in bunker price and foreign exchange rate, ever-occurring geo-political conflicts, or natural or man-made disasters like Tsunami, earthquakes, Covid-19 and pirates' attacks, etc. In all circumstances, however, I have an objective view that the best alternative for market players is to make their organization or individuals "lean" always and remain "agile, resilient, and disciplined" to pre-warn them in their best efforts and respond to such changes highly effectively, and turn the volatile events into opportunities in their favor. There is nothing to complain about them, but to outmaneuver them, at most, proactively or, at least, reactively, utilizing the response-capacity. I term this alternative "Volatility-Responsive Capital".

So, the most effective virtue to win the market is to remain lean, disciplined, and resilient.

The characteristics of trees have much in common with those of humans. Trees make the second growth after disturbances such as forest fires, insect infestation, timber harvest or wind throw. It shows resilience by resuming a new beginning in the face of the disturbances. Humans are affected by adverse conditions or broken down in even worse conditions during which there is nothing more effective than being lean, disciplined, and resilient.

It can be also referred to as the progressive stages of birth-growth-peak-decline-collapse and new birth. People, especially young adults, must make their own second growth by jumping from the old curve to a new curve of growth when the stage passes the peak of the old curve. In the act of jumping, it is crucial to find the right moment to call for a leap.

Meanwhile, the older generations need to play a role of assisting the young adults by reforming a set of structured problems. As the world changes rapidly, responding to the changes should come on apace. As rear streams push the front stream into the big river (in Chinese, 長江後浪推前浪), the old generation makes space for the young generation in due course of generation shift.

The second growth of the trees is combined with a thriving understory of seedlings to make the canopy of trees great.

(4) Be watchful about motions in the motionless appearance

When things are stable and sound, it is time for you to keep calm and get your brain working. Stay grounded, focus on reality, and get your wits about the reality surrounding you and take the juice out of it..

I had my personal experience in the work at the Juwang National Park as a term-based contracted worker from late 2021 to early 2023. In December 2021, my assigned work was to search for a wild hog, live or dead, inside the mountain to find if the hog was contaminated with the contagious disease, so-called, African Swine Fever which affects livestock fatally

On a day in December, I made a solo trip into the no-man's land deep inside the mountain for the search, the winterly cold and strong wind denuded the trees, and visibility in all directions was pretty high under the cloudless sky (By regulations., the solo-search is not recommended, but my companion was sick-off that day, so I made the solo trip with due prior report to the park office and turning on auto-positioning device).

Along the search, the only sounds that I could hear were the wind blowing and rustles of dry leaves under my feet. It was cold and tranquil, and nothing was in motion on the ground and in the sky. With no special intent, I paused, leaned on a tree, and stood still for a moment. I kept standing there motionless for not less than thirty minutes.

Then I was really surprised that I began to hear something moving around, sounding meek, and finally hustle and bustle in all areas of the mountain. All forms of wild animals, big and small, slow and fast, started to move around after the time of pause and watch in the alert of an uninvited human. They got louder and their movements were visible.

When they felt that humans could be a threat or they could not confirm that the humans were not hostile to them, they stopped doing their work and put all activities in abeyance. This offered me the thought that we routinely see or hear something in our daily lives, but they are not all and final. There exists something invisible or inaudible in it, and they also do guesswork about who we are and what we are doing.

We don't have to hustle and bustle, and we get along with the inactivity or even enjoy it when it gets by, but we should not forget that there is something in motion in the motionless state, and they start to move when they feel the time is up, just late enough to check it out, but not enough to be too late for their routine works.

Don't get impatient and be complacent in unnoticeable situations, take time to rest and be prepared for the time when it is tuned into a burst of activities.

One of the major reasons some people or organizations fail to sustain the adversities in the market is that they lack time to prepare for it as most of their days are spent more on routine tasks.

The shipping industry had significant fluctuations for years before the 2008 global financial crisis. The overdemand trend began in the early 2000s when the market's demand for vessels was significantly greater than its supply. The situation worsened until 2008, and the charter rate of vessels spiked weekly and then daily. Because each charter arrangement in the chain generated enormous profits, many shipowners created a chain of charter agreements recklessly with the same vessel among themselves i.e. a circulation of charter transactions.

When the global financial crisis struck, the market rate tumbled, the chains fell apart, and most of such contracts collapsed, leaving so many contractors in turmoil and many of them bellied up. A few years later, when the dust had settled, the market people remarked ruefully, "We shouldn't have worked until late at night every day." It indicates that while everyone was crazy for earnings, they paid little attention to what was happening at the bottom of the market. The lesson from it was that people occasionally need to stop, reflect, and then act.

So, take time, think and know what is set in motion and how it will develop.

(5) Be determined to be positive when in uncertainty

Doomsayers often have been wrong because difficult situations have made people devise solutions in advance or during the progress into the mishap could make us stronger or weaker. We have seen many times that tough times never lasted, but tough people did.

Believe in the innovative capacity of people especially when they are stuck in an enervating stalemate or directionless anomaly. They are supposed to create a breakthrough as far as they can endure or persist. So, the rules of the game are to keep changing with a mindset of optimism.

Even if you attempt to make creative actions laterally or choose to take the incremental course of actions to get things done, you may encounter a dead end, stand up against the wall or be cornered in an unanticipated turn of events. Some opponents may provoke fear in you, you are thrown off balance, and you may be led into self-abasement.

In this circumstance, you'd better give a benefit of the doubt to the points at stake, and deliberately focus more on opportunities rather than downside factors which will give you greater chances of success. Meanwhile, humans have evolved to connect, but communication is tricky, or it tends to be ricocheted. The intent (focusing on opportunities) in confusion brings frustration (communication breakdown).

Personally, I have seen many occasions of confusion and collapses when there were systemic failures of business operations in the cases of the IMF-bailout crisis in 1998 in Korea, the global financial crisis in 2008, and the breakdown of normalcy and entire hullabaloo induced by the Covid-19 in 2020.

The bottom line is to assume the best in people and things. We live our lives following our conscience and we have to be responsible for our decisions in life. We may encourage ourselves to believe that most people are decent and kind. We need to devise a plan that benefits all stakeholders in an issue, or at least a plan that has losses mitigated or compensated.

2) Do yourself

Time and space are key elements in decision-making and actions for all kinds of people in all manner of responses. Specifically, space is variable and relative depending on the individuals, but time is universal and absolute to all.

In mind that we make all conditions favorable to the Case C, a set of principles in the action-sets are presented:

- Actions speak louder than words of obnoxious loudmouth. It means that a decision for the actions is very important, and it should be effective for actions.

- Doubt your sanity, stay sanguine, and get away from being sanctimonious. It cannot be too thorough in assessing the condition to decide for actions and stay focused and humble in mind.

- The amount of time is in direct proportion to the gravity of action. This means that people need the same lapse of time as the significance of the action.

In the context of making the right decision applying the principles, we explore the cases of time for three seconds, 100 days, and three years. People will do what they shouldn't do when they don't do what they should do. Ideas change the world only when we change our behavior.

(1) Exercise the **three seconds**-rule

This is the time for empathy, tolerance, cooperation, and avoiding accidental mishaps of confusion, misunderstanding, and conflicts. It helps create situational advantages to move on to the next action phase.

- In daily routine lives, we come into a specific situation to make us do a transient halt, for example, we stand in a queue that is much slower to dwindle than the other queues beside us, bump into a person or things that stand in our way when we are in a hurry, get stuck in a packed cabin in the commuting trains, or the buses depart when we get to the bus stop or they arrive late when we are already there. The situation may be uncomfortable that we come across by chance because the adverse fortuity stands in our way.

- Everybody has their intent or situation that has the person act like it, and we need to find out what it is before we react to it. All these instances may happen to us when the situation is fluid, and the people are mobile.

    As an instant reaction, we may feel at a loss on how to deal with it, and then we tend to make a spur-of-the-moment decision to overtake it, bypass it, take no heed of it, or stand aside from it absent-mindedly. Many cases of careless mistakes or misunderstandings of the people take place in the action on impulse with no proper patience.

- Rather than making the decision impulsively in such instances, we should train ourselves so that we take stock of the situation, find the most appropriate way to respond, and then talk or act compatible with it. This may sound imprudent to practice it in such a short time, but it is trainable and well-established when repeated.

    The exercise of attentive patience shall pay off with benefits to all including, most notably, the doers of patience and attention. Actions in either haste or indolence are most likely to make waste, and vice versa, timely actions with attentive patience shall bring about benefits. In that sense, exercising attentive patience for three seconds without doing an impulsive reaction may save us time and cost, and it may turn the frowning mischance into a pleasant happenstance.

- However, let me make the point that such an unexpected situation does not happen so frequently every hour, but it happens infrequently at an unexpected spot. It is up to us whether we make it a momentous and favorable opportunity for the benefit of our counterparts including ourselves, or it is just one of such instances that elapses in our lack of attention or impulsive indifference that may eventually end up with a perception that brings us into disrepute.

Attention or fastidiousness may make a meaningful difference in our perception and cognition.

- My experiences tell me that Koreans, including myself, are less accustomed to exercising patience and attention in such tricky situations. We tend to make a nuisance of ourselves wittingly or unwittingly in public places. This phenomenon has caused disturbances, annoyance, and conflict of others who normally responded to it in a fit of pique.

In the aspect of social consequences, the effect of patience and attention for three seconds can be found in traffic accidents in Korea. The number of deaths in traffic accidents was 5,092 in 2013 and it has steadily decreased to 2,551 in 2023 which saved many lives. Decades ago, the traffic lights were oftentimes breached in the streets of Seoul when there is little traffic or none of pedestrians.

The impatient drivers were negligent to abide by the traffic rules and they didn't feel compunction with such reckless demeanors. But these days it is hardly possible to spot automobiles that disregard traffic regulations outrageously. It can be attributed not only to heightened civility that makes patience and attention a social decorum but fines and penalties from surveillance of many speed cameras force the patience and attention of the drivers.

- This is relevant to a situation where we are supposed to make a response in a strained relationship, tense conversation, or acute mental pressure. Our emotions are getting at odds with our reason to deliberate the issue at stake. We feel like blurting out what is on our minds and expressing our dissatisfaction with the issue. In this situation, the unaffectionate emotion is instantly attached to the person who advocates it.

Hereby, we notice a typical situation where it leads to tension or conflict: reddened face, harsh and raspy voice, menacing gesture and facial expressions, disparaging eye gaze, and boisterous head movement. It cross-escalates in the exchange of confrontational remarks and gestures, and the arguers finally begin to slur and cast aspersions on the alleged malignant attitude or misconduct of the counterpart which is not relevant to the topic. Amid the scene of hoarseness, emotion replaces reason.

- In such a situation of tetchy relations, tense conversation, or acute mental pressure, we may be able to reduce the probability of an argument in such a disgrace by employing a tactic of interposing mitigating remarks between the tension and the argument.

When we start with the proper prelude, buffer expression, or empathetic remarks, it shall give the counterpart time to think of the issue and prepare for a response. When the speaker relates to the prelude or remarks, they should be delivered as clearly as possible in a courteous manner. At any rate, they shouldn't be fictitious, superficial, and domineering. Do not jump into an abrasive talk abruptly and without warning unless it is intended to develop an argument for argument, or you have relation with the person close enough to have a free chance of tête-à-tête.

> Split the person from the points of problems. Respect the personality of the counterpart first and then deal with the points. Empathy and compassion make the talk productive or conciliatory even when the mood of the talk is tense.

- It is not exceptional in Korea to notice the ever-deepening polarity of thought, wealth, and opportunities. People are not readily induced to debate over the topics of politics, religion, and sensitive social issues because it typically leads nowhere and everywhere in disarray. This takes the form of freedom but not license, but it nurtures the elephant in the room.

This is not a healthy society, nor we cannot shy away from the debate for action because the future of young adults requires action at present to make it sustainable. The people in contemporary society should debate, conclude, and act with specific intentions to serve the purpose of enhancing sustainability.

In this sense, the three seconds should be used to detail the prelude or opening remarks in an attempt to develop productive debate.

Again, words and actions in either haste or indolence make waste.

(2) Exercise the three **one hundred days-rule**

"The fisher who draws in his net too soon, Won't have any fish to sell; The child who shuts up his book too soon, Won't learn any lessons well. If you have your learning to stay, Be patient – don't learn too fast; The man travels a mile each day, May get round the world at last" McGuffey Readers.

Every new beginning in contact with new people and things poses a challenge to get the person familiarized with those who are involved. The difference in perception builds a peculiar view, and the relationship is relative depending on the stance of counterparts.

The one-hundred-day rule is meant to get yourself patient, position yourself in the new social setting, and settle down in the new situation during which you reprogram your brain in fly-on-the-wall style.

This can develop in two directions:

A good case is that the person positions in the seamless way of social interaction which shall help secure relational advantage. This helps build rapport with the people with whom the person shall engage.

A bad case is that conflict takes place when a relationship gets sour, and the distinction between the person and the problems gets blurred. Some irritating or frustrating experiences at the outset develop unfriendly or even malevolent relationships spurred by premature judgment, sheer misconception, or the heat of the emotion. When the feeling of intense distaste or disgust develops, the bona fide tolerance at the inception of relationships evaporates and conflicts take root where the issue is missing, but the emotion prevails.

This is the point in the 100 day-rule that people need an amount of time to get to know one another and understand why some people act in that way. There in scientific specifics that justify the amount of time e.g. 100 days, but my empirical evidence directs me to say, at least, more than three months to serve the purpose which would be long enough to understand one another and to avoid precocious misjudgment.

- Most humans are self-protective beings. The character becomes apparent when a new competing person steps into the inner group and tries to settle in it. A stage of exchanging perceptions among the people kicks in.

- During the time of 100 days, you don't have to make a final judgment and act upon it. Every person or every situation may have its cogent reasons underlying or behind the scenes. The one hundred days may reveal something that you couldn't find at the beginning of the period.

- Everything is in a state of flux and upheaval. No one knows what the situation surrounding them will change, individually or collectively. In real life, needs have priority over emotions which means that people in emotional tension may have to mend the estrangement because of the needs. We need to keep a door open for a need to use it. In this context, we should cherish people and never lose them.

Again, decisions and actions in either haste or indolence make waste.

(3) Exercise **three years-rule**

The three-year period is utilized to secure transactional advantage. Specifically, it is the time to define the strategy and implement it. It allows us to have a thorough understanding of the assets we are dealing with, to set an effective timetable, and to achieve a goal we are aiming for.

Let me illustrate this point by drawing on my experience in two shipping companies over three decades, which has taught me the virtue of patience in finding the right time for profitable action.

- It is said that when it comes to buying ships in the sale and purchase market, the best deals have the worst cash flow, and we generally do not get a good price and a good cash flow at the same time. This means that a good price for a buyer, i.e. a cheaper price when the market is slow, cannot generate a good cash flow after it has been invested in companies in the spot transport market.

  In the shipping market, there are two factors, the buying and selling price, and the operating profit, and it is unlikely that these two factors will move in the same direction, except in a few cases where the market undergoes a systemic change of boom and bust over a certain period of time, which is not common in the normal state of the market.

- In theory, therefore, the best decision on the part of the buyer to buy or sell ships is to make an anti-cyclical decision. If the purchase price is low and the operating profit is miserable, then buy the ships and operate them at a certain operating loss. The bold buyer takes his time and suffers the loss until the price rises when the owner can sell the ships or make an operating profit that compensates for the losses together with an additional profit.

According to the same market mechanism, a seller cannot sell the vessel at a good price, i.e. a higher price than in the past, and at the same time replace it with an alternative vessel at a lower price on the market in order to make a good operating profit from the transport of goods. They are players in the game, they aren't riding a tandem bike pedaling at the same tempo and time, and in the same direction, but they work in the pattern of staggered hours and move in a counter-cyclical way.

In other words, it is the time of market change that bridges the gap between the low purchase price and the high operating profit. When one is high, the other is low, and vice versa. This means that the best purchase price can be timed to coincide with the worst earnings and that the worst purchase is made when the market is at its peak.

- Another salient feature of the market is that there is no objective justice in the shipping market; rather, there is merely subjective belief. This typifies the fact that there are buying and selling transactions daily, and all parties have an equal opportunity of success in these transactions. On each side of the transaction, some buyers and sellers genuinely believe that they are acting in a morally and legally sound manner.

    As any market player knows, margin counts for everything, and it is about timing, not fortuitous but calculated timing. If the timing is right, some will make a profit and if the timing is wrong, the others will never make any money, even if they are very clever. However, it is easier said than done that a counter-cyclical investment or divestment decision will make a profit.

    The key is to take the time to understand the ever-changing market, to be decisive in picking the right time to make a deal, to outthink the competition that is trying to do the same thing, and to be persistent in staying the course as the market changes. Usually, greed and impatience distort the process, and the wrong decision ends in a loss.

    In the contingent flow of market changes, the time of three years of understanding the market and choosing the time of action would be a necessary condition to make a net profit from the transaction sufficient result.

    Again, haste makes waste, but perseverance makes a profit.

- The challenge is to find a solution that balances the dual mandates as in the case of the FED (the Federal Reserve, the central bank of the United States) which aims for full employment and price stability. Concurrently, we must address other considerations such as corporate profitability and service quality, the security of the rescuers and the rescued, and fiscal requirements and budgetary constraints.

    These two objectives are mutually exclusive and cannot be achieved simultaneously. The optimal solution is to enhance the flexibility of each element in addressing challenges. For instance, we are maintaining a lean, agile, and cash-rich organization to respond to the need for human resources, capital expenditure, and expanding investments.

    Once the targets have been achieved, restructuring should be undertaken to eliminate any excess, redundancy, and overcapacity in order to regain the flexibility to meet future needs.

    This rigorous work to think bigger, do more original and finish the audacious works need time at least for more than three months, i.e. 100 days, with intensive attention and persistent actions.

(4) Defy it. Never take the status of underdogs for granted

There is an adage *"Letum quam lutum,"* which translates to "death before defeat." It implies that the baron would prefer to resign from his post rather than face disgrace or death at the hands of his colleagues.

In human societies, there have been two types of individuals who have exploited the underdog and who suffered from their actions. The former group represents a minority of individuals who have benefited from social privilege and have been determined not to allow the exploited to gain the upper hand. In contrast, the latter groups is the majority who have suffered from exploitation among which some refused to play dead or act dumb cowardly and defied the social conventions that compelled submission and obedience.

In the context of the authoritative social convention, social interaction can be viewed as a social struggle between two opposing forces, represented by the characters of Achilles in the Iliad of Greek epic poems. In some cases, *metis* (wisdom, skill) may be able to compensate for a lack of bie (strength, force).

In particular, *metis* is most valuable in situations where circumstances are fluid, fast-paced, unfamiliar, and uncertain. In such cases, there is no set formula or predictable behavior that can benefit from richer experiences from the past, a stronger grasp on the present, and a more expansive view of the future. Those who seek to take advantage of others are often in a position of greater advantage, which allows them to exploit the metis.

People got a sense of defiance from the experiences of toils and manipulation after being sucked dry by extortion for expensive and stultifying superstructures of the privileged class built primarily for their immediate benefits or ultimate interests. They brainwashed the unprivileged by tradition and convention who came to take the trials and tribulations as an obligation or destiny.

If the necessity for implementing coercive measures arises, it may entail a gradual and systematic approach to identifying the target's threshold of pain. This may involve a pattern of graduated escalation, progressing from mere nuisance, through real pain, and ultimately to absolute dread. It employs threats to persuade the abused to yield.

For those underdogs who are disadvantaged and abused by the upper hands, they should defy it in strategic and decisive ways. People cannot navigate for new horizons until they lose sight of the shore from which they just sailed off. Once you launch, never look back, get fixed in direction and firm in purpose, and free yourself from the backward conventions and institutions of society.

The sense of defiance in such a condition of being abused is the be-all and end-all of their existence.

- The initial task is to understand the nature of the abuse and how to respond to it. Those in a disadvantaged position assess situations, craft a practical strategy, and execute it to defy the malpractice of the abuse. We may refer to the duel between David and Goliath. David exercised foresight in vigilance, made keen analysis, and armed him with his most skilled tools in deceit against gigantic Goliath who was a man completely lacking in guile.

  David maintained a clear focus on the objective even in the face of humiliation and outwardly disadvantage. He concentrated on hitting the point of weakness rather than accepting the disadvantage.

- Cunning is a strategy for underdogs to exercise in fighting a larger and more powerful opponent. The underdogs must utilize their intellect to achieve even a modicum of success by combining tact and finesse with effective strategy. David chose his most competitive tactics. Success is not solely dependent on the initial blow; he also administered the *coup de grâce* to make the initial victory permanent by cutting off the head of Goliath after he fell on his face to the ground.

- It is crucial to never take the status of an underdog for granted. They should challenge the status quo and any malpractices that are enforced on them. It is not just of talk in defiance, but of tenacity, of insatiable questioning of authority, of determined solidarity combined with a brave attitude of embracing the risk of failure.

The underdogs have historically responded to these challenges in three distinct ways.

- A positive case

    Martin Luther translated the Bible into German to exclude himself from power and authority.

    At the Imperial Diet of the Holy Roman Empire, convened by Emperor Charles V and held in the Imperial Free City of Worms in 1521, Martin Luther presented a robust defense of his beliefs.

    The Catholic Church excommunicated him, and Luther's territorial ruler, Frederick the Wise, relocated Luther to the castle at Wartburg for 10 months (4 May 1521–3 March 1522) for his safety.

    While sequestered from actual power, Luther completed the translation of Erasmus's Greek New Testament into German in only eleven weeks. This is an exceptional achievement, regardless of the circumstances, which further solidifies his position as a pivotal figure in Christian history. His translation is known as the September Bible and had a formative impact on the German language.

    The September Bible was released in September 1522 and sold approximately five thousand copies in the first two months. He made the Bible the people's book, ensuring its presence in churches, schools, and homes. The democratization of access to sacred texts had a significant impact on the role of Scripture in guiding faith in Germany.

    He demonstrated an ability to convey the original meaning in a way that was accessible to the language spoken around him. His objective was to present the teachings and examples of Christ and the Apostles in a way that resonated with the German people, using language that was accessible and engaging. For the German audience, it was a form of republication of the gospel, as Luther produced idiomatic German rather than a literal translation.

    Luther proceeded with his translation of the Old Testament and completed the entire Bible in 1534. The printing press, invented by Johannes Gutenberg (1398-1468) in the 1450s, played a pivotal role in the Protestant Reformation by facilitating the dissemination of new belief system and the Bible, which encouraged independent thought, on a wider scale. He fought on rather than settled for half-measures.

- A neutral case

    The perspective is provided by Niccolo Machiavelli in his work, The Prince, which offers food for thought on the subject.

    Niccolo Machiavelli (1469-1517) was a Florentine bureaucrat, diplomat, and political advisor.

His book, The Prince, was drafted in 1513 as a reference guide for those in positions of authority. It was not published until 1532, five years after the author's passing. He highlighted Machiavelli's suitability for the role of an advisor in the context of significant instability and risk in Italian affairs.

The prose in The Prince reflected the urgency of the situation and the concern about the political implications for Florence in the context of formidable French and Spanish capabilities. He sought to enhance the military capabilities of the state in order to defend its interests and extend its power. Unfortunately, the Florentine militia he helped establish was defeated in battle with the Spanish at Prato in 1512. Machiavelli's lack of involvement in the actual power structure allowed him the opportunity to focus on theoretical approaches to exercising power.

It was emphasized that a competent and loyal army is essential for ensuring security and creating diplomatic freedom of action. He provided advice on how to gain and retain power that was notably cynical in nature. This advice involved engaging in a range of private transactions while maintaining a public image of integrity and rectitude. The underlying message was that pursuing virtue in both word and deed would result in adverse consequences.

The overarching objective is to ensure survival. This meant that the prince had to be flexible in his approach, changing his tack to suit the circumstances and, where necessary, prepared to act in ways that might not align with traditional moral standards. He presented the question of whether it is preferable to be loved or feared, or if the two can coexist. The answer is that it would be ideal to be both, but it is more advantageous to be feared than loved if that is not possible.

It is not uncommon for people to display ungrateful, fickle, dishonest, risk-averse, and profit-seeking behaviors while princes provide protection and treatment. The Exodus in the Bible shows the features that the Egyptians forgot the ten accidents (ten plagues) and the Israelites forgot the miracles of mercy (ten interruptions).

They would assert that they would be willing to sacrifice their blood, risk their property, and even their lives for the prince, provided that the danger is not imminent.

Although the term 'Machiavellian' is often used to describe strategies based on deceit and manipulation, Machiavelli's approach was actually far more balanced. He indicated that the more leaders rely on devious methods, the less likely it would be that they succeed. It is wise to exercise power under the pretext of harsh punishments.

- A negative case

Adolf Hitler, a controversial figure in history, wrote Mein Kampf while imprisoned. Hitler was arrested for his involvement in the coup, also known as the Beer Hall Putsch, and sentenced to five years in prison on November 11, 1923. He served his sentence in Landsberg prison, located west of Munich. During this period, Hitler dictated the text of the book Mein Kampf to his aide Rudolf Hess, with whom he shared a cell. On December 20, 1924, the Bavarian Supreme Court granted Hitler a pardon, resulting in his release from prison.

The book was published on July 18, 1925, and sold 9,473 copies. Thereafter, sales decreased annually: 6,913 in 1926, 5,607 in 1927, and 3,015 in 1928. In 1929, sales rose slightly to 7,664, then increased with the rise of the Nazi Party and the introduction of an inexpensive one-volume edition to 54,086 in 1930, 50,808 in 1931, and 90,351 in 1932.

Over the seven years between 1925 and 1932, Hitler's royalties constituted his primary source of income. However, they were insignificant in comparison to the sums he received in 1933, following his appointment as Chancellor. In his first year of office, Mein Kampf sold a million copies, generating over one million marks in royalties (approximately $300,000), making him the most prosperous author in Germany and the first to become a millionaire.

In the book, Hitler outlined the blueprint for the Third Reich, which conquered Europe between 1939 and 1945. This blueprint was not only to restore a defeated and chaotic Germany but also to build a new kind of state. He planned for the state to be based on the Aryan race and for living space outside Germany's frontiers to be established. The Nazi regime was responsible for inflicting catastrophic losses on innocent people in an appalling and crude manner.

It should be noted that not every German purchased the book. It was challenging to read the entire 782-page document. It could be argued that had foreign statesmen read it, they would have been better equipped to understand Hitler's personality and political philosophy before 1933, when the Nazis came to power. Had they done so, they could have thwarted the Nazi plot to expand its influence in Europe in the late 1930s.

In addition, he presented his concept of worldview, or "*Weltanschauung*," in a bold and engaging style. It was evident that the ill-conceived and incoherent blend of an uneducated and neurotic individual was at odds with the prevailing mindset of the 20th century. It is crucial to understand that this ideology was embraced with unwavering fervor by the German people, leading to the devastation of Germany and the loss of millions of innocent lives outside its borders.

Similarly, Hitler espoused the theory of evolution put forth by Darwin, which posits that all life forms are engaged in a constant struggle for survival and that the fittest are the ones that prevail. These were the ideas that Adolf Hitler set forth from his prison cell in Landsberg. Was it a sadistic fantasy, irresponsible egoism, or megalomania? To some extent, it was a combination of all three. The ideas of Hitler were not simply aberrations; they had roots that lay deep in German experience and thought. Nazism and the Third Reich were a natural progression of German history.

(5) Build a bridge, not the wall

It has been observed that humans tend to emulate and turn on one another. They are brought into a trap of conflict that has a contagious effect. The conflict trap makes it incredibly hard for us to dig ourselves out once we get stuck, and the other sides do, too. Both sides become so close, and the tension is so intense that they cannot budge or wiggle out of it. The formidable forces that pulled into the trap take the form of blind prejudice, inveterate bias, binary choices, social confrontation, communication breakdown, and mutual dehumanization.

When we are stuck in the conflict trap, the first task for all in the trap is to stop voicing their concerns rancorously, start to listen attentively, and demonstrate a range of openness to consider a breakthrough. To persuade, one must first understand. To understand, one must listen. To listen, one must open the mind. Conclusively. It is imperative to move beyond a binary system of thought and strive for compromise or agreement before moving on to confront confrontation reflexively.

Such actions should contribute to fostering a more tolerant environment. If not, the world would be a circumstance of *"bellum omnium in omnes"* (a condition of war of all against all).

- First, the key to a sustainable society is effective leadership. The leader should not exploit people's worst instincts, but he should call the people to do their best. The leader establishes a vision for a sustainable future, develops a strategy to achieve that vision, executes the strategy following the defined action plans, leads change management, and achieves the overarching vision of a sustainable future. He must manage or endure public scorn and the inevitable tribulations of political life.

  For a leader, communication is of the essence in which some effective ideas should be made stickier. Chip Heath and Dan Heath indicated ways of making ideas stickier by leaders in their book, Made to Stick, page 72, that a good process for making ideas stickier is: (a) identify central message, that is, find the core, to communicate, (b) figure out what is counter-intuitive message (which is contrary to common sense), and (c) break audience's guessing along the counter-intuitive dimension.

  History has shown that unity in diversity is essential to achieve this goal, for example, Cyrus the Great (r.550–530 BC) founded the Persian Empire (550–330 BC) in the principle. Leaders must set an example to show tolerance, concessions, and sacrifices within an organization or society to foster unity. Without them, conflicts, disorientation, and indiscipline may arise. While selfishness permeates society, it is unsustainable. The leader positions himself more as a moderator than a pugilist.

- Second, go the extra mile. The people take constant consciousness of scarcity and adversity and do more to make it good. They should contain their ego individually and form a unity collectively. Accept that there will always be people who have opposing views or sour relationships because it is not extraordinary to have such opponents. You must stay calm, rational, and principled in dealing with them, and turn their dissatisfaction to improve the problems, not add the problems.

  Some of the *Paradoxical Commandments* by Kent M. Keith in 1968 may help find personal meaning in the face of success as well as adversity.

  a. People are illogical, unreasonable, and self-centered - **Love them anyway.**

  b. If you are successful, you will win false friends and true enemies - **Succeed anyway.**

  c. People favor underdogs but follow only top dog - **Fight for a few underdogs anyway.**

  d. What you spend years building may be destroyed overnight - **Build anyway.**

  e. Give the world the best you have, and you'll get kicked in the teeth - **Give the world the best you have anyway.**

- Third, it is important to foster positive humanizing interactions by increasing tolerance. If the individual has been dehumanized by being viewed as a means to an end or as incorrigible deviants, rather than as a whole person, it is important to rehumanize them.

No matter how the world or other individuals treat you, it is beneficial to adhere to the principle of "Malice toward none, Charity for all." This approach will ultimately prove advantageous, as it makes them work together more effectively as teams and provides tight connections within the community.

In their conversations, say conducive talks by changing from a question of "if" to a matter of "when", treat possibilities ("theoretical") as probabilities ("realistic"), stop saying "I wish" and start saying "I will".

The biggest leap in growth is produced by encouraging meta-ideas (ideas for ideas) that increase the generation and spread of ideas.

The late President Reagan of the U.S. provides an illustrative example> He was a former American actor and politician, and became the 40th President, serving from 1981 to 1989. He is renowned for his role as a leader who achieved the goal of "peace through strength". He had a lively with penetrating eyes and an unaffected eloquence. Despite facing a great deal of criticism and personal attacks throughout his career, Reagan remained composed, responded with a smile and a witty remark, or burst into peals of laughter. He moved with cool precision and absolute determination, and he was firm on matters of substance but avoided personal confrontation.

Abraham Lincoln delivered the Gettysburg Address to commemorate the fallen soldiers in the battleground in which he said *"The world will little note, nor long remember, what we say here, but it can never forget what they did here"* It applies to the same people who dedicate their time and opportunities for the common good, especially, the reformers who make the future sustainable despite resistance and criticism.

Some individuals may be reluctant to propose a peace offering initially, concerned that it may be perceived as a sign of weakness, potentially leading to further demands for concessions. Each objection reinforces existing biases and stereotypes, preventing a unified and balanced perspective on the matter. The distorted perception and unbalanced humanity wreak havoc on communal interactions.

It has been said that *"Death and life are in the power of the tongue, and those who love it will eat its fruit.* Proverbs 18:21". This proverb highlights the significant impact of words. The power of our words can elicit a positive or negative response, depending on how they are used. It can facilitate the development of a relationship or impede it.

My experiences indicate that individuals with a sheep-type personality are more likely to cultivate a positive human network to facilitate success in a competitive environment overcoming social fragmentation beyond binaries. In contrast, individuals with a goat-type personality are adept at fostering suspicion, stoking contention, inciting hatred, and maintaining abrasive relationships in pursuit of their interests.

In other experiences of sitting in a busy coffee shop, I often accidentally overheard the talks of the people around me. In my guess, the subjects and contents of their talks are much more about finding the faults of someone than speaking well of someone or mediating some conflicts. They might have good reasons for the dialogue, but it is something quizzical to see that the portion of bad-mouths of gossiping or backstabbing is preponderantly higher than those who praise or mediate. It is something that we need to ponder if it is more habitual than understandable.

The success of those who adopt a goat-like approach would be a spectacular failure. Ultimately, we must decide where we will be positioned and what we will be doing in the long term. The Great Wall made the Chinese empire the largest open-air prison that the world has seen a truth that immobility faces dangers.

We must choose between planting a seed for a sustainable future or a perishable one. Young adults must recognize that a mentally corrupt individual is unlikely to respond positively to corrective measures, but those who are reform-minded personalities can make the world sustainable.

(6) Vote for the Reformer

As roofs and breakwaters always need mending, any society needs reform to be sustainable, and thus reform is the leitmotif running through the whole contents of this book.

Those who say big and good words, and drag heels for reform are usually revolutionaries in speech but not in deed. In the face of resistance, we must not lose our sense of proportion by knowing what is important and what is not, and what is urgent and what is not.

Key to the success of making the future sustainable is to make purpose-driven reforms by crafting the VSP (Vision-Strategy-Policy) set-up and executing it most efficiently and powerfully to achieve the reforms by overcoming misperception, antipathy, or apathy of the public. The gist of the VSP set-up and the way for reform are, I firmly believe, to "**vote for the reformer**" decisively.

There is a distinction between the Pygmalion effect and the Golem effect.

- The Pygmalion effect is a psychological phenomenon whereby heightened expectations result in enhanced performance in each area, whereas lowered expectations lead to diminished performance. Belief and devotion can manifest in tangible outcomes and drive meaningful change in the world. The placebo effect is self-serving, whereas the Pygmalion effect is beneficial to others.

- The Golem effect is a psychological phenomenon whereby lower expectations placed upon individuals result in poorer performance. This is a type of Nocebo effect; whereby negative expectations result in poor outcomes. This creates a self-fulfilling prophecy, whereby a vicious circle of mounting negative expectations ultimately leads to the downfall of the entire organization.

The reform should be executed to maximize the Pygmalion effect in the public and concurrently minimize the Golem effect, given that people are hardwired to mirror themselves.

The modern democratic society is challenged by misdemeanors and the people should respond to them to cure the chronic diseases of tired democracies.

- Challenges

    Tenets of democracy are eroded; Citizens no longer trust one another in indifference or disobedience, populism prevails, polarity deepens in career opportunities and wealth building, and inequality soaks the society in exasperation, and people's demands are met with dismissiveness which makes them feel disrespected and dispiriting.

    The fundamental principles of democracy are being undermined not only by political parties themselves but also by the impact they have on society. These parties are entrenched in their own privileged status and the enduring biases of their most dedicated supporters. They prioritize the interests of their supporters over the broader public good. Among political parties, the concept of "live and let live" is no longer a guiding principle, and they are becoming increasingly irrelevant and exclusive to one another.

    Citizens who differ in political propensity do not trust one another. Social interaction among themselves gets contradictory in hatred. Social unity covering all walks of life is rarely possible except, for example, for international soccer games. They forgot the principle that "Being divided, a single man may destroy you; being united, you are a match for the whole world".

    Voters are not only losing interest but also feel indignant in long-brewing frustration whenever new elections are recognized to produce a new cabal of villains in the National Assembly. The voters deplore the fact that they are not given enough options to elect capable, ethical, balanced, and sensible politicians.

    Some members of the National Assembly turned out to be not only corrupt, but also convicted by jurisdictional authority, or some were even sentenced to guilty. It means the lawbreakers make the law. They are so impudent and shameless in the contradiction that it is the common people who are perplexed to feel helpless and hopeless.

    The inequality that is inflicted on the common people arises from the members of the National Assembly who take their domineering privileges for granted and are unassailable. They avow themselves to serve the interest of the people on day one of their four-year tenure, but it evaporates the next day, and the brutal crassness lasts until the days of the next election.

- These challenges should be responded to with counter-actions (Rutger Bregman listed the seven plagues that afflict democracies, and the seven remedies that should be engaged in calm and deliberative dialogues in his book "*Humankind, A Hopeful History, This is What Democracy Looks Like*, p299-308 " to which the part of Seven remedies are referred)

    a. From cynicism to engagement (Let the people come and talk by which they cure the deep divide between the people).

    b. From polarization to trust (Do not abandon anyone, and then more and more people come, band together, and democracy takes root).

    c. From exclusion to inclusion (Represent the minorities, the poor, the less educated, and the sidelined. Do not exclude them), or from apathy and unintelligence to sensibility and solicitude.

    d. From complacency to citizenship (Give people a voice who then get nuanced in politics. Everyone has something worthwhile to contribute)

    e. From corruption to transparency (Know civic affairs, and then it prevents bribery. Participation bridges the divide between politics and people)

    f. From self-interest to solidarity (People feel like real citizens in participation, look beyond their own interest, and overcome social fragmentation)

    g. From inequality to fairness (Treat citizens as ballot fodder and they'll behave like ballot fodder but treat them as adults and they'll behave like adults)

The seven remedies are believed to be the right to describe the solutions, but to be honest, they look a bit remote from reality because the problems are so deeply ingrained in the establishments of politics that they cannot be readily remedied. Moreover, the remedial process, if it is attempted, may cause much more adverse effects of confusion, contradiction, and conflicts in the hotbed of politics.

I, personally, have looked forward to seeing the changes of backwardness of Korean politics from the late 1980s when democracy was set in place in full form, but four decades of waiting and patience have been betrayed by even worse conditions of political serenity, sagacity, and sensibility.

Korean people have exceptionally seen or heard calm and deliberative dialogues in the National Assembly, but most of the time, only the rant and rave, tussle and yelling, of insane people in the name of the National Assembly members. People feel disappointed and futile with the anomaly, and finally take the absurdity as normal, and political culture becomes decadent.

Despite this hopelessness, the politics must be reformed because the backward National Assembly not only delays the required procedures to make the future sustainable but also misleads the public with their own agenda to protect their political interests. The only solution is to vote for the reformers who are cultured and well-rounded in thought and actions.

Meanwhile, an election determines who has the power, not who has the truth. We cannot help feeling tired and frustrated with this discrepancy from the real tenet of democracy that the locus of power is in the people. However, the most politically engaged people are the most mistaken about one another and get blinded by conflict.

When people view the people on the other side as deviant or extreme, then they vote for anyone who can keep the other side out of office. It is catastrophic when the reformer is in one side that is less popular or antagonized, people then vote against the reformer because the people regard him as deviant or extreme.

In this context, we see the sign of the times and what the people across generations need to do to make the socio-political system back to normal because the non-reformers are just crass or complacent cowards, they cut no ice and collapse in the end. They are not only unproductive but dangerous for future sustainability.

- It is first with the older generation and the insolence of the elected.

    Time matters to humans, and when people age, they tend to be molded into a rigidly stultifying conventional pattern or become dysfunctional or disjointed from the main frame of contemporary issues. They normally take the stance that this is our election, but the result is your problem.

    At the end of the road, the ultimate question arises if they become a cornerstone, a steppingstone or a stumbling block. The cornerstone serves as a foundation for future generations and the stepping stone that boosts opportunities for future generations, or the stumbling block that just sits there to impede the progress of young adults.

    It's up to the person to choose a role among them, but the old people should not degenerate into parasitic dependents by extracting values of pension, medical insurance, and social security benefits in their longevity without making contributions to or concessions for the sustainable future of the young adults.

    Another party is the insolent change of attitude after they are elected. Contrary to their commitment to dedication and honesty during election campaigns, they suddenly change their attitude to crave attention and power once they are elected. They naturally regarded themselves as privileged and exclusive and demanded service rather than serving the people.

    They often breach the division of power into three branches (executive, legislative, and judicial). This is typical in the National Assembly of Korea. They betray the fact that being elected is not a symbol of status masquerading privilege and prejudice, but it's a call to further humility. Opportunistic lawmakers normally go the contrary.

- Second, it is the young adults who should act in a mind driven not driven by emotion but by inspiration.

    They should know that politics in nature is long on elocution but short on execution. The young adults should not be deceived by those who say big words only and catch a subtle shift of opinion of the grandiloquent speaker.

    Politics, on the other hand. may make the future sustainable once it is determined to make structural reforms for future sustainability. The reforms of the failed Gracchus (Tiberius Gracchus, 163-133 BC, and Gaius Gracchus, 154-121 BC), and successful Emperor Hadrian (r.117-138, 21 years).

    The solution in the condition of immovability in politics is to vote for reformers no matter how unhinged or divisive and to vote to get rid of those opportunistic lawmakers. Immobility begets dangers, and so the young voters should make a difference by their votes in the grassroots movement.

    In this context, they must take a sense of agency that acknowledges their power to influence by initiating and executing their own volitional actions, and a sense of collegiality that fosters companionship and cooperation between colleagues who share responsibility and do the work together.

- When the direction is set, then the next one is attitude to drive actions in the direction.

John Kotter dealt with the attitude in his book, A Sense of Urgency, that aims for creating a high enough sense of urgency in turbulent era with notions that all starts with urgency, complacency is much common and very often invisible to the people involved, watch out a false or misguided sense of urgency prevalent and insidious, do not mistake real urgency for false urgency, transform false urgency and complacency into a true sese of urgency, take the urgency more seriously because change is shifting from episodic to continuous.

	Complacency, False Urgency, and True Urgency		
	Complacency	False Urgency	**True Urgency**
Roots	Success and wins over a period of time	Failures, problems with short-term results, and incremental decline	**Leadership from top to bottom in hierarchy create true urgency**
People Think	I know what to do, and I do it	What a mess this is	**Great opportunities and hazards are everywhere**
People Feel	Content with the status quo	Very anxious, angry, and frustrated	**A powerful desire to move and win, now**

As shown above, we need to distinguish between constructive true urgency from destructive false urgency by dropping complacency and false urgency and move and act with a true sense of urgency in carrying out the "Be Yourself, Do Yourself and Vote for the reformer".

7.3 Conclusion

I have gone through history, visited contemporary issues and tapped into the future to find out the points that may help young adults develop their own future in the 21st century. I earnestly seek forgiveness for my probable excesses, deficiencies and mistakes that lurk in the corners of the contents.

Before I conclude my work with this book, let me add some words that I want to deliver to the readership of the young adults.

First, I wish them to consider the principles in the Be Yourself and Do Yourself with the recognition of the Ten Critical Issues. They may feel moral confusion when they are situated in the polarized and entrenched world of politics and economy, however, they need to get a clear understanding of moral reasoning, moral deviations, and moral choices. I have an opinion that the future will be a battleground of morality.

Those who are agile, principled, and resilient can sustain the uncertainty and vicissitudes now and in the future, and those who are not only striving to reform structured problems, but also making all-out efforts to make the future sustainable. They make themselves reformers and support other reformers who run the risk of adverse public response or unwarranted victimization. All these boil down to a statement that "think deep, and when in a move, act like hunter-gatherers in agile, principled, and resilient manner.

Second, I wish them to consider that they vote for reformer preceding any ideological bent or personal preferences in politics. They will see some populist non-reformers deliberately and unduly delay the reforms for any reason and justify the non-reforming. They tend to be hypocritical crying crocodile tears. In their minds, let me say, they would rather live with guilt than die innocent. They are like vile sycophants who grovel when they are desperate before elections, relentless and brazen when they feel secure after winning the election.

Laying the basis for reform is sometimes daunting and time-consuming compared to the immediate gains from inactivity of reform actions, but its result will be stifling of opportunities for sustainable future and laying down of deep-rooted problems that will fester over time.

The 21st century, especially the next three decades (2025-205), that young adults will be navigating will be a time of transition at the crossroads, if not an end, during which they will be positioning themselves in a choice between "neophilia" to break off the rut to reform the structured problems for a sustainable future and "neophobia" to decline to explore breakthroughs beyond ken of conventional knowledge and rather cocoon themselves in the complacency of the status quo.

Marcel Proust, French novelist, has told us that "The true voyage of discovery is not seeking new landscapes but in having new eye". In my belief, the first action with the new eyes is to "Be Yourself" and "Do Yourself" in themselves, and second one is to "Vote for the Reformer" externally to make their future.

Bibliography

A.Barrie Pittock, Climate Change, Earthscam, 2005

Arun Sundararfajan, The Sharing Economy, The MIT Press, 2016

Barbara W. Tuchman, The March of Folly, Random House, 2014

Brett l. Walker, A Concise History of Japan, Cambridge University Press, 2019

Brian Dumaine, Bezonomics-How Amazon is Changing Our Lives, Scribner, 2020

Bruce Cummings, The Korea's Place in the Sun: A Modern History, W.W. Norton & Company, 2005

Chip Heath & Dan Heath, Made to stick, Random House, 2008

Chris Harman, A People's History of the World: From the Stone Age to the New Millennium, Verso, 2008

Claire Breay. Magna Carta Manuscript and Myths, British Library, 2002

Colonel J.J.Graham, On War , Skyhorse Publishing, 2013

Daron Acemoglu and James A. Robinson, Why Nations Fail, Currency New York

David Halberstam, The Coldest Winter, The Amateurs Ltd., 2007

Edward Luce, The Retreat of Western Liberalism, Atlantic Monthly Press, 2017

Gerald Messadié, Great Inventions Through History, W&R Chambers Ltd., 1991

Greg Woolf, Rome An Empire's Story, Oxford University Press, 2012

Harvey C. Mansfield, Manliness, Yale University Press, 2006

Ian Kershaw, Hitler, Penguin Books, 2009

Ian Morris, Foragers, Farmers and Fossil Fuels, Princeton University Press, 2015

Ian Morris, Why The West Rules – For Now, Farra, Straus and Giroux, , 2010

Ian Whitelaw., History's Biggest Blunders, Metro Books New York, 2012

J. M. Roberts, The Penguin History of the World: Sixth Edition, Rowman & Littlefield, 2017

Jared Diamond, The World Until Yesterday. Vikings. 2012

Joerg Baten, A History of the Global Economy, Cambridge University Press, 2016

John P. Kotter, A Sense of Urgency, Harvard Business Press, 2008

John Toland, The Rising Sun, The Modern Library, New York, 2003

Jonathan Haidt, The Righteous Mind: Why Good People Are Divided by Politics and Religion, Pantheon Books, 2012

Joonbum Bae and Andrew Natsios, How to Avoid Famine and Mass Migration, FOREIGN AFFAIRS SNAPSHOT, 2018

Lawrence Freedman, Strategy, Oxford University Press, 2013

M.Cary, A History of Rome, Macmillian and Company Limited, 1954

Matthew McCleery, The Shipping Man A Novel, Marine Money, 2011

Mauro F. Guillén, 2030-How Today's Biggest Trends Will Collide and Reshape the Future of Everything, 2020

Max Weber, The Protestant Ethic and The "Spirit" of Capitalism and Other Writings, Penguin Books, 2002

Michael Breen, The New Koreans, Penguin Random House UK, 2017

Michael R. Auslin, The End of the Asian Century, Yale University Press, 2017

Michael R. J. Vatikiotis, Blood and Silk, Power and Conflict in modern SE Asia, 2017

Norman Davies, Europe A History, Oxford University Press, 1996

Ohn Chang-Il, Abstract of The Causes of the Korean War, 1950-1953 (Vol. XIV, No. 2)

Paul Kleinman, Philosophy 101, Adam's Media, 2013

Paul Roberts, The End of Oil, Bloomsbury Publishing, 2005

Peter Frankopan, The Silk Roads, Alfred A. Knopf, 2016

Peter McPhee, Liberty or Death: The French Revolution, Yale University Press, 2016

Peter N.Sterns, Michael Adas, Stuart B.Schwartz, Marc J.Gilbert, World Civilizations, The Global Experience, Pearson Education Inc., 2008

Phaidon Press Limited. 30,000 years of ART, 2007

Richard J. Evans, The Coming of the Third Reich, Penguin Books, 2005

Richard Overy, Blood and Ruins, Viking, 2022

Robert B. Marks, The Origins of the Modern World, Rowman & Littlefield, 2017

Robert B. Strassler, The Landmark Herodotus, Anchor Books, 2009

Rutger Bregman, Humankind, A Hopeful History, Bloomsbury Publishing, 2021

Sheila Miyoshi Jager, Brothers At War, W.W.Norton & Company, 2013

Susan Wise Bauer, The History of The Ancient World, W. W. Norton & Company, 2007

Susan Wise Bauer, The History of The Medieval World, W. W. Norton & Company, 2010

Susan Wise Bauer, The History of The Renaissance World, , W. W. Norton & Company, 2013

Volker Ullrich, HITLER Downfall 1939-1945, Vintage, 2020

Walter Scheidel, The Great Leveler, Princeton University Press, 2017

Willaim L. Shirer, The Rise and Fall of the Third Reich, Book Club Associates, 1960

Willian J. Bennett, The Book of Virtues, Simon & Schuster, 1996

Yuval Noah Harari, Homo Deus: A Brief History of Tomorrow, HarperCollins Publisher, 2017

Yuval Noah Harari, Sapiens: A Brief History of Tomorrow, HarperCollins Publisher, 2015

VOTE FOR THE REFORMER I

Byeong-Soo Min

Born in Cheongju, Korea, in 1963.
I have a wife, two sons and a daughter, and my educational background is Shing-Heung High School in Cheongju, Hankuk University of Foreign Studies (German Literature & Language) and the KDI School of Public Policy and Management, Master of Foreign Direct Investment ("MFDI") 2007, in Seoul.

I have 32 years of experiences working for two Korean shipping companies, Hyundai Merchant Marine Co., Ltd. (HMM) and EUKOR Car Carriers Inc. (EUKOR), from 1989 to 2020, I worked on corporate strategy, ship finance and new-building, sale and purchase of used ships, and corporate performance management during that time. For two years (2021-23) thereafter, I ventured to work for the Korea National Park Service with the jobs of customer-cares in camping sites & parking lot, and park ranger.

As I've progressed through my profession with personal setbacks and rueful mistakes as well as some achievements along the vicissitude of events and situations, I've come to concentrate on how individuals, businesses, and countries may become sustainable by learning from the stories of the past and imagining the future that next generations will live in a dissimilar way that my generation has done for the past several decades.

In order to help young adults choose their future, particularly over the next three decades (2025–2055), this book is dedicated to the young adults and those who are excited with ideas for the sustainable future of the young adults which, I believe, is boiled down to the conduct of the book title, "Vote for the Reformer I".

In the 2020s, I have my vision to assess the progress made toward a sustainable future for the young adults and determine whether my suggestions of "Be Yourself, Do Yourself, and Vote for the Reformer" are practical and effective for achieving that goal. Following this, I plan to produce a sequel, "Vote for the Reformer II," in 2030, which will have a more structured format and bibliographic references in the contents.

Vote for the Reformer I

written by Byeong-Soo Min
publication date November 20, 2024
publication company AppleBook Publishing Co., Ltd
I S B N 979-11-93285-51-0 (13370)

This book is protected by copyright law
It prohibits unauthorized reproduction and unauthorized copying.